C & Data Structures

Third Revised Edition

C & DATA STRUCTURES

Third Revised Edition

Prof. P. Padmanabham

M.Tech. (A.E), M.Tech (C.S) Ph.D (Computer Science)

Principal, Bharat Institute of Engineering and Technology,
Mangalpally, Hyderabad

Formerly, Professor & Director Incharge,
School of Informational Technology,
JNTU, Hyderabad.

BSP **BS Publications**

A unit of **BSP Books Pvt., Ltd.**

4-4-309/316, Giriraj Lane, Sultan Bazar,
Hyderabad - 500 095
Phone : 040 - 23445605, 23445688

Published by :

BSP BS Publications
A unit of **BSP Books Pvt., Ltd.**

4-4-309/316, Giriraj Lane, Sultan Bazar,
Hyderabad - 500 095
Phone : 040 - 23445605, 23445688
e-mail : info@bspbooks.net

ISBN : 978-93-52300-43-3 (HB)

Dedicated to

My Beloved Father

Late Sri P. S. Sagar

(Rtd. District & Session Judge)

JAWAHARLAL NEHRU TECHNOLOGICAL UNIVERSITY HYDERABAD

Kukatpally
Hyderabd - 500 085
Andhra Pradesh (India)
Phone : 040-23156109 (O)
Fax : 040-23156112
E-mail : vcjntu@yahoo.com
WWW.jntuh.ac.in

Prof. DN. Reddy
B.E., M.Tech., Ph.D., FIE,MISME, MSESI, MIIPE, MISTE.,
VICE-CHANCELLOR

FOREWORD

I have gone through the book entitled 'C and Data Structures' authored by Prof. P. Padmanabham, specifically to suit the requirements of first year engineering students. I am confident that the book will be welcomed by one and all. This textbook satisfies a long felt need of the first year Engineering students of JNTU - Hyderabad. It has been particularly written keeping in view of the objectives of the syllabus and the requirements of the students. The style and presentation throughout have been lucid and kept within the reach of the readers. The highlight of the book is the large number of programming examples that covers every aspect of 'C' language and Data Structures. These programs will improve the programming skills and perceptions of the students.

The author is a former professor of JNTU and is presently the Principal of Bharat Institute of Engineering and Technology. Prof. Padmanabham is a teacher, writer and researcher. I wish that many more books of this kind would flow from his erudite pen. I am sure that the students will love to be the proud owners of this book. This textbook, in fact, has a universal relevance since 'C' and Data Structures' are useful and valid for all levels of engineering students and technical professionals.

I am certain that all the readers especially students will benefit immensely from the book.

Prof. D.N. Reddy

PREFACE TO THIRD REVISED EDITION

This book provides a comprehensive introduction to C language and data structures and is written to suit the syllabus of the subject "computer Programming & Data structures" of first year B.tech curriculum of JNTU Hyderabad. The primary goal of this book is to present the features of C language in a very lucid fashion to the first year engineering student and to give the basic approach to the learning of data structures Many pedagogical examples are incorporated to assist the student in learning basic concepts. A comprehensive lab manual is also added at the end to help the student to program the lab exercises as per JNTUH syllabus. The contents of each chapter have been matched to the contents of each unit in JNTUH syllabus of the subject "Computer Programming & Data Structures"

Chapter 1 deals with the basic introduction to computers, flow charts, algorithms and problem solving methodology. Chapter 2 contains a lucid presentation of fundamentals of C programming including control structures. Many worked out examples are presented here as the student is baptized to programming in C . Chapter 3 presents briefly about functions, arrays, and storage classes. Chapter 4 explains clearly the concept of pointers apart from presenting how to handle "Strings" in C. Chapter 5 describes the use of structures in C. chapter 6 presents a brief picture of input/output operations. Chapter 7 presents the sorting and searching techniques in detail. Chapters 8 & 9 together cover unit VIII of the JNTUH syllabus. A very precise introduction to Data structures along with implementation/applications of important data structures such as stacks and queues is presented.

I hope that the book will help both students and teachers in accomplishing their respective goals. I sincerely request all the readers to give me a feed back about the book to my email id ppadmanabham@yahoo.com The students are welcome to write to me about their doubts and I assure that them that I will certainly reply .

- Author

PREFACE TO THIRD EDITION

I take this opportunity to express my gratitude to the vast reader-community, especially Students and Teachers for the keen interest shown in the book.

Since the launch of the Second Edition of this book in 2005, I have received considerable feedback from different people including students, teachers and colleges. In serious consideration of this feedback, several changes are made in this edition. Much emphasis is laid on simple explanations of Programming Concepts.

Keeping in view the readers' interest; exhaustive explanations were included with suitable pedagogical examples to make the readers understand the basic concepts. The preliminary chapters of earlier edition have been further expanded with more material and examples for easy understanding.

I request the readers to interact with me on my email ppadmanabham@yahoo.com for any doubts or problems in implementing programmes in 'C'.

While I assure my continuous efforts to improve the quality of the book, I thank the publishers for their sumptuous efforts in making the book to reach the student community.

August 2007 ***- Author***

PREFACE TO FIRST EDITION

This book was motivated by my experience in teaching the course 'C & Data Structures' to the post graduate students of Institute of Postgraduate Studies and Research (IPGSR), Jawaharlal Nehru Technological University, Hyderabad. The primary goal of this book is to promote learning of C language and to apply right kind of techniques to implement the most useful data structures in computer science. The book has two parts. The first part deals with the C language. A lot of effort was put to bring out all the essential features of C in a manner that could be easily understood even by a beginner. In the second part of the book the data structures are presented in a simple and lucid way. No prior knowledge of programming is necessary to understand and implement these data structures. One of the specialties of this book is that every program written is explained line by line so that the student is never left in doubt about how the program works. Over 85 programs are given in this book and all of them are tested under Turbo/Borland C++ compiler. The output of each program is given at the end of the program to enable the student to fully explore the implementation. If you face any problems in implementing these programs on any other platform you are welcome to get in touch with me at my website (http://www.ppadmanabham.com) or through email (p_padmanabham@hotmail.com).

One cannot learn programming just by reading this book. It is a skill that must be developed by practice. Nevertheless, the programs written in this book are to be analyzed, understood and should be used in your own way in practice. This book presents material identified as curriculum for first year students of engineering of JNT University. The book is self-contained as a textbook. At the end of each chapter I have provided set of self-testing questions, which will help the student to check how far he/she has understood the material presented. The answers to the self-testing questions are provided at the back of the book. The student is advised to implement and test all the programming exercises given at the end of each chapter.

Chapter 1 introduces the student to simple C programming. Chapter 2 deals with Functions, Arrays, Strings and Pointers. Chapter 3 is the last chapter of part I and includes Bitwise Operators, Structures, Unions and Files. It is difficult to cover entire C language in three chapters. However, I have given only the essential features of C that are necessary for a beginner to implement data structures. The part II of the book starts with chapter 4 where Data structures are introduced and implemented. Chapter 5 extensively deals with linked lists and their applications. Chapter 6, is once again a long drawn chapter, where I have introduced implementation of several interesting algorithms in Trees and Graphs. The 7th and the last chapter of the book presents several searching and sorting techniques.

I propose to interact with teachers and students as frequently as possible to get their feeling about the book. I earnestly request everyone to frankly and promptly send their feed back to me either by visiting my website or by email. This could be of immense help to me to revise the book.

September 2002 ***- Author***

CONTENTS

1

Introduction to Computers

2

Introduction to C Programming

3
Functions, Arrays & Strings

4
Pointers

5

Structures & Unions

6

Console File I/O

7

Searching & Sorting

8

Introduction to Data Structures

9

Linked Lists

1

Introduction to Computers

1.1 INTRODUCTION

A computer is a device capable of performing computations and making logical decisions at speeds of millions and even billions of times faster than human beings can. For example, many of today's personal computers can perform hundreds of millions of arithmetic and logical operations per second. A person operating a desk calculator might require decades to complete the same number of calculations that a powerful personal computer can perform in one second. Today's fastest *supercomputers* can perform hundreds of billions of additions per second – about as many calculations as hundreds of thousands of people could perform in one year! Moreover, trillion instruction-per-second computers are already in use in research laboratories!

Computers process **data** under the control of sets of instructions called **computer programs**. These programs guide the computer through orderly sets of actions specified by people called **computer programmers**.

1.2 COMPUTER SYSTEMS

A computer comprises of various devices such as keyboard, screen, mouse, disks, memory, CD-ROM and processing units that are referred to as **hardware**. The computer programs that run on a computer are referred to as **software**. Hardware costs have been declining dramatically in recent years, to the point that personal computers have been rising steadily as programmers develop more powerful and complex applications.

1.2.1 Hardware

Regardless of differences in physical appearances, virtually every computer may be divided into six logical units as shown in the Fig. 1.1.

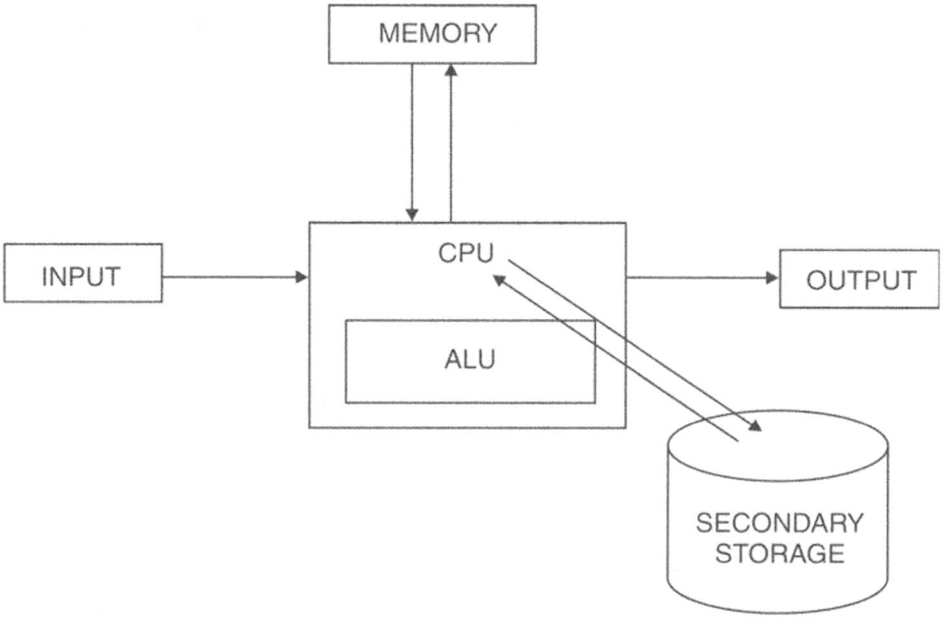
MEMORY
CPU
INPUT
OUTPUT
ALU
SECONDARY
STORAGE

Fig.1.1 Block diagram of computer system

1. **Input unit**

   This is the receiving section of the computer. It obtains information (data and computer programs) from various input devices and places this information at the disposal of the other units so that the information may be processed. Most information is entered into computers today through keyboards and mouse devices. Information can also be entered by speaking to your computer and by scanning images.

2. **Output unit**

   This section of the computer takes information that has been processed by the computer and places it on various output devices to make the information available for use outside the computer. Most information output from computers today is displayed on screens, printed on paper, or used to control other devices.

3. **Memory unit**

   It retains information that has been entered through the input unit so that it may be made immediately available for processing when it is needed. The memory unit also retains processed information until that information can be placed on output devices by the output unit. The memory unit is often called either **Memory** or **Primary Memory**.

4. **Arithmetic and logic unit**

   This section of computer is responsible for performing calculations such as addition, subtraction, multiplication and division. It contains decision mechanisms that allow the computer to complete tasks such as comparing two items from the memory unit to determine whether or not they are equal. Usually ALU is a part of CPU.

5. **Central Processing Unit (CPU)**

   This section of the computer is responsible for supervising the operation of the other sections. The CPU tells the input unit when information should be read into the memory unit, tells the arithmetic and logic unit (ALU) when information from the memory unit should be used in calculations and tells the output unit when to send information from the memory unit to certain output devices.

6. **Secondary storage unit**

   This is the long term, high capacity storage section of the computer. Programs or data not actively being used by the other units are normally placed on secondary devices (such as disks) until they are again needed, possibly hours, days, months or even years later. Information in secondary storage takes much longer to access than information in primary memory. The cost per unit secondary storage is much less than the cost per unit of primary memory.

1.2.2 Software

A set of instructions to the computer (or physical components of the computer) is called programs or software. These sets of instruction or programs can be mainly divided into **System Software** (Operating System) and **Application Software**.

1. **System Software (Operating System)**

   Early computer were capable of performing only on **job** or **task** at a time. This form of computer operation is often called single-user **batch processing**. The computer runs a single program at a time while processing data in groups or **batches**. In these early systems, users generally submitted their jobs to a computer center on decks of punched cards. Users often had to wait hours or even days before printouts were returned to their desks.

Software systems called **operating systems** were developed to help make it more convenient to use computers. Early operating systems managed to transition between jobs. This minimized the time it took for the computer operators to switch between jobs and hence increased the amount of work or **throughput**, computers could process.

As computers became more powerful, it became evident that single user batch processing rarely utilized the computer's resources efficiently because most of the time was spent waiting for slow input/output devices to complete their tasks. Instead, it was thought that many jobs or tasks could be made to **share** the resources of the computer to achieve better utilization. This is called **multiprogramming**. Multiprogramming involves the **simultaneous** operation of many jobs on the computer – the computer shares its resources among the jobs competing for its attention. With early multiprogramming operating systems, users still submitted jobs on decks of punched cards and waited hours or days for results.

In the 1960s, several groups in industry and the universities pioneered **timesharing** operating systems. Timesharing is a special case of multiprogramming in which users access the computer through **terminals**, typically devices with keyboards and screens, sharing the computer at once. The computer does not actually run jobs of all the users simultaneously. Rather, it runs a small portion of one user's job and then moves on to service the next user. The computer does this so quickly that it may provide service to each user several times per second. Thus the users programs **appear** to be running simultaneously. An advantage of timesharing is that the user receives almost immediate responses to requests rather than having to wait long periods for results as with previous modes of computing.

2. Application Software

   Programs or set of instruction to the computer which will assist the user in performing specific tasks are called *Application Software*. Some examples of application software are MS Office, Tally, Oracle, and Adobe Photoshop. MS Office is used for creating documents, spread sheets, presentations, database creation etc... Tally is used for accounting purposes in business applications. Oracle is used for database creation and maintenance. Adobe Photoshop is used for photo editing and creation.

1.3 COMPUTING ENVIRONMENTS

Computers can be used in different environments. An environment describes a situation. There are basically three types of computing environments depending on the way the computer are used. They are:

- Personal Computing
- Distributed Computing
- Client/Server Computing

1.3.1 Personal Computing

In 1977, Apple Computer popularized the concept of **personal computing**. Initially, it was a hobbyist's dream. Computers became economical enough for people to buy them for their own personal or business use. In 1981, IBM, the world's largest computer vendor, introduced the IBM Personal Computer. Literally overnight, personal computing became legitimate in business, industry and government organizations.

1.3.2 Distributed Computing

Computers were **stand-alone** units – people did their work on their own machines and then transported disks back and forth to share information (this is often called **sneaker net**). Although early personal computers were not powerful enough to timeshare several users, these machines could be linked together in computer networks, sometimes over telephone lines and sometimes in **local area networks (LANs)** within an organization. This led to the concept of **distributed computing**, in which an organization's computing, instead of being performed strictly at a central computer installation, is distributed computers were powerful enough to handle the computing requirements of individual users and to handle the basic communications tasks of passing information back and forth electronically.

1.3.3 Client/Server Computing

Today's most powerful personal computers are as powerful as the million dollar machines of just a decade ago. The most powerful desktop machines – called **workstations** – provide individual users with enormous capabilities. Information is easily shared across computer networks, where computers called **file servers** offer a common store of programs and data that may be used by client computers distributed throughout the networks, hence the term **client/ server computing**. C and C++ have become the programming languages of choice for writing software for operating systems, which include UNIX, LINUX AND MICROSOFT WINDOWS – based systems.

1.4 COMPUTER LANGUAGES

Programmers write instructions in various programming languages, some directly understandable by the computer and others that require intermediate **translation** steps. Hundreds of computer languages are in use today. These may be divided into three general types:

1. Machine Languages
2. Assembly Languages
3. High-level Languages

1.4.1 Machine Languages

Any computer can directly understand only its own **machine language**; machine language is the **natural language** of a particular computer. It is defined by the hardware design of the computer. Machine languages generally consist of strings of numbers (ultimately reduced to 1s and 0s) that instruct computers to perform their most elementary operations one at a time. Machine languages are **machine dependent**, i.e., a particular machine language can be used on only one type of computer. Machine languages are cumbersome for humans and therefore can not be easily used for programming. For example, a machine level program to add allowance to basic pay could comprises of series of instructions with 0s and 1s.

1.4.2 Assembly Languages

As computers became more popular; it became apparent that machine language programming was too slow, tedious and error prone. Instead of using strings of numbers that computers could directly understand, programmers began using English-like abbreviations formed the basis of **assembly languages**. **Translators programs** called **assemblers** were developed to convert assembly language programs to machine language at computer speeds. The following section of an assembly language program also adds allowance to basic pay and stores the result in gross pay, but more clearly than is done in machine language.

LOAD BASEPAY

ADD ALLOWANCE

STORE GROSSPAY

Although such code is clearer to humans, it is incomprehensible to computers until translated to machine language.

1.4.3 High-level Languages

Computer usage increased rapidly with the advent of assembly languages, but these still required many instructions to accomplish even the simplest tasks. To speed the programming process, **high-level languages**, in which single statements accomplish substantial tasks, were developed. Translator programs called **compilers** convert high-level language programs into machine language. High-level languages allow programmers to write instructions that look almost like everyday English and contain commonly used mathematical notations. A payroll program written in a high level language might contain a statement such as:

grosspay=basepay+allowance

Obviously, high-level languages are much more desirable from the programmer's stand point than either machine languages or assembly languages. C and C++ are among the most powerful and most widely used high-level languages.

1.5 CREATING AND RUNNING PROGRAMS

The process of compiling a high-level language program into machine language can take a considerable amount of computer time. This problem was solved by the development of **interpreter** programs that can directly execute high-level language programs without needing to compile them into machine language. Although compiled programs execute faster than interpreted programs, interpreters are popular in program development environments in which programs are changed frequently as new features are added and errors are corrected. Once a program is develop, a compiled version can be produced to run most efficiently.

What is an Interpreter?

An **interpreter** reads an executable source program written in high level programming language as well as data for this program, and it runs the program against the data to produce some results. Interpreter executes one instruction at a time as you enter the instruction.

Eg. Unix Shell Interpreter, which runs operating system commands interactively and Visual Basic Interpreter.

What is a Compiler?

A **compiler** is a program that translates a source program written in some high level programming language (such as C) into machine code for some computer architecture (such as the Intel Pentium architecture). The generated machine code can be later executed many times against different data each time.

Eg. Turbo 'C' Compiler and Borland 'C' Compiler.

1.6 SOFTWARE DEVELOPMENT STEPS

Before we go further it is better we look at a systematic program development and problem solving. In order to accomplish computerizing the solution to a problem the following six steps are needed:

1. *Specifying requirements:* The problem whose solution is to implemented on a computer through a program should be thoroughly specified and understood.
2. *Analysis:* The problem must be analyzed to determine the inputs and outputs needed.
3. *Designing algorithm:* A solution must be conceived and must be represented step by step by using algorithmic/pseudo code notations or flow chart symbols. This will help thoroughly verifying the correctness of the solution to the problem.
4. *Implementation:* The flow charts and algorithms developed in the previous steps are converted into actual programs in the high level languages like C. Next translate the program in high level language into machine code. This process is known as **Compilation.**

Syntactic errors are found quickly at the time of compiling the program. These errors occur due to the usage of wrong syntaxes for the statements.

Eg. x=a*y+b

There is a syntax error in this statement, since, each and every statement in 'C' language ends with a semicolon(;).

Most of high level language compiler implementations will generate diagnostic messages when syntax errors are detected during compilation.

5. *Testing:* This deals with the proper and correct execution of the program. The program is executed with input data. In this phase, we may encounter two types of errors.

   Runtime errors:

   These errors may occur during the execution or programs even though the program is successfully compiled without syntax errors. The most common types of runtime errors are:

   Eg. 1. Array range out of bound

   2. Divided by zero

   Logical errors:

   These errors occur due to incorrect usage of the instructions in the program. These errors are neither detected during compilation or execution nor cause any stoppage to the program execution. They only produce incorrect outputs. When the program ends up with incorrect outputs the logical errors are to be identified and rectified.

6. *Maintenance and updation:* After the software is delivered to the customer and installed at the premises of the customer, the customer may ask for some changes after using the software for some time. This calls for updation of the software with some changes.

   This approach makes us to visualize the logic involved in the solution to the problem and further allows you to complete the task of program writing and successful execution.

1.7 ALGORITHM/PSEUDOCODE

Pseudocode is an artificial and informal language that helps programmers develop algorithms. An algorithm is a step-by-step procedure for solving a problem using a psedocode. The pseudocode we present here is particularly useful for developing algorithms that will be converted to structured C programs.

Pseudocode is similar to everyday English; it is convenient and user-friendly although it is not an actual computer programming language. Pseudocode programs are not actually executed on computers. Rather, they merely help the programmer "***think out***" a program before attempting to writ it in a programming language such as C.

Example 1. An Algorithm / pseudo code to add two numbers.

```
Step 1  :  Start
Step 2  :  Read the two numbers into a, b
Step 3  :  c = a + b
Step 4  :  Write/print c
Step 5  :  Stop.
```

Example 2. An Algorithm/ Pseudo code to find whether a given number is odd number or a even number.

```
Step 1  :  Start
Step 2  :  Read the number n
Step 3  :  If (n % 2) = 0 (i.e. the remainder is zero) then.
           Write 'n is even number' Go to step 5
Step 4  :  Write 'n is odd number'
Step 5  :  Stop.
```

Example 3. An algorithm/pseudocode to read three numbers and to determine the maximum, second highest and the minimum.

```
Step 1 :   Read the three numbers into a, b, c
Step 2 :   If a > b and a > c
              Max = a;
              If b > c
                    Max2 = b, Min = c
              Else
                    Max2 = c, Min = b
                    Goto Step 5
              Else
                    Goto Step 3
Step 3 :   If b > c then do the following else goto Step 4
              Max = b;
              If( a > c )
                    Max2 = a, Min = c
              Else
                    Max2 = c, Min = b;
              Goto Step 5
Step 4 :   Max = c;
              If ( a > b )
                    Max2 = a, Min = b
              Else
                    Max2 = b, Min = a
                    Goto Step 5.
Step 5 :   Print Min, Max2, Max;
Step 6 :   Stop.
```

1.8 FLOW CHART

A flowchart is a graphical representation of an algorithm or a portion of an algorithm. Flowcharts are drawn using certain special-purpose symbols such as rectangles, diamonds, ovals and small circles as shown in Table 1.1. These symbols are connected by arrows called flowlines. Like pseudocode, flowcharts are useful for developing and representing algorithms, although, pseudocode is preferred by most programmers. Flowcharts clearly visually show how control structures operate in a program. The most common symbols used in drawing flow charts are in Table 1.1.

***Table 1.1** Flow Chart Sysmbols*

Oval	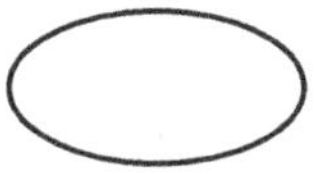	Terminal	Start/Stop/Begin/End.
Parallelogram		Input/Output	Making Data available for processing (Input) or recording of the processed Information (Output).
Document	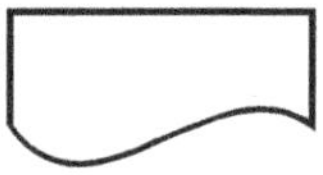	Print Out	Show Data Output in the form of Document.
Rectangle		Process	Any Processing to be done. A Process changes or moves Data. An Assignment Operation.
Diamond		Decision	Decision or Switching type of Operations.
Circle		Connector	Used to connect different parts of Flowchart.
Arrow		Flow	Joins two symbols and also represents flow of Execution.

Example 1. Flowchart for addition of two numbers.

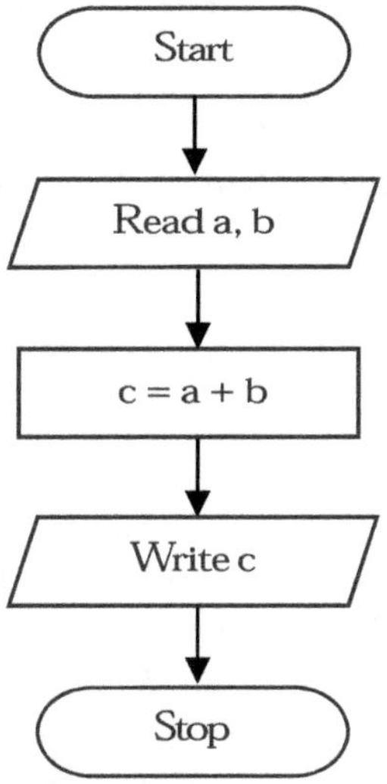
Start
Read a, b
c = a + b
Write c
Stop

Example 2. Flowchart to find whether a given number is odd or even.

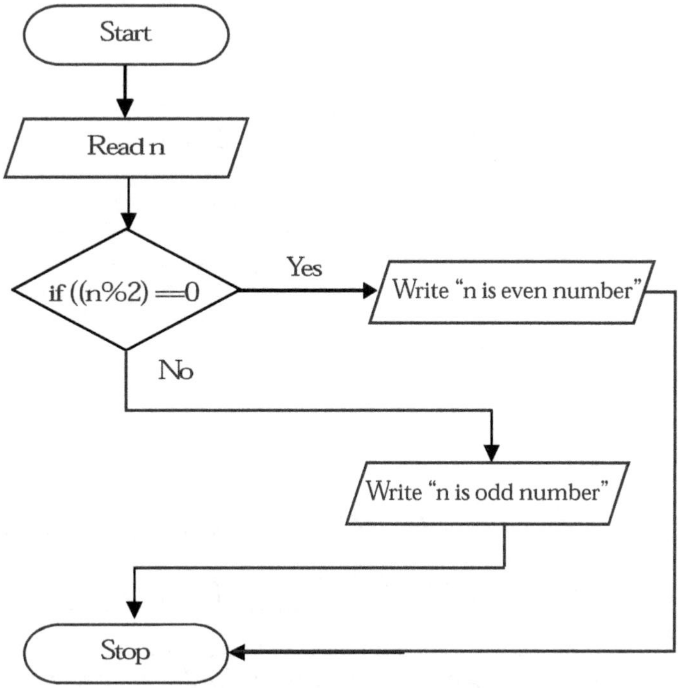
Start
Read n
if ((n%2) ==0
Yes
Write "n is even number"
No
Write "n is odd number"
Stop

1.9 SOFTWARE DEVELOPMENT LIFE CYCLE

The Systems Development Life Cycle (SDLC) or Software Development Life Cycle in software engineering is the process of creating or altering systems (softwares) and the models and methodologies that people use to develop these systems (softwares).

Different phases of SDLC are as follows:

1. Initiation/Planning and requirements collection
2. Analysis
3. Design
4. Build or coding
5. Testing
6. Maintenance and updation

These steps are similar to what we have discussed in earlier section. In software engineering the SDLC concept supports many kinds of software development methodologies (models). These methodologies form the framework for planning and controlling the creation of an information system. One such model, which is frequently used and very much similar to SDLC is Water Fall Model.

Water fall model is a sequential software development model in which progress is seen as flowing steadily downwards (like a waterfall) through the phases of initiation or planning and requirements collection, analysis, design, build or coding, testing and maintenance and updation. The phases SDLC in water fall model are represented in the Fig. 1.2.

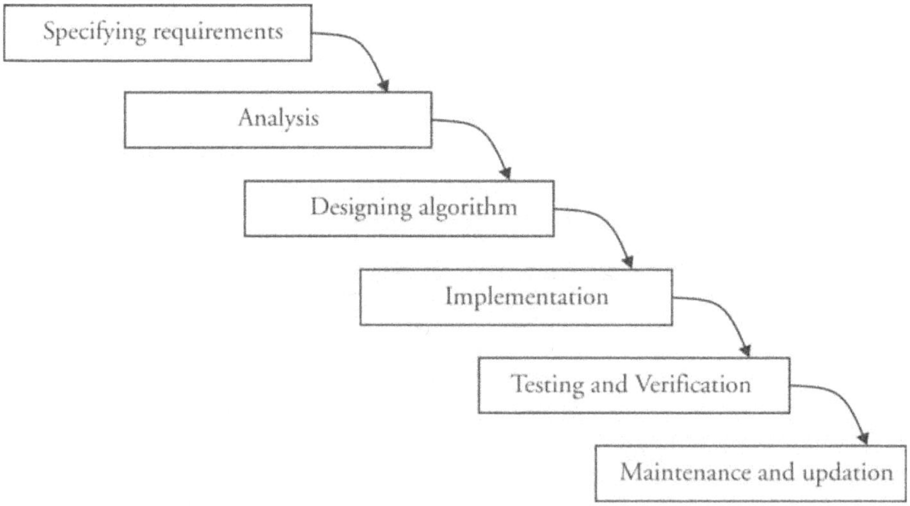
Specifying requirements
Analysis
Designing algorithm
Implementation
Testing and Verification
Maintenance and updation

Fig.1.2 Representation of SDLC phases in water fall model

1.10 APPLICATION OF SOFTWARE DEVELOPMENT METHOD

An example problem is presented in this section to illustrate how to apply software development method. After the problem statement in the analysis we identify the data requirements of the problem including the inputs and desired outputs. Next an algorithm is designed and refined to solve the problem.

Finally we implement the algorithm as a program written in C language. We also indicate how to test the program. Though the problem being taken is a trivial one, the student is urged to observe the process and adopt similar steps in solving other problems.

Problem:

You would like design a program that converts temperature in Fahrenheit to temperature in centigrade.

Analysis:

You should be very clear about the problem before you try to solve it. In this problem we are asked to convert the measurement of temperature from one system to another. You should be clear that the convention is from Fahrenheit to centigrade and not vice-a-versa. Therefore the problem input is temperature in $^{o}{}_{F}$ and the problem output is temperature in $^{o}{}_{C}$. The data requirements and the conversion formula are listed below:

Data requirements

Input: temperature in °F(f)

Output: temperature in °C(c)

Conversion formula: $c=((f-32)x5)\div9$

Design:

We now need to formulate the algorithm (step by step procedure)

Algorithm:

Begin

Step 1: Read the temperature in °F

Step 2: Convert the temperature into °C

Step 3: Display the temperature in °C

End

The above is the 1st phase of the design. We observe that Step 2 can be further subdivided into

2.1 Subtract 32 from °F

2.2 Multiply the result of Step 2.1 by 5

2.3 Divide the result of Step 2.2 by 9

Thus incorporating the method of conversion from °F to °C.

Flow Chart:

Phase 1:

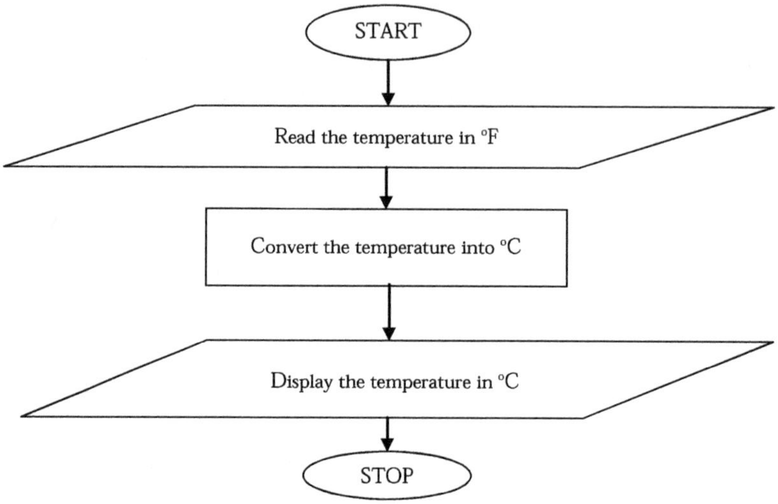
START
Read the temperature in °F
Convert the temperature into °C
Display the temperature in °C
STOP

Fig.1.3 Temperature conversion flow chart

After Refinement

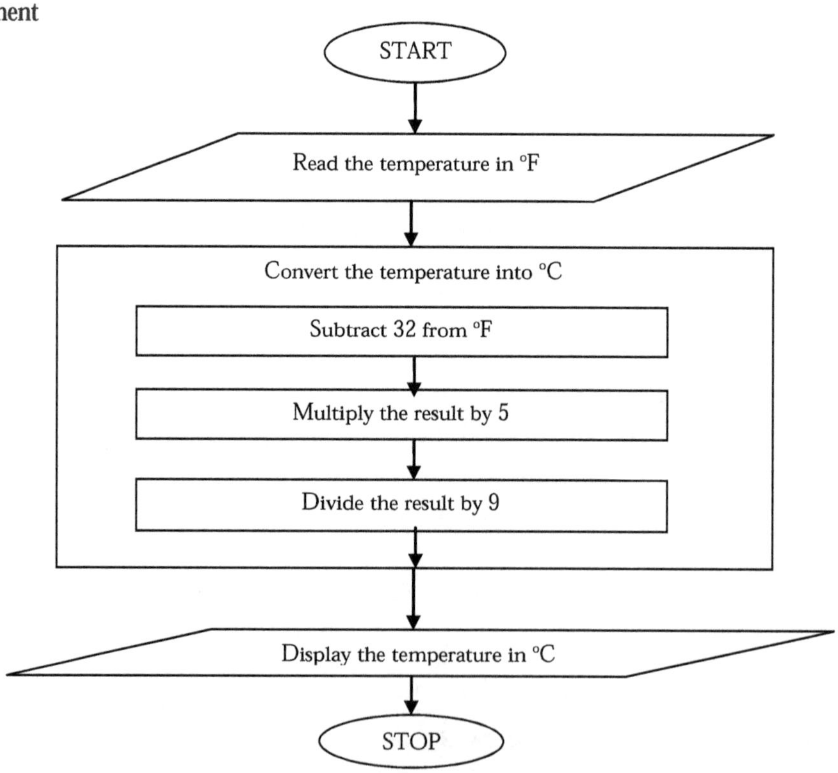
START
Read the temperature in °F
Convert the temperature into °C
Subtract 32 from °F
Multiply the result by 5
Divide the result by 9
Display the temperature in °C
STOP

Fig.1.4 Retined temperature conversion flowchart

Implementation:

The next step is implementation where we convert the algorithm/flow chart into a C program.

```
1. #include<stdio.h>
2. void main()
3. {
4. float f,c;
5. printf("Enter the temperature in Fahrenheit:");
6. scanf("%f", &f);
7. c=f-32;
8. c=c*5;
9. c=c/9;
10. printf("Celsius=%f\n",c);
11. }
```

Output:

```
Enter the temperature in Fahrenheit:60
Celsius=15.555555
```

Fig. 1.5 Sample program with, sample execution results

Fig. 1.5. shows the C program with sample execution results. However the above c program can be refined as the three steps at lines 7 to 9 can be combined to one line since the conversion formula can be directly coded as an expression. Fig. 1.6. shows the revised.

```
1. #include<stdio.h>
2. void main()
3. {
4. float f,c;
5. printf("Enter the temperature in Fahrenheit:");
6. scanf("%f", &f);
7. c=((f-32)*5)/9;
8. printf("Celsius=%f\n",c);
9. }
```

Fig. 1.6 Refined sample program

Testing:

To verify that the program works properly, enter a few more values of temperature in ^{o}F and verify whether you are getting the correct results or not. You may try some negative temperature also. Typical test cases are to be designed for more complex programs to unearth any runtime or logical errors that may occur.

Maintain and update:

This deals with the proper maintenance of the software after delivering it to the customer. And if there are any requirements that are found while maintaining the software they can be programmed and updation of the software is done.

This is how the software development method can be applied to any problem to solve it using computers (computer programming language (high-level language)).

PROBLEMS & EXERCISES

1. Write algorithm/pseudo code and flow charts for the following problems.
   (a) Finding largest number in two numbers.
   (b) Roots of quadratic equation.
   (c) To generate all even numbers between two given numbers.
   (d) Finding the average of n numbers.

2

Introduction to C Programming

2.1 INTRODUCTION TO 'C' LANGUAGE

'C' language facilitates a very efficient approach to the development and implementation of computer programs. The history of 'C' started in **1972** at the **BELL Laboratories**, USA., where ***Dennis M. Ritchie*** proposed this language. The growing popularity of 'C', the changes in the language over the years and the creation of compilers by groups not involved in its design, combined to demonstrate a need for a more precise and more contemporary definition of the language. In **1983**, the ***American National Standards Institute*** (ANSI) established a committee whose goal was to produce "*An unambiguous and machine-independent definition of the language 'C'*" while still retaining its spirit. The result is the ANSI standard for 'C'.

In this book, almost all the programs follow the ANSI standards. We start with simple 'C' programs and later on present several examples that illustrate various important features of 'C'. We analyze each program one line at a time. In this chapter, we present the development of 'C' programs using the fundamental control structures, which are normally available in most of the high level languages. More advanced concepts in 'C' programming will be introduced in later chapters.

2.2 STRUCTURE OF A SIMPLE 'C' PROGRAM

We begin by considering a simple 'C' program presented program listing 2.1. This program illustrates basic structure of 'C' program. We consider each line of this program in detail. Each program presented in this book will have line numbers for readers convenience. The reader should note that these line numbers are not part of the program.

```
1.    /* Program Listing 2.1 :  welcome.c
2.    A Simple Program in 'C' */
3.
4.    #include <stdio.h>
5.    main()
6.    {
7.          printf("Welcome to C Programming!!\n");
8.    } /* End of main()*/
```

```
Welcome to C Programming!!
```

Program Listing 2.1 A Simple Program in 'C'

Actually Line 7,

```
printf("Welcome to C Programming!!\n");
```

does the real work, displaying the text line *Welcome to C Programming!!* on the screen (monitor). The output of the program is shown at the bottom of the program listing 2.1. But then, what for the are other lines? Let us explain.

We begin with Line 1,

```
/* Program Listing 2.1 :  welcome.c
```

which starts with /* indicating the beginning of comments. Programmers insert comments to document programs and improve their readability. Comments also help other people to read and understand your programs. The comments started at Line 1 end at Line 2 with */.

```
A Simple Program in 'C' */
```

If the comment is not terminated properly, the 'C' compiler will give an error. Comments do not cause the computer to perform any action, when the program is run. Thus, the 'C' compiler will ignore line 1 and line 2 of program listing 2.1. The comments simply indicate the program listing number, file name and what the program does, in brief. These two lines are optional and not compulsory. Line 3 is a blank line which is used here to improve the readability of the program.

You may include any number of blank lines in your 'C' program since 'C' compilers ignore all of the blank lines and spaces, when the program is compiled. A good programming practice is to begin every program with a comment, describing the purpose of the program and other details and improve the readability by using the blank lines and spaces. One of the common programming errors is forgetting to delimit a comment.

Line 4,

```
#include <stdio.h>
```

begins with a **#include** and specifies a header file **stdio.h** within the angular brackets. The usual practice in C is external declaration of variables and functions in separate files, historically called **header files** that are included by the **#include**. The suffix **.h** is a conventional for header names and definitely not compulsory. The functions of the standard input/output library are declared in the header file **stdio.h**. The header file indicates to the compiler, the nature of the library functions being used in your program like the function **printf()**.

Every 'C' program, in general, consists of one or more functions. Each of this functions, perform certain specified task(s). Any 'C' program, can execute only when a function called **main()** is included in the program. The function **main()** starts with its name followed by an open parenthesis '(' and a closed parenthesis ')'. You may be wondering why the empty parenthesis exists after **main**. In general, a function may receive parameters, when the function is called. For now you don't have to worry. We shall present the details of the functions in the second chapter. But be sure that you don't forget the empty parenthesis after **main()**.

The open brace '{' at line 6, indicates the starting of the body of the function **main()**. Every 'C' function, should be written, within the open brace '{' and Closed Brace '}' as shown below.

```
funtion()
{
        statement 1
        statement 2
        . . . . . . . . .
        . . . . . . . . .
}
```

printf() at Line 7,

```
printf("Welcome to C Programming!!\n");
```

is a library function in standard input/output library, which is used for the purpose of printing (outputting) the information from the program onto the screen. Several such functions for inputting and outputting exist in standard 'C' library, which we shall see later in this chapter. The information within the double quotes, which is known as ***string*** is passed as a parameter to the function **printf()**. Strings will be explained in chapter 3.

'**\n**' represents the new line character indicating that the string *Welcome to C Programming!!* will be printed on a single line. Notice that '**\n**' represents only a single character. This is commonly reffered as an ***Escape Sequence***, which provides an extensible mechanism for representing hard to write or invisible characters. Among others, that 'C' language provides are '\t' for tab and '**\b**' for backspace etc. A full list of the escape sequences are listed in Table 2.1.

Table 2.1 Escape Sequences

Escape Sequence	Description
\a	Alert (Bell Character)
\b	Backspace
\f	Form Feed
\n	New Line
\r	Carriage Return
\t	Horizontal Tab
\v	Vertical Tab
\\	Backslash
\?	Question Mark
\'	Single Quote
\"	Double Quote
\ooo	Octal Number
xhh	Hexadecimal Number

The semi-colon (;)at the end indicates the statement terminator (separator). At line 8,

```
} /* End of main()*/
```

the closing brace indicates the end of the function **main()**. You must have already noticed that the rest of the line is a comment.

You can key in this program, on a personal computer using Turbo C / Turbo C++, where these softwares are integrated with editors, compilers, etc. These softwares also provide an interactive environment for compiling and executing your programs. You can also key in and execute this program, on a multi-user operating system like **UNIX**, **SOLARIS**, **LINUX** etc., You need to invoke a text editor like '**vi**' to key in the program. The program can be compiled using a command cc, gcc or invoking any other 'C' compiler available under the operating system.

2.3 VARIABLES

A quantity that can vary during the execution of a program is known as a ***variable***. To identify a quantity through out the program, we name the variable. For example, *number1*, *number2* and *sum* are the names chosen to represent the first number, second number and the sum in program listing 2.2. In 'C', the names of the variables and other program elements such as functions, arrays, etc., which are known as ***identifiers***, can be chosen as per the programmer's choice following the rules given below.

- *Identifiers can consist of alphabets(both upper and lower cases), digits and an underscore (_), in any order except the first character must always be an alphabet or an underscore.*

- *An Identifier can be of any arbitrary length.*
- *The Identifier should not be a keyword. (Refer Table 2.2)*

Eg. : name, ptr, etc.

In C, all variables must be declared before use.

2.4 CONSTANTS

A quantity that does not vary during the execution of a program is known as a Constant. C supports two types of constants namely numeric constants and character constants.

An example for an integer constant is 786, –123. A long constant is written with a terminal l or L. For example 123456789L is a long constant. Unsigned constants are written with a terminal u or U, and the suffix ul and UL indicates unsigned long. The advantage of declaring an unsigned constant is to increase the range of storage. Refer Table 1.4.

Floating point constants contain a decimal point or an exponent or both. For example, 123.4, 1e–2, 1.4E–4, etc. The suffixes f or F indicate a float constant while the absence of f or F indicates the double; l or L indicate a long double.

The value of an integer can be specified in octal or hexadecimal instead of decimal. A leading 0 on an integer constant means octal; a leading 0x or 0X means hexadecimal. For example decimal 31 can be written as 037 in octal and 0x1f or 0X1F in hex. Octal and hexadecimal constants may also be followed by L to make them long and U to make them unsigned. For example, 0XAUL is an unsigned long constant with value 10 decimal.

A character constant is written as one character within single quotes, such as 'a'. The value of a character constant is the numeric value of the character (usually ASCII) in the machine's character set. For example, in the ASCII character set the character constant '0' has the value 48, which is unrelated to the numeric 0. Character constants participate in numeric operations just as any other integers which is illustrated later in Chapter 2. Certain character constants can be represented by escape sequences like '\n' (Refer Table 1.2). These sequences look like two characters, but represent only one.

String constants or String Literal is a sequence of 0 or more characters surrounded by a double quote. Example, "I am a little boy". Note that the quotes are not a part of the string. Be careful to distinguish between a character constant and a string that contains a single character. Example, 'a' is not same as "a". 'a' is an integer used to produce the numeric value of letter a in the machines character set, while "a" is an array of characters containing one character and a '\0' as a string in C is an array of characters terminated by NULL. More explanation about strings is given in Chapter 3.

There is one another kind of constant, the enumeration constant. An enumeration is a list of constant integer values, as in

```
enum color { RED, GREEN, BLUE }
```

The first name in the enum has the value 0 and the next 1 and so on unless explicit values are specified.

If not all values are specified, unspeficied values continue the progression from the last speficied value. For example,

```
enum months { JAN = 1, FEB, MAR, ..., DEC}
```

where the value of FEB is 2 and MAR is 3 and so on.

Enumerations provide a convenient way to associate constant values with names.

2.5 KEYWORDS

There are certain words, called **keywords** (reserved words) that have a predefined meaning in C language. These keywords are only to be used for their intended purpose and not as identifiers.

The 'C' standard key words are listed in Table 2.2. Note that the keywords are all ***lowercase***. Since C is a case sensitive language, the keywords with at least one uppercase letter can be used as an identifier, though, this practice is not usually recommended.

Table 2.2 Keywords

auto	break	case	char	const	continue
default	do	double	else	enum	extern
float	for	goto	if	int	long
register	return	short	signed	sizeof	static
struct	switch	typedef	union	unsigned	void
volatile	while				

2.6 DATA TYPES

To be able to represent different types of data in a C program, we need different data types. A data type is essential to identify the storage representation and the type of operations that can be performed on that data. C supports four different classes of data types namely (1) Basic Data Types, (2) Derived Data Types, (3) User-defined Data Types and (4) Pointer Data Types.

The basic data types, their storage size and range are listed in Table 2.3. All arithmetic operations such as addition, subtraction, etc are possible on basic data types.

Eg :
```
int a, b;
char c;
```

Derived data types are used in C to store a set of data values. Arrays and Structures are examples for derived data types.

Eg :
```
int a[10];
char name[20];
```

Contd ...

C provides a facility called ***typedef*** for creating new data type names defined by the user. For example, the declaration,

```
typedef  int Integer;
```

makes the name Integer a synonym of int. Now the type Integer can be used in declarations, casts, etc., like,

```
Integer  num1, num2;
```

which will be treated by the C compiler as the declarion of num1 and num2 as int variables. "typedef" is more useful with structures and pointers which will be discussed later.

Lastly a pointer data type is necessary to store the address of a variable. A detailed discussion, is presented in Chapter 4.

2.6.1 Using Basic Datatypes

Now let us look at another 'C' program given in program listing 2.2.

```
1.    /* Program Listing 2.2 :  add2int.c
2.    A Program to add Two Integers in 'C'  */
3.    main()
4.    {
5.          int number1, number2, sum;
6.          printf("Enter a First Number ...");
7.          scanf( "%d", &number1);
8.          printf("Enter a Second Number ...");
9.          scanf( "%d", &number2);
10.            sum = number1 + number2;
11.            printf("The Sum of the Numbers %d and %d  is %d", number1,
                                                   number2, sum);
12.      } /* End of main()*/
```

```
Enter a First Number ...10
Enter a Second Number ...20
The Sum of the Numbers 10 and 20 is 30
```

Program Listing 2.2 Program to add two numbers

Line 1 and Line 2

```
/* Program Listing 2.2 :  ADD2INT.c
A Program to add to Two Integers in 'C' */
```

are comments stating the figure number, file name etc.

Line 3 and Line 4,

```
main()
{
```

are the starting of **main()**. Line 5,

```
int number1, number2, sum;
```

declares variables *number1*, *number2* and *sum* as integer data type which means that these variables hold integer values (whole numbers). The variables that follow keyword **int** are considered as integer data type. The other basic data types apart from **int** will be introduced later.

Line 6,

```
printf("Enter a First Number ...");
```

is introduced to prompt the user to enter the first number. In any programming, user interaction is a very important criteria as it increases the usability of the program. Since the '**\n**' is not used at the end of the string, the message ***Enter the First Number ...*** is printed on to the screen and the cursor waits at the end of this message. The cursor wait is due to the statement at Line 7,

```
scanf( "%d", &number1);
```

scanf() is a library function (defined in **stdio.h**) that accepts input from the keyboard. This function needs a format string (which is given within the quotes) and the address of the variable to which the accepted value is to be assigned. In this example, we intend to accept an integer value to variable number1. The **%d** within the quotes is required to tell **scanf()** that the input we are going to accept is a decimal number. Other commonly used **scanf()** conversions are given in Table 2.4. The ampersand '&' prefixing the variable number1 represents the address of the variable in the memory. All variables in a C program are allocated memory locations as per the size of the variable while the program is executing. The sizes of various data types used in C/C++ are listed in Table 2.3.

However, there could be a variation in the size depending on the operating systems under which you are working, and the type of compiler used.

***Table 2.3** Basic Data Types, Bits, Ranges*

Type	Length	Range		
unsigned char	8 bits	0	to	255
char	8 bits	-128	to	127
short int	16 bits	-32,768	to	32,767
unsigned int	32 bits	0	to	4,294,967,295
int	32 bits	-2,147,483,648	to	2,147,483,647
unsigned long	32 bits	0	to	4,294,967,295
enum	16 bits	-2,147,483,648	to	2,147,483,647
long	32 bits	-2,147,483,648	to	2,147,483,647
float	32 bits	3.4×10^{-38}	to	$3.4 \times 10^{+38}$
double	64 bits	1.7×10^{-308}	to	$1.7 \times 10^{+308}$
long double	80 bits	3.4×10^{-4932}	to	$1.1 \times 10^{+4932}$

To know the actual sizes of various basic data types, the student is advised to write a small C program using **sizeof**(*data type*) which gives the size of the *data type* in **bytes**. For example, **printf**("Size of an Integer = %d\n", **sizeof(int)**); prints the size of the integer data type in the environment in which the program is executed.

Line 8 and Line 9,

```
printf("Enter a Second Number ...");
scanf( "%d", &number2);
```

will allow you to interactively accept the second number.

Line 10,

```
sum = number1 + number2;
```

allows you to compute the sum of *number1* and *number2* and assign the result to the variable *sum*. *number1* + *number2* is known as an ***arithmetic expression*** which involves only one arithmetic operator namely "+".

Line 11,

```
printf("The Sum of the Numbers %d and %d  is %d", number1,
        number2, sum);
```

prints the two numbers which we have accepted using **scanf()** and their sum using the library function **printf()**. Observe the format string in which all the formats are chosen as **%d** which means all the three variables *number1*, *number2* and *sum* are to be printed as decimal numbers. **printf()** provides printing of numeric and non-numeric data in different formats as listed in Table 2.5.

Table 2.4 Basic ***scanf()*** *Conversion*

Type	Expected Input
d, D	Decimal integer
e,E	Floating point
f	Floating point
g,G	Floating point
o, O	Octal integer
i, I	Decimal, octal, hexadecimal integer
u, U	Unsigned decimal integer
x, X	Hexadecimal integer
s	Character string
c	Character

*Table 2.5 Basic **printf()** Conversion*

Type	Expected Input	Format of Output
d	Integer	signed decimal integer
i	Integer	signed decimal integer
o	Integer	unsigned octal integer
u	Integer	unsigned decimal integer
x,	Integer	unsigned hexadecimal int (with a, b, c, d, e, f)
X	Integer	unsigned hexadecimal int (with A, B, C, D, E, F)
f	Floating point	signed value of the form [-]dddd.dddd.
e	Floating point	signed value of the form [-]d.dddd or e[+/-]ddd
g	Floating point	signed value in either e or f form, based on given value and precision. Trailing zeros and the decimal point are printed if necessary.
E	Floating point	Same as e; with E for exponent.
G	Floating point	Same as g; with E for exponent if e format used.
c	Character	Single character
s	String pointer	Prints characters until a null-terminator is pressed or precision is reached

Line 12,

```
} /* End of main()*/
```

the closing brace and the comment (optional) indicates the end of the program. Notice that we have eliminated **#include <stdio.h>** in the program listing 2.2 since, most of the compilers assume the inclusion of this basic header file in every 'C' program.

2.7 OPERATORS IN 'C'

C uses several operators. They can be mainly classified into eight classes as follows :

1. *Arithmetic Operators*
2. *Assignment Operators*
3. *Relational Operators*
4. *Logical Operators*
5. *Increment & Decrement Operators*
6. *Conditional Operators*
7. *Bitwise Operators*
8. *Comma Operators*

2.7.1 Arithmetic Operators

The binary arithmetic operators are +, -. *, / and %. The % operator cannot be applied to float or double. If % is used to negative operands the result is system dependent. The binary + and - operators have the same precedence, which is lower than the precedence of *, / , and %, which is in turn lower than unary + and - arithmetic operators associate left to right.

```
 # include < stdio.h >
main ( )
{
        int a, b, c, d, e, f, g;
        printf (" enter the values of a & b");
        scanf ("  %d", &a, &b);
        c = a + b;    /* Addition of 2 values */
        printf ("c = %d", c);
        d = a-b;    / * Subtraction * /
        printf ("d = % d", d);
        e = a * b;    /* Multiplication */
        printf ("\n e = % d", e);
        f = a/b;    /* Division */
        printf ("  f = %e", f)
        g = a%b;    /* Modulo Division */
        printf ("g = %d", g)
    }
```

```
Enter the values of a & b:  4 2
c = 6      d = 2
e = 8      f = 2     g = 0
```

Program Listing 2.3 A program involving all arithmetic operators

Note: In the above program, the operator '/ 'is going to return the quotient value of division while the % operator is going to return the remainder.

2.7.2 Assignment Operators

"=" is known as a ***simple assignment operator*** which means that the result of the expression on the right hand side will be assigned to the variable on the left hand side. Therefore the left hand side should always contain only one variable, which should properly type matched to the computed result of the right hand side. The usual statement separator (;) is present at the end of each statement.

'C' provides several assignment operators for abbreviating assignment expressions. For example, the statement i = i + 5 can be abbreviated with an addition assignment operator += as i += 5;

The += operator adds the value of the expression on the right of the operator to the value of the variable on the left of the operator and stores the result in the variable on the left of the operator.

Any statement of the form,

<variable> = <variable><operator>**<expression>;**

where operator is one of the binary operator +, –, *, / or % can be written in the form,

<variable><operator>= **<expression>;**

Thus an assignment **i** *= 5, multiplies the current value of **i** with 5 and assigns the result to **i**. Program listing 2.3 illustration use of all arithmetic operators.

2.7.3 Relational Operators

These operators are used to distinguish between two values depending on their relationship. These operators provide the relationship between two expressions. If the relation is true then it returns a value 1 (true) otherwise 0 (false). The relational operators with description given Table 2.6.

Table 2.6

Operator	Description
>	Greater than
<	Less than
< =	Less than or equal to
> =	Greater than or equal to
= =	Equal to
! =	Not equal to

In the program listing 2.4 the true conditions return 1 and false condition returns 0.

```
# include < stdio.h >
main ( )
{

        printf (" \n condition : Return values  \n");
        printf ("\n 6 > 5    : % 4d", 6>5);
        printf (" \n 5 < 6   : %4d", 5<6);
        printf (" \n 5< = 5   : %4d", 5< = 5);
        printf (" \n 5> = 4   : %4d", 5> = 4);
        printf (" \n 6 = = 5   : %4d", 6 = = 5);
        printf (" \n 6 ! = 4    : %4d", 6 ! = 4);
}
```

```
Condition  :  Return Values
  6>5      :     1
  5<6      :     0
  5< = 5   :     1
  5> = 4   :     1
  6 = = 5 :      0
  6! = 4   :     1
```

Program Listing 2.4 A program to illustrate the use of relational operators

2.7.4 Logical Operators

The logical relationships between the two expressions are checked with logical operators. The logical operators available in 'c' language are logical AND (& &), logical OR (!!) and logical NOT (!).

The following rules are used while evaluating expressions using logical operators.

1. The logical AND (&&) operator provides true (1) result then both expressions are true otherwise 0.

   i.e., if we consider expressions p,q then p & & q value is true (1) only if both p and q are true otherwise it is false (0).

2. The logical OR (11) operator provides true result when one of the expressions is true otherwise 0.

3. The logical NOT operator (!) Evaluater to 0 if the expression is true otherwise to 1.

```
#include < stdio.h >
     main ( )
     {
           printf ("\n condition : Return values \n");
           printf ("\n 4>3 && 4<10 : %4d", 4>3 && 4<10);
           printf ("\n 8>5 !! 0<2 : % 5d", 8>5 !! 0<2);
           printf ("\n ! (5 = = 5) : % 5d", ! (5 = = 5);
     }

           Condition      :      Return values
           4>3 && 4<10    :            1
           8>5 !! 6<2     :            0
           ! (5 = = 5)    :            0
```

Program Listing 2.5 A program to illustrate the use of logical operators

In the program lists 2.5 example the first condition is true i.e 4 is greater than 3 which evaluates to true and 4 is less than 10 which also is evaluated to be true. So as per the rule the expression returns a value one. Similarly the remaining statements are evaluated to false.

```
        #include<stdio.h>
main()
{
  int a,b,c,k;
  int x,y,z;
  a=0,b=3,c=4;
  x=1,y=3;
  printf("\n first case\n");
  k=a && ++b;
  printf("\na=%d",a);
  printf(" b=%d",b);
  printf(" k=%d",k);
  printf("\n second case \n");
  k=b && ++c;
  printf("\n b=%d",b);
  printf("  c=%d",c);
  printf("  k=%d",k);
  printf("\n third case \n");
  z=x || ++y;
  printf("\n x=%d",x);
  printf("  y=%d",y);
  printf("  z=%d\n",z);
}

        first case
                a=0     b=3     k=0
        second case
                b=3     c=5     k=1
        third case
                x=1     y=3     z=1
```

Program Listing 2.6 A program to illustrate short circuit evaluation

In the Program Listing 2.6 in the statement k = a && ++b the value of the variable **a** is considered first which is 0 so the next part of the expression is not evaluated because the resulte is any way false (0). This is known as short circuit evaluation. In the case of "OR" if the first expression us true(1) then the second expression is not evaluater.

2.7.5. Increment & Decrement Operators

'C' provides the increment operator ++ and the decrement operator -- which are summarized in Table 2.7.

Table 2.7 The Increment and Decrement Operators

Operator	Called	Sample Expression	Explanation
++	Preincrement	++a	Increment **a** by 1, then use the new value of **a** in the expression in which a resides.
++	Postincrement	a++	Use the current value of **a** in the expression in which **a** resides, then increment **a** by 1.
--	Predecrement	--a	Decrement **a** by 1, then use the new value of **a** in the expression in which a resides.
--	Postdecrement	a--	Use the current value of **a** in the expression in which **a** resides, then decrement **a** by 1.

If a variable **i** is incremented by 1, the increment operator ++ can be used rather than the expression **i** = **i** + 1 or **i** += 1. If an increment or decrement operator is placed before a variable, it is referred to as the ***preincrement*** or ***predecrement***, respectively. If an increment or decrement operator is placed after a variable, it is referred to as the ***postincrement*** or ***postdecrement***, respectively.

Preincrementing (predecrementing) a variable causes the variable to be incremented (decremented) by 1, then the new value of the variable is used in the expression in which it appears. Postincrementing (postdecrementing) the variable causes the current value of the variable to be used in the expression in which it appears, then the variable value is incremented (decremented) by 1.

The program listing 2.7 illustrates the short cut assignment operators, postincrement and preincrement.

```
/* Program Listing 2.7 : incoper.c */
/*   A Program that illustrates Increment  & Short cut assignment
Operator   */

#include <stdio.h>
main()
{
      int i = 5;
      printf("\ni = %d", i);
      printf("\nAfter preincrement i = %d", ++i);
      printf("\ni = %d", i);
      printf("\nAfter postincrement i = %d", i++)
      printf("\ni = %d", i);
      i *= 2;
      printf("\ni = %d", i);
```

Contd....

```
15.  }
```

```
i = 5
After Preincrement i = 6
i = 6
After Postincrement i = 6
i = 7
i = 14
```

Program Listing 2.7 Program to Illustrate Shortcut Assignment Operators

Line 7,

```
int i = 5;
```

declares **i** as an integer and assigns it a value 5. In C it is possible to assign a value to a variable at the time of declaration. This is known as ***initialization***.

Line 8,

```
printf("\ni = %d", i);
```

prints the current value of **i**, i.e., 5. Line 9,

```
printf("\nAfter preincrement i = %d", ++i);
```

prints 6, while preincrement the current value i by 1. Line 10,

```
printf("\ni = %d", i);
```

prints the current value of **i**, i.e., 6. Line 11,

```
printf("\nAfter postincrement i = %d", i++)
```

prints the value of i as 6 and then increments i since it is a postincrement.

Line 12,

```
printf("\ni = %d", i);
```

prints 7 the current value of i.

```
i *= 2;
```

multiplies the current value of **i**, i.e., 7 with 2 and assigns a value 14 to **i**.

```
printf("\nI = %d", i);
```

prints the current value of **i**, i.e., 14.

2.7.6 Conditional Operator

The conditional operator also known as ternary operator contains a condition followed by two expressions. If the condition is true the first expression is evaluated otherwise the second is executed.

Syntax : Condition? (expression 1) :(expression 2)

Two expressions are separated by a colon .If the condition is true expression 1 gets evaluated otherwise expression 2 is evaluated.

```
# include < stdio.h >
main ( )
{
    int  a,b,c;
    printf (" enter the value of a & b");
    scanf (' %d ", & a,&b);
    c = a > b ? a : b;
    printf (" /n the greatest of two number is %d",c);
}
```

```
Enter the value of a & b : 2  3
The greatest of two numbers is:3
```

Program Listing 2.8 Program to find greatest of two numbers using conditonal operator

In the program listing 2.8 the statement c = a > b? a : b; first the condition a > b is checked for , if (a>b) then a is assigned to c else the value b is assigned to c.

The conditional operator can be nested for

Eg: - k = (a>b)? (a>c? a: c) :(b>c? b: c);

The above statement can be used to find the largest of 3 numbers a, b, c and assign it to a.

2.7.7 Bitwise Operators

'C' provides six operators for bit manipulation. These operators may only be applied to char, short, int, and long, whether signed or unsigned.

The following are the bitwise operators:

&	bitwise AND
|	bitwise OR
^	bitwise Exclusive OR (XOR)
<<	Left Shift
>>	Right Shift
~	One's Complement(UNARY)

The bitwise AND operator & is often used to mask off some set of bits. For example the statement,

n = n & 0177;

sets to zero all but the low-order 7 bits of n. Note that the leading zero in 0177 indicates an octal number.

The bitwise OR operator | is used to turn bits on. For example the statement,

x = x | 0177;

sets to lower-order 7 bits to one in x.

The bitwise Exclusive OR (**XOR**) operator ^ sets a one in each bit position where its operands have different bits, and zero where they are the same.

One must distinguish the bitwise operators & and | from the logical operators && and ||. For example, if x is 1 and y is 2, then x & y is zero while x && y is one(true).

The shift operators << and >> perform left and right shifts of their left operand by the number of bit positions given by the right operand, which must be positive. Thus x << 2 shifts the value of x left by two positions, filling vacated bits with zero; this is equivalent to multiplication by 4. Right shifting an unsigned quantity always fills vacated bits with zero. Right shifting a signed quantity will fill with sign bits ("Arithmetic Shift") on some machines and with 0-bits ("Logical Shift") on others.

The unary operator ~ yields the ones's complement of an integer; that is, it converts each 1-bit into a 0-bit and vice versa. For example the statement,

x = x & ~077

sets the last six bits of x to zero. Note that x & ~077 is independent of word length.

As an illustration of bitwise operators, let us present a program in program listing 2.9.

```
/* Program Listing 2.9 : BITWISE.c
Illustrates the Bitwise Operators  */
#include <stdio.h>
#define MASK 077
#define BITSET 0XFF


void main(void)
{
      unsigned int n1 = 03736, n2 = 0X03AB, n5=0XFF00, n6=0X0AFF;
      short int n3 =19,n4=21;

      printf("\nInitial Value Of n1= %04o(Octal)", n1);
      printf("\nInitial Value Of n2= %04X(Hex)", n2);
      printf("\nInitial Value Of n3= %d(Dec)", n3);
      printf("\nInitial Value of n4= %d(Dec)", n4);
      printf("\nInitial Value Of n5= %04X(Hex)", n5);
```

Contd....

```
        printf("\nInitial Value Of n6= %04X(Hex)", n6);
        printf("\n");
        /* Bitwise AND Operator */
        n1 &= MASK; /*set all bits to zero except the lower 6 bits*/
        printf("\nAfter Bitwise AND Operation n1=%04o(Octal)", n1);

        /* Bitwise OR Operator */
        n2 |= BITSET; /* set the lower 8 bits to ones */
        printf("\nAfter Bitwise OR Operation n2=%04X(Hex)", n2);

        /*  one left shift is equal to multiplying with 2  */
        n3 <<= 1;
        printf("\nAfter 1 Left Shift Opertion ...n3=%d(Dec)",n3);

        /* one Right Shift is equal to division by 2 */
        n4 >>= 1;
        printf("\nAfter 1 Right Shift Opertion ...n4 =%d(Dec)",n4);

        /* bit wise one's complement changes 1s to 0s and 0s to 1s */
          n5 = ~n5;
          printf("\nAfter Bitwise Complement ...n5=%04X(Hex)", n5);
        /* bit wise X-OR */
          n6 ^= BITSET;
          printf("\nAfter Bitwise XOR ...    n6 =  %04X(Hex)", n6);

    }
```

```
Initial Value Of n1  = 3736 ( Octal )
Initial Value Of n2  = 03AB( Hex )
Initial Value Of n3  = 19( Dec )
Initial Value of n4  = 21( Dec )
Initial Value Of n5  = FF00( Hex )
Initial Value Of n6  = 0AFF( Hex )
After Bitwise AND Operation n1  =  0036(Octal)
After Bitwise OR Operation n2   =  03FF(Hex)
After 1 Left Shift Opertion ...n3     =  38(Dec)
After 1 Right Shift Opertion ...n4 =  10(Dec)
After Bitwise Complement ...n5     =  00FF(Hex)
After Bitwise XOR ...   n6         =  0A00(Hex)
```

Program Listing 2.9 Program to Illustrate BITWISE Operators

At Line 8,

```
unsigned int n1 = 03736, n2 = 0X03AB, n5=0XFF00, n6=0X0AFF;
```

we have declared six-integer n1, n2, n3, n4, n5, n6 and each is initialized with a value. We have initialized n1 with 03736, octal value. In C we can use, octal (base 8) and hexadecimal (base 16) numbers along with decimal (base 10) numbers. An Octal Constant when assigned should always proceed with 0 and hexadecimal should proceed with 0x (0X). Note that each digit in an octal number should not be greater than 7. The octal/hexadecimal numbers are specially chosen in this program to reflect the bit pattern of the numbers being manipulated by the bitwise operators. The student may refer **Appendix B** to know more about the number systems. At Line 8, n2, n5, n6 are all initialized with hexadecimal numbers. At Line 9,

```
short int n3 =19,n4=21;
```

n3 and n4 are initialized as decimal values. We can also use **scanf()** to accept octal / hexadecimal numbers(refer the Table 2.5). At Lines 11 to 16,

```
printf("\nInitial Value Of n1= %04o(Octal)", n1);
printf("\nInitial Value Of n2= %04X(Hex)", n2);
printf("\nInitial Value Of n3= %d(Dec)", n3);
printf("\nInitial Value of n4= %d(Dec)", n4);
printf("\nInitial Value Of n5= %04X(Hex)", n5);
printf("\nInitial Value Of n6= %04X(Hex)", n6);
```

the initial values of n1 through n6 are printed. Note the formatted printing of octal and hexadecimal numbers. At Line 19,

```
n1 &= MASK;   /* set all bits to zero except the lower 6
bits*/
```

the number n1 is ANDed with MASK. At Line 2,

```
#define MASK 077
```

MASK is defined as 077. Actually at line 19, we have used a shortcut assignment operator to & (and) MASK with n1. Instead you can as well use,

n1 = n1 & MASK

This ANDing will result in MASKing (or making 0s) all BITS in n1 except the lower order 6 bits. Thus, n1 becomes 0036 (octal).

At Line 23,

```
n2 |= BITSET; /* set the lower 8 bits to ones */
```

n2 is bitwise ORed with BITSET. At Line 3,

```
#define BITSET 0XFF
```

BITSET is defined as 0xFF (hex). The OR operation sets all the lower order 8 bits to 1s leaving the other bits unaltered. Thus, n2 becomes 03FF (hex).

At Line 27,

```
n3 <<= 1;
```

the left shift operator, which is equal to multiplication by 2, makes the value of n3 as 38 (2 × 19).

At Line 31,

```
n4 >>= 1;
```

the right shift operator, which is equal to division by 2, makes the value of n4 as 10 (21 / 2).

Note that in right shift, least significant bit, which is 1, is lost. The student is advised to write 21 in binary form (in 16bits) and right shift by adding a zero at the most significant position and discarding the least significant bit and check the result.

At Line 35,

```
n5 = ~n5;
```

n5 is bitwise complemented (one's complement), i.e., interchanging 0s with 1s and 1s with 0s. Thus n5 becomes 00FF(hex).

At Line 38,

```
n6 ^= BITSET;
```

n6 is exclusive ORed with BITSET making n6 0A00 (hex). The student is advised to write the binary forms of n6 and MASK, then perform XOR operation (remembering that 1 ^ 1 = 0) and check the result.

We shall now present a program in Program Listing 2.10, that uses the bitwise operators to print the bit pattern (the internal representation of the number as described in Appendix B.) of a short int.

```
/* Program Listing 2.10 : BINEQ.c
Illustrates the Bit Pattern   */
#include <stdio.h>
#define MASK 077

void bineq(short int a);

void main(void)
{
/* program to print the internal representation of a short int */
      short int x = 100, z = -100;
```

Contd....

```
10.         bineq(x);
11.         bineq(z);
12.  }
13.
14.  void bineq(short int a)
15.  {
16.         int i, y;
17.         printf("\nThe BIT pattern of %d is ", a);
18.         for(i = 0;i < 16;i++)
19.         {
20.                y = a;
21.                y <<= i;    /* left shift i times */
22.                y &= 0x8000; /* mask all bits except the first */
23.                if(y)
24.                       printf("1 ");
25.                else
26.                       printf("0 ");
27.         }
28.            printf("\n");
29.     }
```

```
The BIT pattern of 100 is 0 0 0 0 0 0 0 0 0 1 1 0 0 1 0 0
The BIT pattern of -100 is 1 1 1 1 1 1 1 1 1 0 0 1 1 1 0 0
```

Program Listing 2.10 Program to display the bit pattern of a short int.

The function bineq takes a short integer and prints the bit pattern. At Line 18,

```
for(i = 0;i < 16;i++)
```

the **for** loop inside the function operates for 16 times since the short int is of 16 bit wide. At Line 21,

```
y <<= i;    /* left shift i times */
```

each time the number is shifted i times, to get i^{th} bit of the number into the most significant position. At Line 22,

```
y &= 0x8000; /* mask all bits except the first */
```

each time y is ANDed with 8000 (hex) to make all other bits 0 except the most significant bit. At Lines 23 to 26,

```
if(y)
       printf("1 ");
else
       printf("0 ");
```

y is tested with an if statement. A '1' is printed if the most significant bit of y is 1 and '0' is printed if the most significant bit of y is 0. Thus the for loop prints bit by bit of all the 16 bits of the number. Note that at Line 20,

```
y = a;
```

y is always restored to original value a, so that the shifting of bits will be correct.

Observe the result of this program where the binary equivalent of 100 and –100 are printed. –100 is printed in 2's complement, which is the form used by a computer, to represent the negative numbers (Refer Appendix B).

2.7.8 Comma Operators

The comma operator is used to separate two or more expression. The comma operator has the lowest priority among all the operators. A pair of expressions separated by a comma is evaluated left to right,and the type and value of the result is the type and value of the right

Eg: z = (x = 5, y = 2, x - y);

First assigns the value 5 to x, than assigns 2 to y, and finally assigns 3 (i.e. 5 - 2) to z.

In for statement, it is possible to place multiple expressions in the various parts by using comma operator only.

Eg: for (i = 1, j = 10; i< = j; i ++, j —)

Note : Comma operator is not a statement separator.

Table 2.8 Precedence and Associativityof Operators

<table>
<tr><th>Operators</th><th>Associativity</th></tr>
<tr><td>() [] -> .</td><td>left to right</td></tr>
<tr><td>! ~ ++ – – + – * & (type) size of</td><td>right to left</td></tr>
<tr><td>* / %</td><td>left to right</td></tr>
<tr><td>+ –</td><td>left to right</td></tr>
<tr><td><< >></td><td>left to right</td></tr>
<tr><td>< <= >=</td><td>left to right</td></tr>
<tr><td>= = !=</td><td>left to right</td></tr>
<tr><td>&</td><td>left to right</td></tr>
<tr><td>^</td><td>left to right</td></tr>
<tr><td>|</td><td>left to right</td></tr>
<tr><td>&&</td><td>left to right</td></tr>
<tr><td>||</td><td>left to right</td></tr>
<tr><td>?:</td><td>right to left</td></tr>
<tr><td>= += –= *= /= %= &= ^= |= <<= >>=</td><td>right to left</td></tr>
<tr><td>,</td><td>left to right</td></tr>
</table>

2.8 EXPRESSION EVALUATION IN 'C' LANGUAGE

In general, an expression in C is constructed using operators, variables and/or constants.

```
x + y * 3.5
```

However, the type of expression depends on the type of variables and the operators you choose. The above example is an arithmetic expression provided x and y are declared as numeric variables (int, float, double, etc.). The following are the examples of relational and logical expressions.

```
x < y
x < y && x > 5
```

An expression in 'c' is evaluated following the procedence and association of operation as shown in Table 2.7.

For example the expression

2 + 3 * 5 is evaluated as 17 and not as 25, since * has higher precedure than +. The student is advised to workout more examples.

2.8.1 Using Arithmetic Expressions

In this section, we present a program, which enables you to understand the use of floating-point data types and how to write an arithmetic expression with several operators. The program listing 2.11, computes and prints the celsius equivalent of fahrenheit temperature entered by the user.

```
/* Program Listing 2.11 :  f2c.c
A Program to compute Celsius of Fahrenheit temperature   */
#include <stdio.h>
main()
{
      float cel, fah;
      int icel;
      printf("Enter Temperature in Fahrenheit Degrees ...");
      scanf( "%f", &fah);
         cel = 5 * ( fah - 32.0 ) / 9;
         icel = (int)cel;
         printf("%6.2f degrees of Fahrenheit is equivalent to %6.2f
                                degrees of Celsius", fah, cel);
         printf("Truncated Celsius Temperature is %06d", icel);
   } /* End of main()*/
```

```
Enter Temperature in Fahrenheit Degrees ...100
100 degrees of Fahrenheit is equivalent to 37.78 degrees of Celsius
Truncated Celsius Temperature is 000037
```

Program Listing 2.11 Conversion Temperature from Fahrenheit to Celsius

Lines 1 to 9,

```
/* Program Listing 2.11 :  f2c.c
A Program to compute Celsius of Fahrenheit Temperature  */
#include <stdio.h>
main()
{
   float cel, fah;
   int icel;
   printf("Enter Temperature in Fahrenheit Degrees …");
   scanf( "%f", &fah);
```

allows the program to accept the temperature in degrees Fahrenheit entered by the user and assign it to floating point variable **fah**.

Notice the declaration of floating point variable **fah** and **cel** at Line 6 using the key word **float**. Also notice the format string **%f** of **scanf()** function at Line 9 which allows you to accept a floating point number.

Line 10,

```
   cel = 5 * ( fah - 32.0 ) / 9;
```

computes the Celsius equivalent of the Fahrenheit temperature. The whole expression consists of several arithmetic operators. Following the precedence of the operators indicated in the Table 1.8, we will show how the expression is evaluated.

Step 1 : First (fah – 32.0) is computed as the highest precedence is for the expression enclosed in the parenthesis.

Step 2 : The result of Step 1 is multiplied by 5.

Step 3 : Finally the result of Step 2 is divided by 9. Since * and / have the same priority, but the associativity is from Left to Right.

Observe the numbers **5** and **9** in the expression, which are ***integer constants*** while **32.0** is a ***floating point constant***. Constants in a program do not assume different values during the execution of the program as the variables do. The outcome of the computation of the expression will be a floating point number. Although, we have used some integer constants in the expression, the expression will finally evaluate to a floating point number. Thus the left hand side should also be a floating point variable in order not to loose any information.

As a general rule, C allows mixed data types in arithmetic expressions. When an operator has operands of different types, they are all converted to a common type. In general, the only automatic conversions are those that convert a ***narrower*** operand into a ***wider*** one without losing information, such as converting an integer to floating point in an expression like f + i.

Expressions may lose information, like when assigning a longer integer type such as long to a short or a floating point type to an integer, may draw a warning, but they are not illegal. The warning is just to tell the programmer that what he is doing is not correct. However, under the circumstances where the programmer is confident that there will not be any worthwhile loss of information by doing so, can silence the compiler by using **type casting.** This is illustrated in Line 11.

```
icel = (int)cel;
```

This assignment forces cel which is a floating point to be assigned to icel which is an integer and therefore, the fraction part of the cell will be lost. Observe the output printed.

A char data type is just a small integer So chars may be freely used in arithmetic expressions. This permits considerable flexibility in certain kinds of character transformations. Such examples can be seen later.

Lines 12 and Line 13,

```
printf("%6.2f degrees of Fahrenheit is equivalent to %6.2f
                            degrees of Celsius", fah, cel);
printf("Truncated Celsius Temperature is %06d", icel);
```

are needed to print the outputs of the program. Notice the format conversion **%6.2f** in Line 12 and **%06d** in Line 13 of the **printf()** functions. The first one is the floating-point conversion that specifies at least six digits wide and two after decimal point. The second one prints as decimal integer at least six digits wide with leading zeroes if the number is less than six digits. Observe the output of the program.

2.9 CONTROL STRUCTURES

Any computer program when compiled and executed will get executed sequentially. However, the sequential execution of a program is not sufficient to solve many problems. As such, every programming language supports control structures which allow, the program control make a different path than proceeding sequentially. In general, the control of a program is either sequential or selective or iterative. The example for selective control is the *if* statement and the example for iterative control is *while.* C also uses selective control structures (*if, if-else, switch-case*) and iterative control structures (*for, while, do-while*).

2.10 THE if STRUCTURE

This section introduces a simple version of C's if structure that allows a program to make a decision based on the truth or falsity of some ***condition.*** If the condition is met (i.e., the condition is ***true***) the statement in the body of the if structure is executed. If the condition is not met (i.e., the condition is ***false***) the body statement is not executed. However in 'c the if straightline can be constructed using any expression in place of condition. This is explained later in this section.

Conditions in if structures can be formed by using the ***Equality Operators*** (==, !=) and ***Relational Operators*** (<, <=, >, >=) summarized in Table 2.6. The relational operators all have the same level of precedence and associate from left to right. The equality operators both have the same level of precedence, which is lower than the precedence of the relational operators. The equality operators also associate from Left to Right. The student should note carefully this hierarchy as this will be helpful in evaluating a relational expression. A relational expression contains both arithmetic operators and relational operators. We shall now present a program in program listing 2.12 that reads the value of x and evaluates the following function using if statements.

$$y = \begin{cases} 1 & \text{for} \quad x > 0 \\ 0 & \text{for} \quad x = 0 \\ -1 & \text{for} \quad x < 0 \end{cases}$$

```
1.    /* Program Listing 2.12 :  feval.c
2.    A Program that will read the value of x and evaluate the following
      function   */
3.    #include <stdio.h>
4.    main()
5.    {
6.       int x, y;
7.       printf("Enter value of x ...");
8.       scanf("%d", &x);
9.       if( x > 0 ) y = 1;
10.         if( x == 0) y = 0;
11.         if( x < 0 ) y = -1;
12.         printf("Value of x = %d, Value of y = %d", x, y);
13.      } /* End of Main Program  */
```

```
Enter value of x ...10
Value of x = 10, Value of y = 1
```

Program Listing 2.12 Program for Evaluation of a Simple Function

The program listing 2.12 uses three if statements to test the value of x and decide the corresponding value of y. The user enters the value of x. If the condition in any of these ***if*** statements is satisfied, the assignment statement associated with that if is executed. The ***if*** statements at lines 9 to 11, are mutually exclusive, i.e., only one condition could be true. It is always necessary for an if statement to use the parenthesis to enclose the condition or relational expression.

Most Common mistake in relational expression is to use the assignment operator "=" instead of the equality operator "==". Unfortunately, the C compiler will not find out this as a syntax error. In C, the condition in if statement, need not compulsorily be a relational expression. It could be a simple arithmetic expression. If an arithmetic expression is used, C will consider it false if the expression evaluates to 0 or NULL and true otherwise. For example, at line 10, if the statement is changed to **if(x = 0) y = 0;** will be compiled without any error and the program gets executed. However, at line 10, x is always assigned a value 0 and since the expression evaluates to 0, it is taken as false and the assignment statement in the body of this if statement, will never get executed.

2.11 *if/else* SELECTION STRUCTURE & NESTED *if/else* STRUCTURE

The if selection structure performs the indicated action only when the condition is true, (i.e., when the expression evalluater to 1 otherwise the action is skipped. The if / else selection structure allows the programmer, to specify a different action to be performed, when the condition is false and thus allowing a two way decision. The if/else structure and the flowchart is shown in Fig. 2.1.

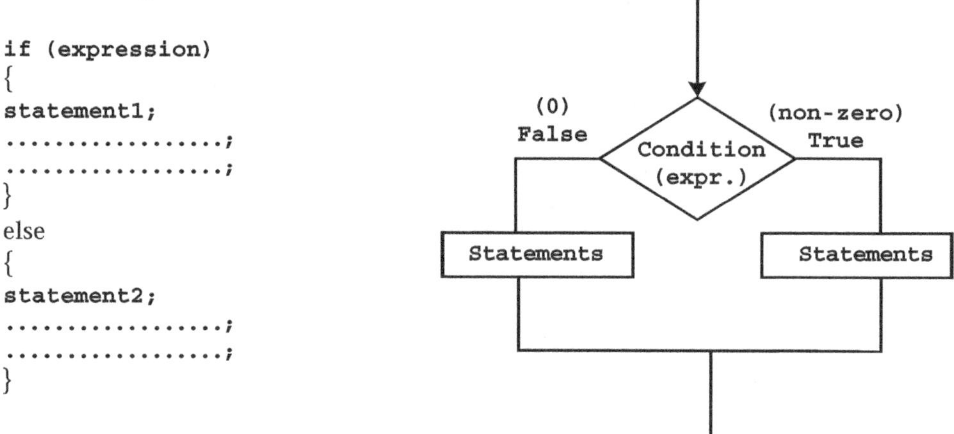

```
if (expression)
{
statement1;
..................;
..................;
}
else
{
statement2;
..................;
..................;
}
```

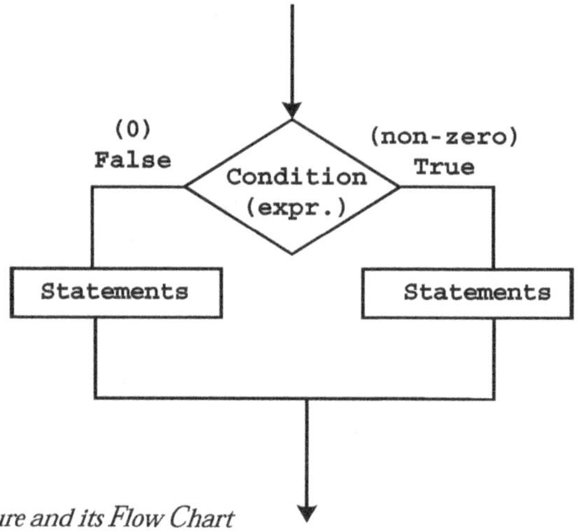
(0)
False
Condition
(expr.)
(non-zero)
True
Statements
Statements

Fig. 2.1 The if/else Structure and its Flow Chart

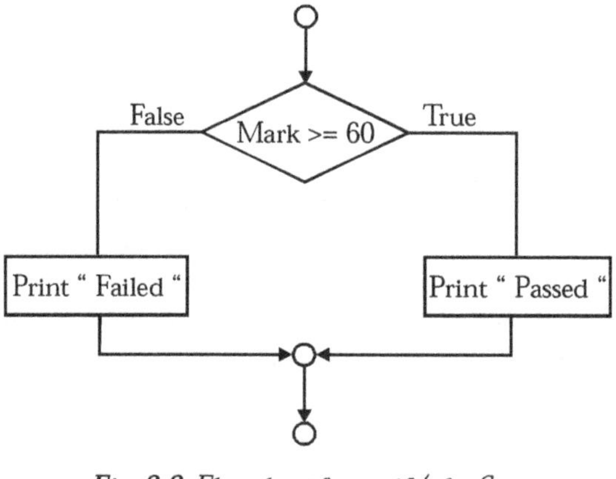
False
Mark >= 60
True
Print " Failed "
Print " Passed "

*Fig. 2.2 Flowchart for an **if/else** Structure*

The equivalent pseudocode of Fig. 2.2 is shown in Fig. 2.3. Thus if the student gets marks 50 or above the action namely ***Print "Pass"*** is performed and otherwise the action ***Print "Fail"*** is performed.

```
If The Student Marks Is Greater Than Or Equal To 50
     Print "Pass"
Else
     Print "Fail"
```

Fig. 2.3 Pseudocode for an if/else Structure

The conditional operator "? :" is closely related to if - else. The preceding if else statement can be written as a conditional expression in the following manner :

```
mark >= 50 ? printf("Pass") : printf("Fail");
```

Nested if / else structure tests the multiple cases by placing if / else structures inside if / else structures. We shall now consider an example, where three distinct numbers are inputted to a program and the program has to decide the largest, second largest and the least and print the numbers in an ascending order.

To be able to use the nested if / else statements effectively, we shall follow the procedure of writing a **flowchart** or a **pseudocode** (algorithm) to solve the problem. The flowchart for the problem stated above is shown in Fig. 2.4.

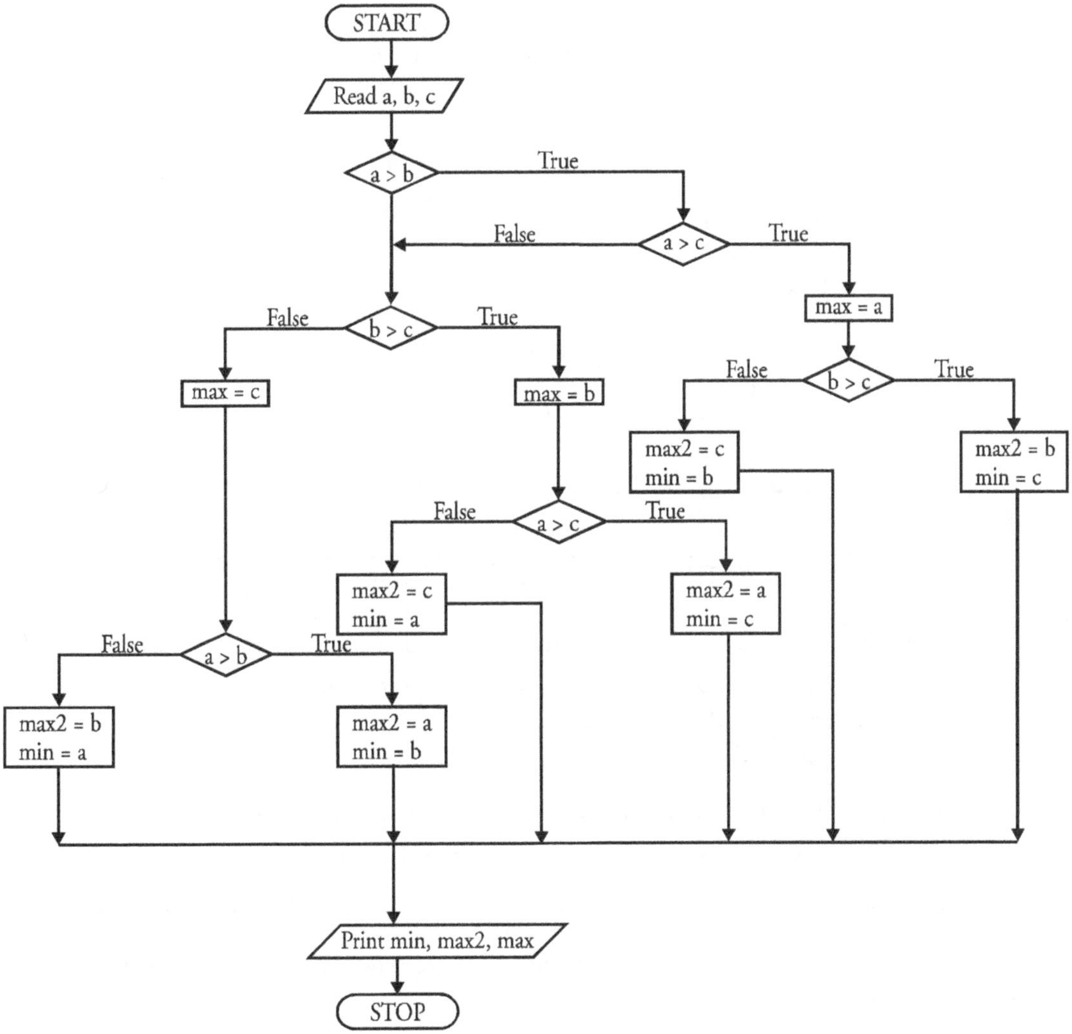
START
Read a, b, c
a > b
True
False
a > c
True
max = a
b > c
False
True
max = c
max = b
b > c
False
True
max2 = c
min = b
max2 = b
min = c
a > c
False
True
max2 = c
min = a
max2 = a
min = c
a > b
False
True
max2 = b
min = a
max2 = a
min = b
Print min, max2, max
STOP

Fig. 2.4 Flowcharting the Program Listing 2.3

The **pseudocode** (**algorithm**) for the above problem is shown in Fig. 2.5.

```
Step 1 :     Read the three numbers into a, b, c
Step 2 :     If a > b and a > c
               Max = a;
               If b > c
                    Max2 = b, Min = c
               Else
                    Max2 = c, Min = b
               Goto Step 5
            Else
               Goto Step 3
Step 3 :     If b > c then do the following else goto Step 4
               Max = b;
               If( a > c )
                    Max2 = a, Min = c
               Else
                    Max2 = c, Min = b;
               Goto Step 5
Step 4 :     Max = c;
               If ( a > b )
                    Max2 = a, Min = b
               Else
                    Max2 = b, Min = a
                    Goto Step 5.
Step 5 :     Print Min, Max2, Max;
Step 6 :     Stop.
```

Fig. 2.5 Pseudocode for Program Listing 2.13

The program listing 2.13 implements the pseudocode of the Fig. 2.5. Lines 5 & 6,

```
printf("\nEnter the Three Number (a, b, c):");
scanf("%d%d%d",&a,&b,&c);
```

Step 1 of the pseudocode is implemented.

The implementation of Step2 of the pseudocode starts at line 8,

```
if( a > b && a > c ){    /* if a is the largest */
```

```
     /* Program Listing 1.13 :  ascord.c
     A Program that will read three values and find maximum number*/
1.   #include <stdio.h>
2.
```

```
3.   main()
4.   {
5.         int a,b,c,max,max2,min;
6.         printf("\nEnter the Three Number (a, b, c):");
7.         scanf("%d%d%d",&a,&b,&c);
8.         if( a > b && a > c ){    /* if a is the largest */
9.               max=a;
10.                 if( b > c ){ /*decide second largest and the least*/
11.                       max2=b; min=c;
12.                 }
13.                 else {
14.                       max2=c; min =b;
15.                 }
16.        }
17.        else if( b > c ){/*if a is not the largest check if b could be*/
18.              max=b;
19.              if( a > c ){/*decide the second largest and the least*/
20.                    max2=a; min=c;
21.              }
22.              else {
23.                    max2=c; min=a;
24.              }
25.        }
26.        else {/*then c is the largest or at least as large as a or b*/
27.              max=c;
28.              if(a>b){    /* decide the second largest and the least*/
29.                    max2=a;min=b;
30.              }
31.              else {
32.                    max2=b; min=a;
33.              }
34.        }
35.        printf("The Ascending Order is %d, %d, %d", min, max2, max);
36.  }
```

```
Enter the Three Number (a, b, c):3 4 1
The Ascending Order is  1, 3, 4
```

Program Listing 2.13 *Program that will read three values and find maximum number*

Observe the if condition with relational and logical operators. Both the conditions should become true for the body of the if statement to be executed. The body of this if statement runs from opening brace "{" at Line 8 to the closing brace "}" at Line 16. There are two binary logical operators. Expression connected by logical and "&&" and logical or "||" are evaluated left to right. Note that && has a higher priority than ||. The only unary logical operator in C is "!" (not), which has the highest priority among the logical operators.

The if statement at Line 8, decides whether **a** is the largest among the three numbers i.e., If **a** is the largest, the body of the if statement is executed otherwise the control goes to Line 17.

At line 17,

```
else if( b > c ){/*if a is not the largest check if b could be*/
```

it is tested whether **b** could be the largest if **a** is not largest. Notice that **b** is only compared with **c**. If **b** is the largest then the body of this if starting from Line 18 to Line 25 will be executed. Otherwise the control goes to line 26 where obviously **c** is taken the largest without any comparison since **a**, **b**, **c** are distinct numbers. However the above program will work even if the numbers entered are not distinct.

Each of the if / else nesting blocks have got inner if / else statements to decide the second largest and the least, once the largest is established.

2.12 THE switch MULTIPLE SELECTION STRUCTURE

We have discussed the **if** single selection structure and the **if** / **else** double selection structure. When a multiway decision is needed, we used nested **if** / **else** statements (refer to program listing 2.13). Another elegant solution for multi selection is the switch statement in C language.

The **switch** statement is a multi-way decision that tests whether an expression matches one among a number of constant integer values, and branches accordingly. The general form of the switch structure is shown in Fig. 2.6.

```
    switch( expression
)
    {
       case <const-
expr1>:
          <statements>;
       case <const-
expr2>:
          <statements>;
       default:
          <statements>;
    }
```

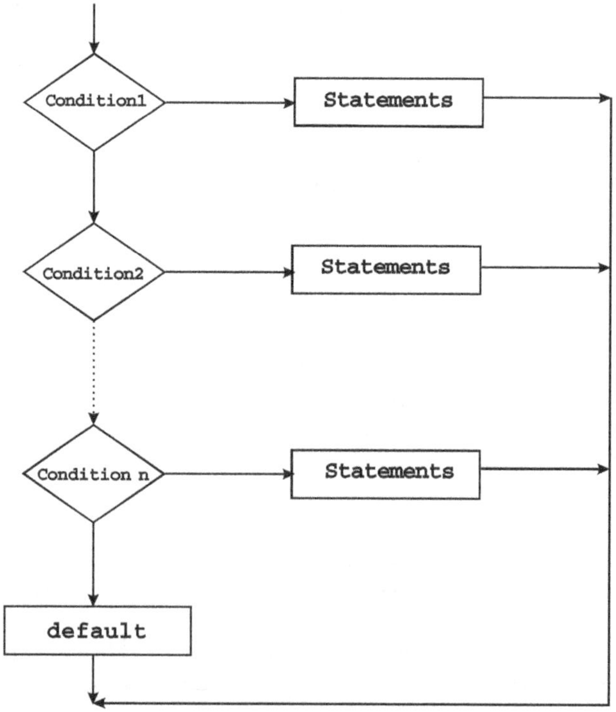
Condition1
Statements
Condition2
Statements
Condition n
Statements
default

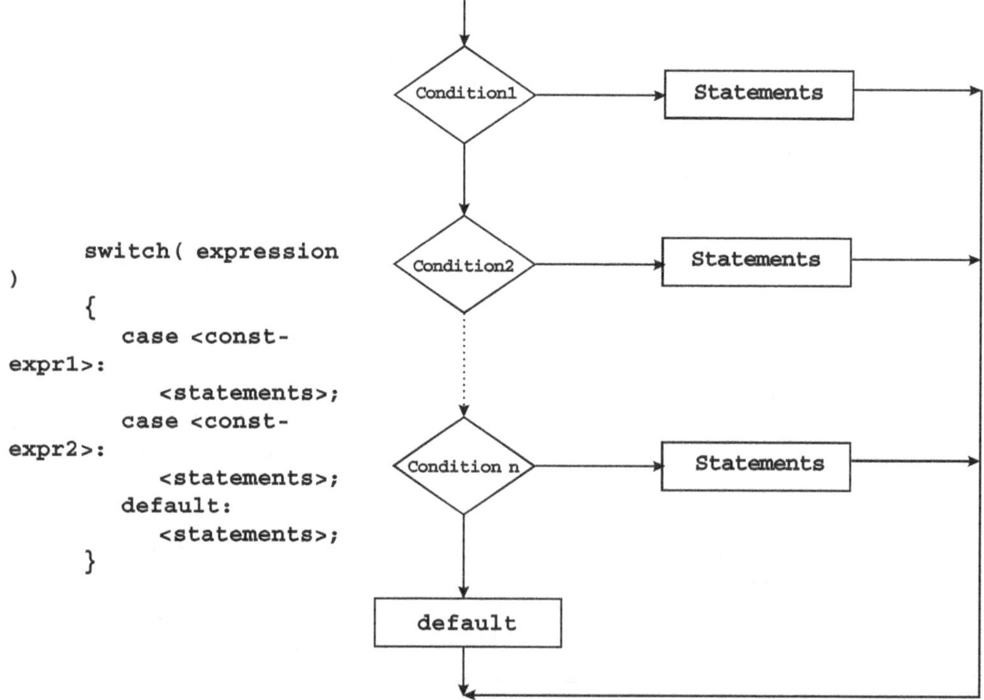

*Fig. 2.6 Structure and Flowchart of a **switch/case** statement*

Each case is labeled by one or more integer-valued constants or constant expressions. If a case matches the expression value, execution starts at that case. All case expressions must be different. The case labeled default is executed if none of the other cases are satisfied. A default is optional; if it isn't there and if none of the cases match, no action takes place. Cases and the default clause can occur in any order. Note that **default** need not be the last label. But usually many programmers prefer it to be the last label. Let us illustrate the use of switch statement by writing a C program, which takes two integer operands and one operator from the user, performs the operation and then prints the result in Program Listing 2.14. We will only consider the operator +, –, *, /, %.

```
/* Program Listing 2.14 : switch.c */
/*   A Program that illustrates switch / case Statement */
#include <stdio.h>
#include <stdlib.h>
void main(void)
{
      char oper;
      int num1, num2, result;
      printf(“Enter the Num1 Oper Num2( 23 + 28 ) ...”);
      scanf(“%d %c %d”, &num1, &oper, &num2);
      switch( oper )
      {
            case ‘+’:
                  result = num1 + num2;
                  break;
            case ‘-’:
                  result = num1 - num2;
                  break;
            case ‘*’:
                  result = num1 * num2;
                  break;
            case ‘/’:
                  result = num1 / num2;
                  break;
            case ‘%’:
                  result = num1 % num2;
                  break;
            default:
                  printf(“Unknown Operator ...”);
                  exit(0);
```

```
29.        }
30.            printf("%d %c %d = %d", num1, oper, num2, result);
31.    }
```

```
Enter the Num1 Oper Num2( 23 + 28 ) ...43 + 43
43 + 43 = 86
```

Program Listing 2.14 Program to illustrate ***switch*** *structure*

When the flow control reaches the switch structure at line 9,

```
switch( oper )
```

the controlling expression, *oper* in the parentheses following the keyword switch, is evaluated.

Note that the value of this expression must evaluate to a integral value of type **char**, **int**, **short**, **long** etc., As stated earlier (in section 1.4) in C **char** is also treated as a small integer. This value is compared with each case label.

For example, let us assume that the user has entered the following 23 + 28, thus making the value of the num1 as 23, oper as '+' and num2 as 28. The variable oper will evaluate to '+' (which is always interpreted as number equivalent ASCII Code of "+" which is 43). This is compared with each of the case labels. Since the first case label matches the expression, the statement following that case label *result = num1 + num2* will be executed. The variable result is set to 51. Following this, there is a break, which takes the control out of the switch structure i.e., line 30

```
printf("%d %c %d = %d", num1, oper, num2, result);
```

which prints results.

It is important to use the **break** statement to take the control out of the **switch** structure. Otherwise, all the statements from this case label to the end of the switch statement will be executed. The break statement is further explained in section 1.20. Now suppose that the user has inputted 23 × 45. The variable oper now evaluates to 'X' and thus, does not match with any of the case labels. The switch expression evaluates to 'X' and as this does not match any of the case label, the control enters the default case label and executes the statements following this label. In this example, it prints the error message and exits from the program(***exit(n)*** causes the program to terminate). Note that it is not essential to use ***exit(0)*** in a default case. If ***exit(0)*** is removed, the control goes to the end of case. Since we want to prevent it to print statement at Line 30, we used an ***exit(0)*** here. Here we have used **default** as the last statement in the switch structure, which is not essential. Note that the **default** case label is optional.

2.13 THE while REPETITION STRUCTURE

A repetition structure allows the programmer to specify that an action is to be repeated while some condition remains true. One such repetition structure is while. The while repetition structure is shown in Fig. 2.7.

```
while( expression )
{
   statement1;
   statement2;
   .................;
   .................;
}
```

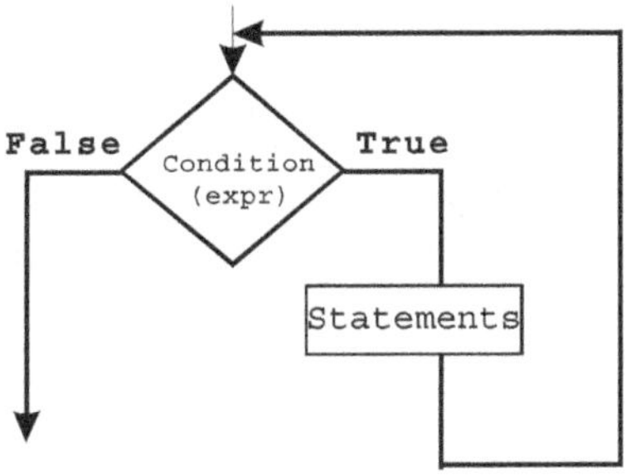
False
True
Condition
(expr)
Statements

Fig. 2.7 The while Repetition Structure and its Flow Chart

The expression is evaluated and if it is non-zero (true) the statements inside the body of the while are executed. The expression is re-evaluated at the end of the body of the while. The cycle continues until the expression evaluates to 0 / NULL (i.e., false). At this point execution resumes at the first statement after the end of the body of the while.

Let us illustrate the functioning of a while repetition structure. The Program Listing 2.15 sums n natural numbers using while repetition structure. The value of n is entered by the user interactively at lines 8 and 9.

```
1.    /* Program Listing 2.15 : while.c   */
2.    /*    A Program for sum of n natural numbers   */
3.
4.    #include <stdio.h>
5.    main()
6.    {
7.          int n, count = 1, sum = 0;
8.          printf("Enter the value of N: ");
9.          scanf("%d", &n);
10.         while(count <= n)
11.         {
12.               sum += count;
13.               count++;
14.         }
15.         printf("Sum is %d", sum);
16.   }

      Enter the value of N: 5
      Sum is 15
```

Program Listing 2.15 Program for Sum of N Natural Numbers

Line 10,

```
while(count <= n)
```

where the while loop starts, the expression within the parenthesis is evaluated. As long as the value of the count is less than or equal to n, the expression evaluates to 1(i.e., true) and the while is entered.

Line 12,

```
sum += count;
```

adds the value of count to sum. Thus every time the while loop is entered, sum goes up by the value of count. Note that the sum is initialized to 0.

Line 13,

```
count++;
```

increments the value of the count by 1. At Line 13, even you can use **++count** and it makes no difference. Infact, Lines 12, 13 can be combined in a single statement as follows, sum += count++;

2.13.1 The Sentinel Control vs Counter Control Loops

Consider a problem of averaging an arbitrary number of floating point numbers. In general, if a while loop is designed to handle the arbitrary number of processes, how can the program determine when to exit from the while loop? One way to solve this problem is to use a special value called ***sentinel value*** (dummy value) to indicate the end of *data entry*. The user types in arbitrary number of floating point numbers and at the end enters the chosen sentinel value say 0 to end the loop. Program Listing 2.16 illustrates Sentinel Control Loop.

```
/* Program Listing 2.16 : sentinel.c  */
/*    A Program that illustrates Sentinel Control Loop    */

#include <stdio.h>
main()
{
        float x, avg = 1, sum = 0;
        int n = 0;
        printf("Enter a value or 0 to terminate ...");
           scanf("%f", &x);
           while(x != 0)
           {
                 sum += x;
```

```
14.             n++;
15.             printf("Enter a value or 0 to terminate ...");
16.             scanf("%f", &x);
17.         }
18.         if ( n > 0)
19.             avg = sum / n;
20.         else avg = 0;
21.             printf("Average is %f", avg);
22.     }
```

```
Enter a value or 0 to terminate ...4
Enter a value or 0 to terminate ...5
Enter a value or 0 to terminate ...6
Average is 5
```

Program Listing 2.16 Program for Sentinel Control

The while loop condition at Line 11,

```
while(x != 0)
```

should never be allowed to be tested without accepting the first value of x. Therefore, at line 9 & 10,

```
printf("Enter a value or 0 to terminate ...");
scanf("%f", &x);
```

the first value of x is accepted. This is essential to allow controlling the while loop properly. The other way to solve this problem is to initialize x to a non-sentinel value and manipulate the while loop which is not an elegant solution. Of course, the do-while loop, which is going to be presented later on, will handle this problem, most elegantly. Lines 18 to 20,

```
if ( n > 0)
    avg = sum / n;
else avg = 0;
```

compute the average of the numbers entered, after ensuring that atleast one number is entered. Otherwise the average is kept at 0.

2.13.2 Example using Integer Division and Modulo Operator

The Modulus Operator '%' gives the remainder in a division. Thus expression **x** % y produces the remainder when x is divided by y i.e., 0 when y divides x exactly. In C, '%' operator cannot be applied to float or double.

Some other languages like Java accept the '%' operator for float and double. Integer division, truncates any fractional part. Thus the expressions, 5 / 3 is evaluated to 1 and 5 % 3 is evaluated to 2.

Let us now present a C program that uses the integer division and the modulus operator. The program listing 2.17, reverses the digits of the inputted number. For example, if 1234 is inputted to the program, it should be able to produce 4321.

```
1.    /* Program Listing 2.17 : reverse.c   */
2.    /*   A Program that Reverses the given Number   */
1.    #include <stdio.h>
2.    void main(void)
3.    {
4.          long n, rev = 0;
5.          printf("Enter any Number ...");
6.          scanf("%ld", &n);
7.          while( n != 0 )
8.          {
9.                rev = rev * 10 + n % 10;
10.               n /= 10;
11.         }
12.         printf("Reverse = %ld", rev);
13.   }
```

```
Enter any Number ...1234
Reverse = 4321
```

Program Listing 2.17 Program to Reverse the digits of a Number

At Line 7,

```
while( n != 0 )
```

the while loop is entered initially for a given n except 0. At Line 9,

```
rev = rev * 10 + n % 10;
```

the partially reversed number is shifted by one digit (**rev * 10**)and the next digit (**n % 10**) is added. Notice that n ultimately becomes 0 when all the digits are reversed.

For example, if n is **123** during the first iteration, **rev** becomes **3** and n becomes 12. In the second iteration, rev becomes 32 and n becomes 1. In the third iteration rev becomes 321 and n becomes 0. Notice that the number of iterations for the while loop is equal to the number of digits.

2.14 THE for REPETITION STRUCTURE

The ***for*** repetition structure essentially is a counter controlled loop. The following are the requirements of a counter control repetition.

1. *The name of a controlled variable (or loop counter).*
2. *The initial value of the control variable.*
3. *The increment (or decrement) by which the control variable is modified each time through the loop (also known as each iteration of the loop).*
4. *The condition that tests for the final value of the control variable (i.e., whether looping should continue or not).*

The ***for*** repetition structure essentially handles all the requirements of the counter control repetition. The general form of for structure is shown in Fig. 2.8.

```
for( expression1; expression2; expression3 )
{
   statement1;
   statement2;
   ..................;
   ..................;
}
```

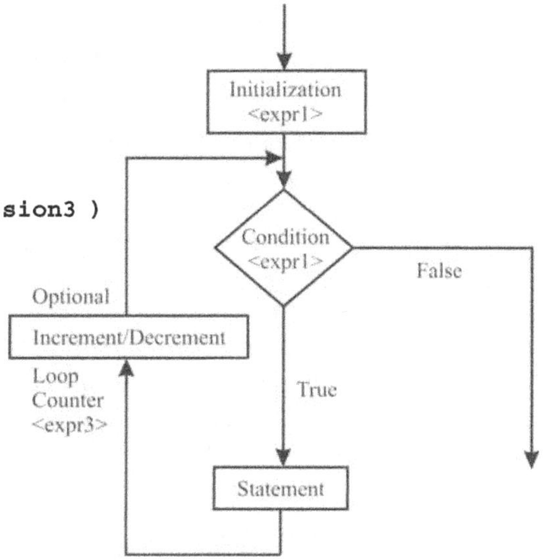
Initialization
<expr1>
Condition
<expr1>
False
Optional
Increment/Decrement
Loop
Counter
<expr3>
True
Statement

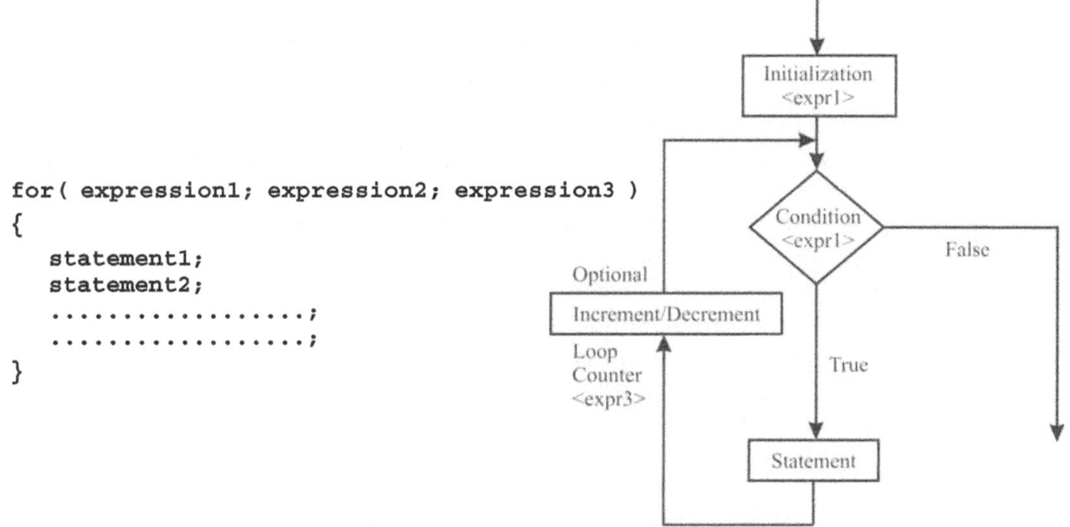

*Fig. 2.8 General Structure of a **for** statement and Flowchart*

where ***expression1*** provides initial value for the **loop - control variable(s)**; ***expression2*** is the **loop - continuation condition(s)** (containing the control variable's final value) and ***expression3*** increments/decrements/alters the control variable. In most cases the for structure can be represented with an equivalent while structure with ***expression1***, ***expression2*** and ***expression3*** placed as shown in Fig. 2.9.

```
expression1;

while(expression2)
{
   statement1;
   statement2;
   ..................;
   ..................;
   expresstion3;
}
```

*Fig. 2.9 A **while** equivalent for **for***

There is one exception with this behavior when a ***continue*** is used in the body of the ***for***. This will be explained later after we look into ***continue*** statement. Though all the three components of the for loop are expressions, most commonly ***expression1*** and ***expression3*** are assignments or function calls and ***expression2*** is a relational expression. Any of the three parts can be omitted although the semicolons remain. For example, ***for(; ;) {..................;}*** is an infinite loop, presumably to be broken by other means, such as a ***break*** or ***return***.

Sometimes ***expression1*** and ***expression3*** in a for structure are comma separated lists of expressions that enable the programmer to use multiple initialization expressions and / or multiple increment expressions. For example, there may be several control variables in a single for structure that must be initialized and incremented. We shall see an example of this later.

Let us write a C program using ***for*** statement to find the following from a given set of five integers.

1. *Total number of even integer and their sum.*
2. *Total number of odd integer and their sum.*

```
/* Program Listing 2.18 : sumofE_O.c  */
/*   A Program that finds the even or odd number  and sum */
#include <stdio.h>
void main(void)
{
      int i, n, even_sum, even_numbers, odd_sum, odd_numbers;
      even_sum = even_numbers = odd_sum = odd_numbers = 0;
      for( i = 1; i <= 5; i++ )
      {
            printf("Enter the number ...");
            scanf("%d",&n);
```

```
12.             if( n%2 == 0 )
13.             {
14.                   even_sum += n;
15.                   even_numbers++;
16.             }
17.             else
18.             {
19.                   odd_sum += n;
20.                   odd_numbers++;
21.             }
22.       }
23.       printf("No. of Even Numbers = %d\n Sum of Even Numbers = %d\n
                 No. of Odd Numbers = %d\n Sum of Odd Numbers = %d",
                 even_numbers, even_sum, odd_numbers, odd_sum);
24.  }
```

```
Enter the number ...1
Enter the number ...5
Enter the number ...6
Enter the number ...3
Enter the number ...4
No. of Even Numbers = 2
Sum of Even Numbers = 10
No. of Odd Numbers = 3
Sum of Odd Numbers = 9
```

Program Listing 2.18 *Program for finding Even & Odd numbers and their Sum*

Observe the for loop at line 8.

```
for( i = 1; i <= 5; i++ )
```

The initialization expression is i = 1, the loop control variable is i, the loop continuation condition is n <= 5. Line 11,

```
scanf("%d",&n);
```

accepts one number at a time. Line 12,

```
if( n%2 == 0 )
```

decides whether the number is even and if so increments even sum by n at line 14,

```
even_sum += n;
```

and increments the number of even numbers by 1 at Line 15.

```
even_numbers++;
```

The else part from lines 17 to 21,

```
else
{
        odd_sum += n;
        odd_numbers++;
}
```

of the if statement obviously takes care of the odd numbers, since a number is not even it should be odd

2.15 THE do / while REPETITION STRUCTURE

The **do / while** is similar to the while structure. In the while structure, the loop - continuation condition is tested at the beginning of the loop before the body of the loop is performed. Observe the flow chart for do/while given in Fig. 2.10. The **do / while** structure tests the loop - continuation condition after the loop body is performed. Therefore, the loop body is always executed at least once. When a **do / while** terminates, execution continues with the statement after the **while** clause. Note that it is not necessary to use braces in the **do / while** structure if there is only on statement in the body. However, the braces are usually included to avoid confusion between the **while** and **do / while** structures. For example,

```
while( condition )
```

is normally regarded as the header to a while structure. A **do / while** with no braces around the single statement body appears as,

```
do
      statement;
while( condition );
```

which can be confusing. The last line

```
while(condition);
```

may be misinterpreted by the reader as a **while** structure containing an empty statement (the semicolon by itself). Thus, the **do / while** even with one statement is often written as follows to avoid confusion.

```
do
{
   statement;
}
while(condition);
```

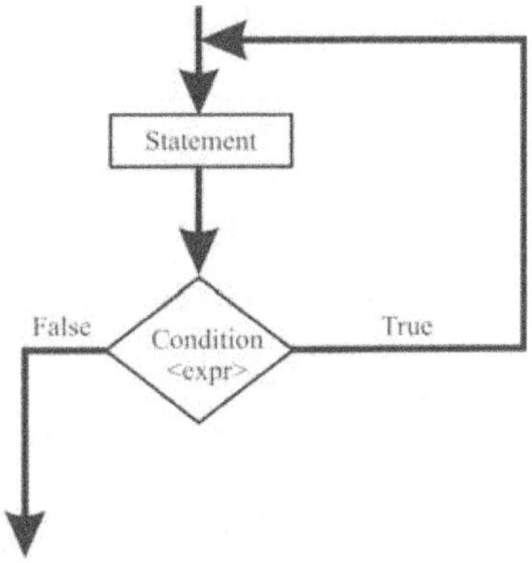
Statement
False
Condition
<expr>
True

Fig. 2.10 The do/while Structure and its Flow Chart

Experience shows **do / while** is much less used than **while** and for. However, sometimes it could be valuable. We shall rewrite the program of summing arbitrary number of floating - point number of Section 2.14 using **do / while** loop. We would like to avoid reading the value of x outside the while loop once (refer program listing 2.7). The same program using the **do / while** loop is presented in program listing 2.19.

```
/* Program Listing 2.19 : sentinel.c  */
/*   A Program that illustrates Sentinel Controls */

#include <stdio.h>
main()
{
      float x, avg = 1, sum = 0;
      int n = 0;
      do
         {
               printf("Enter a value or 0 to terminate …");
               scanf("%f", &x);
               if(x != 0)
               {
                     sum += x;
                     n++;
               }
         } while( x != 0 );
         if ( n > 0)
         {
               avg = sum / n;
         }
      else
            avg = 0;
```

```
25.         printf("Average is %f", avg);
26.     }
```

```
Enter a value or 0 to terminate ...4
Enter a value or 0 to terminate ...5
Enter a value or 0 to terminate ...6
Average is 5
```

Program Listing 2.19 SENTINEL.C

Observe that all the values of **x** are read within the loop. Since, do / while loop tests the condition only at the end of the loop, the problem of reading **x** outside the loop has been successfully avoided. Lines 13 to 17,

```
if(x != 0)
{
        sum += x;
        n++;
}
```

will allow only the numbers other than the sentinel value (0) to be summed and counted for average. The **do / while** loop exits when a 0 is entered by the user and prints the average. In this program the **do / while** is necessary or at least convenient since at least one value of **x** must be accepted before x is tested (even if it is a 0).

2.16 THE break & continue STATEMENTS

It is sometimes, convenient to exit from the middle of the loop rather than at the end by testing loop condition at the top or the bottom. The **break** statement provides an early exit from **for**, **while**, **do / while** and **switch** structures and the execution continues with the first statement after the structure. The program listing 2.20 illustrates the use of **break** statement. This program is an other version of computing the average of arbitrary number of floating point numbers using a sentinel value controlled loop.

```
/* Program Listing 2.20 : break.c  */
/*   A Program that illustrates break Statement */

#include <stdio.h>
main()
{
        float x, avg = 1, sum = 0;
        int n = 0;
```

```
9.          do
10.           {
11.                printf("Enter a value or 0 to terminate …");
12.                scanf("%f", &x);
13.                if(x == 0)
14.                     break;
15.                sum += x;
16.                n++;
17.           } while(1);
18.           if ( n > 0)
19.           {
20.                avg = sum / n;
21.           }
22.           else
23.                avg = 0;
24.           printf("Average is %f", avg);
25.    }
```

```
Enter a value or 0 to terminate …4
Enter a value or 0 to terminate …5
Enter a value or 0 to terminate …6
Average is 5
```

Program Listing 2.20 Program to Illustrate ***break*** *Statement*

Observe the do / while loop from Line 9 to Line 17.

```
do
{
     printf("Enter a value or 0 to terminate …");
     scanf("%f", &x);
     if(x == 0)
          break;
     sum += x;
     n++;
} while(1);
```

The while statement at Line 17, makes the loop infinite (forever), since the expression within the parenthesis always evaluates to 1. In the place of 1 any other number other than 0, would result in the same effect. At Line 14, the only way to exit this loop is through the **break** statement. When a sentinel value 0 is entered by the user, the loop breaks and the control is transferred to Line 18.

```
if ( n > 0)
```

where from the program executes the usual way.

The **continue** statement used in a **while**, **for**, ***do / while*** loop, skips the remaining statements in the body of that structure and proceeds with the next iteration of the loop. In **while** and **do / while** structures, the loop continuation test is evaluated immediately after the **continue** statement is executed. Whereas, in a **for** loop, the increment operation is executed, then the loop continuation test is evaluated.

Earlier, we stated that the **while** structure could be used in most cases to represent the **for** loop. The one exception occurs when the increment expression in the ***while*** structure occurs after the **continue** statement. In this case, the increment does not execute before the repetition continuation condition is tested, and the **while** does not execute in the same manner as the **for**.

The equivalent **while** loop of the **for** loop was shown in Fig. 2.9 in Section 2.10. If a ***continue*** statement is used in a **for** loop, then the equivalent **while** loop will not be correct, since the **while** loop will miss ***expression3***, which is responsible for loop increment / decrement. On the other hand, when the ***continue*** statement executes, program control continues with the increment/decrement of the control variable in the **for** structure.

The program listing 2.21 illustrates the use of **continue** statement in a program that allows entry of marks for 5 students and finds the number of students who have passed (marks >= 50) and their average ignoring the failed students.

```
/* Program Listing 2.21 : continue.c  */
/*   A Program that illustrates continue Statement */
#include <stdio.h>
void main(void)
{
      int i, marks, passed = 0, sum_marks_passed = 0;
      float avg = 0;
      for( i = 1;i <= 5;i++ )
      {
            printf("Enter the mark of the candidate(%d)...", i);
            scanf("%d", &marks);
            if( marks < 50 )
                  continue;
            sum_marks_passed += marks;
            passed++;
         }
         if(passed > 0)
         {
```

```
17.             avg = (float)sum_marks_passed / passed;
18.         }
19.         printf("No. of Students passed = %d\nSum = %d\nAverage =
                %f", passed, sum_marks_passed, avg);
20.     }
```

```
Enter the mark of the candidate(1)...35
Enter the mark of the candidate(2)...55
Enter the mark of the candidate(3)...25

Enter the mark of the candidate(4)...15
Enter the mark of the candidate(5)...45
No. of Students passed = 1
Sum = 55
Average = 55.000000
```

*Program Listing 2.21 Program to illustrate **continue** statement*

The for loop from Line 6 to Line 14,

```
for( i = 1;i <= 5;i++ )
{
    printf("Enter the mark of the candidate(%d)...", i);
    scanf("%d", &marks);
    if( marks < 50 )
        continue;
    sum_marks_passed += marks;
    passed++;
}
```

will allow the entry of marks for 5 students. At Line 11, the **continue** statement is executed only when the marks are less than 50 (failed). Whenever continue is executed, Lines 12 to 14 which are computing the sum of the marks for the passed candidates and the number of passed candidates will be skipped and the for loop is resumed at Line 6. Notice that i will be incremented even when continue is executed.

At Line 17,

```
avg = (float)sum_marks_passed / passed;
```

the average is computed after ensuring that at least one candidate has passed the examination otherwise the average is zero. This is necessary to avoid dividing by zero if all the candidates fail. At Line 19,

```
printf("No. of Students passed = %d\nSum = %d\nAverage = %f",
    passed, sum_marks_passed, avg);
```

the number of students passed, sum and average is printed.

MORE EXAMPLES

1. Write a Program to determine whether a given year is a Leap Year or not. Under our current (Gregorian) Calendar, a year is said to be a leap year if it is divisible by 400 or if it is divisible by 4 but not by 100. For example, the year 1996 is a leap year, whereas, 1900 is not.

```
#include <stdio.h>
#define TRUE 1
#define FALSE 0
void main(void)
{
      int y;
      printf("\nEnter any Year: ");
      scanf("%d", &y);
      if(y % 400 == 0)
            printf("The given Year %d is a Leap Year.\n", y);
      else if(y % 100 == 0)
            printf("The given Year %d is not a Leap Year.\n", y);
      else if(y % 4 == 0)
            printf("The given Year %d is a Leap Year.\n", y);
      else
            printf("The given Year %d is not a Leap Year.\n", y);
}
OUTPUT:
            Enter any Year: 1996
            The given Year 1996 is a Leap Year.
```

2. Write a Program to print a diamond of stars using a pair of nested *for loops.*

```
#include <stdio.h>
void main(void)
{
      int i, j, n;
      printf("\nEnter the Value of N: ");
      scanf("%d", &n);
```

```
        for(i = 0;i <= 2*n;i++)
        {
            for(j = 0;j <= 2*n;j++)
            {
                if(i <= n)
                    if(j < n-i || j > n+i)
                        printf(" ");
                    else
                        printf("*");
                else
                    if(j < i-n || j > 3*n-i)
                        printf(" ");
                    else
                        printf("*");
            }
            printf("\n");
        }
    }
```

OUTPUT:

```
        Enter the Value of N: 10
                          *
                         ***
                        *****
                       *******
                      *********
                     ***********
                    *************
                   ***************
                  *****************
                 *******************
                *********************
                 *******************
                  *****************
                   ***************
                    *************
                     ***********
                      *********
                       *******
                        *****
                         ***
                          *
```

3. Write a Program to determine whether a given positive integer is Prime or not.

```
#include <stdio.h>
void main(void)
{
      int num, i;
      printf("Enter a Number: ");
      scanf("%d", &num);
      i = 2;
      while(i <= num - 1)
      {
            if(num % i == 0)
            {
                  printf("\nThe Given Number %d is not a Prime Number.\n",
                                                                    num);
                  break;
            }
            i++;
      }
      if(i == num)
            printf("\nThe Given Number %d is a Prime Number.\n", num);
}
OUTPUT:
            Enter a Number: 5
            The Given Number 5 is a Prime Number.
```

4. Write a Program to print a Series of Prime Number upto the given number.

```
#include <stdio.h>
#include <math.h>
void main(void)
{
      int num, i, j, flag = 1;
      printf("Enter a Number: ");
      scanf("%d", &num);
      printf("\nThe Prime Number upto Given Range: %d are.\n", num);
      for(i = 1;i < num;i++)
      {
            if(i == 1 || i == 2)
```

```
                printf("%d\t", i);
            else
            {
                j = 2;
                while(j <= (int)ceil((sqrt(i))))
                {
                    if(i % j == 0)
                    {
                        flag = 0;
                        break;
                    }
                    j++;
                }
                if(flag == 1)
                    printf("%d\t", i);
            }
            flag = 1;
        }
    }
    OUTPUT:
            Enter a Number: 20
            The Prime Number upto Given Range: 20 are.
            1     2     3     5     7     11     13     17     19
```

5. Write a program to convert Decimal Number to Binary Number.

```
#include <stdio.h>
void main(void)
{
    int dec, bin = 0, decimal, digit, base = 1;
    printf("\nInput a Decimal Number: ");
    scanf("%d", &decimal);
    dec = decimal;
    while(decimal)
    {
        digit = decimal % 2;
        bin += digit * base;
```

```
            base *= 10;
            decimal /= 2;
      }
      printf("\nBinary Equivalent of Decimal Number %d = %d\n", dec,
bin);
}
OUTPUT:
            Input a Decimal Number: 7
            Binary Equivalent of Decimal Number 7 = 111
```

6. Write a program to convert Decimal Number to Octal Number.

```
#include <stdio.h>
void main(void)
{
      int dec, oct = 0, decimal, digit, base = 1;
      printf("\nInput a Decimal Number: ");
      scanf("%d", &decimal);
      dec = decimal;
      while(decimal)
      {
            digit = decimal % 8;
            oct += digit * base;
            base *= 10;
            decimal /= 8;
      }
      printf("\nOctal Equivalent of Decimal Number %d = %d\n", dec,
oct);
}
OUTPUT:
            Input a Decimal Number: 9
            Octal Equivalent of Decimal Number 9 = 11
```

7. Write a program to convert Decimal Number to Hexa-Decimal Number.

```
#include <stdio.h>
void main(void)
{
      int n, i = 0, j, base = 16, rem, num;
      char a[15];
```

```
        printf("Input a Decimal Number: ");
        scanf("%d", &n);
        num = n;
        do
        {
              rem = n % base;
              switch(rem)
              {
                    case 10:
                          a[i++] = 'A';
                          break;
                    case 11:
                          a[i++] = 'B';
                          break;
                    case 12:
                          a[i++] = 'C';
                          break;
                    case 13:
                          a[i++] = 'D';
                          break;
                    case 14:
                          a[i++] = 'E';
                          break;
                    case 15:
                          a[i++] = 'F';
                          break;
                    default:
                          a[i++] = '0'+ rem;
              }
              n /= base;
        }
        while(n != 0);
        a[i] = '\0';
        printf("\nHexa-Decimal Equivalent of Decimal Number %d = %d\n",
  num, strrev(a));
  }
```

OUTPUT:

```
            Input a Decimal Number: 123
            Hexa-Decimal Equivalent of Decimal Number 123 = 7B
```

8. Write a program to convert Binary Number to Decimal Number.

```
#include <stdio.h>
void main(void)
{
      int bin, binary, decimal = 0, digit, base = 1;
      printf("\nInput a Binary Number: ");
      scanf("%d", &binary);
      bin = binary;
      while(binary)
      {
            digit = binary % 10;
            decimal += digit * base;
            base *= 2;
            binary /= 10;
      }
      printf("\nDecimal Equivalent of Binary Number %d = %d\n", bin,
                                                          decimal);
}
OUTPUT:
            Input a Binary Number: 1001
            Decimal Equivalent of Binary Number 1001 = 9
```

9. Write a program to convert Octal Number to Decimal Number.

```
#include <stdio.h>
void main(void)
{
      int oct, octal, decimal = 0, digit, base = 1;
      printf("\nInput a Octal Number: ");
      scanf("%d", &octal);
      oct = octal;
      while(octal)
      {
            digit = octal % 10;
            decimal += digit * base;
            base *= 8;
            octal /= 10;
      }
```

```
        printf("\nDecimal Equivalent of Octal Number %d = %d\n", oct,
                                                            decimal);
}
OUTPUT:
        Input a Octal Number: 11
        Decimal Equivalent of Octal Number 111 = 9
```

10. Write a program to compute Cosine Series.

$$\text{COS(X)} = \frac{x^2}{2!}+\frac{x^4}{4!}-\frac{x^6}{6!}+\ldots+\frac{x^n}{n!}$$

```
#include <stdio.h>
void main(void)
{
    float x, y, t, sum;
    int i, n = 20;
    printf("Input X: ");
    scanf("%f", &x);
    y = x;
    x = x*3.1412/180;
    t = sum = 1;
    for(i = 1;i < n + 1;i++)
    {
        t = t * pow((double)(-1),(double)(2*i-1))*x*x/(2*i*(2*i-1));
        sum += t;
    }
    printf("COS( %f ) = %7.3f ", y, sum);
}
OUTPUT:
        Input X: 60
        COS( 60.000000 ) =   0.500
```

11. Write a program to compute Sine Series.

$$\text{SIN(X)} = x-\frac{x^3}{3!}+\frac{x^5}{5!}-\frac{x^7}{7!}+\ldots+\frac{x^n}{n!}$$

```
#include <stdio.h>
void main(void)
{
```

```
        float x, y, t, sum;
        int i, n = 20;
        printf("Input X: ");
        scanf("%f", &x);
        y = x;
        x = x*3.1412/180;
        t = sum = x;
        for(i = 1;i < n + 1;i++)
        {
                t = (t * pow((double)(-1),(double)(2*i-1))*x*x)/
(2*i*(2*i+1));
                sum += t;
        }
        printf("SIN( %f ) = %7.3f ", y, sum);
}
OUTPUT:
                Input X: 30
                SIN( 30.000000 ) =   0.500
```

12. Write a program to print Pascal Triangle using Binomial Theorem.

```
#include <stdio.h>
void main(void)
{
        int binom = 1, p, q = 0, r, x;
        printf("Enter the number of Rows : ");
        scanf("%d", &p);
          while(q < p)
          {
            for(r = 40 - 3*q;r > 0;--r)
            {
                printf(" ");
            }
            for(x = 0;x <= q;++x)
            {
                if((x==0) || (q == 0))
                     binom = 1;
                else
                     binom = (binom * (q-x+1))/x;
```

```
                printf("%6d", binom);
            }
            printf("\n");
            ++q;
        }
        printf("\n");
}
```

```
OUTPUT:
        Enter the number of Rows : 8

                                      1
                                  1       1
                              1       2       1
                          1       3       3       1
                      1       4       6       4       1
                  1       5      10      10       5       1
              1       6      15      20      15       6       1
          1       7      21      35      35      21       7       1
      1       8      28      56      70      56      28       8       1
  1       9      36      84     126     126      84      36       9       1
```

13. Write a program to print Pyramid of Digits

```
#include <stdio.h>
void main(void)
{
    int p, m, q, n;
    printf("Enter the number of Lines : ");
    scanf("%d", &n);
    for(p = 1;p <= n;p++)
    {
        for(q = 1;q <= n - p;q++)
            printf("    ");
        m = p;
        for(q = 1;q <= p;q++)
            printf("%4d", m++);
        m -= 2;
```

```
            for(q = 1;q < p;q++)
                printf("%4d", m--);
            printf("\n\n");
        }
        printf("\n");
}
```

OUTPUT:

```
            Enter the number of Lines : 8

                                       1
                                   2   3   2
                               3   4   5   4   3
                           4   5   6   7   6   5   4
                       5   6   7   8   9   8   7   6   5
                   6   7   8   9  10  11  10   9   8   7   6
               7   8   9  10  11  12  13  12  11  10   9   8   7
           8   9  10  11  12  13  14  15  14  13  12  11  10   9   8
```

14. Write a program to print Pyramid of Digits in Reverse

```
#include <stdio.h>
void main(void)
{
        int p, m, q, n, r;
        printf("Enter the number of Lines : ");
        scanf("%d", &n);
        for(p = n;p >= 1;p--)
        {
            for(q = n - p;q >= 1;q--)
                printf("    ");
            m = p;
            for(q = p;q >= 1;q--)
                printf("%4d", m++);
            m -= 2;
            for(q = p;q > 1;q--)
                printf("%4d", m--);
            printf("\n\n");
```

```
        }
        printf("\n");
    }
OUTPUT:
            Enter the number of Lines : 8

        8   9  10  11  12  13  14  15  14  13  12  11  10   9   8
            7   8   9  10  11  12  13  12  11  10   9   8   7
                6   7   8   9  10  11  10   9   8   7   6
                    5   6   7   8   9   8   7   6   5
                        4   5   6   7   6   5   4
                            3   4   5   4   3
                                2   3   2
                                    1
```

SELF-REVIEW EXERCISES

1. Calculations are normally performed by .... statements.
2. The .... standard library function displays information on the screen.
3. The escape sequence '**\n**' represents the .... character which causes the cursor to position to the begining of the next line on the screen.
4. The .... standard library function is used to obtain data from the keyboard.
5. The conversion specifier .... is used in a **scanf()** format control string to indicate that an integer will be input and in a **printf()** format control string to indicate that an integer will be output.
6. The .... statement is used to make decisions.
7. All programs can be written in terms of three control structures: ...., ... and ....
8. The .... selection structure is used to execute one action when a condition is true and another action when the condition is false.
9. Several statements grouped together in braces ({ and }) are called a ....

10. The process of setting certain variables to specific values at the beginning of a program is called ....

11. A special value used to indicate "**End of Data Entry**" is called a .... value.

12. A .... is a graphical representation of an algorithm.

13. Counter-controlled repetition is also known as .... repetition because it is known in advance how many times the loop will be executed.

14. The .... statement, when executed in a repetition structure causes the next iteration of the loop to be performed immediately.

15. The .... is used to test a particular variable or expression for each of the constant integral values it may assume.

EXERCISES

1. Write a program that prints the numbers 1 to 4 on the same line. Write the program using the following statements.
    1. *Using one printf statement with no conversion specifiers*
    2. *Using one printf statement with four conversion specifiers*
    3. *Using four printf statements.*

2. Write a program that reads in the radius of a circle and prints the circle's diameters, circumference and area. Use the constant value 3.14159 for π. Do each of these calculations inside the printf statement(s) and use the conversion specifier %f.

3. Write a program that reads in five integers and then determines and prints the largest andthe smallest integers in the group. Use only the programming techniques you have learned in this chapter.

4. Write a program that reads in two integers and determines and prints if the first is a multiple of the second. (Hint: Use the modulus operator)

5. Input an integer containing only 0s and 1s (i.e., a **binary** integer) and print its decimal equivalent.

6. Write a program that reads an integer and determines and prints how many digits in the integer are 7s.

7. Write a program that reads three nonzero float values and determines and prints if they could represent the sides of a triangle.

8. Write a program that estimates the value of the mathematical constant ***e*** by using the formula :

(a) $$e = 1+\frac{1}{1!}+\frac{1}{2!}+\frac{1}{3!}+\ldots$$

(b) $$e^x = 1+\frac{x}{1!}+\frac{x^2}{2!}+\frac{x^3}{3!}+\ldots$$

9. Calculate the value of π from the infinite series

$$\pi = 4-\frac{4}{3}+\frac{4}{5}-\frac{4}{7}+\frac{4}{9}-\frac{4}{11}+\ldots$$

10. Write a program that prints a table of the binary, octal and hexadecimal equivalents of the decimal numbers in the range 1 through 256. If you are not familiar with these number systems, read Appendix C first if you would like to attempt this exercise.

11. Write a program to print prime numbers between 1 and 500.

3

Functions, Arrays & Strings

3.1 WHAT IS A 'C' FUNCTION?

In the previous chapter, we have introduced several control structures and writing of C programs using these structures. As described in Section 2.2, C program can contain one or more functions and we have introduced you to the function **main()**. The function **main()** is a specific function, where the execution of C program starts. The user may write more functions to improve the modularity and reuse of the programs.

A function is a self - contained program segment that carries out some specific well - defined task(s). If a program contains multiple functions, their definitions may appear in any order. C is not a block - structured language in the same sense as Pascal or similar language, because in C functions may not be defined within another function. On the other hand variables can be defined in a block-structured fashion within a function. We shall see more about the block-structure and scope of these variables later on. So far we have used only library functions like **printf()**, **scanf()** that have been provided for us by the C library. Now it is time to write a few C functions of our own. We shall start with a simple example.

3.2 WRITING & USING A SIMPLE 'C' FUNCTION

We shall present a C function, which computes the factorial of **n** (**n** < 12) in Program Listing 3.1.

```
1    long factorial(int n)
2    {
3          long fact = 1;
4          int i;
5          if(n < 1 )
6                return 0;
7          for( i = 2;i <= n;i++ )
8                fact *= i;
9          return fact;
10   }
```

Program Listing 3.1 A function that computes factorial of a number

The general form of function as per the ANSI Standards is shown below.

```
<return-type><function name>( <parameter declarations, if any> )
{
      declarations;
      statements;
}
```

The general form of a function

where ***<return-type>*** represents the data type of the value, which is returned by the function, and ***<function name>*** represents the function name which is to be chosen following the same rules which you use for an identifier (refer to Section 1.7).

In the Program Listing 3.1, Line 1,

```
long factorial(int n)
```

gives the definition of the function. The *<return type>* is long, the *<function name>* is factorial and there is only one parameter n, which is an integer.

Whenever this function is called by an other function, the function call must specify the value of the parameter. So any call to this function of the form, factorial(8), factorial(x) where x is already initialized to some integer value or factorial(2 + x) are all valid calls. Let us suppose that this function is invoked with a function call factorial(4), then the body of the function is executed with n as 4.

Line 3,

```
long fact = 1;
```

declares the local integer variables fact, i and fact is initialized to 1.

Line 5,

```
if(n < 1 )
```

we have chosen to return 0, because factorial of any number zero or less is zero by convension.

Line 7,

```
for( i = 2;i <= n;i++ )
```

the for loop operates 2 to n times, each time the fact is multiplied by i (i.e., n – 1 times). Thus when n is 4, the sum is 1 x 2 x 3 x 4 = 24.

Line 9,

```
return fact;
```

returns the value of fact, which in this case is 24 to the calling program.

We will now present a program which calls this function factorial, to compute the following series

$$Y(x) = 1 + \frac{x^2}{2!} + \frac{x^4}{4!} + \frac{x^6}{6!} + \ldots + \frac{x^n}{n!}$$

The value of x is inputted by the user. Since C has no exponential operator (like Fortran's **), let us write a function, power(float x, int n) to raise some floating point number x to the power of a positive integer n which could be used in the computation of the above series. The program listing 3.2 is for computing the above series upto 10 terms.

```
/*    Program Listing 3.2 : expr1.c
      Program to evaluates the given Series */
#include <stdio.h>
#include <math.h>
double power(float x, float n)
{
      int i;
      double p = 1.0;
      for(i = 1;i <= n;i++)
            p *= x;
      return p;
}
```

```
13    double factorial(int n)
14    {
15          double fact = 1;
16          int i;
17          if(n < 1 )
18                return 0;
19          for(i = 1;i <= n;i++)
20                fact *= i;
21          return fact;
22    }
23    main()
24    {
25          double x, y = 1, a, b;
26          int i;
27          printf("Enter any Value ...");
28          scanf("%lf", &x);
29          for(i = 2;i <= 20;i += 2)
30          {
31                a = power(x, i);
32                b = factorial(i);
33                y += a/b;
34          }
35          printf("Y = %lf", y);
36    }
```

```
Enter any Value ...5
Y = 74.209946
```

Program Listing 3.2 Program for evaluation of a given Series

Notice that the return type of the power is double to accommodate large return values. Suppose we call this function as power(2, 4) then the for loop at Line 8, operates for 4 times and multiplies 2, 4 times and returns the value 16 which is 2^4.

Now let us use the two functions factorial and power in program listing 3.2 to compute the series. The series is to be computed up to 10 terms, requiring us to compute factorial 20. Since factorial 20 is a 19 digit number, the data type long is insufficient to hold this number. So the function factorial is modified to return a double instead of a long whose range will accommodate factorial 20.

The student is advised to refer the range of long and double given in Table 2.3. However, this may appear slightly awkward as the factorial of an integer should be an integer. Probably we shall later on discuss how to compute factorial of very large number even beyond the range of the double (factorial(500)!!). For now we shall compromise with a return type double for the function factorial.

Both the functions are presented from line 5 to 22,

```
double power(float x, float n)
{
        int i;
        double p = 1.0;
        for(i = 1;i <= n;i++)
                p *= x;
        return p;
}
double factorial(int n)
{
        double fact = 1;
        int i;
        if(n < 1 )
                return 0;
        for(i = 1;i <= n;i++)
                fact *= i;
        return fact;
}
```

before the function main(). In the main() the value of x is accepted at line 28 using scanf()

```
scanf("%lf", &x);
```

The for loop at Line 29

```
for(i = 2;i <= 20;i += 2)
```

calls the power() at Line 31,

```
a = power(x, i);
```

with x and i to compute x^i and store the return value in the variable a. The function factorial is called at Line 32,

```
b = factorial(i);
```

to compute i! and store it in b.

At Line 33,

```
y += a/b;
```

the value of y is computed by adding a/b to the current value of y. Notice the initial value of y is 1 and i is 2 and the for loop runs 10 times for the values of i = 2, 4, 6, 8, 10, …, 20 as required by the series.

Observe the order in which the functions are declared namely power(), factorial() and main(). This is not compulsory. These functions can be in any order, provided we include a formal declarations in the beginning before we use the function. We rewrite the program presented in program listing 3.2 including the function declarations and present it in program listing 3.3

```
/*    Program Listing 3.3 : expr2.c
      Improved version of Program Listing 2.2*/
#include <stdio.h>
double factorial(int);
double power(float, float);
void main(void)
{
      double x, y = 1, a, b;
      int i;
      printf("Enter Any Value ...");
      scanf("%lf", &x);
      for(i = 2;i <= 20;i += 2)
            y += power(x, i) / factorial(i);
      printf("Y = %lf", y);
}
double factorial(int n)
{
      double fact = 1;
      int i;
      if(n < 1 )
            return 0;
      for(i = 1;i <= n;i++)
            fact *= i;
      return fact;
}
```

```
24    double power(float x, float n)
25    {
26          int i;
27          double p = 1.0;
28          for(i = 1;i <= n;i++)
29                p *= x;
30          return p;
31    }
```

```
Enter any Value ...5
Y = 74.209946
```

Program Listing 3.3 Improved version of Program Listing 3.2

The lines 2 and 3 in program listing 3.3,

```
double factorial(int);
double power(float, float);
```

are the formal declaration of the functions factorial() and power() which are used in main(). Now the functions can appear after the main() because by formal declaration, we are telling the compiler, that the functions do exist somewhere in the same file and have the same return type, name and arguments. Notice some more changes that we made in the program, like we have eliminated the variables a and b straight away computed the value of y. This is more desirable than using a & b.

3.3 MORE ABOUT FUNCTIONS

In general, a C program is just a set of definitions of variables and functions. Communication between the functions is by arguments and values returned by the function, and through external variables (which will be discussed later). In any programming language, functions or sub-programs or sub-routines are quite common. Usually, the calling function passes certain values (parameters) to the called function. There are several ways of passing parameters. But more importantly there are two common mechanisms namely call-by-value and call-by-reference used by most of the languages. As an example, PASCAL uses both these mechanisms. Call-by-value means, the called function is given the values of its arguments in temporary variables rather than the originals. Call-by-reference means, the called routines has access to the original argument, not a local copy. However, C uses only call-by-value mechanism though it is possible to pass explicitly the address of the variable to the called function which enables the called function to access the original copy of the parameter through this address. This should not be interpreted as call-by-reference. More explanation about this is given in subsequent sections.

One advantage with functions you might have observed is that you can call the function any number of times to do a specific task, anywhere in the program without repeating the code. This property is refered as ***modularity***. Another obvious advantage with functions is, you would never write once again those functions you have written earlier, should you need them in some other programs. This property is known as ***reusability***. At this point, you should note that it is possible to call functions in your programs that are not present in the same file. This property of C is discussed later under Storage Classes.

Another point to be noted at this stage is that, if a function does not return any value, the return type should be indicated as **void**. Further, **void** can also be used within the parentheses of the function, if the function does not expect any arguments. Thus, at Line 4,

```
void main(void)
```

of Program Listing 3.3 indicates that **main()** does not return anything, as well as it does not expect any arguments. In most of the programs from now, we will be using functions, to improve the ***modularity*** and ***reusability***.

3.4 RECURSIVE FUNCTIONS

When a function calls itself directly or indirectly is known as ***recursive function***. C functions may also be used recursively. Let us illustrate the idea of recursive functions, by writing a recursive function to compute factorial of a given number. The function, we have written in earlier section, is known as a iterative function, since, we have used a for loop, to iterate (repeat a number of times) to compute the factorial (1 * 2 * 3 * 4 * …n). Let us now think about the same problem in a recursive way. Consider the following

```
n * ( n - 1 ) * ( n - 2 ) * …. 1 * 2 * 3
```

which is nothing but factorial of n and can be written as n * (n – 1)! Thus the factorial of (n – 1) can be written as (n – 1) * (n – 2)! This kind of expressions are known as ***recurrence relations***. Computing n! by knowing (n – 1)! and computing (n – 1)! by knowing (n – 2)! and so on computing 2! by knowing 1! is known as a ***recursive computation***. Since 1! is known to be 1, this forms the terminating condition for the recursion. Now let us present the recursive function that computes n! in program listing 3.4.

```
double rfactorial(int n)
{
      if(n <= 1) return 1.0;
      return (n * rfactorial( n - 1 )) ;
}
```

Program Listing 3.4 *Recursive function for computing factorial n*

The function declaration at line 1 is same as that of a non-recursive function. At line 3,

```
if(n <= 1) return 1.0;
```

is the base or the terminating condition, which allows the recursion to wind up. You should be sure that this condition is met somewhere down the recursive calls, otherwise the recursion will go on infinitely and will never terminate.

Lines 5,

```
return (n * rfactorial( n - 1 )) ;
```

makes the recursive call, to compute (n – 1)! and takes the return value of rfactorial(n – 1) multiplies with n and returns the value to the calling function.

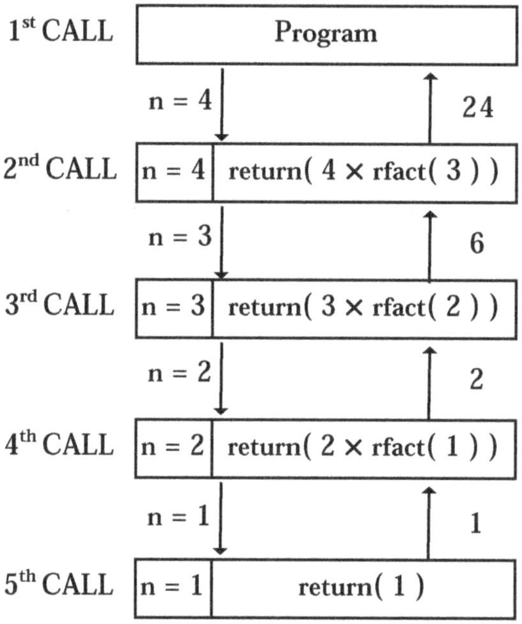
1st CALL
Program
n = 4
24
2nd CALL
n = 4
return(4 × rfact(3))
n = 3
6
3rd CALL
n = 3
return(3 × rfact(2))
n = 2
2
4th CALL
n = 2
return(2 × rfact(1))
n = 1
1
5th CALL
n = 1
return(1)

Fig 3.1 Recursive Calls of rfactorial for n = 4

Assume that the rfactorial() is called with n = 4 by some function. Let us trace the steps and find how the recursive calls progress and eventually terminate when the base condition is met. Figure 3.1 indicates the complete sequence of events that take place when a call of rfactorial(4) is made. Each box represents one copy of the function invoked with the value n indicated in the box. Notice how the recursive call is terminated when the base condition is met and the return value of each copy of the function.

Let us now present another example for computing n^{th} Fibonacci number. The fibonacci sequence starts as,

0, 1, 1, 2, 3, 5, 8, 13, 21, 34, 55 ...

Each new term of the series is obtained by taking the sum of the two previous terms. If we call the first and second term of the sequence as F_0 and F_1 then $F_0 = 0$, $F_1 = 1$ and in general,

$$F_n = F_{n-1} + F_{n-2}$$

The above equation is known as a ***recurrence relation***, which means, to generate n^{th} fibonacci number, we should compute $(n - 2)^{th}$ and $(n - 1)^{th}$ fibonacci numbers. The Program Listing 3.5 contains two functions fib() (an iterative or non-recursive function) and rfib() (a recursive function) to compute n^{th} fibonacci number.

```
/*    Program Listing 3.5 : fib.c
      Evaluates the Fibonacci Series  */
#include <stdio.h>

typedef unsigned long  big;

big rfib(int);
big fib(int);

void main(void)
{
      int i,m;
      printf("Enter the Number: ");
      scanf("%d",&m);
      for(i=0;i<=m;i++)
            printf("%ld  ", fib(i));
      printf("\n");
      for(i=0;i<=m;i++)
            printf("%ld  ", rfib(i));
}
big rfib(int n){   /* recursive program */
      if( n<=0 ) return(0);
      if( n==1 ) return(1);
      return (rfib(n-1) + rfib(n-2));
}
big fib(int n){ /* iterative  or non-recursive program */
      big fn,fnm1,fnm2,i;
      if( n<=0 ) return(0);
      if( n==1 ) return(1);
      fnm1=1; fnm2=0;
      for(i=2;i<=n;i++){
```

```
30.             fn= fnm1+fnm2;
31.             fnm2=fnm1;
32.             fnm1=fn;
33.         }
34.         return fn;
35.     }
```

```
Enter the Number: 10
0 1 1 2 3 5 8 13 21 34 55
0 1 1 2 3 5 8 13 21 34 55
```

Program Listing 3.5 Program to generate n^{th} Fibonacci Number

Both these function compute the nth Fibonacci number, taking n as an input parameter. Notice that the return type is selected as big which is not a standard data type of C. However at line 3 by using the statement,

```
typedef unsigned long  big;
```

we have defined unsigned long as big. By doing so, the compiler will replace unsigned long where ever big occurs. Note that typedef is a keyword through which this is achieved.

At lines 5 and 6

```
big rfib(int);
big fib(int);
```

define fib() and rfib() prototypes. At line 12 in the ***main()***,

```
scanf("%d",&m);
```

the value of m is accepted. The for loop at line 13,

```
for(i=0;i<=m;i++)
```

calls the function fib(), the iterative version to compute the nth fibonacci number and generates the fibonacci sequence up to m. The for loop at line 16,

```
for(i=0;i<=m;i++)
```

calls the function rfib(), the recursive version to compute the nth fibonacci number and generates the fibonacci sequence up to m. The first two lines of interative as well as recursive version are same, since the first two fibonacci numbers $F_0 = 0$, $F_1 = 1$ are given rather than computed. In the recursive version, these two lines are used as the base conditions to terminate recursion, while in the iterative version, they are used as starting values. Suppose we call rfib() with n = 4, then the recursive calls are depicted in the Figure 3.2.

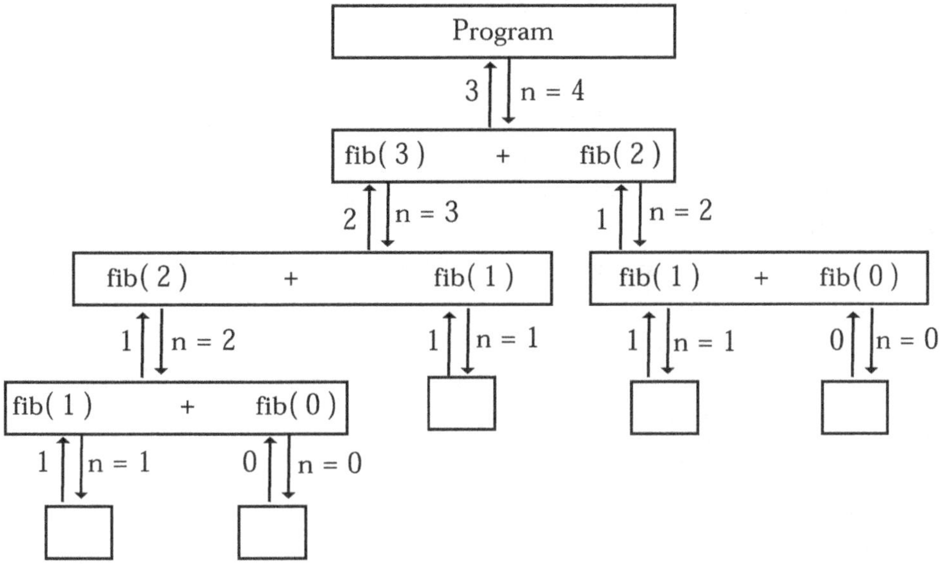
Program
3
n = 4
fib(3) + fib(2)
2
n = 3
1
n = 2
fib(2) + fib(1)
fib(1) + fib(0)
1
n = 2
1
n = 1
1
n = 1
0
n = 0
fib(1) + fib(0)
1
n = 1
0
n = 0

Fig 3.2 Recursive Calls of rfib() for n = 4

The final value returned is F_4 which is equal to 3. You must have already noticed that each rfib() call in turn generates two recursive calls as against rfactorial(), which generates only one recursive call (Fig. 3.1). In the iterative version, the nth fibonacci number is computed by using a for loop to generate F_2, F_3, . . ., F_n by initializing fnm1 as $F_0(0)$, and fnm2 as $F_1(1)$. The student is advised to run with n = 35 and see the output. You will certainly observe that the generation of fibonacci numbers using recursive function will be very slow in comparison with that of the iterative function. This is obviously expected as the value of n grows, the depth of recursion increases and results in huge number of function calls. Thus recursion is very inefficient as far as the speed of execution is concerned. Then why recursion? Notice the logic of fib() and rfib(). rfib() reveals, the recursive formulation of the fibonacci series while fib() does not. For certain problems in computer science, it is much easier to conceive a recursive solution rather than an iterative solution. Since every recursive function, has an equivalent iterative function, even if the solution to a problem is best conceived recursively, the equivalent non-recursive function can be developed to increase the execution speed. Almost all the algorithms of ***binary trees*** (discussed in chapter 6, TREES & GRAPHS), will be developed using recursion. However, some equivalent iterative programs will also be discussed in chapter 6, to make the student understand how to write a non-recursive version for a recursive program.

3.5 SINGLE DIMENSIONAL ARRAYS

Many applications require to process multiple data items that have common characteristics. In such situations, it is often convenient to place the data items into an array, where they will share the same name. However, the individual data items, should be of same type and ***Storage Class***. C provides the facility to declare an array of any size and all C compilers guarantee contiguous allocation of memory to all the data items that belong to the same array. For example, if a character array x of size 10 is declared then the compiler reserves 10 bytes of contiguous memory to hold these character. Each array element is referred through, by specifying the array name followed by a index enclosed in square brackets ([]). Each index must be expressed as a non-negative integer constant / expression. Thus, the elements in the character array x are referenced as x[0], x[1], x[2], ..., x[9]. Notice that in C, the indexing starts from 0 and not from 1.

Arrays are declared in much the same manner as ordinary data types, except that each array must be accompanied by the size specification within the square brackets. In general, a one dimensional array may be declared as follows

```
<storage class><data type> <array name>[<size>].
```

where *<storage class>*, which is optional, could be ***static***, ***auto*** or ***extern*** (will be discussed later in this chapter). The ***<data type>*** could be a standard C data type like ***int***, ***char***, ***float***, etc., or user defined data type like ***struct***, ***union***, etc.,(will be discussed later). Array name should be selected as per the rules specified earlier for an identifier. With these simple ideas, let us now present program for the following problem using arrays.

A company pays its sales person on a commission basis. The sales person receives $200 per week + 9% of the gross sales for that week. For example, a person whose gross sale is $5000 in a week, receives $200 + 9% of 5000 or a total of $650. Determine how many of the sales persons earned salaries in each of the following range. Assume each sales person's salary is truncated to an integer amount).

(a) *Range 1 is $200-$299*
(b) *Range 2 is $300-$399*
(c) *Range 3 is $400-$499*
(d) *Range 4 is $500-$599*
(e) *Range 5 is $600-$699*
(f) *Range 6 is $700-$799*
(g) *Range 7 is $800-$899*
(h) *Range 8 is $900-$999*
(i) *Range 9 is $1000 and over.*

To solve the above problem, we need to compute the salary of each sales person as the sales amount is inputted and increment a counter corresponding to the range in which the sales person's salary falls. Since there are nine ranges, we need nine counters to be declared and initialized to zero. By using an array range_counter of dimension 9, we will present an elegant solution for the above problem. The solution is presented in program listing 3.6.

```
/*   Program Listing 3.6 : array.c
     Evaluates the Range of Counter in Arrays   */
#include <stdio.h>

void main(void)
{
     int range_counter[9], comm, sale, sal;
     int i;
     for(i = 0;i < 9;i++)
          range_counter[i] = 0; /* initialize array to 0   */
     do
     {
          printf("\nEnter Weekly Sales or -1 to Exit: ");
          scanf("%d", &sale);
          if(sale >= 0)
          {
               comm = (int)(0.09 * sale);
               sal = 200 + comm;
               if(sal < 1000)
                    range_counter[sal/100 - 2]++;
               else
                    range_counter[8]++;
          }
     }
     while(sale >= 0);
     for(i = 0;i< 9;i++)
          printf("Range of Counter[%d] = %d\n", i,
               range_counter[i]);
}
```

```
Enter Weekly Sales or -1 to Exit: 2500
Enter Weekly Sales or -1 to Exit: 3500
```

```
Enter Weekly Sales or -1 to Exit: 950
Enter Weekly Sales or -1 to Exit: 750
Enter Weekly Sales or -1 to Exit: 5000
Enter Weekly Sales or -1 to Exit: 7000
Enter Weekly Sales or -1 to Exit: 150

Range of Counter[1] = 3
Range of Counter[2] = 0
Range of Counter[3] = 1
Range of Counter[4] = 1
Range of Counter[5] = 1
Range of Counter[6] = 0
Range of Counter[7] = 1
Range of Counter[8] = 0
Range of Counter[9] = 0
```

Program Listing 3.6 Program to illustrate the use of arrays

Line 5,

```
int range_counter[9], comm, sale, sal;
```

declares the array range_counter and other variables required. Line 7,

```
for(i = 0;i < 9;i++)
    range_counter[i] = 0; /* initialize array to 0    */
```

initializes all the 9 locations of range_counter to 0. This is essential since we are going to increment each of these counters after computing the salary. The first part of ***do / while*** loop from Line 9 to Line 23,

```
do
{
    printf("\nEnter Weekly Sales or -1 to Exit: ");
    scanf("%d", &sale);
    if(sale >= 0)
    {
        comm = (int)(0.09 * sale);
        sal = 200 + comm;
        if(sal < 1000)
            range_counter[sal/100 - 2]++;
        else
            range_counter[8]++;
    }
}
while(sale >= 0);
```

allows you to accept the weekly sale value of a sales person and compute the commission and salary. Notice that the commission is truncated at line 15, using int as the casting operator. The if statement at line 13, will allow the computation of commission(comm), salary(sal) only when the sale is greater than or equal to zero and terminates the ***do / while*** loop if a negative sale is entered (sentinel value). The inner if statement at Line 17, will increment the respective range counter depending on the sal. Observe the expression sal / 100 - 2 at Line 18. This will be evaluated to 0 if the sal is between 200 and 299 and to 1 if sal is between 300 and 399 and so on up to 7 if sal is between 900 and 999. In the case of 1000 and over (range 9) is handled in the else part by incrementing the last counter (range_counter[8]++). The ***for*** loop and ***printf()*** at line 24 and 25,

```
for(i = 0;i< 9;i++)
      printf("Range of Counter[%d] = %d\n", i,
                                   range_counter[i]);
```

print the counter values of ranges from 1 to 9. The student at this stage should understand how we have handled, the subscript range 0 through 8 of range_counter to represent ranges 1 to 9.

3.6 PASSING ARRAYS AS ARGUMENTS TO FUNCTIONS

In C, all function arguments are passed by value. This means the called function is given values to its arguments into temporary variables rather than originals, by the calling function, unlike some other programming languages like FORTRAN, where original copy is handed over to the function. The later method of passing the parameters is known as ***call by reference*** which is not supported by C. For example, while calling the function fib() in program listing 3.5, the value of n is passed by the calling function ***main()*** by value which means, the value is copied into the temporary variable n. The life of this temporary variable n is only limited to the execution of the function and cannot be referenced outside the function. Such variables are known as ***Local (Automatic) Variables.***

The mechanism of passing an array is different from that of the basic data types. Actually in C, an array name can be used as an argument to a function. By convention the name of the array represents the starting address of the array, which means the called function will get the address of the original array passed by a calling function. Thus the called function, can manipulate the elements of the original array. Many authors sometimes incorrectly call this as ***call by reference.*** And the student should note that C does not support call by reference in the sense that FORTRAN or PASCAL do. Probably, this mechanism (Passing the Address of the Array) has been adapted in C to avoid making a local copy in a function.

Let us now illustrate, how an array can be passed as an argument to a function, by writing a function that takes n number of integers in an array and returns the largest integer from the array in program listing 3.7.

```c
/*  Program Listing 3.7 : arrlst.c
    Evaluates the Largest Number in Array*/
#include <stdio.h>

int maxm(int[], int);

void main(void)
{
    int a[20], i, n;
    printf("Enter the number of elements(not more than 20)...");
    scanf("%d", &n);
    for(i = 0;i < n;i++)
    {
        printf("\nEnter %d Value ...", i+1);
        scanf("%d", &a[i]);
    }
    printf("The Largest Number is %d ...", maxm(a, n));
}

int maxm(int arr[], int m)
{
    int largest, i;
    largest = arr[0];
    for(i = 1;i < m;i++)
    {
        if(arr[i] > largest)
            largest = arr[i];
    }
    return(largest);
}
```

```
Enter the number of elements(not more than 20)...5
Enter 1 Value ...8
Enter 2 Value ...6
Enter 3 Value ...10
Enter 4 Value ...7
Enter 5 Value ...2
The Largest Number is 10 ...
```

Program Listing 3.7 *Program to illustrate passing of array to a function.*

At Lines 18 to 28 the function maxm(),

```
int maxm(int arr[], int m)
{
        int largest, i;
        largest = arr[0];
        for(i = 1;i < m;i++)
        {
                if(arr[i] > largest)
                        largest = arr[i];
        }
        return(largest);
}
```

receives the address of the array which has been created in the main(). Notice the call to this function, at Line 15, in ***main()***

```
        printf("The Largest Number is %d ...", maxm(a, n));
```

The arguments passed are **a** the address of the array and **n** the number of elements of the array. In the function, maxm(), we can reference any element of array **a** by subscripting arr. For example, while the function is executing arr[0] refers to the first element of the array **a**. The for loop at line 22, runs through the array and determines the largest number by comparing each value to **largest**. Notice that the variable largest is initialized to the first value of the array outside the for loop and the for loop runs from 1 to n – 1 comparing the rest of elements. Line 27, returns the largest value.

It is possible to initialize an array in C, like you initialize other data types. The program listing 2.8, initializes an array list and passes the same to a function where the average of the numbers contained in the array is computed and returned.

```
/*      Program Listing 3.8 : ARRAVG.c
        Evaluates the Average of the Values in Array */
#include <stdio.h>

void main(void)
{
        float average(int, int[]);
        int list[] = {0, 1, 2, 3, 4, 5, 6, 7, 8, 9};
        float avg;
        avg = average(10, list);
        printf("\nThe Average is %f ...", avg);
}
```

```
11.
12.  float average(int  m, int x[])
13.  {
14.        int sum = 0, i;
15.        for(i = 0;i < m;i++)
16.              sum = sum + x[i];
17.        printf("\nSum = %d", sum);
18.        return((float)sum / (float)m);
19.  }
```

```
Sum = 45
The Average is 4.500000 ...
```

Program Listing 3.8 Program to illustrate initialization of an array.

At Line 6,

```
int list[] = {0, 1, 2, 3, 4, 5, 6, 7, 8, 9};
```

an array is declared and initializes with 10 values. Notice that all the values are separated by commas and are enclosed in braces. There is no need to indicate the dimension as the initialization itself determines the dimension. At Lines 12 to 19,

```
float average(int m, int x[])
{
      int sum = 0, i;
      for(i = 0;i < m;i++)
            sum = sum + x[i];
      printf("\nSum = %d", sum);
      return((float)sum / (float)m);
}
```

the function average() computes the average by adding n elements of the array using a for loop and dividing by n. At Line 5,

```
float average(int, int[]);
```

is the prototype declaration of the function average() which is now included in the main(). There is no great difference, as against earlier declarations made outside the ***main()***. Since we have included the declaration in the ***main()***, only main() knows the prototype of the function average(). This is known as the ***scope of the declaration*** which will be discussed at the end of this chapter.

3.7 MULTI - DIMENSIONAL ARRAYS

Multi – Dimensional Array means having more than one dimension. C allows multi dimensional arrays of virtually any number of dimensions subject to the memory constraints. However, the most important of the multi dimension arrays is the two dimensional arrays, used usually to represent a table of values (a matrix of information), arranged in rows and columns.

To identify a particular two dimensional array element, we must specify two subscripts. By convention the first identifies the row and the second identifies the column. Arrays that require two subscripts, to identify a particular element are called double subscripted arrays.

Let us look into a simple problem of writing the transpose of a matrix. When the rows and columns of the matrix are interchanged, the resultant matrix is called the transpose of the original matrix. If the given matrix is of the size m ´ n, i.e., m rows and n columns, the transpose will be of the size n ´ m, i.e., n rows and m columns.

In the example, we shall consider only a square matrix. However the program in program listing 3.9 works for any matrix.

```
/*    Program Listing 3.9 : ARRTRN.c
      Program to transpose a matrix*/
#include <stdio.h>

void transpose(int x[] [3], int r, int c);
void print_mat(int x[] [3], int r, int c);

void main(void)
{
      int a[] [3] = {  {1, 2, 3},
                       {4, 5, 6},
                       {7, 8, 9}
                    }; /* declaration of a 2 dimensional array
                          and intialisation */
      print_mat(a, 3, 3);
      transpose(a, 3, 3);
      printf("\n");
      print_mat(a, 3, 3);
}
```

```
void transpose(int x[][3], int r, int c) /* passing a 2D array to
                               a function by conventional method */
{
      int t, i, j;
      for(i = 0;i < r;i++)
      {
            for(j = i;j < c;j++)
            {                   /* Inplace Transpose */
                  t = x[i][j];
                  x[i][j] = x[j][i];
                  x[j][i] = t;
            }
      }
}

void print_mat(int y[][3], int r, int c)
{
      int i, j;
      for(i = 0;i < r;i++)
      {
            for(j = 0;j < c;j++)
            {
                  printf("%5d", y[i][j]);
            }
            printf("\n");
      }
}
```

```
    1    2    3
    4    5    6
    7    8    9
    1    4    7
    2    5    8
    3    6    9
```

Program Listing 3.9 Program to transpose a matrix

At line 8,

```
int a[] [3] = { {1, 2, 3},
                {4, 5, 6},
                {7, 8, 9}
              }; /* declaration of a 2 dimensional array
                    and intialisation */
```

a two dimensional array is declared and initialized with 3 rows and 3 columns. Notice that the second dimension is always needed as the compiler should know this essentially to determine the storage pattern. At lines 3 & 4,

```
void transpose(int x[] [3], int r, int c);
void print_mat(int x[] [3], int r, int c);
```

we find the formal declaration of two functions namely transpose and print_mat. Both the functions take 3 parameters, the matrix, the number of rows and the number of columns.

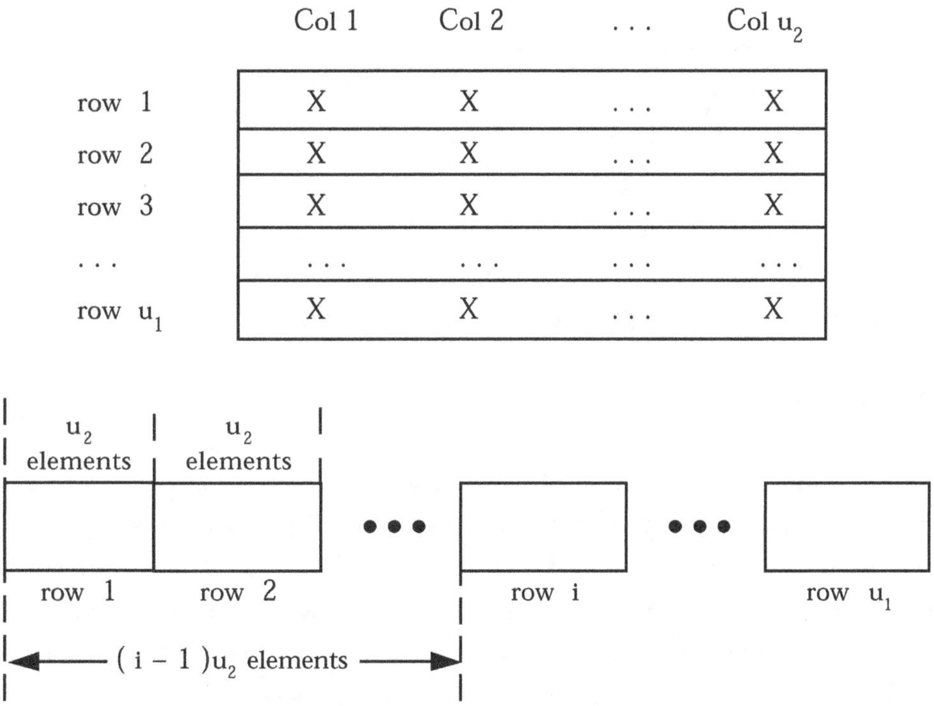
Col 1
Col 2
Col u_2
row 1
row 2
row 3
row u_1
u_2 elements
u_2 elements
row 1
row 2
row i
row u_1
(i – 1)u_2 elements

Fig. 3.3 Distribution of elements in the Memory

Note that the argument that receives the two dimensional array should have the specification of the second dimension or the number of elements in each row, since the actual representation of two dimensional array in the memory will be a row major representation, i.e., the elements are distributed in the memory row-wise as shown in the Fig.3.3.

When an element of a two dimensional array is referenced as a[i][j]; the compiler has to locate the jth element in the ith row. The compiler has to skip (i – 1) * (the number of elements in each row) to reach the ith row and then from there it should find the jth element (see Fig. 3.9). Obviously, the compiler needs the number of elements in a row. And therefore it has to be passed to the function. At line 23 & 26,

```
for(i = 0;i < r;i++)
{
    for(j = i;j < c;j++)
    {                   /* Inplace Transpose */
```

the function transpose uses two for statements one within the other to run through all the elements of the two dimensional array to effect the exchange of the columns and rows. The ***inplace exchange*** of elements is done at lines 27 to 29

```
t = x[i][j];.
x[i][j] = x[j][i];
x[j][i] = t;
```

with the use of a temporary variable t. Notice that the inside for loop starts from j = i, so that already transposed elements of each row are not disturbed. The student is advised to check the logic of the inner loop by actually performing on an example matrix.

3.8 STRINGS

The most common type of array in C is the array of characters which is known as string. In C, there is no separate data type available to represent a string. As stated strings are treated as arrays of characters and are terminated with ASCII NULL.('\0'). Thus an array, which is filled with characters and not terminated with a NULL, is known as an array of characters and the one that is terminated with NULL is known as a string. However several functions such as scanf(), gets() which input strings to a program will automatically place a NULL character at the end.

Several functions such as ***strlen()***, ***strcpy()*** etc., are defined in the header file **string.h** to handle various operations on the strings. String constants are always represented within double quotes as against the character constants that are represented in single quotes. For example, let us look into the program listing 3.10, wherein several concepts about strings have been introduced.

Line 5,

```
char name1[] = "Computer Science";
```

declares a character array name1 and assigns it a string constant “Computer Science”. Notice that no ‘\0’ explicitly need be put into the string. Automatically, it will be placed at the end of the string. Line 6,

```
char name2[] = { 'C', 'o', 'm', 'p', 'u', 't', 'e', 'r', '
                 ', 'S', 'c', 'i', 'e', 'n', 'c', 'e', '\0'
                 };
```

initializes name2 in a conventional way by putting characters in each location. Notice that the last character we have placed is ‘\0’ which is necessary if we want to treat name2 as a string.

```
        /*  Program Listing 3.10 : STRING1.c
            Evaluates the Size of Strings*/
1.      #include <stdio.h>
2.
3.      void main(void)
4.      {
5.          char name1[] = "Computer Science";
6.          char name2[] = { 'C', 'o', 'm', 'p', 'u', 't', 'e', 'r', '
                             ', 'S', 'c', 'i', 'e', 'n', 'c', 'e', '\0'
                             };
7.          char name3[20], name4[20];
8.
9.          printf("Enter any String ...");
10.         scanf("%s", name3);
11.
12.         fflush(stdin);
13.
14.         printf("Enter any Other String ...");
15.         gets(name4);
16.
17.         printf("\nName1 = %s", name1);
18.         printf("\nName2 = %s", name2);
```

```
19.         printf("\nName3 = %s", name3);
20.         printf("\nName4 = ");
21.         puts(name4);
22.
23.         printf("Size of Name1 = %d", sizeof(name1));
24.         printf("\nSize of Name2 = %d", sizeof(name2));
25.         printf("\nSize of Name3 = %d", sizeof(name3));
26.         printf("\nSize of Name4 = %d", sizeof(name4));
27.   }
```

```
Enter any String ...India
Enter any Other String ...Andhra
Name1 = Computer Science
Name2 = Computer Science
Name3 = India
Name4 = Andhra
Size of Name1 = 17
Size of Name2 = 17
Size of Name3 = 20
Size of Name4 = 20
```

Program Listing 3.10 Program that demonstrates several characteristics of strings

Line 7,

```
char name3[20], name4[20];
```

declares two more character arrays, that will be used to accept strings through the library functions scanf() and gets().

Line 12,

```
fflush(stdin);
```

is used between ***scanf()*** and ***gets()*** to clear the input buffer.

At Line 10,

```
scanf("%s", name3);
```

scanf() accepts the string leaving the carriage return delimiter in the input buffer, which you would have entered while terminating the string.

If the input buffer is not cleared by fflush() at this stage gets() takes a NULL string, from the input buffer assuming this carriage return as a delimiter. Thus you will not be able to enter the second string into name4.

One another point to be noted is the sizes of various character arrays declared at Line 5, 6, and 7.

The size of name1 is printed as 17 though the total numbers of characters in the string are 16. Note that the 17th location is utilized to place '\0' automatically by the compiler.

We write a function in program listing 3.11 that will take a character string passed as an argument and convert all the lower case alphabets to uppercase leaving all other characters without change.

```
/*    Program Listing 3.11 : STR.c
      Converts all the small case Alphabets to Capitals  */
#include <stdio.h>

void to_str_upper(char []);

void main(void)
{
      char str[100];
      printf("Enter the String: ");
      gets(str);

      to_str_upper(str);
      printf("Changed to %s",str);
}

void to_str_upper(char s[])
{
      int i = 0;
      while(s[i])    /* loop continues till *s is '\0' */
      {
            /*to check s is a lower case letter and if so replace
                                             with upper case*/
```

```
21.             if((s[i] >= 'a')&&(s[i] <= 'z')) s[i] -= 32;
22.                 i++;
23.         }
24.   }
```

```
Enter the String: AbCd;l123
Changed to ABCD;L123
```

Program Listing 3.11 Program to convert all lowercase alphabet to uppercase

At Line 9,

```
gets(str);
```

accepts the string into str and keeps the required NULL value at the end. At Line 11,

```
to_str_upper(str);
```

the function to_str_upper() is called by passing str as a parameter. Notice that ***str*** is the address of the character array and it is passed to the calling function. At lines 15 to 24,

```
void to_str_upper(char s[])
{
        int i = 0;
        while(s[i])     /* loop continues till *s is '\0' */
        {
                /*to check s is a lower case letter and if so replace
                                                          with upper case*/
                if((s[i] >= 'a')&&(s[i] <= 'z')) s[i] -= 32;
                        i++;
        }
}
```

the function to_str_upper() is presented. A local variable i is used to run through the string character by character in a while loop. Each character is examined, and if it is an alphabet of lower case it is changed to uppercase by subtracting 32.

The student is advised to refer the ASCII character listing given in Appendix A to make sure that the difference in ASCII value of uppercase and lowercase is 32. The while loop terminates when s[i] equals to the last character '\0'. Note that the expression within the paranthesis of while at line 18, can be replaced with s[i] != '\0' or s[i] != 0, since the ASCII value of the NULL character '\0' is 0.

3.9 STORAGE CLASSES & SCOPE OF VARIABLES

In C several keywords together with the context of an object of declaration specifies its storage class. The storage class specifiers are

auto **register** **static** **extern** **typedef**

Automatic objects are local to a block and are discarded on exit from the block. The keyword auto is not necessary when you declare a local variable with in a block, yet it will be treated as automatic. The auto and register specifiers give the declared objects automatic storage class and may be used only within the functions.

A register declaration is equivalent to an auto declaration, but hints that the declared objects will be accessed frequently. There is no guarantee given by the compiler that these variables are kept in the processor registers. Actually, only a few register variables declared by the user may be placed into registers depending on the implementation. However, if an object is declared as a register variable, the unary operator & (i.e., Address Operator) may not be applied to it as it will be meaningless to compute the address of a variable stored in a register. The following code may be illegal.

```
register int a;
int *x;
a = 23;
x = &a;
```

However, many compilers may consider register variables as automatic and may not consider the above code as a illegal.

Static objects may be local to a block or external to all blocks. But either case, retain the value across exit and re-entry to the functions and blocks. The static declaration applied to a local(automatic) variable will allow this variable to retain its value even if the function exits. We shall show the use of this declaration in later chapters.

Because automatic variables come and go with function invocation, they do not retain their values from one call to the next (unless declared static) and must be explicitly set upon each entry. If they are not set they will contain garbage.

As an alternative to automatic variables, it is possible to define variables that are external to all functions, that is, variables that can be accessed by name by any function. Because external variables are globally accessible, they can be used instead of argument lists to communicate data between function. Furthermore, because external variables remain in existence permanently, rather than appearing and disappearing as functions are called and exited, they retain their values even after the functions that set them have returned.

An external variable must be defined, exactly once, outside of any function; this sets aside storage for it. The variable must also be declared in each function that wants to access it; this states the type of variable.

The extern modifier is used to indicate that the actual storage and initial value of a variable, or body of a function, is defined in a separate source code module. For example, if the following delcaration occurs in a source file

```
extern int a;
extern double val[];
```

For the rest of the source file, a is declared as an int and val as a double arrary(whose size is defined elsewhere). But the above declaration does not create the variables or reserves storage for them. Note that there must be only one definition of the external variables among all the files that make up the C source program. Other files may contain extern declaration to acess it. Array sizes must be specified with the definition but are optional with an extern declaration. The use of extern may not be necessary, if you are not splitting the source code into several files. Functions declared with extern are visible throughout all source files in a program, unless you redefine the function as a static. The static declaration applied to an external variable or function, limits the scope of that object to the rest of the source file being compiled.

The typedef specifier doesnot reserve storage and is called a storage class specifier only for syntactic convenience and has already been discussed in Section earlier in this chapter.

3.10 BLOCK-STRUCTURE OF C

We have been using { and } in a C program to group declarations and statements together. This is usually referred as a block in C. Note that there is no semi-colon is used after the end of }, since, semi-colon is only a statement separator.

We have already stated, C is not a block-structured language in the sense of PASCAL or similar languages. However, variables can be defined in a block-structured fashion within a C block. Declarations of variables (including initializations) may follow a { that starts the block. Variables declared in this way, hide any identically named variables in outer blocks and remain in existence until matching }.

As an example, consider the program listing 3.12. The scope of variable i which is declared in the true branch of if is unrelated to the i declared in the main(). Notice that within the inner block the i value varies from 0 to 4 while the i value in the outer block remains as 2. A variable declared and initialized in a block is initialized each time the block is entered.

```
#include <stdio.h>
main()
{
   int i = 2, n;
   printf("\nEnter a number...");
   scanf("%d", &n);
   if(n > 0)
   {
      int i;
         for(i = 0;i < n;i++)
            printf("%d", i); printf("\nThe block ends here.\n");
      }
      printf("%d", i); printf("\ni value outside the block.\n");
}
```

```
Enter a number... 3
0 1 2
The block ends here.
2
i value outside the block.
```

Program Listing 3.12 Program to illustrate Block Structure & Scope of Variables

3.11 HEADER FILES

It is very convenient to divide large C programs into several modules. Consider dividing a calculator program into several source files. The main() will go into one file which we will call as main.c. Code for computing each arithmetic operations go into a second file, arithmetic.c. Code for Inputting from keyboard goes into third file, input.c and code for outputting on to the screen goes to the fourth file, output.c.

In such a software design, each of these modules can be compiled separately. However, there is one thing to worry about-the definitions and declarations shared among the files. As much as possible, we want to centralize this, so that there is only one copy to get right and keep right as the program evolves. Accordingly, we will place this common material in a header file, calc.h, which will be included as necessary. The resulting program then looks like as shown in Fig. 3.4.

Up to some moderate program size, it is probably best to have one header file that contains everything that is to be shared between any two parts of the program; that is the decision we made here. For a much larger program, more organization and more headers would be needed.

calc.h

```
#define Number '0'
void push(double);
double pop(void)
int getop(char []);
int getch (void);
void ungetch(int);
```

main.c

```
#include <stdio.h>
#include <stdlib.h>
#include <calc.h>
#define MAXOP 100
main()
{
   . . .
}
```

input.c

```
#include <stdio.h>
#include <ctype.h>
#include "calc.h"
getop()
{
   . . .
}
```

arithmetic.c

```
#include <stdio.h>
#include "calc.h"
#define MAXVAL 100
int sp = 0;
double val[MAXVAL];
void push(double)
{
   . . .
}
double pop(void)
{
   . . .
}
```

output.c

```
#include <stdio.h>
#define BUFSIZE 100
char buf[BUFSIZE];
int bufp = 0;
void getch(void)
{
   . . .
}
double ungetch(void)
{
   . . .
}
```

Fig.3.4 Header Files

3.12 C PREPROCESSORS

A pre-processor in C is the first step in compilation. Certain facilities are provided by the pre-processor. The two most frequently used preprocessor features are #include and #define. We will now discuss a number of preprocessor features

File Inclusion

#include is to include the contents of a file during compilation. The following examples describe file inclusion. For example,

```
#include "filename"
```

or

```
#include <filename>
```

is replaced by the contents of the file filename. If the filename is quoted, searching for the file typically begins from the directory where the source program was found. If it is not found there, or if the name is enclosed in < and >, searching follows an implementation-defined rule to find the file (usually the include directory specified by the path). An included file may itself contain #include lines.

There are often several #include lines at the beginning of a source file, to include common #define statements and extern declarations, or to access the function prototype declarations for library function from header files like stidio.h

#include is the preferred way to tie the declarations together for a large program as shown in calculator program above. It guarantees that all the source files will be supplied with the same definitions and variable declarations, and thus eliminates any bugs. When an included file is is changed, all files that depend on it must be recompiled.

MACRO Substitution

A definition has the form

```
#define name    replacement text
```

#define is to replace a token by an arbitrary sequence of characters. For example,

```
#define MAXSIZE 512
int buffer[MAXSIZE];
   ... ... ... ...
```

While compilation of the above segment of program, MAXSIZE is replaced in statement 2 is replaced by 512. Note that, if MAXSIZE is used anywhere in the program subsequently, will also be replaced by 512.

#define is not only used to replace simple strings but also can be used to replace an entire program statement. This kind of replacement is known as MACRO Substitution. #define has the same form as a variable name; the replacement text can be arbitrary long. A long definition may be continued into several lines by placing a \ at the end of each line to be continued. The scope of a name defined with #define is from its point of definition to the end of the source file being compiled. A definition may use previous definitions. Substitutions are made only for tokens, and do not take place within quoted strings. For example,

```
#define YES 1
printf("YES\n");
```

Here, YES is not replaced with the value 1. Any name can be defined with any replacement text. It is possible to define macros with arguments so that the replacement text may be different for different calls of macro. As an example, define a macro called MAX

```
#define MAX(A, B)  ((A) > (B) ? (A) : (B))
```

Although it looks like a functions call, a use of max expands into in-line code. Each occurrence of a formal parameter (here A, B) will be replaced by the corresponding actual argument. Consider the following example,

```
#define MAX(A, B)  ((A) > (B) ? (A) : (B))
... ... ... ... ... ... ... ...
... ... ... ... ... ... ... ...
x = MAX(p+q, r+s)
... ... ... ... ... ... ... ...
... ... ... ... ... ... ... ...
y = MAX(m*2, n+s)
... ... ... ... ... ... ... ...
... ... ... ... ... ... ... ...
z = MAX(i++, j++)
... ... ... ... ... ... ... ...
... ... ... ... ... ... ... ...
```

The statement,

```
x = MAX(p+q, r+s)
```

is replaced by

```
x = ((p+q) > (r+s) ? (p+q) : (r+s))
```

and the statement,

```
y = MAX(m*2, n+s)
```

is replaced by

```
x = ((m*2) > (n+s) ? (m*2) : (n+s))
```

by the pre-processor before the actual compilation takes place. Now consider the statement,

```
z = MAX(i++, j++)
```

is replaced by

```
z = ((i++) > (j++) ? (i++) : (j++))
```

Note that this statement will no doubt assign z the larger of i and j, but, increments the larger twice.

Consider another example. When the macro

```
#define square(a)  a * a
... ... ... ... ... ... ... ...
... ... ... ... ... ... ... ...
x = square(p)
... ...  ... ... ... ... ...
... ... ... ... ... ... ... ...
```

```
y = square(m+2)
... ... ... ... ... ... ... ...
... ... ... ... ... ... ... ...
```

The statement,

```
x = square(p)
```

is replaced by

```
x = p * p
```

which correctly computes square of p. However, consider the other statement,

```
y = square(m+2)
```

is replaced by

```
y = m+2 * m+2
```

which is definitely not equal to the square of m+2 as the 2 * m is first computed then m and 2 are added to the result, since * has higher precedence than +. To eliminate this problem the macro has to be declared as

```
#define square(a)  (a) * (a)
```

#undef usually ensures that the routine is really a function and not a macro. Normally, getchar is defined as a macro in stdio.h. After the statement,

```
#undef getchar
int getchar(void)  { ... }
```

the getchar will not be replaced by the macro in stdio.h and the function will be as it is will be compiled.

Conditional Inclusion

In C, it is possible to control pre-processing itself with conditional statements which are evaluated during the pre-processing. This provides a way to include code selectively depending on the value of conditions evaluated during compilation. As an example, consider the following pre-processor code.

```
#if   !defined(NULL)
   #define NULL  0
#endif
```

These directives determine if NULL is to be defined or not. The expression defined(NULL) evaluates to 1 if NULL is defined; 0 otherwise. If the result is 0, !defined(NULL) evaluates to 1 and NULL is defined. Otherwise, the #define directive is skipped. Every #if construct ends with #endif. Directives #ifdef and #ifndef are shorthand for #if defined (name) and #if !defined (name). A multiple-part conditional pre-processor construct may be tested by using the #elif (the equivalent of else if in an if structure) and the #else (the equivalent of else in an if structure) directives.

The # and ## pre-processor operators are available in standard C. The # operator causes a replacement text token to be converted to a string surrounded by quotes. Consider the following macro definition:

```
#define HELLO(x)   printf("Hello, " #x "\n");
```

When HELLO(World) appears in a program file, it is expanded to

```
printf("Hello, "World" "\n");
```

The string "World" replaces #x in the replacement text.

Strings separated by white space can be concatenated during pre-processing, so the preceding statement is equivalent to

```
printf("Hello, World\n");
```

Note that the # operator must be used in a macro with arguments because the operand of # refers to an argument of the macro.

The ## operator concatenates two tokens. Consider the following macro definition:

```
#define CONCAT(x, y) x ## y
```

When CONCAT appears in the program, its arguments are concatenated and used to replace the macro. For example, CONCAT(Hello, World) is replaced by HelloWorld in the program. The ## operator must have two operands.

MORE EXAMPLES

1. Write a function that implements the following Algorithm (*known as Babylonian Algorithm*) to compute the square root of x > 0.

```
#include <stdio.h>
double f(double x)
{
        double TOL = 5e-15;
        double y;
        if(x <= 0)
                return(0.0);
        y = (x > 2 ? x/2 : 1);
        do
        {
                y = (y + x/y)/2;
        }
        while(x > y*y + TOL || y*y > x + TOL);
        return(y);
}
void main(void)
{
        double x, y;
        for(x = 0.0;x <= 10.0;x += 0.25)
        {
                y = f(x);
                printf("X = %lf\tY = %lf\n", y, y*y);
        }
}
OUTPUT:
                X = 0.000000  Y = 0.000000
                X = 0.500000  Y = 0.250000
                X = 0.707107  Y = 0.500000
                X = 0.866025  Y = 0.750000
                X = 1.000000  Y = 1.000000
                X = 1.118034  Y = 1.250000
```

```
X = 1.224745  Y = 1.500000
X = 1.322876  Y = 1.750000
X = 1.414214  Y = 2.000000
X = 1.500000  Y = 2.250000
X = 1.581139  Y = 2.500000
X = 1.658312  Y = 2.750000
X = 1.732051  Y = 3.000000
X = 1.802776  Y = 3.250000
X = 1.870829  Y = 3.500000
X = 1.936492  Y = 3.750000
X = 2.000000  Y = 4.000000
X = 2.061553  Y = 4.250000
X = 2.121320  Y = 4.500000
X = 2.179449  Y = 4.750000
X = 2.236068  Y = 5.000000
X = 2.291288  Y = 5.250000
X = 2.345208  Y = 5.500000
X = 2.397916  Y = 5.750000
X = 2.449490  Y = 6.000000
X = 2.500000  Y = 6.250000
X = 2.549510  Y = 6.500000
X = 2.598076  Y = 6.750000
X = 2.645751  Y = 7.000000
X = 2.692582  Y = 7.250000
X = 2.738613  Y = 7.500000
X = 2.783882  Y = 7.750000
X = 2.828427  Y = 8.000000
X = 2.872281  Y = 8.250000
X = 2.915476  Y = 8.500000
X = 2.958040  Y = 8.750000
X = 3.000000  Y = 9.000000
X = 3.041381  Y = 9.250000
X = 3.082207  Y = 9.500000
X = 3.122499  Y = 9.750000
X = 3.162278  Y = 10.000000
```

2. Write a function that implements that returns the *Integral Binary Logarithm* of a given positive number (the number of times it can be divided in two). For example, f(500) would return 9.

```
#include <stdio.h>
int lg(double x)
{
        int y = 0;
        while(x > 1)
        {
                x /= 2;
                ++y;
        }
        return(y);
}
void main(void)
{
        int n, m;
        printf("\nEnter any value: ");
        scanf("%d", &n);
        m = lg(n);
        printf("\nBinary Logarithm of %d is %d", n, m);
}
OUTPUT:
                Enter any value: 500
                Binary Logarithm of 500 is 9
```

3. Write a program that implements the following algorithm (*known as Horner's Method*) to evaluate a polynomial

$$p(x) = a_0 + a_1x + a_2x^2 + a_3x^3 + . . . + a_nx^n$$

by using its equivalent form

$$p(x) = a_0 + x(a_2 + x(a_3 + . . . + x(a_n) . . .)))$$

For example, the polynomial,

$$p(x) = 4x^3 - 8x + 5$$

would be evaluated as

$$p(x) = 5 + x(-8 + x(0 + x(4)))$$

```
#include <stdio.h>
void main(void)
{
      double a[] = {16, -32, 24, -8, 1}, y;
      int i, n = 4;
      y = a[n];
      for(i = n - 1;i >= 0;i--)
      {
            y = y * 0.5 + a[i];
      }
      printf("%lf\n", y);
}
OUTPUT:
            5.062500
```

4. Write a function that returns the sum of digits of a positive integer. For example, sums(12345) would return 6.

```
#include <stdio.h>
int sums(int num)
{
      int digit, sum = 0;
      while(num)
      {
            digit = num % 10;
            sum += digit;
            num /= 10;
      }
      return(sum);
}
void main(void)
{
      int n, num, sum = 0;
      printf("\nInput a Number: ");
      scanf("%d", &num);
      do
      {
            sum = sums(num);
```

```
            n = sum;
            sum = sums(n);
        }
        while(sum >= 10);
        printf("\nSum of the Given Number %d = %d = %d\n", num, n, sum);
}
```

OUTPUT:

```
            Input a Number: 12345
            Sum of the Given Number 12345 = 15 = 6
```

5. Write a function that finds the GCD of two numbers.

```
#include <stdio.h>
int gcd(int p, int q)
{
        int rem;
        rem = p - (p / q * q);
        if(rem == 0)
            return q;
        else
            gcd(q, rem);
}
void main(void)
{
        int a, b, igcd;
        printf("\nEnter any two Numbers: ");
        scanf("%d %d", &a, &b);
        igcd = gcd(a, b);
        printf("GCD of %d and %d is %d.\n", a, b, igcd);
}
```

OUTPUT:

```
            Enter any two Numbers: 45 55
            GCD of 45 and 55 is 5.
```

6. Write a program to find the Mean, Variance and Standard Deviation of the elements of an array. The *Mean* of a sequence of n numbers is the number m defined by the formula,

$$m = \frac{x_0 + x_1 + x_2 + \ldots + x_{n-1}}{n}$$

The *Varianace* of a sequence of n numbers is the number s defined by the formula,

$$v = \frac{(x_0 - m)^2 + (x_1 - m)^2 + (x_2 - m)^2 + \ldots + (x_{n-1} - m)^2}{n}$$

The *Standard Deviation* of a sequence of n numbers is the number s defined by the formula,

$$s = \frac{\sqrt{(x_0 - m)^2 + (x_1 - m)^2 + (x_2 - m)^2 + \ldots + (x_{n-1} - m)^2}}{n}$$

```
#include <stdio.h>
#include <math.h>
void main(void )
{
      int i, n;
      float a[50], mean, variance, sdn;
      float sumsq, sum;
      sumsq = sum = 0.0;
      printf("Enter the size of Array: ");
      scanf("%d", &n);
      for(i = 0;i < n;i++)
      {
            printf("Enter the Element in [%d] location :", i);
            scanf("%f", &a[i]);
            sum += a[i];
      }
      printf("Elements in the Array:\n");
      for(i = 0;i < n;i++)
            printf("%8.2f", a[i]);
      mean = sum/(float)n;
      for(i = 0;i < n;i++)
            sumsq = sumsq + (mean - a[i]) * (mean - a[i]);
      variance = sumsq/(float)n;
      sdn = sqrt(variance);
      printf("\nMean of %8d Elements: %8.2f", n, mean);
```

```
    printf("\nVariance                  : %8.2f", variance);
    printf("\nStandard Deviation        : %8.2f", sdn);
}
```

OUTPUT:

```
        Enter the size of Array: 7
        Enter the Element in [0] location : 32
        Enter the Element in [1] location : 11
        Enter the Element in [2] location : 90
        Enter the Element in [3] location : 34
        Enter the Element in [4] location : 52
        Enter the Element in [5] location : 24
        Enter the Element in [6] location : 7
        Elements in the Array:
            32.00   11.00   90.00   34.00   52.00   24.00   7.00
        Mean of        7 Elements:    35.71
        Variance                  :   685.92
        Standard Deviation    :    26.19
```

7. Write a function that rotates an array of integers by the given number of positions.

```
#include <stdio.h>
void rotate(int a[9], int n, int k)
{
    int temp[9], i;
    for(i = 0;i < k;i++)
        temp[i] = a[n - k + i];
    for(i = k;i < n;i++)
        temp[i] = a[i - k];
    for(i = 0;i < n;i++)
        a[i] = temp[i];
}
void main(void)
{
    int a[] = {1, 2, 3, 4, 5, 6, 7, 8, 9}, i, n = 9;
    for(i = 0;i < n;i++)
        printf("%5d", a[i]);
    rotate(a, n, 2);
    printf("\n");
```

```
    for(i = 0;i < n;i++)
        printf("%5d", a[i]);
}
```

OUTPUT:

```
        1    2    3    4    5    6    7    8    9
        8    9    1    2    3    4    5    6    7
```

8. Write a program that determines whether a given array is sorted or not.

```
#include <stdio.h>
#include <stdlib.h>
void main(void)
{
    int i, n, a[50];
    printf("Enter the size of Array: ");
    scanf("%d", &n);
    for(i = 0;i < n;i++)
    {
        printf("Enter the Element in [%d] location :", i);
        scanf("%d", &a[i]);
    }
    printf("Elements in the Array:\n");
    for(i = 0;i < n;i++)
    {
        printf("%8d", a[i]);
    }
    for(i = 1;i < n;i++)
    {
        if(a[i-1] > a[i])
        {
          printf("\nThe Array Elements are not in Sorted Order.\n");
          exit(0);
        }
    }
    printf("\nThe Array Elements are in Sorted Order.\n");
}
```

OUTPUT:

```
        Enter the size of Array: 5
```

```
Enter the Element in [0] location : 1
Enter the Element in [1] location : 2
Enter the Element in [2] location : 3
Enter the Element in [3] location : 4
Enter the Element in [4] location : 5
Elements in the Array:
     1        2        3        4        5
The Array Elements are in Sorted Order.
```

9. Write a program to find the Trace of a Matrix

```
#include <stdio.h>
void main(void)
{
      int a[10][10], i, j, n, trace = 0;
      printf("Enter the order of Matrix A: ");
      scanf("%d", &n);
      for(i = 0;i < n;i++)
            for(j = 0;j < n;j++)
            {
               printf("Enter the Elements in Matrix A[%d][%d]: ", i, j);
               scanf("%d", &a[i][j]);
            }
      for(i = 0;i < n;i++)
      {
            for(j = 0;j < n;j++)
                  printf("%5d", a[i][j]);
            printf("\n");
      }
      for(i = 0;i < n;i++)
            trace += a[i][i];
      printf("\nTrace = %5d", trace);
}
OUTPUT:
            Enter the order of Matrix A: 3
            Enter the Elements in Matrix A[0][0]: 1
            Enter the Elements in Matrix A[0][1]: 2
            Enter the Elements in Matrix A[0][2]: 3
```

```
Enter the Elements in Matrix A[1][0]: 4
Enter the Elements in Matrix A[1][1]: 5
Enter the Elements in Matrix A[1][2]: 6
Enter the Elements in Matrix A[2][0]: 7
Enter the Elements in Matrix A[2][1]: 8
Enter the Elements in Matrix A[2][2]: 9
     1    2    3
     4    5    6
     7    8    9
Trace =    15
```

10. Write a program to find the Norm of a Matrix

```
#include <stdio.h>
#include <math.h>
void main(void)
{
      int i, j, m, n;
      float sum, norm, a[10][10];
      sum = norm = 0.0;
      printf("Enter the Row & Column Matrix A: ");
      scanf("%d %d", &n, &m);
      for(i = 0;i < n;++i)
            for(j = 0;j < m;++j)
            {
               printf("Enter the Elements in Matrix A[%d][%d]: ", i, j);
               scanf("%f", &a[i][j]);
            }
      for(i = 0;i < n;++i)
      {
            for(j = 0;j < m;++j)
                  printf("%8.2f", a[i][j]);
            printf("\n");
      }
      for(i = 0;i < n;++i)
            for(j = 0;j < m;++j)
                  sum += a[i][j] * a[i][j];
      printf("\nSum  = %8.2f", sum);
      norm = sqrt((double)sum);
      printf("\nNorm = %8.2f", norm);
}
```

```
OUTPUT:
        Enter the Row & Column Matrix A: 3 3
        Enter the Elements in Matrix A[0][0]: 1
        Enter the Elements in Matrix A[0][1]: 2
        Enter the Elements in Matrix A[0][2]: 3
        Enter the Elements in Matrix A[1][0]: 4
        Enter the Elements in Matrix A[1][1]: 5
        Enter the Elements in Matrix A[1][2]: 6
        Enter the Elements in Matrix A[2][0]: 7
        Enter the Elements in Matrix A[2][1]: 8
        Enter the Elements in Matrix A[2][2]: 9
            1.00    2.00    3.00
            4.00    5.00    6.00
            7.00    8.00    9.00
        Sum  =   285.00
        Norm =    16.88
```

11. Write a program to find the Whether a Matrix is Orthogonal or not
Identity Matrix = Matrix A * Transpose A

```
#include <stdio.h>
#include <math.h>
void main(void)
{
    int i, j, k, m, flag = 0;
    float a[10][10], b[10][10], c[10][10];
    printf("Enter the Size of the Matrix A: ");
    scanf("%d %d", &m);
    for(i = 0;i < m;++i)
        for(j = 0;j < m;++j)
        {
          printf("Enter the Elements in Matrix A[%d][%d]: ", i, j);
          scanf("%f", &a[i][j]);
        }
    for(i = 0;i < m;++i)
    {
        for(j = 0;j < m;++j)
            printf("%8.2f", a[i][j]);
        printf("\n");
    }
```

```
        printf("\nTranspose of the Given Matrix is:\n");
        for(i = 0;i < m;i++)
                for(j = 0;j < m;j++)
                        b[i][j] = a[j][i];
        for(i = 0;i < m;++i)
        {
                for(j = 0;j < m;++j)
                        printf("%8.2f", b[i][j]);
                printf("\n");
        }
        for(i = 0;i < m;++i)
        {
                for(j = 0;j < m;++j)
                {
                        c[i][j] = 0;
                        for(k = 0;k <= m;k++)
                                c[i][j] += a[i][k] * b[k][j];
                }
        }
        for(i = 0;i < m;++i)
        {
                for(j = 0;j < m;++j)
                {
                        if((int)c[i][i] == 1 && (int)c[i][j] == 0)
                                flag = 1;
                }
        }
        printf("\nIdentity Matrix = Matrix A * Transpose A\n");
        for(i = 0;i < m;++i)
        {
                for(j = 0;j < m;++j)
                        printf("%8.2f", c[i][j]);
                printf("\n");
        }
        if(flag == 1)
                printf("\nThe given Matrix is ORTHOGONAL\n");
        else
                printf("\nThe given Matrix is not ORTHOGONAL\n");
}
```

```
OUTPUT:
          Enter the Size of the Matrix A: 3 3
          Enter the Elements in Matrix A[0][0]: 1
          Enter the Elements in Matrix A[0][1]: 0
          Enter the Elements in Matrix A[0][2]: 0
          Enter the Elements in Matrix A[1][0]: 0
          Enter the Elements in Matrix A[1][1]: 1
          Enter the Elements in Matrix A[1][2]: 0
          Enter the Elements in Matrix A[2][0]: 0
          Enter the Elements in Matrix A[2][1]: 0
          Enter the Elements in Matrix A[2][2]: 1
               1.00    0.00    0.00
               0.00    1.00    0.00
               0.00    0.00    1.00
          Transpose of the Given Matrix is:
               1.00    0.00    0.00
               0.00    1.00    0.00
               0.00    0.00    1.00
          Identity Matrix = Matrix A * Transpose A
               1.00    0.00    0.00
               0.00    1.00    0.00
               0.00    0.00    1.00
          The given Matrix is ORTHOGONAL
```

12. Write a program to find the Saddle Point of a Matrix

```
#include <stdio.h>
#include <math.h>
void main(void)
{
     int i, j, m, n, p, q, a[10][10], min, max, flag = 1;
     printf("Enter the Size of the Matrix A: ");
       scanf("%d %d", &n, &m);
     for(i = 0;i < n;++i)
          for(j = 0;j < m;++j)
          {
            printf("Enter the Elements in Matrix A[%d][%d]: ", i, j);
            scanf("%d", &a[i][j]);
          }
```

```
        for(i = 0;i < n;++i)
        {
              for(j = 0;j < m;++j)
                    printf("%5d", a[i][j]);
              printf("\n");
        }
        for(i = 0;i < n;i++)
        {
              min = a[i][0];
              p = i;
              q = 0;
              for(j = 0;j < m;j++)
              {
                    if(min > a[i][j])
                    {
                          min = a[i][j];
                          p = i;
                          q = j;
                    }
              }
              for(j = 0;j < n;j++)
              {
                    if(a[j][q] > a[p][q])
                    {
                          flag = 0;
                    }
              }
              if(flag)
              printf("\nSaddle Point a[%d][%d] = %d\n", p+1, q+1, a[p][q]);
              else
                    printf("\nNo Saddle Point in Row %d\n", i+1);
              flag = 1;
        }
}
OUTPUT:
              Enter the Size of the Matrix A: 3 3
              Enter the Elements in Matrix A[0][0]: 7
              Enter the Elements in Matrix A[0][1]: 5
```

```
Enter the Elements in Matrix A[0][2]: 5
Enter the Elements in Matrix A[1][0]: 10
Enter the Elements in Matrix A[1][1]: 5
Enter the Elements in Matrix A[1][2]: 8
Enter the Elements in Matrix A[2][0]: 6
Enter the Elements in Matrix A[2][1]: 3
Enter the Elements in Matrix A[2][2]: 3
     7    5    5
     10    5    8
     6    3    3
Saddle Point a[1][2] = 5
Saddle Point a[2][2] = 5
No Saddle Point in Row 3
```

13. Write a program to traversal a matrix Helically.

```
#include <stdio.h>
#include <math.h>
void main(void)
{
      int i, j, n, a[20][20];
      printf("Enter the Order of the Matrix A: ");
      scanf("%d", &n);
      for(i = 1;i < n + 1;++i)
            for(j = 1;j < n + 1;++j)
            {
              printf("Enter the Elements in Matrix A[%d][%d]: ", i, j);
              scanf("%d", &a[i][j]);
            }
      for(i = 1;i < n + 1;++i)
      {
            for(j = 1;j < n + 1;++j)
                  printf("%5d", a[i][j]);
            printf("\n");
      }
      printf("\nThe Required Traversal is: ");
      i = 1;
```

```
        while(n > 0)
        {
            for(j = i;j < n + 1;j++)
                printf("%5d", a[i][j]);
            for(j = i + 1;j < n + 1;++j)
                printf("%5d", a[j][n]);
            for(j = n - 1;j > i - 1;j--)
                printf("%5d", a[n][j]);
            for(j = n - 1;j > i;j--)
                printf("%5d", a[j][i]);
            i += 1;
            n -= 1;
        }
        printf("\n");
    }
OUTPUT:
            Enter the Order of the Matrix A: 3
            Enter the Elements in Matrix A[1][1]: 1
            Enter the Elements in Matrix A[1][2]: 2
            Enter the Elements in Matrix A[1][3]: 3
            Enter the Elements in Matrix A[2][1]: 4
            Enter the Elements in Matrix A[2][2]: 5
            Enter the Elements in Matrix A[2][3]: 6
            Enter the Elements in Matrix A[3][1]: 7
            Enter the Elements in Matrix A[3][2]: 8
            Enter the Elements in Matrix A[3][3]: 9
                1    2    3
                4    5    6
                7    8    9
            The Required Traversal is: 1  2  3  6  9  8  7  4  5
```

14. Write a program to Multiply two Matrices

```
#include <stdio.h>
#include <math.h>
void main(void)
{
    int i, j, k, m, n, q;
    float a[10][10], b[10][10], c[10][10];
```

```
printf("Enter the Size of the Matrix A: ");
scanf("%d %d", &m, &n);
printf("Enter the Size of the Matrix B: ");
scanf("%d %d", &k, &q);
if(n == k)
{
    for(i = 0;i < m;++i)
      for(j = 0;j < m;++j)
      {
      printf("Enter the Elements in Matrix A[%d][%d]: ", i, j);
      scanf("%f", &a[i][j]);
      }
    for(i = 0;i < m;++i)
    {
        for(j = 0;j < m;++j)
            printf("%8.2f", a[i][j]);
        printf("\n");
    }
    for(i = 0;i < k;++i)
      for(j = 0;j < q;++j)
      {
      printf("Enter the Elements in Matrix B[%d][%d]: ", i, j);
      scanf("%f", &b[i][j]);
      }
    for(i = 0;i < m;++i)
    {
        for(j = 0;j < m;++j)
            printf("%8.2f", b[i][j]);
        printf("\n");
    }
    for(i = 0;i < m;++i)
    {
        for(j = 0;j < m;++j)
        {
            c[i][j] = 0;
            for(k = 0;k <= m;k++)
                c[i][j] += a[i][k] * b[k][j];
        }
    }
```

```
            printf("\nElements after Multiplication.\n");
            for(i = 0;i < m;++i)
            {
                  for(j = 0;j < m;++j)
                        printf("%8.2f", c[i][j]);
                  printf("\n");
            }
      }
      else
            printf("\nColumn of Matrix A must be EQUAL TO Row of Matrix B.\n
                        Hence, Multiplication cannot be performed.\n");
}
```

OUTPUT:

```
Enter the Size of the Matrix A: 3 3
Enter the Size of the Matrix B: 3 3
Enter the Elements in Matrix A[0][0]: 1
Enter the Elements in Matrix A[0][1]: 2
Enter the Elements in Matrix A[0][2]: 3
Enter the Elements in Matrix A[1][0]: 4
Enter the Elements in Matrix A[1][1]: 5
Enter the Elements in Matrix A[1][2]: 6
Enter the Elements in Matrix A[2][0]: 7
Enter the Elements in Matrix A[2][1]: 8
Enter the Elements in Matrix A[2][2]: 9
      1.00    2.00    3.00
      4.00    5.00    6.00
      7.00    8.00    9.00
Enter the Elements in Matrix B[0][0]: 1
Enter the Elements in Matrix B[0][1]: 2
Enter the Elements in Matrix B[0][2]: 3
Enter the Elements in Matrix B[1][0]: 4
Enter the Elements in Matrix B[1][1]: 5
Enter the Elements in Matrix B[1][2]: 6
Enter the Elements in Matrix B[2][0]: 7
Enter the Elements in Matrix B[2][1]: 8
Enter the Elements in Matrix B[2][2]: 9
      1.00    2.00    3.00
      4.00    5.00    6.00
      7.00    8.00    9.00
Elements after Multiplication.
     30.00   36.00   42.00
     66.00   81.00   96.00
    102.00  126.00  150.00
```

15. Write a program to find the Inverse of a Matrix

```
#include <stdio.h>
#include <math.h>
#define N 10
void write_matrix(float matrix[][N], int order)
{
      int row, column;
      for(row = 0;row < order;++row)
      {
            for(column = 0;column < order;++column)
                  printf("%10.2f", matrix[row][column]);
            printf("\n");
      }
}
void exchange_rows(float matrix[][N], float inverse[][N], int row1,
                                                  int row2, int order)
{
      int column;
      float temp;
      for(column = 0;column < order;++column)
      {
            temp = matrix[row1][column];
            matrix[row1][column] = matrix[row2][column];
            matrix[row2][column] = temp;
            temp = inverse[row1][column];
            inverse[row1][column] = inverse[row2][column];
            inverse[row2][column] = temp;
      }
}
int invert(float matrix[][N], float inverse[][N], int order)
{
      int row, column, current, singular = 0;
      float ratio;
      for(row = 0;(row < order) && !singular;++row)
      {
            if(matrix[row][row])
                  for(current = 0;current < order;++current)
```

```
                    if(current == row)
                    {
                       ratio = matrix[row][row];
                       for(column = 0;column < order;++column)
                       {
                          matrix[row][column] /= ratio;
                          inverse[row][column] /= ratio;
                       }
                    }
                    else
                    {
                       ratio = matrix[current][row]/matrix[row][row];
                       for(column = 0;column < order;++column)
                       {
                 matrix[current][column] -= ratio * matrix[row][column];
              inverse[current][column] -= ratio * inverse[row][column];
                       }
                    }
                    else
                    {
                       singular = 1;
          for(current = row + 1;(current < order) && singular;++current)
                          if(matrix[current][row])
                          {
                             singular = 0;
                    exchange_rows(matrix, inverse, current, row,order);
                             --row;
                          }
                    }
      }
      return !singular;
}
void main(void)
{
      char answer;
      int order, row, column;
      float matrix[N][N], inverse[N][N];
```

```
    do
    {
        printf("\n\n                MATRIX INVERSION");
        printf("\n                  ----------------\n");
        do
        {
            printf("\nEnter the Size of Matrix: ");
            scanf("%d", &order);
        }
        while((order <= 0) || (order > N));
        for(row = 0;row < order;++row)
        {
            for(column = 0;column < order;++column)
            {
  printf("Enter the Elements into Matrix - A[%d][%d]: ", row, column);
              scanf("%f", &matrix[row][column]);
              inverse[row][column] = 0.0;
            }
            inverse[row][row] = 1.0;
        }
        printf("\nThe given Matrix is: \n");
        write_matrix(matrix, order);
        if(invert(matrix, inverse, order))
        {
            printf("\nThe Matrix after Inversion is: \n");
            write_matrix(inverse, order);
        }
        else
            printf("\nThe given matrix is singular and hence it's
                                        inverse does not  exist.\n");
        printf("\nAgain? (y/n): ");
        do
            answer = getchar();
        while((answer != 'y') && (answer != 'Y') &&
              (answer != 'n') && (answer != 'N'));
    }
    while((answer == 'y') || (answer == 'Y'));
}
```

OUTPUT:

```
MATRIX INVERSION
----------------------------
Enter the Size of Matrix: 3
Enter the Elements into Matrix - A[0][0]: 2
Enter the Elements into Matrix - A[0][1]: 3
Enter the Elements into Matrix - A[0][2]: 1
Enter the Elements into Matrix - A[1][0]: 4
Enter the Elements into Matrix - A[1][1]: 6
Enter the Elements into Matrix - A[1][2]: 5
Enter the Elements into Matrix - A[2][0]: 1
Enter the Elements into Matrix - A[2][1]: 2.25
Enter the Elements into Matrix - A[2][2]: 0.75
The given Matrix is:
     2.00      3.00      1.00
     4.00      6.00      5.00
     1.00      2.25      0.75
The Matrix after Inversion is:
     1.50      0.00     -2.00
     -0.44     -0.11     1.33
     -0.67      0.33     0.00
Again? (y/n): n
```

16. Write a program to find whether a Matrix is Magic Square or Not.

```
#include <stdio.h>
#include <math.h>
void main(void)
{
     int i, j, n, a[20][20], old, sum, x, y, k;
     printf("Enter the Order of the Matrix A: ");
     scanf("%d", &n);
     for(i = 1;i < n + 1;i++)
          for(j = 1;j < n + 1;j++)
          {
             printf("Enter the Elements in Matrix A[%d][%d]: ", i, j);
             scanf("%d", &a[i][j]);
          }
```

```
for(i = 1;i < n + 1;i++)
{
      for(j = 1;j < n + 1;j++)
            printf("%5d", a[i][j]);
      printf("\n");
}
old = 0;
for(i = 1;i < n + 1;i++)
      old += a[i][i];
for(i = 1;i < n + 1;i++)
      sum += a[i][n + 1 - i];
if(sum != old)
      k = 1;
i = 1;
while(i <= n)
{
      sum = 0;
      for(j = 1;j < n + 1;j++)
            sum += a[i][j];
      if(sum != old)
            k = 2;
      ++i;
}
i = 1;
while(i <= n)
{
      sum = 0;
      for(j = 1;j < n + 1;j++)
            sum += a[j][i];
      if(sum != old)
            k = 3;
      ++i;
}
x = 1;
while(x <= n)
{
      y = 1;
```

```
            while(y <= n)
            {
                  for(i = 1;i < n + 1;i++)
                        for(j = 1;j < n + 1;j++)
                              if(!(x == i && y == j) && a[i][j] == a[x][y])
                                    k = 4;
                  ++y;
            }
            ++x;
      }
      if(k == 1 || k == 2 || k == 3 || k == 4)
            printf("\nThe given matrix is not a Magic Square ...");
      else
            printf("\nThe given matrix is a Magic Square ...");
}
OUTPUT:
            Enter the Order of the Matrix A: 3
            Enter the Elements in Matrix A[1][1]: 4
            Enter the Elements in Matrix A[1][2]: 3
            Enter the Elements in Matrix A[1][3]: 8
            Enter the Elements in Matrix A[2][1]: 9
            Enter the Elements in Matrix A[2][2]: 5
            Enter the Elements in Matrix A[2][3]: 1
            Enter the Elements in Matrix A[3][1]: 2
            Enter the Elements in Matrix A[3][2]: 7
            Enter the Elements in Matrix A[3][3]: 6
                  4     3     8
                  9     5     1
                  2     7     6
            The given matrix is a Magic Square ...
```

17. Write a program to find the Rank of a Matrix.

```
#include <stdio.h>
#include <math.h>
#define N 10
void write_matrix(float matrix[][N], int nor, int noc)
{
      int row, column;
```

```
        for(row = 0;row < nor;++row)
        {
              for(column = 0;column < noc;++column)
                    printf("%10.2f", matrix[row][column]);
              printf("\n");
        }
  }
  void exchange_rows(float matrix[][N], int row1, int row2, int noc)
  {
        int column;
        float temp;
        for(column = 0;column < noc;++column)
        {
              temp = matrix[row1][column];
              matrix[row1][column] = matrix[row2][column];
              matrix[row2][column] = temp;
        }
  }
  int rank(float matrix[][N], int nor, int noc)
  {
        int row, column, current;
        float ratio;
        for(row = 0;row < noc;++row)
        {
              if(matrix[row][row])
                    for(current = 0;current < nor;++current)
                          if(current != row)
                          {
                             ratio = matrix[current][row]/matrix[row][row];
                             for(column = 0;column < noc;++column)
                 matrix[current][column] -=  ratio * matrix[row][column];
                          }
                          else
                                ;
                          else
                          {
                             for(current = row + 1;current < nor;++current)
```

```
                                    if(matrix[current] [row])
                                    {
                                  exchange_rows(matrix, row, current, noc);
                                        break;
                                    }
                                    if(current == nor)
                                    {
                                        --noc;
                                  for(current = 0;current < nor;++current)
                                            matrix[current] [row] =
                                                  matrix[current] [noc];
                                    }
                                    --row;
                            }
            }
            return noc;
      }
      void main(void)
      {
            char answer;
            int transpose, nor, noc, row, column;
            float matrix[N] [N], temp;
            do
            {
                  printf("\n\n                    RANK OF A MATRIX");
                  printf("\n                      ----------------\n");
                  do
                  {
                        printf("\nEnter the Size of Matrix: ");
                        scanf("%d %d", &nor, &noc);
                  }
                  while((nor <= 0) || (noc <= 0) || (nor > N) || (noc > N));
                  transpose = (nor < noc);
                  for(row = 0;row < nor;++row)
                        for(column = 0;column < noc;++column)
                        {
            printf("Enter the Elements into Matrix - A[%d] [%d]: ", nor, noc);
                              scanf("%f", &temp);
```

```
                    if(transpose)
                        matrix[column][row] = temp;
                    else
                        matrix[row][column] = temp;
                }
            if(transpose)
            {
                row = nor;
                nor = noc;
                noc = row;
   printf("\nThe Rank of a Matrix is not affected by Transposition.\n");
            }
   printf("\nThe given Matrix of Order %d x %d is\n\n", nor, noc);
            write_matrix(matrix, nor, noc);
   printf("\nThe Rank of the Matrix is %d\n", rank(matrix, nor, noc));
            printf("\nAgain? (y/n): ");
            do
                answer = getchar();
            while((answer != 'y') && (answer != 'Y') && (answer != 'n')
                                                      && (answer != 'N'));
        }
        while((answer == 'y') || (answer == 'Y'));
}
```

OUTPUT:

```
            RANK OF A MATRIX
            ----------------------------
            Enter the Size of Matrix: 3 3
            Enter the Elements into Matrix - A[3][3]: 2
            Enter the Elements into Matrix - A[3][3]: 3
            Enter the Elements into Matrix - A[3][3]: 1
            Enter the Elements into Matrix - A[3][3]: 4
            Enter the Elements into Matrix - A[3][3]: 6
            Enter the Elements into Matrix - A[3][3]: 5
            Enter the Elements into Matrix - A[3][3]: 1
            Enter the Elements into Matrix - A[3][3]: 2.25
            Enter the Elements into Matrix - A[3][3]: 0.75
            The given Matrix of Order 3 x 3 is
                2.00      3.00      1.00
                4.00      6.00      5.00
                1.00      2.25      0.75
            The Rank of the Matrix is 3
            Again? (y/n): n
```

18. Write a program to find whether a Matrix is Singular or Not.

```
#include <stdio.h>
#include <math.h>
void main(void)
{
      int i, j, k, m, n;
      float a[10][10], b[10][10], partial, psum, nsum, sum = 0.0;
      printf("Enter the Size of the Matrix A: ");
      scanf("%d", &n);
      for(i = 0;i < n;++i)
            for(j = 0;j < n;++j)
            {
               printf("Enter the Elements in Matrix A[%d][%d]: ", i, j);
                  scanf("%f", &a[i][j]);
            }
      for(i = 0;i < n;++i)
      {
            for(j = 0;j < n;++j)
                  printf("%8.2f", a[i][j]);
            printf("\n");
      }
      if(n < 3)
            sum = a[0][0] * a[1][1] - a[0][1] * a[1][0];
      else
      {
            for(k = 0;k < n;k++)
                  for(m = 0;m < n;m++)
                        b[k][m] = a[k][m];
            for(k = 0;k < n;k++)
                  for(m = n;m < ( 2 * n - 1);m++)
                        b[k][m] = a[k][m - n];
            for(j = 0;j < n;j++)
            {
                  partial = 1;
                  for(i = 0;i < n;i++)
                        partial *= b[i][i + j];
                  psum += partial;
            }
```

```
            for(j = n - 1;j < ( 2 * n - 1);j++)
            {
                  partial = 1;
                  for(i = 0;i < n;i++)
                        partial *= b[i][j - i];
                  nsum += partial;
            }
            sum = psum - nsum;
      }
      printf("\nDeterminant = %8.2f", sum);
      if(sum == 0)
            printf("\nThe Given Matrix is Singular.\n");
      else
            printf("\nThe Given Matrix is not Singular.\n");
}
OUTPUT:
            Enter the Size of the Matrix A: 3
            Enter the Elements in Matrix A[0][0]: 1
            Enter the Elements in Matrix A[0][1]: 2
            Enter the Elements in Matrix A[0][2]: 3
            Enter the Elements in Matrix A[1][0]: 4
            Enter the Elements in Matrix A[1][1]: 5
            Enter the Elements in Matrix A[1][2]: 6
            Enter the Elements in Matrix A[2][0]: 7
            Enter the Elements in Matrix A[2][1]: 8
            Enter the Elements in Matrix A[2][2]: 9
                  1.00     2.00     3.00
                  4.00     5.00     6.00
                  7.00     8.00     9.00
            Determinant =      0.00
            The Given Matrix is Singular.
```

19. Write a program to find the Row Sum and Column Sum of a Matrix.

```
#include <stdio.h>
#include <math.h>
void main(void)
{
      int i, j, m, n, a[10][10];
```

```
        printf("Enter the Row & Column Matrix A: ");
        scanf("%d %d", &n, &m);
        for(i = 1;i < n + 1;++i)
              for(j = 1;j < m + 1;++j)
              {
                 printf("Enter the Elements in Matrix A[%d][%d]: ", i, j);
                 scanf("%d", &a[i][j]);
              }
        for(i = 1;i < n + 1;++i)
        {
              for(j = 1;j < m + 1;++j)
                    printf("%5d", a[i][j]);
              printf("\n");
        }
        for(i = 1;i < n + 1;++i)
        {
              a[i][m + 1] = 0;
              for(j = 1;j < m + 1;++j)
                    a[i][m + 1] = a[i][m + 1] + a[i][j];
        }
        for(j = 1;j < m + 1;++j)
        {
              a[n + 1][j] = 0;
              for(i = 1;i < n + 1;++i)
                    a[n + 1][j] = a[n + 1][j] + a[i][j];
        }
  printf("Matrix - A, Column Sum ( last row ) & Row Sum ( Last Column
                                                                   ):\n");
        for(i = 1;i < n + 1;++i)
        {
              for(j = 1;j < m + 2;++j)
                    printf("%5d", a[i][j]);
              printf("\n");
        }
        i = n + 1;
           for(j = 1;j < m + 1;++j)
              printf("%5d", a[i][j]);
        printf("\n");
  }
```

```
OUTPUT:
          Enter the Row & Column Matrix A: 3 3
          Enter the Elements in Matrix A[1] [1]: 1
          Enter the Elements in Matrix A[1] [2]: 2
          Enter the Elements in Matrix A[1] [3]: 3
          Enter the Elements in Matrix A[2] [1]: 4
          Enter the Elements in Matrix A[2] [2]: 5
          Enter the Elements in Matrix A[2] [3]: 6
          Enter the Elements in Matrix A[3] [1]: 7
          Enter the Elements in Matrix A[3] [2]: 8
          Enter the Elements in Matrix A[3] [3]: 9
               1    2    3
               4    5    6
               7    8    9
       Matrix - A, Column Sum ( last row ) & Row Sum ( Last Column ):
               1    2    3    6
               4    5    6    15
               7    8    9    24
               12   15   18
```

20. Write a program to find the Sum of elements above and below the main Diagonal of a Matrix.

```
#include <stdio.h>
#include <math.h>
void main(void)
{
     int a[20] [20], i, j, n, csum, dsum;
     csum = dsum = 0;
       printf("Enter the order of Matrix A: ");
     scanf("%d", &n);
     for(i = 0;i < n;i++)
          for(j = 0;j < n;j++)
          {
            printf("Enter the Elements in Matrix A[%d] [%d]: ", i, j);
            scanf("%d", &a[i] [j]);
          }
```

```
        for(i = 0;i < n;i++)
        {
              for(j = 0;j < n;j++)
                    printf("%5d", a[i][j]);
              printf("\n");
        }
        for(i = 0;i < n;i++)
        {
              for(j = 0;j < n;j++)
              {
                    if(i < j)
                          csum += a[i][j];
              }
        }
        printf("\nSum of Elements above the Main Diagonal: %d", csum);
        for(i = 0;i < n;i++)
        {
              for(j = 0;j < n;j++)
              {
                    if(i > j)
                          dsum += a[i][j];
              }
        }
        printf("\nSum of Elements below the Main Diagonal: %d", dsum);
}
```

OUTPUT:

```
Enter the order of Matrix A: 3
Enter the Elements in Matrix A[0][0]: 1
Enter the Elements in Matrix A[0][1]: 2
Enter the Elements in Matrix A[0][2]: 3
Enter the Elements in Matrix A[1][0]: 4
Enter the Elements in Matrix A[1][1]: 5
Enter the Elements in Matrix A[1][2]: 6
Enter the Elements in Matrix A[2][0]: 7
Enter the Elements in Matrix A[2][1]: 8
Enter the Elements in Matrix A[2][2]: 9
    1    2    3
    4    5    6
    7    8    9

Sum of Elements above the Main Diagonal: 11
Sum of Elements below the Main Diagonal: 19
```

21. Write a program to print the Upper and Lower Triangular Elements of the Main Diagonal of a Matrix.

```
#include <stdio.h>
#include <math.h>
void main(void)
{
      int i, j, m, n, a[10][10];
      printf("Enter the Row & Column Matrix A: ");
      scanf("%d %d", &n, &m);
      for(i = 0;i < n;++i)
            for(j = 0;j < m;++j)
            {
               printf("Enter the Elements in Matrix A[%d][%d]: ", i, j);
               scanf("%d", &a[i][j]);
            }
      for(i = 0;i < n;++i)
      {
            for(j = 0;j < m;++j)
                  printf("%5d", a[i][j]);
            printf("\n");
      }
      printf("\nLower Triangular Matrix:\n");
      for(i = 0;i < n;++i)
      {
            for(j = 0;j < m;++j)
            {
                  if(i < j)
                        printf("     ");
                  if(i >= j)
                        printf("%5d", a[i][j]);
            }
            printf("\n");
      }
      printf("\nUpper Triangular Matrix:\n");
```

```
        for(i = 0;i < n;++i)
        {
             for(j = 0;j < m;++j)
             {
                  if(i > j)
                       printf("     ");
                  if(i <= j)
                       printf("%5d", a[i][j]);
             }
             printf("\n");
        }
   }
```

OUTPUT:

```
Enter the Row & Column Matrix A: 3 3
Enter the Elements in Matrix A[0][0]: 1
Enter the Elements in Matrix A[0][1]: 2
Enter the Elements in Matrix A[0][2]: 3
Enter the Elements in Matrix A[1][0]: 4
Enter the Elements in Matrix A[1][1]: 5
Enter the Elements in Matrix A[1][2]: 6
Enter the Elements in Matrix A[2][0]: 7
Enter the Elements in Matrix A[2][1]: 8
Enter the Elements in Matrix A[2][2]: 9
     1    2    3
     4    5    6
     7    8    9
Lower Triangular Matrix:
     1
     4    5
     7    8    9
Upper Triangular Matrix:
     1    2    3
          5    6
               9
```

22. Write a program to find the Symmetry of a Matrix

```
#include <stdio.h>
#include <math.h>
void main(void)
{
    int i, j, n, a[20][20], b[20][20], flag = 0;
    printf("Enter the Order of the Matrix A: ");
    scanf("%d", &n);
    for(i = 0;i < n;i++)
        for(j = 0;j < n;j++)
        {
          printf("Enter the Elements in Matrix A[%d][%d]: ", i, j);
          scanf("%d", &a[i][j]);
        }
    for(i = 0;i < n;i++)
    {
        for(j = 0;j < n;j++)
            printf("%5d", a[i][j]);
        printf("\n");
    }
    for(i = 0;i < n;i++)
    {
        for(j = 0;j < n;j++)
            b[i][j] = a[j][i];
    }
    printf("\nTranspose of a Given Matrix is:\n");
    for(i = 0;i < n;i++)
    {
        for(j = 0;j < n;j++)
            printf("%5d", b[i][j]);
        printf("\n");
    }
    for(i = 0;i < n;i++)
    {
        for(j = 0;j < n;j++)
            if(a[i][j] != b[i][j])
                flag = 1;
    }
```

```
        if(flag)
            printf("\nMatrix is not Symmetric.\n");
        else
            printf("\nMatrix is Symmetric.\n");
}
OUTPUT:
            Enter the Order of the Matrix A: 3
            Enter the Elements in Matrix A[0][0]: 1
            Enter the Elements in Matrix A[0][1]: 2
            Enter the Elements in Matrix A[0][2]: 5
            Enter the Elements in Matrix A[1][0]: 2
            Enter the Elements in Matrix A[1][1]: 3
            Enter the Elements in Matrix A[1][2]: 4
            Enter the Elements in Matrix A[2][0]: 5
            Enter the Elements in Matrix A[2][1]: 4
            Enter the Elements in Matrix A[2][2]: 9
                1    2    5
                2    3    4
                5    4    9
            Transpose of a Given Matrix is:
                1    2    5
                2    3    4
                5    4    9
            Matrix is Symmetric.
```

23. Write a program to insert an element into an Array

```
#include <stdio.h>
#include <math.h>
void main(void)
{
    int i, j, k, n, pos;
    float a[50], item;
    printf("Enter the size of Array: ");
    scanf("%d", &n);
    for(i = 0;i < n;i++)
    {
        printf("Enter the Element in [%d] location :", i);
        scanf("%f", &a[i]);
    }
```

```
    printf("Elements in the Array:\n");
    for(i = 0;i < n;i++)
         printf("%8.2f", a[i]);
    printf("\nElement to be inserted into an array: ");
    scanf("%f", &item);
    printf("\nPosition of Insertion: ");
    scanf("%d", &pos);
  printf("\nPushing Down the Elements in the Array and Inserting\n");
    printf("the new element ...\n");
    n++;
    for(k = n;k >= pos;k--)
         a[k] = a[k - 1];
    a[--pos] = item;
    printf("\n");
    printf("\nArray after Insertion:\n");
    for(i = 0;i < n;i++)
         printf("%8.2f", a[i]);
    printf("\n");
}
```

OUTPUT:

```
        Enter the size of Array: 6
        Enter the Element in [0] location : 1
        Enter the Element in [1] location : 2
        Enter the Element in [2] location : 3
        Enter the Element in [3] location : 4
        Enter the Element in [4] location : 5
        Enter the Element in [5] location : 6
        Elements in the Array:
             1.00    2.00    3.00    4.00    5.00    6.00
        Element to be inserted into an array: 10
        Position of Insertion: 3
        Pushing Down the Elements in the Array and Inserting
        the new element ...
        Array after Insertion:
             1.00    2.00   10.00    3.00    4.00    5.00    6.00
```

24. Write a program to delete an element from an Array

```
#include <stdio.h>
#include <math.h>
void main(void)
{
      int i, j, k, n, pos, num, flag = 0;
      float a[50], item;
      printf("Enter the size of Array: ");
      scanf("%d", &n);
      num = n;
      for(i = 0;i < n;i++)
      {
            printf("Enter the Element in [%d] location :", i);
            scanf("%f", &a[i]);
      }
      printf("Elements in the Array:\n");
      for(i = 0;i < n;i++)
            printf("%8.2f", a[i]);
      printf("\nElement to be deleted from the array: ");
      scanf("%f", &item);
      for(i = 0;i < n;i++)
      {
            if(a[i] == item)
            {
                  flag = 1;
                  for(k = i;k < n;k++)
                        a[k] = a[k + 1];
                  n--;
            }
      }
      if(flag == 0)
            printf("\nElement of Deletion not found.\n");
      else
      {
            printf("\nArray has %d Duplicates\n\n", num - n);
            printf("\nArray after Deletion:\n");
```

```
            for(i = 0;i < n;i++)
                printf("%8.2f", a[i]);
            printf("\n");
        }
    }
```

OUTPUT:

```
            Enter the size of Array: 6
            Enter the Element in [0] location : 1
            Enter the Element in [1] location : 2
            Enter the Element in [2] location : 3
            Enter the Element in [3] location : 4
            Enter the Element in [4] location : 5
            Enter the Element in [5] location : 6
            Elements in the Array:
                1.00    2.00    3.00    4.00    5.00    6.00
            Element to be deleted from the array: 3
            Array has 1 Duplicates
            Array after Deletion:
                1.00    2.00    4.00    5.00    6.00
```

25. Write a program to delete duplicate elements from an Array

```
#include <stdio.h>
#include <math.h>
void main(void)
{
    int i, j, k, n, num, flag = 0;
    float a[50];
    printf("Enter the size of Array: ");
    scanf("%d", &n);
    num = n;
    for(i = 0;i < n;i++)
    {
        printf("Enter the Element in [%d] location :", i);
        scanf("%f", &a[i]);
    }
    printf("Elements in the Array:\n");
```

```
        for(i = 0;i < n;i++)
             printf("%8.2f", a[i]);
        for(i = 0;i < n - 1;i++)
             for(j = i + 1;j < n;j++)
             {
                  if(a[i] == a[j])
                  {
                       n = n - 1;
                       for(k = j;k < n;k++)
                            a[k] = a[k + 1];
                       flag = 1;
                       j -= 1;
                  }
             }
        if(flag == 0)
             printf("\nNo Duplicates found in the Array.\n");
        else
        {
             printf("\nArray has %d Duplicates\n\n", num - n);
             printf("Array after Deleting Duplicates:\n");
             for(i = 0;i < n;i++)
                  printf("%8.2f", a[i]);
             printf("\n");
        }
}
```

OUTPUT:

```
             Enter the size of Array: 6
             Enter the Element in [0] location : 1
             Enter the Element in [1] location : 2
             Enter the Element in [2] location : 1
             Enter the Element in [3] location : 3
             Enter the Element in [4] location : 2
             Enter the Element in [5] location : 4
             Elements in the Array:
                  1.00    2.00    1.00    3.00    2.00    4.00
             Array has 2 Duplicates
             Array after Deleting Duplicates:
                  1.00    2.00    3.00    4.00
```

26. Write a program to Concatanate the two strings using Pointers

```
#include <stdio.h>
#include <malloc.h>
#define length 50
void main(void)
{
      char *s1, *s2, *s3, c;
      int i, j, k;
      s1 = (char *)malloc(length * sizeof(char));
      s2 = (char *)malloc(length * sizeof(char));
      s3 = (char *)malloc(2* length * sizeof(char));
      printf("\nEnter the String One: ");
      scanf("%s", s1);
      printf("\nEnter the String Two: ");
      scanf("%s", s2);
      i = 0;
      while((c = *(s1 + i)) != '\0')
      {
            s3[i] = c;
            i++;
      }
      k = 0;
      while((c = *(s2 + k)) != '\0')
      {
            s3[i + k] = c;
            k++;
      }
      printf("\nConcatenated String is: %s", s3);
}
```

```
OUTPUT:
            Enter the String One: Ravi
            Enter the String Two: Kiran
            Concatenated String is: RaviKiran
```

27. Write a program to find the position of the Pattern String in the Main String.

```
#include <stdio.h>
void main(void)
{
      char mainstr[50], patstr[50];
      int i, j, k, len1, len2, diff, flag;
      printf("Enter Main String: ");
      scanf("%[^\n]", mainstr);
      for(len1 = 0;mainstr[len1] != '\0';len1++);
      printf("\nLength of Main String ( %s ) is %d\n", mainstr, len1);
      printf("Enter Pattern String: ");
      scanf("%s", &patstr);
      for(len2 = 0;patstr[len2] != '\0';len2++);
      printf("\nLength of Pattern String ( %s ) is %d\n", patstr, len2);
      flag = j = 0;
      for(i = 0;i < len1, j < len2;i++)
            if(mainstr[i] != patstr[j])
                  flag = 1;
            else
            {
                  flag = 0;
                  j++;
            }
            if(flag == 0)
                  printf("\nPattern found at position %d\n", i - len2 +
1);
            else
                  printf("\nPattern not Found.\n");
}
OUTPUT:
            Enter Main String: Artificial Intelligence
            Length of Main String ( Artificial Intelligence ) is 23
            Enter Pattern String: tell
            Length of Pattern String ( tell ) is 4
            Pattern found at position 14
```

28. Write a program to extract the substring from a Given String.

```
#include <stdio.h>
void main(void)
{
      char mainstr[50], substr[50];
      int count, pos, i, j, len, num;
      printf("Enter Main String: ");
      scanf("%[^\n]", mainstr);
      for(len = 0;mainstr[len] != '\0';len++);
      printf("\nLength of Main String ( %s ) is %d\n", mainstr, len);
      printf("\nStarting Position of the Substring: ");
      scanf("%d", &pos);
      printf("\nNumber of Characters in Substring? ");
      scanf("%d", &count);
      if(pos <= 0 || count <= 0 || pos > len)
            printf("\n\nExtracted String is EMPTY.\n");
      else
      {
            if(pos + count > len)
            {
               printf("\n\nCharacters to be extracted exceed length.\n");
               num = len - pos + 1;
            }
            else
                  num = count;
            j = 0;
            for(i = --pos;i <= pos + num - 1;i++)
            {
                  substr[j] = mainstr[i];
                  j++;
            }
            printf("\n\nSubstring is: %s\n", substr);
      }
}
OUTPUT:
   Enter Main String: She sells sea shells on the sea shore
   Length of Main String ( She sells sea shells on the sea shore ) is 37
   Starting Position of the Substring: 11
   Number of Characters in Substring? 10
   Substring is: sea shells
```

29. Write a program to insert a substring into a Given String.

```
#include <stdio.h>
void main(void)
{
      char mainstr[50], instr[50], save[50];
      int i, j, k, pos, num, last, len1, len2, len;
      printf("\nEnter the Main String: ");
      scanf("%[^\n]", mainstr);
      for(len1 = 0;mainstr[len1] != '\0';len1++);
      printf("Length of Main String ( %s ) is %d\n", mainstr, len1);
      printf("\nEnter Position of Insertion: ");
        scanf("%d", &pos);
      printf("\nEnter String to be inserted: ");
      scanf("%s", instr);
      for(len2 = 0;instr[len2] != '\0';len2++);
      printf("Length of Insertion String ( %s ) is %d\n", instr, len2);
        if(pos > len1)
      {
            for(i = 0;i < len2;i++)
                  mainstr[len1 + i - 1] = instr[i];
            len = len1 + len2;
      }
      else
      {
            last = pos + len2 - 1;
            j = 0;
            for(i = --pos;i < len1;i++)
            {
                  save[j] = mainstr[i];
                  j++;
            }
            len = j;
            for(i = pos, j = 0;j < len;i++, j++)
                  mainstr[i] = instr[j];
            for(i = 0;i < len;i++)
            {
                  mainstr[last] = save[i];
                  last++;
            }
```

```
        for(i = last;i < len1;i++)
            mainstr[i] = ' ';
    }
    printf("\n");
    printf("\nInserted String is: %s\n", mainstr);
}
OUTPUT:
        Enter the Main String: twinkle little star
        Length of Main String ( twinkle little star ) is 19
        Enter Position of Insertion: 1
        Enter String to be inserted: Twinkle_
        Length of Insertion String ( Twinkle_ ) is 8
        Inserted String is: Twinkle_twinkle little star
```

30 Write a program to replace a portion of string.

```
#include <stdio.h>
void main(void)
{
    char mainstr[50], repstr[50], save[50];
    int i, j, k, pos, num, last, len1, len2, len;
    printf("\nEnter the Main String: ");
    scanf("%[^\n]", mainstr);
    for(len1 = 0;mainstr[len1] != '\0';len1++);
    printf("Length of Main String ( %s ) is %d\n", mainstr, len1);
    printf("\nEnter Position of Replacing: ");
    scanf("%d", &pos);
    printf("\nEnter Number of characters to be Replaced: ");
    scanf("%d", &num);
    printf("\nEnter String to be Replaced: ");
    scanf("%s", &repstr);
    for(len2 = 0;repstr[len2] != '\0';len2++);
    printf("Length of Replacing String ( %s ) is %d\n", repstr, len2);
    if(pos > len1)
    {
        for(i = 0;i < len2;i++)
            mainstr[len1 + i - 1] = repstr[i];
            len = len1 + len2;
    }
```

```
        else
        {
            last = pos + len2 - 1;
            j = 0;
            for(i = pos + num - 1;i < len1;i++)
            {
                save[j] = mainstr[i];
                j++;
            }
            len = j;
            j = 0;
            for(i = --pos;i < last;i++)
            {
                mainstr[i] = repstr[j];
                j++;
            }
            for(i = 0;i < len;i++)
            {
                mainstr[last] = save[i];
                last++;
            }
            for(i = last;i < len1;i++)
                mainstr[i] = ' ';
        }
        printf("\n");
        printf("\nReplaced String is: %s\n", mainstr);
    }
```

OUTPUT:

```
        Enter the Main String: Good Morning!
        Length of Main String ( Good Morning! ) is 13
        Enter Position of Replacing: 6
        Enter Number of characters to be Replaced: 7
        Enter String to be Replaced: Night
        Length of Replacing String ( Night ) is 5
        Replaced String is: Good Night!
```

31. Write a program to convert Hexa-Decimal to Decimal Number.

```
#include <stdio.h>
void main(void)
{
      int n = 0, i = 0, j, base = 1, rem;
      char a[15], b[15], c;
      printf("Input a Hexa-Decimal Number: ");
      scanf("%s", &a);
      strcpy(b, a);
      strrev(b);
      while(b[i] != '\0')
      {
            c = b[i++];
            switch(c)
            {
                  case 'A':
                        n += 10 * base;
                        break;
                  case 'B':
                        n += 11 * base;
                        break;
                  case 'C':
                        n += 12 * base;
                        break;
                  case 'D':
                        n += 13 * base;
                        break;
                  case 'E':
                        n += 14 * base;
                        break;
                  case 'F':
                        n += 15 * base;
                        break;
                  default:
                        n += (c - '0') * base;
            }
            base *= 16;
      }
   printf("Decimal Equivalent of Hexa-Decimal Number %s = %d\n", a, n);
}
OUTPUT:
            Input a Hexa-Decimal Number: 7B
            Decimal Equivalent of Hexa-Decimal Number 7B = 123
```

SELF-REVIEW EXERCISES

1. A variable that is known only within the function in which it is defined is called a ....
2. The .... statement in a called function is used to pass the value of an expression back to the calling function.
3. The storage class specifiers are ...., ..., ... and ....
4. The contents of a particular element of an array is called the .... of that element.
5. The process of placing the elements of an array into either ascending or descending order is called ....
6. When referring to an array element, the position number contained within parentheses is called a ....
7. In a double subscripted array, the first subscript (by convention) identifies the .... of an element and the second subscript (by convention) identifies the .... of an element.
8. The .... operator returns the location in the memory where its operand is stored.
9. The .... operator returns the value of the object to which its operand points.
10. To simulate call by reference when passing a non-array variable to a function, it is necessary to pass the .... of the variable to the function.
11. The number used to refer to a particular element of an array is called its ....
12. A .... should be used to declare the size of an array because it makes the program more scalable.
13. A recursive function typically has two components: One that provides a means for the recursion to terminate by testing for a .... case, and one that expresses the problem as a recursive call for a slightly simpler problem than the original call.
14. Keyword .... is used in a function header to indicate that a function does not return a value or to indicate that a function contains no parameters.

EXERCISES

1. Write a recursive function ***power(base, exponent)*** that when invoked returns ***base***^{exponent}. For example, ***power(3, 4) = 3 * 3 * 3 * 3***. Assume that ***exponent*** is an integer greater than or equal to 1.

2. Computers are playing an increasing role in education. Write a program that will help an elementary school student learn multiplication. Use ***rand*** to produce two positive one-digit integers. It should then type a question such as :

   How much is 6 times 7?

   The student then types the answer. Your program checks the student's answer. If it is correct, print " ***Very Good!!*** " and then ask another multiplication question. If the answer is wrong, print " ***No. Please try again*** " and then let the student try the same question again repeatedly until the student finally gets it right.

3. Write a program that runs 1000 games of craps and answers each of the following questions.

   (a) *How many games are won on the first roll, second roll, ..., twentieth roll and after the twentieth roll?*

   (b) *How many games are lost on the first roll, second roll, ..., twentieth roll and after the twentieth roll?*

   (c) *What are the chances of winning at craps?*

   (d) *What is the average length of a game of craps?*

   (e) *Do the chances of winning improve with the length of the game?*

4. Write your own versions of the functions getchar(), gets(), putchar() and puts().

5. Write a program that reads a series of strings and prints only those strings beginning with the letter " **b** ".

6. Write a function distance that calculate the distance between points (x_1,y_1) and (x_2,y_2). All numbers and return values should be of type double.

7. Write a program to find whether a sub-string exists in a given string.

8. Write a functin that takes an array of integers and returns the index of the largest number in the array.

4

Pointers

4.1 WHAT IS A POINTER ?

We shall now present a very important concept in C – ***the Pointers***. A pointer is a variable that stores the address of a variable. Pointers are very much used in C, partly because sometimes there is no other way except using a pointer and partly because the use of pointer leads to a more compact and efficient code. Like any other variables, pointers must be declared before they are used. The interpretation of pointer declaration is somewhat different than the interpretation of other variable declaration. When a pointer variable is declared, the unary operator asterisk * must precede the variable name. At this stage, you should recall that the binary * operator is used for multiplication and should not be confused with the unary operator *. The * before the variable identifies the fact that the variable is a pointer.

4.2 SIMPLE USE OF A POINTER

The pointer declaration usually may be written as follows

```
<data type> *<ptrvar>
```

where ***<data type>*** refers to any basic data type or user defined data type. The ***<ptrvar>*** is the name of pointer variable which you can select using the same rules applicable for an identifier. Let us now present a program in program listing 4.1 that illustrate several concepts about a pointer.

```
/*    Program Listing 4.1 : PTR.c
      Illustration of Pointers    */

#include <stdio.h>
void main(void)
{
      int i = 10, j = 20, *k, *l;

      printf("Address of i = %X\n", &i);
      printf("Address of j = %X\n\n", &j);

      printf("Address of k = %X\n", &k);
      printf("Address of l = %X\n\n", &l);

      k = &i;
      l = &j;

      printf("k points to  %d\n", k);
      printf("l points to  %d\n\n", l);

      printf("*k = %d\n", *k);
      printf("*l = %d\n", *l);

      *k = 15;
      *l = 25;

      printf("k points to  %X\n", k);
```

```
25.        printf("l points to  %X\n", l);
26.
27.        printf("Value of i = %d\n", i);
28.        printf("Value of j = %d\n", j);
29.  }
```

```
Address of i = 64FE00
Address of j = 64FDFC

Address of k = 64FDF8
Address of l = 64FDF4

k points to  6618624
l points to  6618620

*k = 10
*l = 20

k points to  64FE00
l points to  64FDFC

Value of i = 15
Value of j = 25
```

Program Listing 4.1 Illustration of Pointers

At Line 4, i, j are declared as integer variables and initialized to values 10 and 20 respectively. k, l are declared as integer pointer variables i.e., k and l can hold the address of any integer variable. The initial memory allocation of these four variables is shown in Fig. 4.1.

Notice that k and l hold some garbage. Also note that the memory space required for holding an integer is 4 bytes and the pointer is also 4 bytes. Note that the addresses and the sizes of the variable indicated in the figure 4.3 are only nominal and can considerably vary if the program is run on different hardware and operating systems. Line 12,

```
k = &i;
```

assigns the pointer variable k with the address of i(&i) and Line 13,

```
l = &j;
```

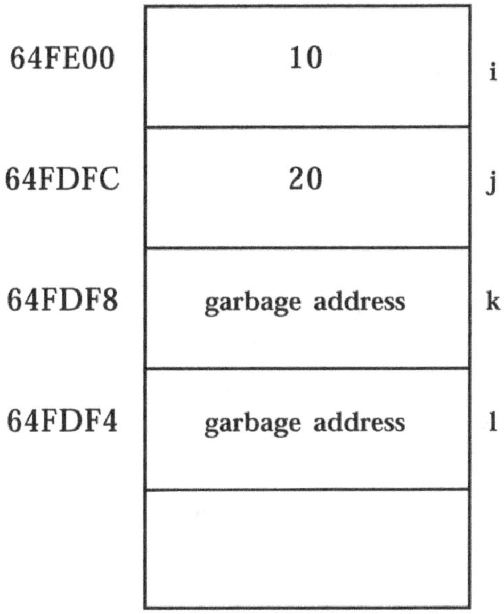
64FE00
10
i
64FDFC
20
j
64FDF8
garbage address
k
64FDF4
garbage address
l

Figure 4.1 Memory Scenario of Program Listing 4.1 before Line 12

assigns the address of j to l. After the execution of these two assignments the snapshot scenario of the memory is shown in Figure 4.2 (a). Since, k contains the address of i and l contains the address of j, we say k points to i and l points to j. Now the usage of *k and *l are meaningful. Obviously *k is 10 and *l is 20. At Line 18 and 19,

```
printf("*k = %d\n", *k);
printf("*l = %d\n", *l);
```

the values of *k and *l are printed. At Line 26 and Line 27,

```
*k = 15;
*l = 25;
```

now we assign new values to *k and *l, Since, k points to i and l points to j, we are changing the values stored by i and j indirectly. The memory scenario after this assignment is shown in Figure 4.2 (b)

Now to bring out the importance of pointers we first present a swap function in program listing 4.2, which actually does not swap (exchange) the value of a and b.

```
/*    Program Listing 4.2 : SWAP.c
      Illustration of Swap function*/
#include <stdio.h>

void swap(int, int);

void main(void)
{
      int a = 10, b = 15;
      printf(“Value of A and B before Swaping”);
      printf(“\nValue of A = %d\nValue of B = %d\n”, a, b);
      swap(a, b);
      printf(“Value of A and B After Swaping”);
      printf(“\nValue of A = %d\nValue of B = %d\n”, a, b);
}

void swap(int x, int y)
{
      int t;
      t = x;
      x = y;
      y = t;
}
```

```
Value of A and B before Swaping
Value of A = 10
Value of B = 15
Value of A and B After Swaping
Value of A = 10
Value of B = 15
```

***Program Listing 4.2** Program for swap() which does not actually swaps*

The function swap() only receives the copies of the values of a and b from main() into its local variables x and y. No doubt the function exchanges the values of x and y but this has no effect on the values of a and b in the main() program. The reason for this is that x and y are only local variables to the function swap() and their scope is only within that function. The snapshot of memory scenario when the program listing 4.2 is executed is shown in Fig. 4.3.

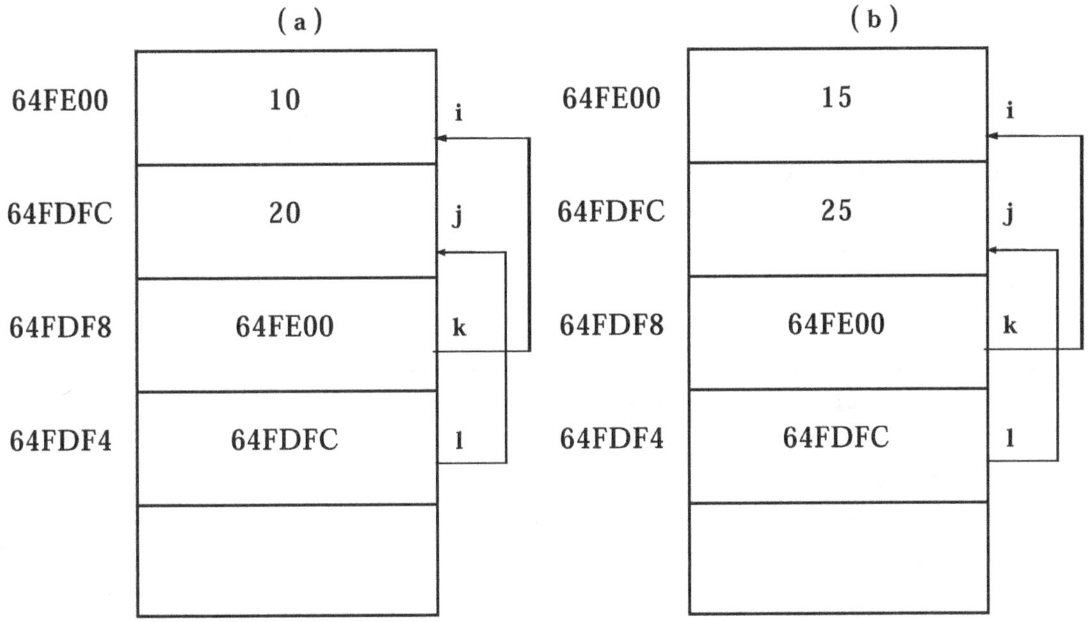
(a)
64FE00
10
i
64FDFC
20
j
64FDF8
64FE00
k
64FDF4
64FDFC
l
(b)
64FE00
15
i
64FDFC
25
j
64FDF8
64FE00
k
64FDF4
64FDFC
l

Figure 4.2 Memory Scenario of Program Listing 4.1 (a) after Line 13; (b) after Line 22

Now let us turn our attention to the correct version of swap() function in Program Listing 4.3, which really exchanges the values of a and b in main() function.

```
/*   Program Listing 4.3 : SWAPPTR.c
     Illustration of Swap function*/
#include <stdio.h>

void swap(int *, int *);

void main(void)
{
     int a = 10, b = 15;
     printf("Value of A and B before Swaping");
     printf("\nValue of A = %d\nValue of B = %d\n", a, b);
     swap(&a, &b);
     printf("Value of A and B After Swaping");
     printf("\nValue of A = %d\nValue of B = %d\n", a, b);
}
```

```
14.
15.  void swap(int *x, int *y)
16.  {
17.          int t;
18.          t = *x;
19.          *x = *y;
20.          *y = t;
21.  }
```

```
Value of A and B before Swaping
Value of A = 10
Value of B = 15
Value of A and B After Swaping
Value of A = 15
Value of B = 10
```

***Program Listing 4.3** Program for swap() which correctly swaps.*

Observe that at Line 10,

```
swap(&a, &b);
```

the address of a and b are passed to swap() function. Since, x and y are declared as pointer variables and will hold the address of a and y will hold the address of b respectively (Figure 4.6). Line 17,

```
int t;
```

the temporary variable t is declared and at Line 18,

```
t = *x;
```

copies the value pointed by x, i.e., the value of a into t. Line 19, copies the value pointed by y to the value pointed by x, i.e., the value of b copied into a(overwriting a's original value of 10).

Line 20,

```
*y = t;
```

copies the value of the t (10) into b (overwriting b's original value of 15). On return to main(), both x and y vanish, but we have achieved the swapping of a and b in the function main().

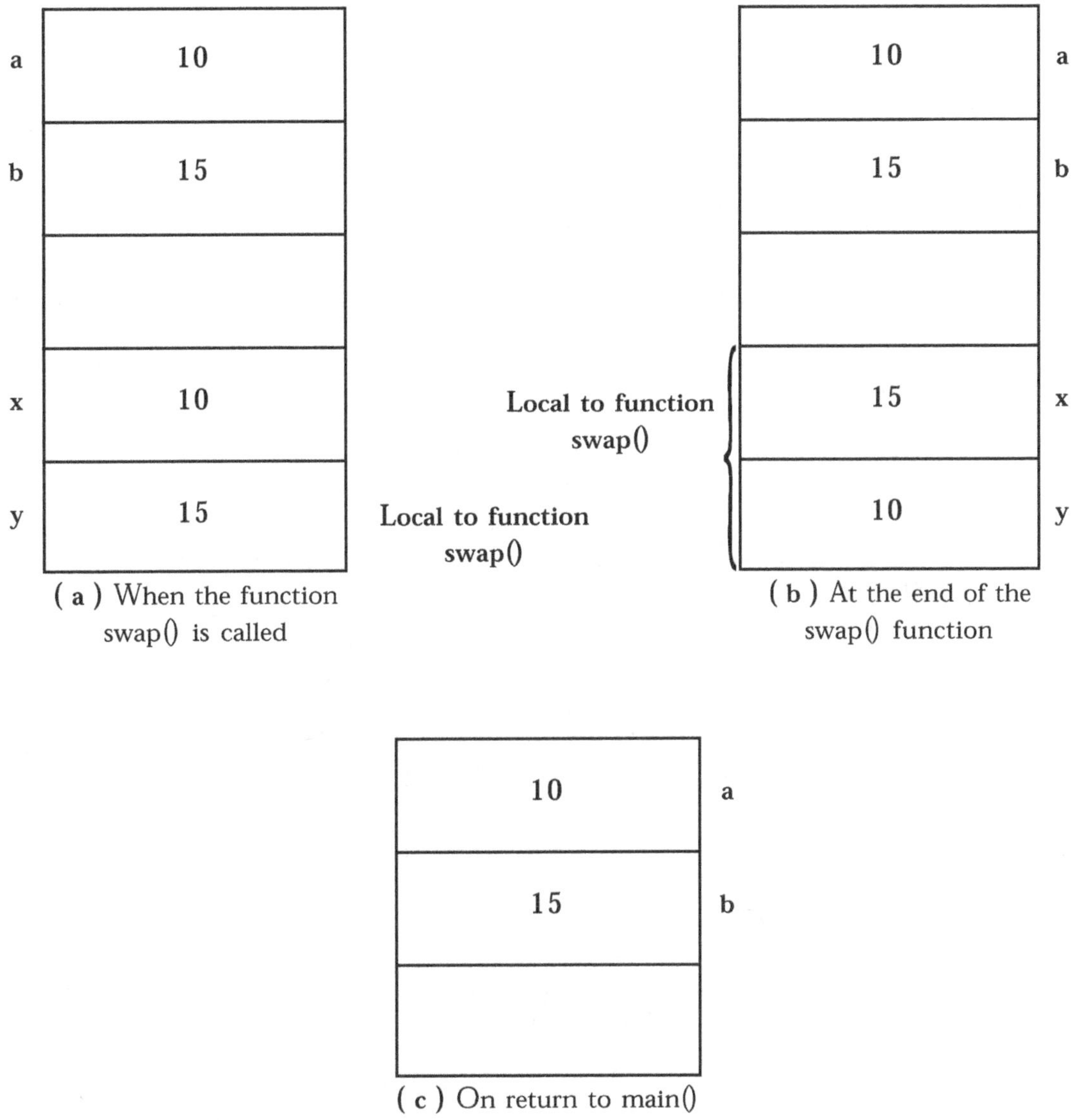
a
10
b
15
x
10
y
15
(a) When the function swap() is called
10
a
15
b
Local to function swap()
15
x
Local to function swap()
10
y
(b) At the end of the swap() function
10
a
15
b
(c) On return to main()

Figure 4.3 Memory Scenario of Program Listing 4.2

The student should convince himself or herself that there is no other alternative in C than to use pointers to achieve the swap through a function. However, if we are swapping a and b within the main() function using a temporary variable, then we have no problem at all. This is where the pointers are absolutely needed.

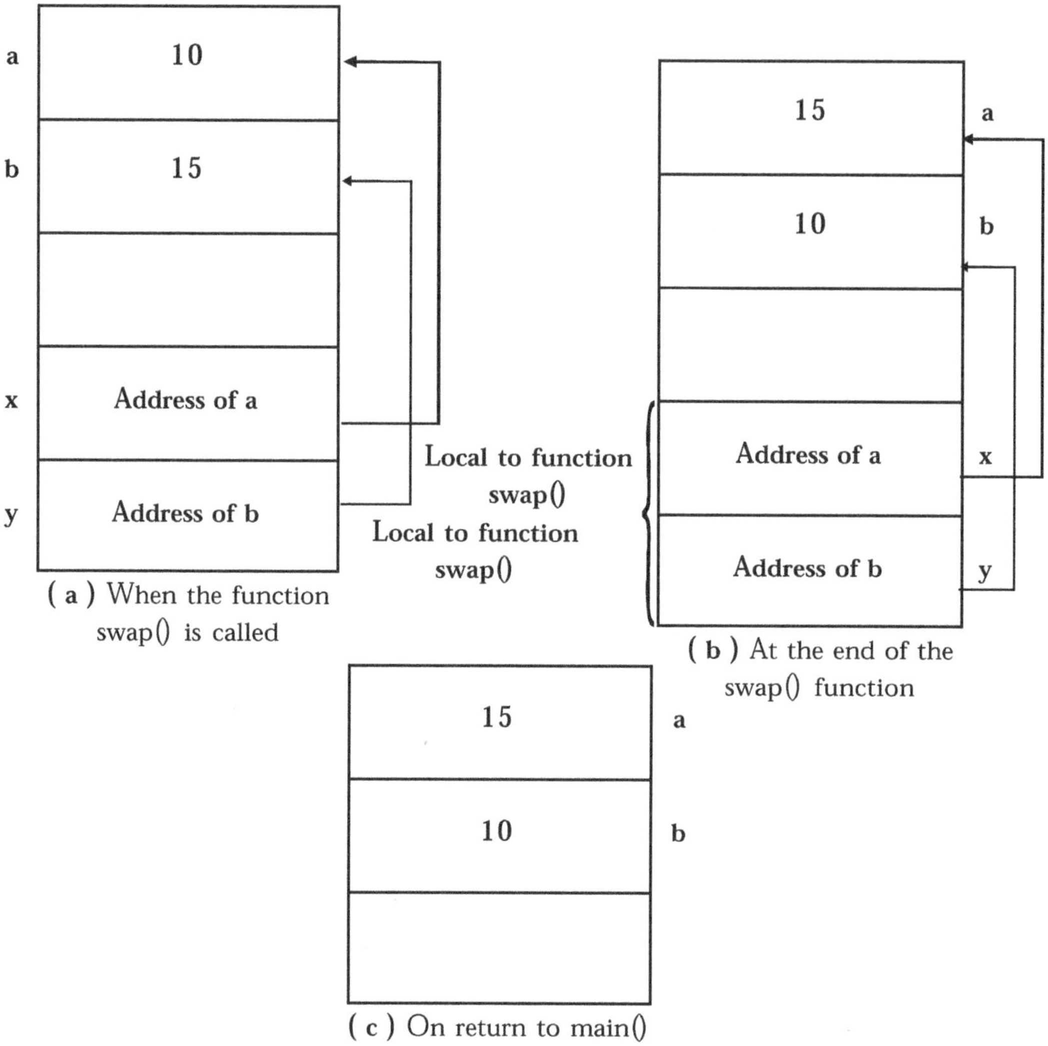
a
10
b
15
x
Address of a
y
Address of b
(a) When the function swap() is called
Local to function swap()
Local to function swap()
15
a
10
b
Address of a
x
Address of b
y
(b) At the end of the swap() function
15
a
10
b
(c) On return to main()

Figure 4.4 Memory Scenario for Program Listing 4.3

4.3 POINTERS AND ARRAYS

Let us begin with a simplified picture of how memory is organized. A typical machine has an array of consecutively numbered or addressed memory cells that may be manipulated individually or in contiguous groups. One common situation is that any byte can be a char, a pair of one-byte cells can be treated as a short integer, and four adjacent bytes form an integer long. A pointer is a group of cells(often four) that can hold an address.

In C there is a strong relationship between pointers and arrays. Any operation that can be achieved by array subscripting can easily be implemented with pointers. The pointer version, in general, will be faster. But somewhat hard to understand. Let us start with the following declaration.

Let us rewrite Program Listing 4.2 in Section 4.2 in which the maxm() returns the largest integer in an array of integers using pointers. The program is illustrated in program listing 4.4

```
/*  Program Listing 4.4 : LARPTR.c
    Illustration of Swap function*/
#include <stdio.h>

int maxm(int *, int);

void main(void)
{
    int a[20], i, n;
    printf("Enter the number of elements(not more than 20)...");
    scanf("%d", &n);
    for(i = 0;i < n;i++)
    {
        printf("\nEnter %d Value ...", i+1);
        scanf("%d", &a[i]);
    }
    printf("The largest Number is %d ...", maxm(a, n));
}

int maxm(int *arr, int n)
{
    int largest, i;
    largest = *arr;
    for(i = 1;i < n;i++)
    {
        if(*(arr + i) > largest)
            largest = *(arr + i);
    }
    return(largest);
}
```

```
Enter the number of elements(not more than 20)...5
Enter 1 Value ...8
Enter 1 Value ...6
Enter 1 Value ...10
Enter 1 Value ...7
Enter 1 Value ...2
The Largest Number is 10 ...
```

Program Listing 4.4 LARPTR.C

At Line 7,

```
int a[20], i, n;
```

defines the array a of size 20, that is, a block of 20 consecutive objects named a[0], a[1], ..., a[19]

At Line 15,

```
printf("The largest Number is %d ...", maxm(a, n));
```

the function maxm() is called, which passes the starting address and the number of elements of the array to the function, which is just similar to the earlier program (program listing 4.7). At Line 18,

```
int maxm(int *arr, int n)
```

the function maxm(), has the first argument as an integer pointer variable ***arr***. When the function is called, ***arr*** gets the value of the starting address of the array, and the memory scenario looks as indicated in Figure 4.5.

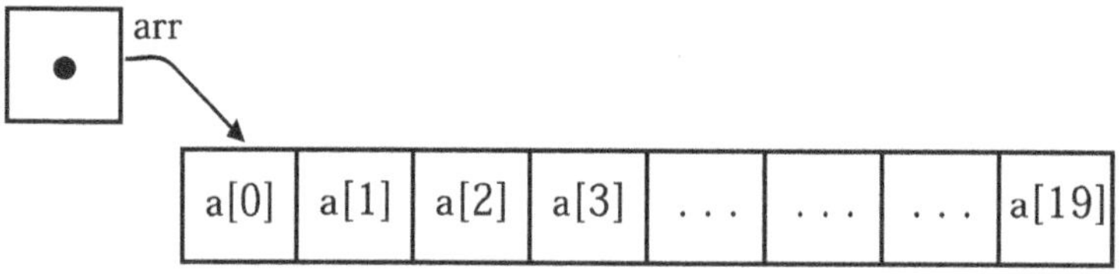
arr
a[0]
a[1]
a[2]
a[3]
...
...
...
a[19]

Figure 4.5 Memory Scenario when the function maxm() is called in program listing 4.4

At Line 22,

```
for(i = 1;i < n;i++)
```

the starting address is used by the for loop to run through the array. One interesting point to note here is the pointer arithmetic. Observe the Line 24,

```
if(*(arr + i) > largest)
```

the expression arr + i is absolutely legal and points to an integer i integers away from the starting address as depicted in Figure 4.6.

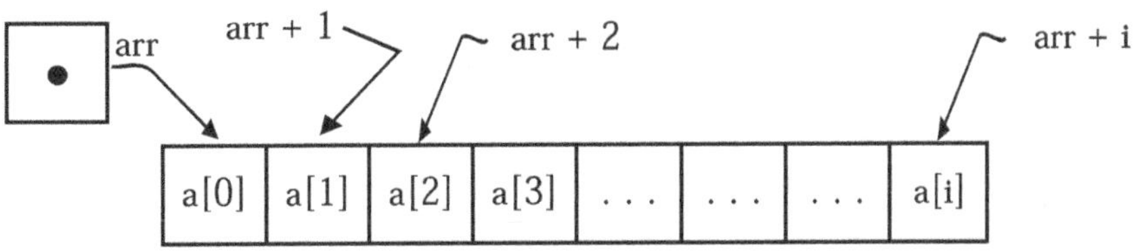
arr
arr + 1
arr + 2
arr + i
a[0]
a[1]
a[2]
a[3]
. . .
. . .
. . .
a[i]

Figure 4.6 Memory Scenario illustrating the pointer arthematic

One need not have to worry about the number of bytes that, the type integer takes since adding 1 to pointer makes it to point to the next element, regardless of the type. Notice that ***arr + i*** is in the parenthesis, since the unary operator * has the highest priority and our intension is to add i first and then take the value it points to. If the parenthesis is omitted, there is no syntax error. Simply what ever is pointed by ***arr*** (i.e., a[0]) will be incremented by 1 and the condition is checked. The program might work, but may not give you the correct result.

4.4 ADDRESS ARITHMETIC

Incrementing / Decrementing a pointer variable, adding and subtracting an integer from pointer variable are all legal and known as ***pointer arithmetic.*** Pointers are valid operands in arithmetic expressions, assignment expressions, and comparison expressions. However, not all the operators normally used in these expressions are valid in conjunction with pointer variables. This section describes the operators that can have pointers as operands, and how these operators are used.

A limited set of arithmetic operations may be performed on pointers. A pointer may be incremented(++) or decremented (—), an integer may be added to a pointer (+ or +=), an integer may be subtracted from a pointer (- or -=), or one pointer may be subtracted from another. However, consider the following example.

Assume that array int v[10] has been declared and its first element is at location 3000 in memory. Assume pointer vPtr has been initialized to point to v[0], i.e., the value of vPtr is 3000. The following figure illustrates this situation for a machine with 4-byte integers. Note that vPtr can be initialized to point to array v with either of the statements

```
vPtr = v;
vPtr = &v[0];
```

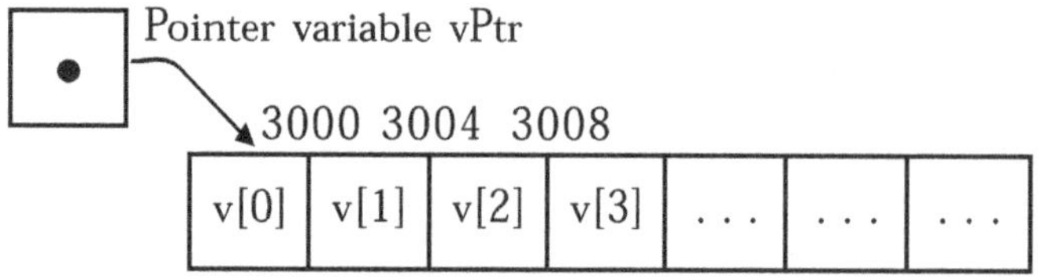
Pointer variable vPtr
3000 3004 3008
v[0]
v[1]
v[2]
v[3]
. . .
. . .
. . .

Fig. 4.7 The array v and a pointer variable vPtr that points to v

In conventional arithmetic, the addition 3000+2 yields the value 3002. This is normally not the case with pointer arithmetic. When an integer is added to or subtracted from a pointer, the pointer is not simply incremented or decremented by that integer, but the integer times the size of the object to which the pointer refers. The number of bytes depend on the object's data type. For example, the statement,

```
vPtr += 2;
```

would produce 3008(3000+2 * 4) assumeing an integer is stored in 4-bytes of memory. In the array v, vPtr would now point to v[2]. If an integer is stored in 2-bytes of memory, then the preceding calculation would result in memory location 3004(3000 + 2 * 2). If the array were of a different data type, the preceding statement would increment the pointer by twice the number of bytes that it takes to store an object of that data type. When performing pointer arithmetic on a character array, the results will be consistent with regular arithmetic because each character is one byte long.

If vPtr had been incremented to 3016, which points to v[4], the statement

```
vPtr -= 4;
```

would set vPtr back to 3000 – the beginning of the array. If a pointer is being incremented or decremented by one, the increment(++) and decrement(––) operators can be used. Either of the statements

```
++vPtr;
vPtr++;
```

increment the pointer to point to the next location in the array. Either of the statements,

```
--vPtr;
vPtr--;
```

decrement the pointer to point to the previous element of the array.

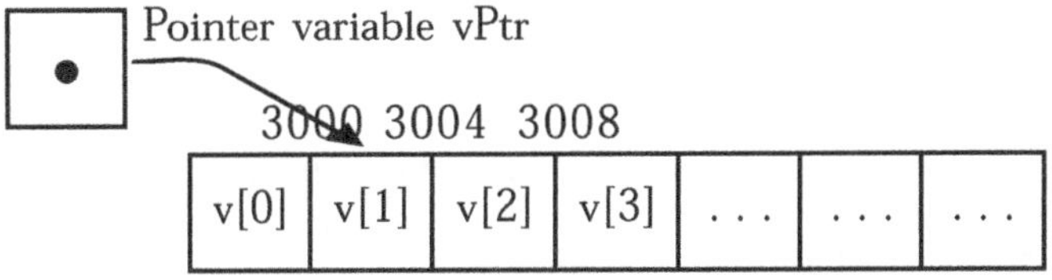
Pointer variable vPtr
3000 3004 3008
v[0]
v[1]
v[2]
v[3]
. . .
. . .
. . .

Figure 4.8 The pointer vPtr after pointer arithmetic

Pointer variables may be subtracted from one another. For example, if vPtr contains the location 3000, and v2Ptr contains the address 3008, the statement,

```
x = v2Ptr - vPtr;
```

would assign to x the number of array elements from vPtr to v2Ptr, in this case, 2 pointer arithmetic is meaningless unless performed on an array. We cannot assume that two variables of the same type are stored contiguously in memory unless they are adjacent elements in an array.

4.5 POINTER TO void

In C, an additional type void * (pointer to void) is defined as a proper type for generic pointer. Any pointer to an object may be converted to type void * without loss of information. If the result is converted back to the original pointer type, the original pointer is recovered and program listing below illustrates these concepts.

```
main()
{
        void *a;
        int n = 2, *m;
        double d = 2.3, *c;
        a = &n;
        m = a;
        printf("\n%d %d %d", a, *m, m);
        a = &d;
        c = a;
        printf("\n%d %3.1f %d", a, *c, c);
}
```

At Line 3,

```
void *a;
```

a is declared as a pointer to void which is used at line 6 to carry the address of an int and line 9 to carry the address of a double.

At Line 7 and 10,

```
m = a;
c = a;
```

the original pointers are recovered without any loss of information. Observe the output of the program.

A pointer to void cannot be dereferenced. In the above program using *a will be an error.

There is one difference between the array name and the pointer that must be kept in mind. Let us suppose that p is a pointer variable and a is an array, both of the same type. Then p = a, p++, p += 2, etc., are all valid and legal, while a = p, a++, a += 2 are all illegal. The reason for this is that a is an address but not an address variable (pointer). Similarly, if p is a pointer variable and a is a variable, both of the same type, p = &a is legal, p = a is also legal, but should be avoided. The reason for this is, it amounts to initializing p with the value of a and not with the address of a which might lead to fatal runtime errors and is not very useful in programming.

However all other arithmetic operations such as *, /, % etc., are illegal. Even with the permitted pointer arithmetic one should be careful not to violate the memory regulations. That is one should not increment, decrement, add or subtract an integer to a pointer if it is not meaningful and exceeds the memory limits. As an example,

4.6 POINTERS AND STRINGS

It is convenient and interesting to use pointers to handle strings in C language. Let us straight away present the pointer version of program listing 2.11 to convert lowercase characters to uppercase characters in Program Listing 4.5.

```
        /*    Program Listing 4.5 : STRPTR.c
              Converts all the small case Alphabets to Capitals */
1.      #include <stdio.h>
2.
3.      void to_str_upper(char *);
4.
5.      void main(void)
6.      {
7.            char str[100];
8.            printf("Enter the String: ");
9.            gets(str);
10.             to_str_upper(str);
11.             printf("%s",str);
12.       }
13.
14.     void to_str_upper(char *s)
15.     {
16.           while(*s){      /* loop continues till *s is '\0' */
17.     /* to check *s is a lower case letter
18.     and if so replace with upper case*/
19.                 if((*s  >= 'a')&&(*s <= 'z'))  *s -= 32;
20.                 s++;
21.           }
22.     }
```

```
Enter the String: AbCd;l123
Changed to ABCD;L123
```

Program Listing 4.5 Program to convert all lowercase alphabet to uppercase using pointers

Observe that there is no change in the main() function. At Line 10,

```
to_str_upper(str);
```

the function to_str_upper() is called from the main() function, passing the starting address of the string (character array, properly terminated with '\0'). At Line 14,

```
void to_str_upper(char *s)
```

the function to_str_upper() receives the starting address of the string in the character pointer variable s. We use this address and pointer arithmetic in the while loop from Line 16 to Line 21,

```
        while(*s){      /* loop continues till *s is '\0' */
    /* to check *s is a lower case letter
    and if so replace with upper case*/
            if((*s  >= 'a')&&(*s <= 'z'))  *s -= 32;
            s++;
        }
```

to run through the string. At Line 20, the pointer is incremented to point to the next location. Notice that the last statement in the routine can be replaced with ++s.

Let us now present a more interesting program using ***strings***. A string is known as a palindrome if and only if when reversed is same as the original string. For example, the string MADAM is a palindrome. The program listing 4.6 takes a string and checks whether the given string is palindrome or not.

```
/*    Program Listing 4.6 : PALIN.c
      Converts all the small case Alphabets to Capitals  */
#include <stdio.h>

void reverse(char *);
void strcopy(char *, char *);
void strlower(char *);
  void strupper(char *);
int compare(char *, char *);
int length(char *);

void main(void)
{
      char str[100], rev[100];

      printf("Enter any String ...");
      gets(str);
      strupper(str);
```

```

	strcopy(str, rev);
	reverse(rev);

	if(compare(str, rev) == 0)
		printf("\nThe string is a Palindrome");
	else
		printf("\nThe string is not a Palindrome");
}

void reverse(char *s)
{
	char *s1;
	char c;
	s1 = s + (length(s) - 1);
	while(s < s1)
	{
		c = *s;
		*s = *s1;
		*s1 = c;
		s++;
		s1—;
	}
}

int compare(char *s1, char *s2)
{
	while(*s1 && *s2)
	{
		if(*s1 > *s2)
			return 1;
		if(*s1 < *s2)
			return -1;
		s1++;
		s2++;
	}
	if(!(*s1) && (*s2))
		return -1;
	if(!(*s2) && (*s1))
		return 1;
```

```
        return 0;
}

int length(char *s)
{
        int len = 0;
        while(*s)
        {
                len++;
                s++;
        }
        return(len);
}

void strcopy(char *s1, char *s2)
{
        while(*s1)
        {
                *s2 = *s1;
                s1++;
                s2++;
        }
        *s2 = ‘\0’;
}

void strupper(char *s)
{
        while(*s)
        {
                if((*s  >= ‘a’)&&(*s <= ‘z’)) *s -= 32;
                        s++;
        }
}

void strlower(char *s)
{
        while(*s)
```

```
94.         {
95.                 if((*s  >= 'A')&&(*s <= 'Z')) *s += 32;
96.                 s++;
97.         }
98.  }
```

```
Enter any String ...English
The string is not a Palindrome
Enter any String ...Madam
The string is a Palindrome
```

Program Listing 4.6 Program to check a string for Palindrome

We make use of several string handling functions in the program namely, reverse, strcopy, strupper, compare and length. Some of these functions probably with different names are available in C library and the prototypes are defined in **string.h**. Refer Appendix B for more details. However, we have chosen to write all these functions to make the student understand and develop the skill to handle strings and pointers together effectively. The function reverse, defined at Line 27,

```
void reverse(char *s)
```

takes a string through a character pointer and reverses the string. At Line 31,

```
s1 = s + (length(s) - 1);
```

the function length is called to obtain the length of the string s and set the char *s1 to the last character of the string. Notice that we have subtracted 1 from the length of the string, since the string indexing starts from 0. During the first iteration, the while loop from Lines 32 to 38,

```
while(s < s1)
{
        c = *s;
        *s = *s1;
        *s1 = c;
        s++;
        s1—;
}
```

exchanges what is pointed by s (first character) with that of what is pointed by s1 (last character). s is incremented and s1 is decremented and the exchange continues until s is less than s1. Thus the string is reversed in place. Note that comparing two pointers is legal. The return type is void for this function since it does not return any value, but simply makes a in place reversal of the string whose starting address is passed to this function.

The function compare() at Line 42,

```
int compare(char *s1, char *s2)
```

compare, compares two strings with starting addresses s1 and s2. It returns +1, if s1 is lexicographically greater than s2, returns –1, if s2 is lexicographically greater than s1 and returns 0, if both the strings are identical. The conditions from Lines 53 to 56,

```
if(!(*s1) && (*s2))
    return -1;
if(!(*s2) && (*s1))
    return 1;
```

are necessary, to check if one of the strings is shorter and up to that point lexicographically same. For example, when two strings ***Amjad*** and ***Amjad Khan*** are passed to the string compare as s1 and s2 respectively, then the function should return –1. The function length at Line 60,

```
int length(char *s)
```

takes the starting address of the string and returns the length of the string. Observe the while loop from Line 63 to 67.

```
while(*s)
{
    len++;
    s++;
}
```

The while loop will terminate when s points to '\0' which is the last character in the string. Thus, rightly, the routine length() returns the actual length of the string and will not include '\0' as this is not a part of the string. Line 71,

```
void strcopy(char *s1, char *s2)
```

the function strcopy, takes two addresses and copies the string pointed by s1 into the consecutive locations starting from s2. The while loop from Line 73 to 78,

```
while(*s1)
{
    *s2 = *s1;
    s1++;
    s2++;
}
```

terminates when s1 points to '\0' and therefore '\0' is not copied to s2.

So this is the reason, we explicitly copy '\0' into s2. At Line 79,

```
*s2 = '\0';
```

At Line 82,

```
void strupper(char *s)
```

the function strupper takes the starting address of a string and converts all the character into Upper Case.

At Line 15 in main(),

```
gets(str);
```

the string is accepted into str. At Line 16,

```
strupper(str);
```

strupper is called to convert the string into upper case. This is essential if the string is given by the user using the Mixed Case Letters. At Line 18,

```
strcopy(str, rev);
```

strcopy is called to create a copy of the string. At Line 19,

```
reverse(rev);
```

reverse is called with a string rev. At Line 21 to 24,

```
if(compare(str, rev) == 0)
     printf("\nThe string is a Palindrome");
else
     printf("\nThe string is not a Palindrome");
```

the if else statement test for the palindrome, calling the compare to compare the strings str and rev.

4.7 POINTERS AND TWO-DIMENSIONAL ARRAYS

We shall now present the relation between a two dimensional arrays and pointers. The program listing 4.7 and program listing 4.8 illustrate how a two dimensional arrays can be passed to a function using pointers. Both these programs are the pointer versions of the inplace transpose of a matrix. The student is advised to carefully follow these program listings. Let us first explain the program listing 4.7.

```
/*    Program Listing 4.7 : ARTRNPTR.c
      Program to transpose a matrix using Pointers */

#include <stdio.h>

   void transpose(int (*)[3], int, int);
   void print_mat(int (*)[3], int, int);

   void main(void)
   {
         int a[][3] = { {1, 2,3},
                      {4, 5,6},
                        {7, 8,9}
                        };
           int (*b)[3];   /* this is only a pointer to a group of
                        one dimensional arrays of size 3
                        if the brackets around *b are elemenated
                      then b becomes an array of 3 interger pointers */
           b = a; /* now you can access elements of a using b*/

           print_mat(b, 3, 3); /* pass a or b no difference */
           transpose(a, 3, 3); /* pass a or b no difference */
           printf("\n");
           print_mat(a, 3, 3); /* pass a or b no difference */
     }

     void transpose(int (*x)[3], int r, int c)
     {
           int t, i, j;
           for(i = 0;i < r;i++)
           {
               for(j = i;j < c;j++)
                 {
                   t = *(*(x+i)+j);/*we can use t=x[i][j]; here */
```

```
32.                     *(*(x+i)+j) = *(*(x+j)+i);/* we can use
                                        x[i][j]=x[j][i]; here */
33.                     *(*(x+j)+i) = t;/*we can use x[j][i]=t; here */
34.                 }
35.             }
36.     }
37.
38.     void print_mat(int (*y)[3], int r, int c)
39.     {
40.         int i, j;
41.         for(i = 0;i < r;i++)
42.         {
43.             for(j = 0;j < c;j++)
44.             {
45.                 printf("%5d", *(*(y+i)+j));/* we can use
                                                  y[i][j] here */
46.             }
47.             printf("\n");
48.         }
49. }
```

```
1   2   3
4   5   6
7   8   9

1   4   7
2   5   8
3   6   9
```

Program Listing 4.7 Program to transpose a matrix using Pointers

At Line 8, an array is declared and initialized. At Line 12,

```
int (*b)[3];   /* this is only a pointer to a group of
                  one dimensional arrays of size 3
                  if the brackets around *b are elemenated
                  then b becomes an arry of 3 interger pointers */
```

observe the declaration of the pointer variable b. b points to an object which is an array of 3 integers. Incase b is incremented by 1, it points to the next object of a 3 element integer array.

Since the square brackets ([]) have higher priority than the indirection operator *, the elimination of the parantheses around *b, the compiler interprets b as an array of 3 integer pointers rather than, a pointer to an array of size 3 integers. We shall see an array of pointers in the next section. Line 16, where a is assigned to b, allows the pointer b to take the starting address of the two dimensional array. At line 24, the function transpose receives this address into x when called from main at line 19. The function transpose manuplates the pointer to affect the change of columns and rows using the two for loops. At Line 31, x[i][j] is referenced as *(*(x + i)+j). x + i is the address of the ith row i.e., this points to the object containing three integers of row i. Within this row we want j^{th} integer. Therefore, we first dereference x + i using a * operator, then add j and once again dereference to get the contents of jth location in i^{th} row. However, you can still continue to reference with the usual notation as x[i][j] in this function.

We shall now look into the next listing where we are passing the starting address of the two dimensional array to the function transpose as a pointer to the integer.

```
       /*   Program Listing 4.8 : ARTRNPTR.c
            Program to transpose a matrix using Address Calculation */
1.     #include <stdio.h>
2.
3.     void transpose(int *, int, int);
4.     void print_mat(int * , int, int);
5.
6.     void main(void)
7.     {
8.          int a[][4] = { {1, 2,3,4},
9.                         { 5,6,7,8},
10.                          {9,10,11,12},
11.                          {13,14,15,16}
12.                        };
13.         int *x;
14.         x=(int *)a; /* forcing the starting address of a 2D array
15.                              into an integer pointer*/
16.
17.         print_mat(x,4, 4); /* passing x as a pointer to integer */
18.         transpose(x, 4, 4);/* passing x as a pointer to integer */
19.         printf("\n");
20.         print_mat(x,4, 4);/* passing x as a pointer to integer */
21.    }
```

```

void transpose(int *x,int r,int c) /* passing 2D array to the
                                      function as a pointer to int */
{
     int t, i, j;
     for(i = 0;i < r;i++)
     {
          for(j = i;j < c;j++)
          {/* address computation assuming row major
                                                   representation*/
               t = *((x+c*i)+j);
               *((x+c*i)+j) = *((x+c*j)+i);
               *((x+c*j)+i) = t;
          }
     }
}

void print_mat(int *y, int r, int c) /* passing 2D array to the
                                        function as a pointer to int */
{
     int i, j;
     for(i = 0;i < r;i++)
     {       /* address computation assuming row major
                                                   representation*/
          for(j = 0;j < c;j++)printf("%5d", *((y+c*i)+j));
               printf("\n");
     }
}
```

```
1    2    3    4
5    6    7    8
9   10   11   12
13   14   15   16

1    5    9   13
2    6   10   14
3    7   11   15
4    8   12   16
```

Program Listing 4.8 Program to transpose a matrix using address calculation

At Line 13, we have declared an integer pointer x. At Line 14, we force the starting address of a 2D array into an integer pointer x. Our idea is to send this integer pointer to the function transpose, and compute the address of x[i][j] using row major representation. A row major representation (which most of the compilers follow) stores the elements of 2D array row wise. That is, if you assume that there are n elements in each row, the first n locations of the memory will be filled with the elements of the first row and the second n locations will be filled by the elements of the second row, and so on. The other representation is known as column major representation, which is not used by many compilers. In this representation instead of storing the elements rowwise, they are stored column wise, i.e., first column followed by second column, etc.

At Line 31, observe that the expression (x+c*i) gives the starting address of the ith row and (x+c*i)+j gives the jth element of the ith row. Dereferencing this now, i.e., *((x+c*i)+j) gives the value of x[i][j].

4.8 ARRAY OF POINTERS & FUNCTIONS THAT RETURN POINTER

We have seen functions returning values like integers, floats, doubles etc., However the functions can also return pointers to different data types. We have also discussed in the previous section, about an array of pointers briefly. We shall now present a program that illustrates both these ideas. The program sends several sets of numbers to a function max_avg which returns a pointer to set that has the maximum average. The program is illustrated in program listing 4.9.

```
/*    Program Listing 4.9 : ARTRNPTR.c
      Program to print the array with largest average */

#include <stdio.h>
 /* to determine the set of nubers with largest average among
                                          several sets of numbers*/
int* max_avg(int *[],int);
void print_max(int *);
void main(void)
{

      int *a[4]; /* declare an array of 4 integer pointers */
      int a1[] = {56,28,84,66,78,23,90,-1};
      int a2[]= {43,56,89,20,46,79,26,56,89,-1};
      int a3[]={44,34,78,98,34,77,84,12,56,90,34,67,-1};
      int a4[]= {23,100,34,78,23,67,98,23,34,28,90,88,3,67,91,-1};
      /* -1 indecates end of data in each set */
      a[0]=a1;a[1]=a2; a[2]=a3;a[3]=a4;  /* each poiter location is
   filled with the starting address of each one dimensional array*/
```

```
16.         print_max(max_avg(a,4));/* prints trhe set that has
                                             largest average */
17.     }
18.
19.     int * max_avg(int *x[],int n)
20.     { /* returns a pointer to the set of numbers that have
21.     the largest average amoung n sets */
22.         int tot, i, j, max;
23.         float max_avg=0;
24.         for(i = 0;i <n;i++)
25.         {
26.             tot=0;j=0;  /* intialize tot and j for each set */
27.             while(*(x[i]+j)!= -1) {tot+=*(x[i]+j); j++;}
28.             /* pick the set having largest average */
29.           if(((float)tot/j)>max_avg){max_avg=(float)tot/j;max=i;}
30.         }
31.         return x[max];
32.     }
33.
34.     void print_max(int *y)
35.     {
36.         while(*y != -1){printf("%5d", *y);y++;};
37.         printf("\n");
38.     }
```

```
56  28  84  66  78  23  90
```

Program Listing 4.9 Program to print the array with largest average

Line 8,

```
int *a[4]; /* declare an array of 4 integer pointers */
```

declares an array of 4 integer pointers. We are going to use these four pointers to send the starting addresses of the set of four one dimensional arrays to the function max_avg. Lines 9 to 12,

```
int a1[] = {56,28,84,66,78,23,90,-1};
int a2[]= {43,56,89,20,46,79,26,56,89,-1};
int a3[]={44,34,78,98,34,77,84,12,56,90,34,67,-1};
int a4[]= {23,100,34,78,23,67,98,23,34,28,90,88,3,67,91,-1};
```

declare 4 one dimensional arrays a1, a2, a3, a4 and each one is initialized with a set of numbers. We have used −1 to indicate the end of the set.

Notice that, each set has a different cardinality (no. of elements). At line 14, each of the starting address of the arrays a1, a2, a3, a4 are filled in the locations 0, 1, 2 and 3 of a, which is an array of 4 pointers. Line 16,

```
                print_max(max_avg(a,4));/* prints trhe set that has largest
average */
```

the function max_avg is called passing the address of a, to the function. At Lines 19 to 32,

```
int * max_avg(int *x[],int n)
{ /* returns a pointer to the set of numbers that have
the largest average amoung n sets */
    int tot, i, j, max;
    float max_avg=0;
    for(i = 0;i <n;i++)
    {
        tot=0;j=0;  /* intialize tot and j for each set */
        while(*(x[i]+j) != -1) {tot+=*(x[i]+j); j++;}
        /* pick the set having largest average */
        if(((float)tot/j)>max_avg){max_avg=(float)tot/j;max=i;}
    }
    return x[max];
}
```

the function max_avg receives the 4 pointers in the array x. At line 24, the for loop runs through each set, while the inner while loop computes the total of each set. The average is computed by dividing the total with the number of elements and is tested at line 29, against max_avg and the variable max is updated accordingly. When the for loop is exited the max contains the index of the address pointing to the set that has the largest average. Therefore, it is returned at line 31. In main this pointer is used and the correct set with the largest average is picked and printed by calling the function print_max.

Now let us look at how an array of strings can be handled using pointers. The following declarations will allow you to store all the names of the months in an year in a array of pointers.

```
char *months[] ={  "January", "February", "March",
                   "April", "May", "June", "July",
                   "August", "September", "October",
                   "November", "December"
                };
```

In program listing 4.6 we have printed the values of various range counters against each range by printing the range as range1, range2, etc., Choose an array of strings and initialize it with different ranges. Use this array to generate an output of the following form.

Range	Counter Value
\$200-\$299	--
\$300-\$399	--
\$400-\$499	--
\$500-\$599	--
\$600-\$699	--
\$700-\$799	--
\$800-\$899	--
\$900-\$999	--
\$1000 and over	--

4.9 POINTERS TO FUNCTIONS

In C, we have already defined pointers for variables of different data types like int, char, double, etc. As all these variables are within the memory of the computer, it is quite meaningful to define a variable to carry their address. A function is also contained in the memory starting at a particular address. The concept here is, *why not have a pointer defined to a function.* Indeed C allows pointers to a function, of course, with certain restrictions. One advantage of defining a pointer to a function is, that it can be passed as a parameter to the other functions. We shall now present a C program to illustrate, how to declare a pointer to function and use it in program listing below.

```
#include <stdio.h>
void main(void)
{
   int n;
   int square(int );
   int cube(int );
   void compute(int(*f)(int ), int );  /* Pointer to function */
   printf("\nEnter a Number: ");
   scanf("%d", &n);
   printf("\nThe Square of n is: ");
   compute(square, n);/*Call using the address of function square*/
```

```
12.        printf("\nThe Cube of n is: ");
13.        compute(cube, n); /* Call using the address of function cube
*/
14.     }
15.     int square(int n)
16.     {
17.        return n*n;
18.     }
19.     int cube(int n)
20.     {
21.        return n*n*n;
22.     }
23.     void compute(int(*f)(int ), int n)
24.     {
25.        int x;
26.        x = (*f)(n); /* Call to appropriate function */
27.        printf("%d", x);
28.     }
```

This program has to functions – square and cube. These functions are chosen to be trivial to add more concentration towards the pointer to function declarations and use. The program accepts a number and calls the function compute which has two parameters – the first is a pointer to a function that returns an int and the second is an int. Note the declaration of the formal parameter *f* (at line 7) which is the function pointer. The general syntax for the declaration of pointers to function is,

```
<return value type> (*fptr)()
```

Consider line 7,

```
void compute(int(*f)(int ), int )
```

declares f as a pointer to a function which has one formal parameter as int and returns an int. At Line 11, compute is invoked with square as the first parameter.

```
compute(square, n);/* Call using the address of function
square */
```

Here square represents the starting address of the function square. Note that this is very similar to an array pointer where the name of the array is the starting address and therefore an & is not necessary before square. Similarly, at Line 13, the compute function is called with the function cube which is the starting address of the cube.

```
compute(cube, n); /* Call using the address of function cube */
```

In compute function, observe line 26 where the function is invoked using a pointer.

```
x = (*f)(n); /* Call to appropriate function */
```

When the function compute is called for the first time, the line 26 is equivalent of

```
x = square(n);
```

and for the second time, it is equivalent to

```
x = cube(n);
```

Notice that the parenthesis around *f* in the declaration at lines 7 and 23. In the absence of these parenthesis the declaration of *f* will be interpreted as a function that returns a pointer to integer and not as a pointer to function.

4.10 goto STATEMENT AND LABELS

C provides goto statement and labels to branch from a statement to any desired statement. However, the goto statement is not necessary, and in practice it almost always easy to write code without it. Except in this section we will not use goto anywhere else in this book. Nevertheless, there are few situations, where goto will find a place. The most common is the place where we cannot get out of a loop by using a break of return. Consider the problem of determining whether two arrays a and b have an element in common? Let us present the code for this problem in program listing 4.10.

```
/*  Program Listing 4.10 : GO_TO.c
    Program to illustrate the use of goto statement */

#include <stdio.h>

void main(void)
{
    int a[] = {5,6,8,12,45,65}, b[] = {4,7,9,13,50, 77, 66, 1},
                                                  i, j, found = 0;
    for(i = 0;i < 6;i++)
    {
        for(j = 0;j < 8;j++)
        {
            if(a[i] == b[j])
            {
                found = 1;
```

```
13.                          goto end;
14.                     }
15.                }
16.           }
17.      end:
18.           if(found)
19.                printf("Common Element is found at %d, %d", i, j);
20.           else
21.                printf("No Common Element is found");
22.      }
```

```
No Common Element is found
```

Program Listing 4.10 Program to Illustrate the use of goto statement

For convenience, At Line 5, we have initialised arrays a and b instead of inputting the arrays by the user. The student can always add code to interactively input the two arrays a and b. The outer for loop at line 6, takes each element of a and compares with all elements of b in the inner for loop. At line 10, If the element is found, we would like to comeout of both the loops to print the result. At line 13,

```
goto end;
```

we have used a goto statement to come out of both the loops to print the result. Instead of goto if a break is used we will be comming out of only the inner loop and not both the loops. However, we can add an if statement in the outer loop and eliminate the goto. This is illustrated in the program listing 3.11. Observe that you need two break statements to come out.

```
/*   Program Listing 4.11 : GO_BRK.c
Program eliminating goto statement from program listing 4.10*/

#include <stdio.h>

void main(void)
{
     int a[] = {5,6,8,12,45,65}, b[] = {4,7,9,13,50, 77, 65, 1},
                                                   i, j, found = 0;
     for(i = 0;i < 6;i++)
     {
          for(j = 0;j < 8;j++)
          {
               if(a[i] == b[j])
               {
```

```
                        found = 1;
                        break;
                    }
                }
                if(found) break;
            }
            if(found)
                printf("Common Element is found at %d, %d", i, j);
            else
                printf("No Common Element is found");
        }
```

```
No Common Element is found
```

Program Listing 4.11 Program eliminating goto from program listing 4.10

4.11 COMMAND LINE PARAMETERS

It is fairly common to pass arguments to a program when the program is invoked from the command line. For instance, if you are using a program that copies one file into another, we use the command "copy in_file out_file". In this case you are passing the names of two files in_file and out_file to the program "copy" as arguments on the command line.

Such arguments are known as ***Command Line Arguments.*** Information about command line arguments is passed by the operating system to the entry function of the invoked program. In the case of C this is the function main().

To make use of the command line arguments which are passed to a program the function main() needs to be told two things. First, how many arguments there are and second where to find them. This is achieved by two special variables. These are the first and second parameters of the function main(). They can be called anything you like, but by tradition they are usually called as **argc** and **argv**. In C these are usually declared as:

```
main(int argc, char *argv[])
```

What we have in the declaration char *argv[] is a declaration of a pointer, which itself points to an array which is made up of pointers each of which points to a string. argc gives the count of arguments passed to the shell (including the command itself as the 0th parameter). The simplest illustration is the program ECHOES, which echoes its command line arguments on a single line separated by blanks spaces. In Program Listing 4.12, the ECHOES program is presented.

```
     /* Program Listing 4.11 :  ECHOES.c
     Echoes the Command Line Arguments on a Single Line */
1.   main(int argc, char *argv[])
2.   {
3.        int i;
4.        printf("No. of Arguments ...%d\n", argc);
5.        for(i = 1;i < argc;i++)
6.             printf("%s ", argv[i]);
7.        printf("\n");
8.   }
```

```
C:\>ECHOES Welcome to C
No. of Arguments ...4
Welcome to C
```

Program Listing 4.12 Program to illustrate command line arguments

At Line 1,

```
main(int argc, char *argv[])
```

main() is declared with 2 arguments argc and argv. When, on the command line, we invoke this program, by typing ECHOES **Welcome to** C prints the output as **Welcome to** C. By convention argv[0] is the name by which the program was invoked, so argc is atleast 1. If argc is 1 there are no command line arguments after the program name. In the above example, argc is 4 and argv[0], argv[1], argv[2], and argv[3] are the strings "ECHOES", "Welcome", "to" and "C" respectively. At Line 4, the number of arguments are printed. At line 5, the for loop, runs through i = 1 to argc – 1, which prints "Welcome to C".

MORE EXAMPLES

1. Write a program to find the Inverse of a Matrix using Pointers

```
#include <stdio.h>
#include <malloc.h>
#include <math.h>
void write_matrix(float *matrix, int order)
{
     int row, column;
```

```
        for(row = 0;row < order;++row)
        {
             for(column = 0;column < order;++column, ++matrix)
                  printf("%8.2f", *matrix);
             printf("\n");
        }
}
void exchange_elements(float *e1, float *e2)
{
        float temp;
        temp = *e1;
        *e1 = *e2;
        *e2 = temp;
}
void exchange_rows(float *matrix, float *inverse, int row1, int row2,
int order)
{
        int column;
        for(column = 0;column < order;++column)
        {
        exchange_elements(matrix + row1 + column, matrix + row2 + column);
    exchange_elements(inverse + row1 + column, inverse + row2 + column);
        }
}
int invert(float *matrix, float *inverse, int order)
{
        int row, column, current, row_offset, last_value, singular = 0;
        float ratio;
        last_value = order * order;
        for(row = 0, row_offset = 0;(row < order) &&
                                        !singular;++row,row_offset += order)
        {
             if(*(matrix + row_offset + row))
                  for(current = 0;current < last_value;current += order)
                       if(current == row_offset)
                       {
                            ratio = *(matrix + row_offset + row);
```

```
                        for(column = 0;column < order;++column)
                        {
                              *(matrix + row_offset + row) /= ratio;
                              *(inverse + row_offset + row) /= ratio;
                        }
                  }
                  else
                  {
   ratio = (*(matrix + current + row))/(*(matrix +  row_offset + row));
                              for(column = 0;column < order;++column)
                              {
                  *(matrix + current + column) -= ratio * *(matrix
                                                + row_offset + column);
                  *(inverse + current + column) -= ratio * *(inverse
                                                + row_offset + column);
                              }
                  }
                  else
                  {
                        singular = 1;
            for(current = row_offset + order;(current < last_value) &&
                                          singular;current += order)
                              if(*(matrix + current + row))
                              {
                                    singular = 0;
                              exchange_rows(matrix, inverse, current,
                                                row_offset, order);
                                    --row;
                                    row_offset -= order;
                              }
                  }
      }
      return !singular;
}
void main(void)
{
      char answer;
      int order, row, column, current;
      unsigned long int matrix_size;
      float *matrix, *inverse, temp;
```

```
do
{
     printf("\n\n                    MATRIX INVERSION");
     printf("\n                      ----------------\n");
     do
     {
          printf("\nEnter the Size of Matrix: ");
          scanf("%d", &order);
     }
     while(order <= 0);
     matrix_size = order * order * sizeof(float);
     matrix = (float *)malloc(matrix_size);
     inverse = (float *)malloc(matrix_size);
     if((matrix == NULL) || (inverse == NULL))
     printf("\nMemory Allocation Failure.  Program Aborted.\n");
     else
     {
          for(row = 0, current = 0;row < order;++row)
          {
               for(column = 0;column < order;++column, ++current)
               {
     printf("Enter the Elements into Matrix - A[%d][%d]: ", row,
                                                              column);
                    scanf("%f", &temp);
                    *(matrix + current) = temp;
                    *(inverse + current) = 0.0;
               }
               *(inverse + row * order + row) = 1.0;
          }
          printf("\nThe given Matrix is: \n");
          write_matrix(matrix, order);
          if(invert(matrix, inverse, order))
          {
               printf("\nThe Matrix after Inversion is: \n");
               write_matrix(inverse, order);
          }
          else
printf("\nThe given matrix is singular and hence it's inverse does
                                                        not exist.\n");
```

```
            printf("\nAgain? (y/n): ");
            do
                answer = getchar();
            while((answer != 'y') && (answer != 'Y') &&
                                    (answer != 'n') && (answer != 'N'));
        }
        free(matrix);
        free(inverse);
    }
    while((answer == 'y') || (answer == 'Y'));
}
```

OUTPUT:

```
        MATRIX INVERSION
        ----------------------------
        Enter the Size of Matrix: 3
        Enter the Elements into Matrix - A[0][0]: 2
        Enter the Elements into Matrix - A[0][1]: 3
        Enter the Elements into Matrix - A[0][2]: 1
        Enter the Elements into Matrix - A[1][0]: 4
        Enter the Elements into Matrix - A[1][1]: 6
        Enter the Elements into Matrix - A[1][2]: 5
        Enter the Elements into Matrix - A[2][0]: 1
        Enter the Elements into Matrix - A[2][1]: 2.25
        Enter the Elements into Matrix - A[2][2]: 0.75
        The given Matrix is:
            2.00      3.00      1.00
            4.00      6.00      5.00
            1.00      2.25      0.75
        The Matrix after Inversion is:
            1.50      0.00     -2.00
            -0.44     -0.11     1.33
            -0.67      0.33     0.00
        Again? (y/n): n
```

SELF-REVIEW EXERCISES

1. A Pointer is a variable that stores the .... of a variable.
2. When a pointer variable is declared, the .... must precede the variable name.
3. Adding & Subtracting an integer from pointer variable is known as ....
4. Any pointer to an object may be converted to type .... without loss of information.
5. A pointer to void cannot be ....
6. When using char[] and char *a as formal parameters while defining a function, these are treated as ....
7. .... will be the equivalent expression for referring the element a[i][j][k][l].
8. The declaration int (*ptr)[10] menas ....
9. A string can be processed only on a .... by .... basis.
10. To make a function return a pointer it has to be .... defined in the .... function.
11. .... is provided by C language to branch from a statement to any desired statement.
12. .... & .... are two special variables used as parameters in the function main().

EXERCISES

1. Write a function using pointers ***power(base, exponent)*** that when invoked returns $base^{exponent}$. For example, ***power(3, 4) = 3 * 3 * 3 * 3***. Assume that ***exponent*** is an integer greater than or equal to 1.
2. Write a program to obtain the determinant value of a 5 × 5 matrix using pointers
3. Write a program to reverse the strings stored in an array of pointers.
4. Write a program to count the number of inputted characters in an array of pointers to strings.
5. Write a program that will print out all the rotations of a string typed into it. For example, rotations of the word "space" are:

   space paces acesp cespa espac

5

Structures & Unions

5.1 STRUCTURES

A **structure** is a collection of one or more variables possibly of different types, grouped together under a single name for convenient handling. A more common word used for structures is **record**. In languages like Pascal, this terminology is more common. A structure (record) allows organizing, a group of related variables to be treated as one unit instead of separate entities. One traditional example of a structure is a payroll record of an employee, which is described with a set of attributes such as name, address, empno, salary, etc. Another example is a complex number, which basically contains real and imaginary parts and can be represented in several forms. We shall look into the program involving complex numbers after we discuss how to define(declare) and use a structure.

We have already seen an array which stores a set of homogeneous (same type) values. However, for several applications, we need to group different types (heterogeneous data) of data together for convenience. The structure is a very useful derived data type defined in C as many systems programs use several structures for handling different types of variables together.

In C, structures may be copied, assigned to, pass to functions and returned by functions. Like arrays structures can also be initialized.

5.2 DECLARATIONS & INITIALIZATION

Like arrays, structures can be initialized specifying the values. The following example illustrates the initialization of structures.

```
#include <stdio.h>
struct student {
      char name[20], course[5];
      int rno;
};
void main(void)
{
   struct student student1 = {"Rama Rao", "MCA", 4};
   struct student student2 = {"Ranga Rao", "BCA", 7};
   struct student student3;
   printf("Enter Student Roll Number: ");
   scanf("%d", &student3.rno);
   printf("Enter Student Name: ");
   scanf("%s", student3.name);
   printf("Enter Student Course: ");
   scanf("%s", student3.course);
   printf("  Rno\t  Name\t\t      Course\n");
   printf("%4d\t%s\t\t%s\n", student1.rno, student1.name,
                                                  student1.course);
   printf("%4d\t%s\t\t%s\n", student2.rno, student2.name,
                                                  student2.course);
   printf("%4d\t%s\t\t%s\n", student3.rno, student3.name,
                                                  student3.course);
}
```

```
Enter Student Roll Number: 1
Enter Student Name: Raja Rao
Enter Student Course: B.Tech
4  Rama Rao   MCA
7  Ranga Rao  BCA
1  Raja Rao     B.Tech
```

Lines 2 to 5,

```
2.   struct student {
3.        char name[20], course[5];
4.        int rno;
5.   };
```

declares a structure student outside the function main. We have not used the tag and declared any variables at this stage. We are taking the option of declaring the inside the function main.

Lines 8 and 9,

```
8.      struct student student1 = {"Rama Rao", "MCA", 4};
9.      struct student student2 = {"Ranga Rao", "BCA", 7};
```

we have declared two structure variables student1 and student2 of the type student and initialized them with the values (similar to arrays). For a change, we have accepted the values of the third structure student3 from the input using scanf() statement. Notice that & is needed only for the first member of the structure (rno) which is declared as int.

Structure declaration is somewhat more complicated than array declaration, since a structure is to be defined in terms of its individual members. In general, the composition of a structure may be defined as shown in Fig. 5.1

```
struct <tag> {
     data item1;
     data item2;
     . . . . . . . . . .
     . . . . . . . . . .
     data item n;
} [ Optional List Of Variables ];
```

Fig. 5.1 General declaration syntax of a ***structure***

In this declaration, **struct** is the required keyword, *<tag>* is a name that identifies structures of this type (i.e., structures having this composition), and *<data item1>*, *<data item2>*, …, *<data item n>* are individual member declarations. The variables of the structure-type can follow optionally the declaration. For example, consider, a typical structure given below:

```
struct emp_rec {
     char name[20];
     int empno;
     float sal;
} emp1, emp2, emp3;
```

The variables ***emp1***, ***emp2*** and ***emp3*** are all declared as of type ***emp*** structure. The individual members of a structure can be ordinary variables, pointers, arrays, or even other structures. The member names within a particular structure must be distinct from one another, though a member name can be the same as the name of variable defined outside the structure. A storage class, however, cannot be assigned to an individual member (i.e., we can't use keywords like static, extern, etc.) and individual members cannot be initialized within a structure.

The variables of a structure need not be declared along with the declaration of the structure. Once the composition of the structure has been defined, individual structure-type variables can be declared later on as follows:

```
<storage-class>struct<tag><variable1>, <variable2>, …, <variable n>;
```

where *<storage-class>* is an optional storage class specifier, struct is a required keyword, *<tag>* is the name that appeared in the structure type declaration, and *<variables 1>* to *<variable n>* are structure variables of type *<tag>*. A typical structure declaration and later declaring variables is shown below:

```
struct emp_rec {
      char name[20];
      int empno;
      float sal;
};
struct emp_rec emp1, emp2, emp3;
```

The members of a structure are usually processed individually, as separate entities. Therefore, we must be able to access the individual structure members. A structure member can be accessed by using the dot (.) operator as *<variable.member>* where variable refers to the name of a *structure-type variable*, and *<member>* refers to the name of a member within the structure. The period (dot) is an operator, which is a member of the highest precedence, and Left to Right associativity (refer Table 1.4). Note that there is no formal distinction between a structure definition and a structure declaration; the terms are used interchangeably.

5.3 PASSING OF STRUCTURES AS ARGUMENTS

As we have stated already, structures can be passed as arguments to functions. To illustrate this, let us now present a program that allows addition, subtraction, multiplication and division of complex numbers presented in program listing 5.1

```
/* Program Listing 5.1 :  COMPLEX.c
Evaluate the complex number      */
#include <stdio.h>
#include <math.h>
#include <process.h>
#include <conio.h>

   struct complex {
      float real, image;
   };

void print_complex(struct complex);
struct complex add_complex(struct complex, struct complex);
struct complex sub_complex(struct complex, struct complex);
struct complex mul_complex(struct complex, struct complex);
struct complex div_complex(struct complex, struct complex);

void main(void)
{
      struct complex a = {2.0, -3.0};
      struct complex b = {-4.0, -7.0};
      struct complex c;
      int choice;

      print_complex(a);
      print_complex(b);
      do
      {
            printf("\n +  for Addition”);
            printf("\n -  for Subtraction”);
            printf("\n *  for Multiplication”);
            printf("\n /  for Division”);
            printf("\nAny other key to Exit ...”);
            choice = getche();
            switch(choice)
            {
               case ‘+’:
                     c = add_complex(a, b);
                     break;
```

```
                case '-':
                    c = sub_complex(a, b);
                    break;
                case '*':
                    c = mul_complex(a, b);
                    break;
                case '/':
                    c = div_complex(a, b);
                    break;
                default:
                    exit(0);
            }
            print_complex(c);
        } while(1);

}

void print_complex(struct complex x)
{
        char sign = '+';
        if(x.image < 0)
        {
            sign = '-';
            x.image = abs(x.image);
        }
        printf("\n%0.2f %c j%0.2f", x.real, sign, x.image);
}

struct complex add_complex(struct complex x, struct complex y)
{
        struct complex temp;
        temp.real = x.real + y.real;
        temp.image = x.image + y.image;
        return temp;
}

```

```
struct complex sub_complex(struct complex x, struct complex y)
{
      struct complex temp;
      temp.real = x.real - y.real;
      temp.image = x.image - y.image;
      return temp;
}

struct complex mul_complex(struct complex x, struct complex y)
{
      struct complex temp;
      temp.real = x.real * y.real - (x.image * y.image) ;
      temp.image = x.real * y.image + (x.image * y.real);
      return temp;
}

struct complex div_complex(struct complex x, struct complex y)
{
      struct complex temp, conj;
      int i;

      conj.real = y.real;
      conj.image = -(y.image);

      temp = mul_complex(x, conj);

      i = conj.real * conj.real + conj.image * conj.image;

      temp.real /= i;
      temp.image /= i;

      return temp;
}
```

```
2.0 -j3.0
-4.0 - j7.00
+  for Addition
```

```
- for Subtraction
* for Multiplication
/ for Division
Any other key to Exit ...+
-2.00 - j10.00
+ for Addition
- for Subtraction
* for Multiplication
/ for Division
Any other key to Exit ...-
6.00 + j4.00
```

Program Listing 5.1 Program to add, subtract, multiply, divide two complex numbers

At Line 6,

```
struct complex {
     float real, image;
};
```

the structure complex is declared. This structure has two members and both of them are floats. ***real*** part and the ***image*** represent the imaginary part of the complex number. Note that the declaration is done outside the main so as to enable all functions to access the definition of the structure. No variables are declared along with the definition. This is the most convenient practice usually adopted. At Lines 18 to 20,

```
struct complex a = {2.0, -3.0};
struct complex b = {-4.0, -7.0};
struct complex c;
```

in the main we have declared three variables and initialized two of them. However, it is possible to accept, these two complex numbers interactively also using **scanf()**, which we shall present in the next program. From Lines 55 to 64,

```
void print_complex(struct complex x)
{
     char sign = '+';
     if(x.image < 0)
     {
          sign = '-';
          x.image = abs(x.image);
     }
     printf("\n%0.2f %c j%0.2f", x.real, sign, x.image);
}
```

the function print_complex takes a complex number and prints the value in the form **x + jy**. At lines 23 and 24,

```
print_complex(a);
print_complex(b);
```

the call to *print_complex()* function passes the structures a and b by value to the called function. The function *print_complex()* handles the structures passed by creating local variables. It is also possible to pass the structures using pointers (address of the structure) which will be presented in the next section. At Line 63, the **printf()** function prints the complex number in the required format. At Line 58,

```
if(x.image < 0)
{
      sign = '-';
      x.image = abs(x.image);
}
```

the proper sign is manipulated for the imaginary part. If the imaginary part is negative, we make the sign as "–" and value positive by calling the library function abs which is defined in **math.h**. Note that this manipulation is only for the purpose of printing only before j. The do / while loop from lines 25 to 51,

```
do
{
      printf("\n +  for Addition");
      printf("\n -  for Subtraction");
      printf("\n *  for Multiplication");
      printf("\n /  for Division");
      printf("\nAny other key to Exit ...");
      choice = getche();
      switch(choice)
      {
            case '+':
                  c = add_complex(a, b);
                  break;
            case '-':
                  c = sub_complex(a, b);
                  break;
            case '*':
                  c = mul_complex(a, b);
                  break;
```

```
                case '/':
                    c = div_complex(a, b);
                    break;
                default:
                    exit(0);
            }
            print_complex(c);
        } while(1);

}
```

is used to display several options to the user such as +, -, *, / to choose one among them. The **switch / case** statement is used to call the appropriate function, depending on the value inputted to choice. For example, if the user enters +, the two complex numbers are added and the result is displayed. At Line 66,

```
struct complex add_complex(struct complex x, struct complex y)
{
    struct complex temp;
    temp.real = x.real + y.real;
    temp.image = x.image + y.image;
    return temp;
}
```

the function add_complex, which receives two complex numbers as structures passed by value and creates local copies x and y. The real and imaginary parts of x and y are added separately and respectively assigned to the real and imaginary parts of a temporary complex structure *temp* declared locally. At Line 71, temp is returned by the function. For this reason we chose the return type of add_complex as struct complex. The other functions sub_complex, mul_complex and div_complex are implemented in the same way.

Notice that the **do / while** loop is a continuous loop and the program can exit only if the user takes a choice other than +, -, *, /. At Line 32, the getche() library function, accepts the keystroke from the user and returns the corresponding the ASCII code as an integer which gets assigned to choice. The following is a brief demonstration of how two complex numbers (a + jb) and (x + jy) are multiplied and divided.

Multiplication of two complex numbers,

$$\begin{aligned}(a + jb)(x + jy) &= ax + j(xb) + j(ya) + j^2(by)\\ &= (ax - by) + j(xb + ya).\end{aligned}$$

Division of two complex numbers,

$$(a + jb)/(x + jy) = ((a + jb)(x - jy)) \ / \ (x + jy)(x - jy)$$
$$= (ax + by + j(xb - ya)) \ / \ (x^2 + y^2)$$
$$= (ax + by) \ / \ (x^2 + y^2) + j(xb - ya) \ / \ (x^2 + y^2)$$

However, the student is advised to analyze how the above complex numbers multiplication and division is made.

5.4 SELF REFERENTIAL STRUCTURES

In C, we have the structures, which can be made self-referential. A self-referential structure is one that includes within its structure at least one member which is a pointer to the same structure type.

With self-referential structures, we can create very useful data structures such as linked lists, trees, etc. The creation and usage of self-referential structures is elaborately discussed in chapters on linked lists, trees and graphs.

However, in the next section we will show using typedef how a node of a binary tree can be defined. Each node of a binary tree has two children left and right which are again binary trees. If we choose to represent a binary tree with a structure, then the structure must contain two pointers to the left sub-tree and the right sub-tree. Therefore, the structure becomes a self-referential structure.

5.5 typedef REVITISED

The use of typedef for creating user defined data types was already introduced in Chapter 1. There typedef was only illustrated for basic data types. We now extend the usage of typedef to other data types such as pointers and structures. The declaration

```
typedef char * string
```

makes string as a data type which is same as character pointer (char *). We can now use declaration and casts such as,

```
string p;     /* p is a character pointer */
```

int strcmp(string, string); /* the prototype for strcmp needs two character pointer parameters)

As an example of more useful typedef declaration, we show the declaration of a self referential structure which is discussed in the previous section.

```
typedef struct tnode *Treeptr;
typedef struct tnode {
                    char *word;
                    int count;
                    Treeptr left;
                    Treeptr right;
                 } Treenode;
```

This creates two new type keywords called Treenode (a structure) and Treeptr (a pointer to structure).

There are two main reasons for using typedefs. The first is to create an easy portability. If typedefs are used for data types that may be machine-dependent, only the typedefs need change when the program is moved on to a different machine.

The second purpose of typedefs is to provide better documentation for a program – a type called Treeptr may be easier to understand than one declared only as a pointer to a complicated structure.

5.6 POINTERS TO STRUCTURES

If a large structure is to be passed to a function, it is generally more efficient to pass a pointer than to copy the whole structure into a local variable in the function. Pointers to structures are just like the pointers to any other variable. For example, in the program listing of fig 5.2 in the main we can declare struct complex *p where p is a pointer to a structure of type struct complex. Now an assignment p = &a makes p point to structure a. The real part of the structure a can now be referenced as (*p).real and the imaginary part can be referenced as (*p).image. The parenthesis are necessary around p because the precedence of the structure member operator dot(.) is higher than *. Pointers to structures are so frequently used that an alternative notation is provided without parentheses as a short hand.

If p is a pointer to a structure *p->member-of-structure* refers to the particular member. Therefore the real part of a could now be referenced as p->real and the imaginary part as p->image instead of (*p).x and (*p).y. Hereafter we shall adopt only this notation rather than the notation with the de-referencing operator *, which needs a parentheses always.

Let us present the program for complex numbers of Program Listing 5.1 , now using pointers to structures in Program Listing 5.2. We shall only implement the add_complex and print_complex and leaving implementation of sub_complex, mul_complex, div_complex as an exercise to the student.

```
/* Program Listing 5.2 :  COMPPTR.c
Evaluate the complex number using pointers */
#include <stdio.h>
#include <math.h>
struct complex {
     float real, image;
};

void print_complex(struct complex *);
struct complex add_complex(struct complex *, struct complex *);

void main(void)
{
     struct complex a, b, c;
     int sign;

     printf(“Enter the real part of First complex numbers ...”);
     scanf(“%f”, &a.real);
printf(“Enter the imaginary part of First complex numbers ...”);
     scanf(“%f”, &a.image);
     printf(“Enter the real part of First complex numbers ...”);
     scanf(“%f”, &b.real);
printf(“Enter the imaginary part of First complex numbers ...”);
     scanf(“%f”, &b.image);

     print_complex(&a);
     print_complex(&b);

     c = add_complex(&a, &b);
     print_complex(&c);
}

void print_complex(struct complex *x)
{
     char sign = ‘+’;
     float t;
     t = x->image;
```

```
36.         if(t < 0)
37.         {
38.              sign = '-';
39.              t = abs(t);
40.         }
41.         printf("\n%0.2f %c j%0.2f", x->real, sign, t);
42.    }
43.
44.    struct complex add_complex(struct complex *x, struct complex *y)
45.    {
46.         struct complex temp;
47.         temp.real = x->real + y->real;
48.         temp.image = x->image + y->image;
49.         return temp;
50.    }
```

```
Enter the real part of First complex numbers ...10
Enter the imaginary part of First complex numbers ...15
Enter the real part of First complex numbers ...10
Enter the imaginary part of First complex numbers ...15
10.00 + j15.00
10.00 + j15.00
20.00 + j30.00
```

Program Listing 5.2 Add two complex numbers using Pointers & Structures

The functions print_complex and add_complex using pointers to structures lines 15 to 22,

```
     printf("Enter the real part of First complex numbers ...");
     scanf("%f", &a.real);
printf("Enter the imaginary part of First complex numbers ...");
     scanf("%f", &a.image);
     printf("Enter the real part of First complex numbers ...");
     scanf("%f", &b.real);
printf("Enter the imaginary part of First complex numbers ...");
     scanf("%f", &b.image);
```

allow the user to accept the complex numbers interactively.

The prototype declarations of print_complex and add_complex are line 7 and 8

```
void print_complex(struct complex *);
struct complex add_complex(struct complex *, struct complex *);
```

and are changed to pointer notation. However, the return type of add_complex is still retained as a structure. The call to add_complex at line 27,

```
c = add_complex(&a, &b);
```

passes the address of a and b to the function. These addresses are assigned to the formal pointer parameters x and y of add_complex() function. In add_complex() function, x->real or (*x).real will have the same value of a.real. At lines 47 & 48,

```
temp.real = x->real + y->real;
temp.image = x->image + y->image;
```

the addition is performed among the real and imaginary parts separately and assigned to temp.real and temp.image respectively. As usual temp is returned to give the complex numbers corresponding to the addition of two complex numbers and is assigned to c in the main at line 27.

The call print_complex function, now at line 28,

```
print_complex(&c);
```

rightly sends the address of c rather than c itself; as is done to print a and b at lines 24 & 25. Note that print_complex() function now uses a temporary variable t to manpulate sign. This is essential because we are not creating local copy of the complex number in print_complex() function rather, we are directly handling the complex number of the calling function through a pointer.

5.7 ARRAY OF STRUCTURES

C provides the facility to declare arrays of structures. These structures can also be initialized just like any other data type. In this way, C is consistent in representing data types. That is how we can consistently define, structures within a structure or an array of structures and so on. This property is referred as ***orthogonality*** of a language. Let us now present a program that counts VOWELS, CONSONENTS, DIGITS and SPECIAL SYMBOLS from a given line of text. We shall use an array of structures to implement this. The program is presented in program listing 5.3.

```
/* Program Listing 5.3 :  VOWEL.c
Counts Number of Vowels, Consonents, Digits etc.,  */
#include <stdio.h>
#include <ctype.h>
#include <conio.h>

```

```
struct oval_counter  {
            char *name;
            int count;
};

void increment(char,struct oval_counter []);
void print_counters(struct oval_counter []);

void main(void)
{
      struct oval_counter x[]=   {
                  {"VOWELS", 0},
                  {"DIGITS", 0},
                  {"COSONENTS", 0},
                  {"SPECIAL SYMBOLS", 0}
      };
      char c;

      printf("Enter the TEXT: ");
      while((c=getche()) != '\r')
            increment(c,x);
      print_counters(x);
}

void print_counters(struct oval_counter x[])
{
      int i;
      for(i=0;i<4;i++)
            printf("\n%-15s  %3d", x[i].name,x[i].count);
}

void increment(char c,struct oval_counter x[])
{
      if(isalpha(c))
            switch(c){
                  case 'a':  /* Vowels */
                  case 'e':
                  case 'i':
```

```
43.                 case 'o':
44.                 case 'u':
45.                 case 'A':
46.                 case 'E':
47.                 case 'I':
48.                 case 'O':
49.                 case 'U':
50.                      x[0].count ++; break;
51.                 default:
52.                      x[2].count ++; /* Consonents */
53.            }
54.        else if(isdigit(c))        /* Digits */
55.            x[1].count ++;
56.        else if(!isspace(c)) /* Spaces */
57.            x[3].count++;
58.  }
```

```
Enter the TEXT: India will be the Best Country by 2010.
VOWELS                 9
CONSONENTS             18
DIGITS                 4
SPECIAL SYMBOLS        1
```

Program Listing 5.3 *Program to count Vowels, Digits, Consonents, Special Symbols*

At lines 5 to 8,

```
struct oval_counter  {
        char *name;
        int count;
      };
```

the structure oval_counter is declared outside the main with two members. The first one is the pointer to a character and the second is an integer. At Lines 15 to 20,

```
struct oval_counter x[] =   {
            {"VOWELS", 0},
            {"DIGITS", 0},
            {"COSONENTS", 0},
            {"SPECIAL SYMBOLS", 0}
};
```

in the main the array of structure oval_counter is declared and initialized with appropriate pairs of names and the counter value 0.

At Line 24 & 25,

```
        while((c=getche()) != '\r')
            increment(c,x);
```

the while loop accepts the text character by character till the carriage return ('\r') is encountered. The character returned by getche() is assigned to c and at the same time tested if it is a carriage return or not. Further, while inputting the text, we should avoid backspaces as getche() inputs every character as you enter. Note that getche() may not be available under all compilers. At line 25, inside the while loop, the function increment is called with two parameters. The first one is the character c and the second one is the array of structures x. At Line 36 to 58,

```
    void increment(char c,struct oval_counter x[])
    {
        if(isalpha(c))
            switch(c){
                case 'a':  /* Vowels */
                case 'e':
                case 'i':
                case 'o':
                case 'u':
                case 'A':
                case 'E':
                case 'I':
                case 'O':
                case 'U':
                    x[0].count ++; break;
                default:
                    x[2].count ++; /* Consonents */
            }
        else if(isdigit(c))        /* Digits */
            x[1].count ++;
        else if(!isspace(c)) /* Spaces */
            x[3].count++;
    }
```

the function increment() is present, which accepts c and x as parameters. At Line 39, the **switch** statement is executed if c is an alphabet. Notice that the upper and lower case vowels are taken care of, in the switch statement. The vowel counter is incremented if c is an vowel otherwise the consonants counter is incremented. If it is not an alphabet then it is tested whether it is a digit and the digits counter is incremented. At Line 56, the last else tests for other symbols (ignoring spaces) and increments special symbols counter.

All the character testing functions like **isalpha()**, **isdigit()**, **isspace()**, used in this program are defined in **ctype.h** which is included in the program at line 2.

```
#include <ctype.h>
```

At Line 26,

```
print_counters(x);
```

the print_counters function is called with x as the parameter. At Line 29,

```
void print_counters(struct oval_counter x[])
{
      int i;
      for(i=0;i<4;i++)
            printf("\n%-15s   %3d", x[i].name,x[i].count);
}
```

the function print_counters runs through the array of structures and the prints the counter name and the counter value. Notice the format %-15s which allows you to print a string in 15 characters left justified. Left justification means if the string is less than the number of characters specified in the format, to the right of the string, spaces are added to make the string match the length specified. If the minus sign is eliminated the string is printed right justified. That is if its length is less than the number of characters specified spaces are include to the left of the string.

5.8 UNIONS

A union is a variable that may hold (at different times) objects of different types and sizes, with the compiler keeping track of size and alignment requirements. Unions provide a way to manipulate different kinds of data in a single area of storage, without embedding any machine-dependent information in the program.

As an example, suppose we want to represent a constant which may be an int, a float, or a character pointer. The value of a particular constant must be stored in a variable of the proper type, yet it is most convenient if the value occupies the same amount of storage and is stored in the same place regardless of its type. This is the purpose of a union – a single variable that can legitimately hold any one of several types. The syntax of an union is similar to the syntax of structures. Thus, the union declaration for the above example is as follows

```
union diff_types {
      int i;
      float f;
      char *s;
} x;
```

The variable x will be large enough to hold the largest of the three types; the specific size is implementation-dependent. Any one of these types may be assigned to x and then used in expressions, so long, as the usage is consistent. The type retrieved must be the type most recently stored. It is the programmer's responsibility to keep track of which type is currently stored in a union; the results are implementation-dependent if something is stored as one type and extracted as another.

Syntactically, members of a union are accessed as

```
<union-name>.<member>
```

or

```
<union-pointer>-><member>
```

just similar to structures. The unions may occur within a structure, arrays and vice versa. The notation for accessing a union in a structure or vice versa is identical to the nested structures. For example, let us consider the following definition of a structure in continuation of earlier union defined.

```
struct xyz {
      int a
      int b
      int c;
      char *name;
      union diff_types y;
} e[10];
```

The reference e[j].y.f is perfectly legal and refers to the floating value, that the union loaded into j^{th} location of the array of structures. For a reference like this the programmer should ensure to fill this location with a floating point value.

Let us now present a program in Program Listing 5.4, which uses union. We have printed the bit pattern of a short int using bitwise operators in the earlier program in program listing 1.11. It is not possible to apply a similar procedure to print a bit pattern of a floating point number. The reason for this is that the bitwise operators cannot be applied to a floating point number. To get over this problem we will declare a union.

```
/* Program Listing 5.4 :  UNION.c
   Illustrates the Internal Representation of Floating Point Number   */
#include <stdio.h>
#define MASK 0X80000000

```

```
void main(void)
{
     /* program to print the internal representation of a float */
     union long_float {
        long int l;
        float f;
     } x;
     long int y;
     int i;
     printf("Size of long int = %d bytes\n",sizeof(long int));
     printf("Size of float= %d bytes\n",sizeof(float));
     printf("Size of Union x= %d bytes\n",sizeof(x));
     printf("Enter a floating point number:");
     scanf("%f",&x.f);
     printf("The IEEE floating point 32 bit pattern representing
            %6.2f is\n",x.f);

     for(i = 0;i < 32;i++)
     {
          y = x.l;
          y <<= i;    /* left shift i times */
          y &= MASK; /* mask all bits except the first */
          if(y)
               printf("1");
          else
               printf("0");
     }
}
```

```
Size of long int= 4 bytes
Size of float    = 4 bytes
Size of Union x = 4 bytes
Enter a floating point number: 3.5
The IEEE floating point 32 bit pattern representing 3.50 is
01000000011000000000000000000000
```

***Program Listing 5.4** Program to Internal Representation of Floating Point Numbers*

At Line 7 to 10,

```
union long_float {
      long int l;
      float f;
} x;
```

a union long_float is declared with two variables l and f. The first one is a long int and the other is a float. Under most of the Operating Systems, the length of long and float is 4 bytes (32 bits). Printing the sizes of the long and float using sizeof function can ensure this. At Line 13 to 15,

```
printf("Size of long int = %d bytes\n",sizeof(long int));
printf("Size of float= %d bytes\n",sizeof(float));
printf("Size of Union x= %d bytes\n",sizeof(x));
```

we have printed various sizes. Note that the size of the union is 4 bytes allowing only one variable (either a long int or float) to be stored. The idea is to store a float in this union x and handle it as a long int to get the bit pattern by applying the bitwise operators, because the long int and the float occupy the same memory locations. At Line 17,

```
scanf("%f",&x.f);
```

we accept a floating point number using scanf() into x.f. At Line 20,

```
for(i = 0;i < 32;i++)
```

the for loop runs for 32 times as the length of the long int or float is 4 bytes or 32 bits. As usual y is restored always at the beginning of the for loop with the value of x.l (in other words x.f). The logic is just similar to the previous program of Program Listing 5.5, in getting bit by bit from the memory representation and printing it. Observe the result of this program, where the bit pattern is printed in **IEEE 32-bit format which is used by most of the personal computers. The student is advised to refer Appendix B for complete information of floating point number representation and IEEE formats.

5.9 BIT FIELDS

In many hardware applications, it is necessary to pack several states of information into a single machine word. For example, the status of a printer could be read as a single word into the program and each bit in this status word could mean some specific state of the printer like paper empty, power off, hardware error, etc. For each of this bits are referred as flags.

The usual way to handle the status word is to define a set of "MASKS" corresponding to relevant bit positions as in,

```
#define PAPEREMTY 01
#define POWEROFF 02
#define HWERROR 04
```

Note that the numbers chosen is a power of 2, since when we bitwise AND with the status word, only the bit at k^{th} position (given by 2^k) is not masked and all other bits will be 0s. Thus, if we test the status word, we know whether the particular bit is set or not. For example,

```
if((flags & POWEROFF) == 1)
… … …
```

where flags is the status word.

Although, this is one way of handling the status word, C offers, the capability of defining and accessing fields within a word directly rather than using bitwise, logical operators. This is possible with the bit fields. A bit-field is a set of adjacent bits with in a single word. Note that the set can contain, 0, 1, 2, …, etc., bits. For example, the above #defines, could be replaced by the definition of three bit fields.

```
struct {
   unsigned int PAPEREMPTY : 1;
   unsigned int POWEROFF : 1;
   unsigned int HWERROR : 1;
} flags;
```

This defines a variable called flags that contains three 1-bit fields. The number following the colon represents the field width in bits. The fields are declared unsigned int to ensure that they are unsigned quantities.

Individual fields are referenced in the same way as other structure members: flags.PAPEREMPTY, flags.POWEROFF, flags.HWERROR, etc. Fields behave like small integers, and may participate in arithmetic expressions just like other integers. Thus the previous example may be written more naturally as,

```
if(flags.POWEROFF == 1)
… … …
```

The following program illustrates the use of bit fields.

```
#include <stdio.h>
struct {
   unsigned int PAPEREMPTY : 1;
   unsigned int POWEROFF : 1;
   unsigned int HWERROR : 1;
} flags;
```

```
void main(void)
{
   flags.PAPEREMPTY = 0;
   flags.POWEROFF = 0;
   flags.HWERROR = 1;
   if(flags.PAPEREMPTY == 1)
      printf("\nNo Paper in the Printer.");
   if(flags.POWEROFF == 1)
      printf("\nNo Power to the Printer.");
   if(flags.HWERROR == 1)
      printf("\nThere is a Hardware Error.");
}
```

In the program we have initialized various bit fields with 0s and 1s. However, in actual practice, the status word will be read into variable flags.

Almost everything about fields is implementation-dependent. Whether a field may overlap a word boundary is implementation-defined. Fields need not be named; unnamed fields (a colon and width only) are used for padding and note that you cannot reference the unnamed fields. The special width 0 may be used to force alignment at the next word boundary. For portability, fields may be declared only as signed or unsigned ints. Bit fields are not arrays and don't have addresses, so the & operator cannot be applied to them.

SELF-REVIEW EXERCISES

1. A .... is a collection of related variables under one name.
2. A .... is a collection of variables under one name in which the variables share the same storage.
3. Keyword .... introduces a structure declaration.
4. A structure member is accessed with the .... operator.
5. The .... and .... operators are used to shift the bits of a value to the left or to the right respectively.
6. The conversion specifiers .... , ... and .... are used to display unsigned integers in octal, decimal and hexadecimal form respectively.
7. The .... and .... streams are normally connected to the computer screen.

EXERCISES

1. Write statements that accomplish each of the following. Assume that the structure

```
struct person {
   char lastname[15], firstname[15], age[4];
};
```

has been defined and that the file is already open for writing.

   (a) *Initialize the file " **nameage.dat**" so that there are 100 records with **lastname** = " **unassigned** ", **firstname** = " " and **age** = " 0 ".*

   (b) *Input 10 last names, first names and ages and write them to the file.*

   (c) *Update a record; if there is no information in the record, tell the user " **No Information** ".*

   (d) *Delete a record that has information by reinitializing that particular record.*

2. Implement complex Numbers - Subtraction, Division and multiplication using pointers.

6

Console File I/O

6.1 INTRODUCTION

There are a number of facilities provided in C language for input and output interaction. Thus far, we have used only a few of them. In this chapter we will study more details about input and output operations including string handling and using files for input and output. The ANSI standard defines the number of library functions for accomplishing input and output. However, input and output facilities are not a part of C language and more dependent on the environment in which C programs are running and the runtime C library. Generally we can classify the I/O into two categories namely,

1. ***Formatted I/O*** *– which makes use of C runtime library.*
2. ***Low-Level I/O*** *– which uses the system calls to Operating System.*

We note here, that the input and output has to be performed in co-ordination with the operating system in which the C program is executed. For example, if we consider the library function scanf – it has to collect the input from the keyboard and evidently keyboard can only be accessed through the operating system and not directly by the C program (scanf()). This means, the library function scanf makes a call to operating system (System Call) which collects the keyboard output and gives it to the C program.

In the formatted or high-level I/O, all this process is hidden (more abstraction) and the C programmer feels as if the C program is directly performing the I/O. However, one can use directly the system calls to perform the I/O which is normally referred as Low-level I/O. One advantage with the Low-Level I/O is it provides the direct interaction with Operating System so as to explore the possibility of using more facilities within the Operating System thus providing faster I/O. But this needs more understanding of the Operating Systems. The obvious disadvantage is the portability. A program which uses low level I/O cannot be ported easily on to a different Operating System unless there is consistency in system calls among them.

In this chapter, we will discuss only the formatted I/O which is Operating System Independent and uses the standard C library, since, the low-level I/O can only be studied along with Operating System like UNIX.

6.2 STANDARD I/O & FILES

In C a file is basically a stream of bytes (more commonly referred as stream), which can be interpreted by a C program. When a C program is started, the Operating System is responsible for opening three files (streams). These files are the **standard input**, the **standard output** and the **standard error**. Normally the **standard input** is connected to the keyboard, the **standard output** and the standard error are connected to the screen. In several earlier examples, we have already handled standard input and standard output through several library functions such as **scanf()**, **getchar()**, **gets()**, **printf()** etc., simple and we are going to present the mechanism of file handling in next few sections.

The next step is to write a program that access files that are not already connected to the program. For example, copying a data file to another data file or appending data to a data file. Usually, the Operating System identifies files with a name (and possibly with an extension). And it is necessary for C programs to use these names, because the C programs have to negotiate with the Operating System to get connected to these files. Now the question is how to arrange the named files to be read or written into by a program. The rules are very simple. Before a file can be read or written, a file has to be opened by the library function **fopen()**.

6.3 BASIC FILE OPERATIONS

fopen() takes an external file name, does some housekeeping, negotiation with the operating system (the details of which are no concern for us), and returns a pointer to be used in subsequent reads or writes of the file. This pointer is called the **File pointer**. This points to a structure containing information about a file such as the location of the buffer, current character position in the buffer, whether the file is read or written and so on.

Once again the users do not need to know the details, because the definition of the file structure is obtained from **stdio.h**. A number of library functions need this file pointer to perform read/write operations. We shall present these functions a little later. The following declaration opens a file named **mydot.dat** in read mode.

```
FILE *fp;
fp = fopen("mydot.dat", "r");
```

The above code says that fp is a pointer to a FILE and fopen() returns a pointer to a FILE. The two arguments of fopen are char *filename and char *mode. The first argument of fopen() is a character string containing the name of the file. The second is the mode also a character string which indicates how one intends to use the file. The allowable modes are shown in Table 6.1.

Table 6.1 FILE MODES

Mode	Description
"r"	Open Text File for Reading
"w"	Create Text File for Writing; discard previous contents if any
"a"	Append; Open or Create Text File for Writing at End of File
"r+"	Open Text File for Update (i.e., Reading & Writing)
"w+"	Create Text File for Update; discard previous contents if any
"a+"	Append; Open or Create Text File for Update, Writing at End

Normally two types of files are handled by the C high-level libraries namely text files and binary files. The text files do not store certain characters like for example a '\0' and a new line character may be interpreted (depending on the Operating System) as a pair of characters new line followed by carriage return. A binary file does not do this kind of interpretation. It stores bytes written into the file as it is. Also the end of file symbol is different for these two files. In text file, the end of file (EOF) is indicated by ^Z (Ctrl + Z) for DOS or ^d (Ctrl + d) for UNIX and may be different for different Operating System as defined in **stdio.h**. In case of binary files, the EOF is generally −1 or as defined in **stdio.h**. Some systems may not distinguish between these two types of files but most do.

In the systems that distinguish, text and binary files, the mode strings given in Table 6.1 work for text files by default. To handle binary files, the letter "**b**" should be appended to the mode string. If a file is opened for writing or appending and if the file does not exist, it is created if possible (if the Operating System permits). Opening an existing file for writing causes the old contents to be discarded, while opening for appending preserves them. Trying to read a file that does not exist is an error. There may be other causes of error as well like trying to read a file when you don't have permission. If there is an error, fopen returns a NULL. The file pointers that corresponds to standard input, standard output and standard error are **stdin**, **stdout**, **stderr**. These are declared in **stdio.h**. So a user can always use these FILE pointers without declaring them or opening these streams using fopen.

The next thing needed, is a way to read or write into a file, once the file is opened. There are several possibilities of which **getc()** or **fgetc()** and **putc()** or **fputc()** are the simplest. The following is the protype along with the description for these functions, declared in the stdio.h.

```
int fgetc(FILE *fp);
```

returns the next character of a file stream pointed by fp as an unsigned char converted to int or EOF, if the end of file or error occurs.

```
int fputc(int c, FILE *fp);
```

writes a character c (converted to an unsigned char), on to the FILE stream pointed by fp. It returns the character written or EOF for error.

```
       int getc(FILE *fp);
and    int putc(int c, FILE *fp);
```

are similar to fputc and fgetc except with some minor differences, which can be ignored at this stage. We shall present more functions available in the standard C library for reading and writing into files (streams). We need the library function fclose() to formally close a file. The prototype of this function is

```
int fclose(FILE *fp);
```

fclose returns 0 on success or EOF if any errors were detected. Now Let us present a simple program that copies a file in program listing 6.1.

```
/* Program Listing 6.1 :  FILE1.c
Copies data from one file to other */

#include <stdio.h>
#include <process.h>

```

```
void filecopy(FILE *, FILE *);

void main(void)
{
      FILE *fp1, *fp2;
      char sr_file[20], dt_file[20];

      printf(“Enter the Source File Name to be Copied ...”);
      gets(sr_file);

      printf(“Enter the Destination File Name ...”);
      gets(dt_file);

      fp1 = fopen(sr_file, “r”);

      if(fp1 == NULL) {
         printf(“Cannot Open %s”, sr_file);
         exit(1);
}
fp2 = fopen(dt_file, “w”);
if(fp2 == NULL) {
   printf(“Cannot Create %s”, dt_file);
   exit(1);
}
filecopy(fp1, fp2);
{
      fclose(fp1);
      fclose(fp2);

      printf(“File Successfully copied ...”);
}

void filecopy(FILE *fp1, FILE *fp2)
{
   int c;
   while((c = fgetc(fp1)) != EOF) {
         fputc(c, fp2);
   }
}
```

```
Enter the Source File Name to be Copied ...BITWISE.C
Enter the Destination File Name ...WISEBIT.C
File Successfully copied ...
```

Program Listing 6.1 Program for copy data from one file to another.

At Line 8,

```
FILE *fp1, *fp2;
```

two FILE pointer fp1 and fp2 are declared to handle the source file and the destination file. At Lines 11 to 15,

```
printf("Enter the Source File Name to be Copied ...");
gets(sr_file);

printf("Enter the Destination File Name ...");
gets(dt_file);
```

we accept the file names interactively by the user as strings into the two variables sr_file and dt_file.

At Line 17,

```
fp1 = fopen(sr_file, "r");
```

the source file is opened in read mode. At Line 19 to 22,

```
if(fp1 == NULL) {
     printf("Cannot Open %s", sr_file);
     exit(1);
}
```

the if statement tests whether the file has been opened successfully. Note fp1 will be NULL, if fopen is not successful. The function exit allows the program to terminate, if the file could not be opened successfully. The value returned here by exit() is 1. We have generally not worried about exit status in our small illustrative programs, but any serious program, should use sensible and useful values in place of 1, especially working in UNIX like operating system.

At Lines 24 to 27,

```
if(fp2 == NULL) {
     printf("Cannot Create %s", dt_file);
     exit(1);
}
```

similarly test the destination file for its successful opening. At Line 28,

```
filecopy(fp1, fp2);
```

the function filecopy is called with two arguments fp1 and fp2.

At Line 36 to 42,

```
void filecopy(FILE *fp1, FILE *fp2)
{
    int c;
    while((c = fgetc(fp1)) != EOF) {
        fputc(c, fp2);
    }
}
```

the function filecopy has a while loop that uses getc (or fgetc) to read character by character from the first file pointed by fp1 and putc (or fputc) to write the character to second file pointed by fp2. The while loop is terminated when an EOF (as defined in stdio.h) is encountered. At Line 30 and 31,

```
fclose(fp1);
fclose(fp2);
```

closes both the files after successful copying.

There are some more functions that can handle the file I/O in using formatted inputs and outputs like fscanf() and fprintf() and line inputs and outputs like fgets() and fputs(). Let us now present a program in program listing 6.2, that copies a file to another file line by line using fgets() and fputs(). The following is the general format of fgets() and fputs().

```
char *fgets(char *s, int n, FILE *fp);
```

fgets reads at most the next n – 1 characters into the array s, stopping if a newline is encountered. The newline is included in the array, which is terminated by '\0'and returns normally. fgets() returns NULL if end of file or error occurs.

```
int fputs(char *s, FILE *fp);
```

fputs writes the string s (which need not contain '\n') on fp. it returns non-negative value, or EOF for an error.

```
/* Program Listing 6.2 :  FILE2.c
Copies data from one file to other line by line */
#include <stdio.h>
#include<process.h>
#define MAXSIZE 100

FILE *fp1, *fp2;

```

```
void main(void)
{
        char sr_file[20], dt_file[20];
            char buff[MAXSIZE];

            printf("Enter the Source File Name to be Copied ...");
            gets(sr_file);

            printf("Enter the Destination File Name ...");
            gets(dt_file);
            fp1 = fopen(sr_file, "r");
            if(fp1 == NULL) {
                    printf("Cannot Open %s", sr_file);
                    exit(0);
            }
            fp2 = fopen(dt_file, "w");
            if( fp2 == NULL) {
                    printf("Cannot Create %s", dt_file);
                    exit(0);
            }
            while(!feof(fp1))
            {
                    fgets(buff,MAXSIZE,fp1);
                    fputs(buff,fp2);
            }
            printf("DONE ");
            fclose(fp1);
            fclose(fp2);
    }
```

```
Enter the Source File Name to be Copied ...BITWISE.C
Enter the Destination File Name ...WISEBIT.C
DONE
```

Program Listing 6.2 *Program to copy data from one file to other using fgets() or fputs().*

At Line 10,

```
char buff[MAXSIZE];
```

a buffer is declared of MAXSIZE to handle the string read by fgets() from the input file (fp1). Same buffer will be used to write the string into the output file (fp2) using fputs(). Note that gets() is nothing but fgets(stdin); and is used to accept strings from the standard input. At Line 27 to 31,

```
while(!feof(fp1))
{
      fgets(buff,MAXSIZE,fp1);
      fputs(buff,fp2);
}
```

the while loop tests for end-of-file condition for fp1. This function returns true (1) if the file currently is at EOF. As long as we don't reach the EOF, the while loop is entered. At Line 29, fgets() reads a line (delimited by \n or EOF) or at most 100 characters into buff, from fp1. At Line 30, fputs() writes the string into fp2. We can also use, the return value of fgets() to test for end-of-file EOF and modify the while loop as follows.

```
while(fgetcs(buff, MAXSIZE, fp1) != NULL)
      fputs(buff,fp2);
```

6.4 SEQUENTIAL FILES

Usually, a data file which contains data is searched for the required data. For example, a file that contains the records of several employees may be searched for the details of a particular employee. There are two ways in searching this data.

1. Sequential Access
2. Random Access

In sequential access, we read record-by-record till such time we access the required record. In random access, we can position the file pointer to the desired position by without reading all the preceding records.

We now present a program in program listing 6.3, to illustrate the creation & accessing a sequential file. We shall create a data file with a set of employee records. Each record gives the following details of an employee.

1. name,
2. empno,
3. salary.

Using fprintf() we will write the records into a file, later we close this file open it again and read record by record using fscanf(). Let us discuss the code.

```
/* Program Listing 6.3 :  EMPFILE.c
Collects the Data from user and Stores in a data file*/
#include <stdio.h>
#include<process.h>
#define MAXSIZE 100

void main(void)
{
    FILE *fp1;
    struct rec{
        char name[30];
          int empno;
          float sal;
  }x;
      char sr_file[20];
      int c;

      printf("Enter the Source File Name to enter data:");
      gets(sr_file);
      fp1 = fopen(sr_file, "w");
      if(fp1 == NULL) {
          printf("Cannot create %s", sr_file);
          exit(0);
      }

      while(1)
      {

          printf("Enter empno(-1 to quit):");
          scanf("%d",&x.empno);
          if(x.empno == -1) break;
          fflush(stdin);
          printf("Enter name:");
          scanf("%[^\n]",x.name);
          printf("Enter salary:");
          fflush(stdin);
          scanf("%f",&x.sal);
          fprintf(fp1,"%d\t%f\t%s\n",x.empno,x.sal,x.name);
      }
```

```
38.         printf("DONE\n ");
39.         fclose(fp1);
40.         fp1 = fopen(sr_file, "r");
41.         if(fp1 == NULL) {
42.             printf("Cannot create %s", sr_file);
43.             exit(0);
44.         }
45.     while(fscanf(fp1,"%d%f%[^\n]",&x.empno,&x.sal,&x.name) != EOF)
46.         printf("%d\t%-30s\t%6.2f\n",x.empno,x.name,x.sal);
47.     }
```

```
Enter the Source File Name to enter data: EMPDATA.DAT
Enter empno(-1 to quit): 001
Enter name: AZIZ
Enter salary: 5000
Enter empno(-1 to quit): -1
DONE
001   AZIZ  5000.00
```

*Program Listing 6.3 Program to handle a file with **fprintf()** & **fscanf()***

At Line 8 to 12,

```
struct rec{
    char name[30];
    int empno;
    float sal;
}x;
```

a structure **rec** is declared to handle the data inputted by the user and write it into the file. At lines 24 to 37,

```
while(1)
{

    printf("Enter empno(-1 to quit):");
    scanf("%d",&x.empno);
    if(x.empno == -1) break;
    fflush(stdin);
    printf("Enter name:");
    scanf("%[^\n]",x.name);
    printf("Enter salary:");
    fflush(stdin);
```

```
                scanf("%f",&x.sal);
                fprintf(fp1,"%d\t%f\t%s\n",x.empno,x.sal,x.name);
        }
```

the while loop allows the user to enter the data. An employee number of –1 (sentinel value) terminates the while loop using the break statemement (line 29). fflush is used between the successive scanf()s to get rid of the new line characters.

At Line 32, Observe the format of the scanf(). The [^\n] allows you to accept string including white spaces till a \n is encountered. If %s is used you may not able to enter a string which contains white spaces and invariablly names contain white spaces. At Line 36, we use **fprintf()** to write the record values into the file. Note that each field is separated by a tab and we have added a \n at the end of each record. Though these are not necessary, this allows us to read using scanf(), rather easily. It is essential to close the file, before you open it in the read mode to read the data and print. At lines 39 & 40,

```
fclose(fp1);
fp1 = fopen(sr_file, "r");
```

the file is closed and reopened. At line 45,

```
while(fscanf(fp1,"%d%f%[^\n]",&x.empno,&x.sal,&x.name) !=
        EOF)
```

the while loop tests the return value of fscanf() for eof. Note that fscanf() returns EOF at the end-of-file and not NULL as with fgets(). At line 46,

```
printf("%d\t%-30s\t%6.2f\n",x.empno,x.name,x.sal);
```

the values read are printed.

6.5 RANDOM FILE ACCESS

Now let us look into some functions, that are important when we wish to access a file randomly. It is often useful to know where you are currently in a file, when you are accessing the file randomly. The following function ftell(),

```
long ftell(FILE *fp);
```

returns the offset of the FILE pointer from the beginning of the file (BOF). So far we have not experienced a need, to know where we are in the file, since we are only doing sequential reads and writes. Even in append mode, we write at the end of the file in a sequential mode. However sometimes it is useful to be able to read or write from some desired locations in the file. This ability to go directly to the desired place in the file, is called Random Access. We will use the function ftell() to record the current position, so that we can get back the current position if needed. We present another function fseek(), which allows us to go to any desired position. The syntax for fseek is

```
int fseek(FILE *fp, long offset, int whence);
```

fseek sets the file pointer associated with stream to a new position that is offset bytes from the file location given by whence.

The possible values for whence are SEEK_SET (beginning), SEEK_CUR (current position) and SEEK_END (end of file). For a text stream, offset must be zero, or a value returned by ftell (in which case origin must be SEEK_SET). fseek returns non-zero on error. If a file is opened in read/write mode ("r+"), there should be a seek between read and write to switch the mode properly.

Keeping all this points in mind, let us present a program in program listing 6.4 that opens a text file in read/write mode and changes every 5th character of the file to Uppercase.

```
/* Program Listing 6.4 :  FSEEK.c
Changes every 5th character of the data file  */
#include <stdio.h>
#include <process.h>

FILE *fp1;

void main(void)
{
        int ch;
        long current_position;
        char fname[20];

        printf("Enter the File Name ...");
        gets(fname);
        fp1 = fopen(fname, "r+");
        if(fp1 == NULL) {
                printf("Cannot Open %s", fname);
                exit(0);
        }
        current_position = ftell(fp1);
        while(!feof(fp1))
        {
                if(((current_position + 1)%5) == 0)
                {
                        ch = getc(fp1);
                        if(ch >= 'a' && ch <= 'z')
                                ch -= 32;
                        fseek(fp1, current_position , SEEK_SET);
                        fputc(ch, fp1);
                        fseek(fp1, 0L, SEEK_CUR);
                }
```

```
31.             else
32.                     ch = getc(fp1);
33.         }
34.         fclose(fp1);
35.  }
```

```
Enter the File Name ...EMPDATA.TXT
```

Program Listing 6.4 Program to change every 5th character in a file to Uppercase in a text file

At Line 14,

```
fp1 = fopen(fname, "r+");
```

the file is opened in read/write mode ("r+"). At Line 20,

```
while(!feof(fp1))
```

the while loop uses feof() to test for end-of-file. At Line 22,

```
current_position = ftell(fp1);
```

the ftell returns the current position and is stored in variable current_position. The if statement tests whether the character position is divisible by five or not. Since, the current_position starts from zero, we have used (current_position + 1)%5, to test this condition. This is because we are counting the characters from 1, 2, 3, 4, . . .etc., whereas ftell counts from zero. At Line 24,

```
ch = getc(fp1);
```

getc reads the current character (wanted current character) and stores into ch. At Line 28,

```
fseek(fp1, current_position , SEEK_SET);
```

since the file pointer advances, we go back to the current position noted earlier by using fseek. Note that the second and third parameters of fseek allows the file pointer to get back to the current position from the beginning of the file. At Line 29,

```
fputc(ch, fp1);
```

fputc overwrites the lowercase letter with uppercase and the file pointer is advanced. At Line 30,

```
fseek(fp1, 0L, SEEK_CUR);
```

a dummy fseek which does not move the file pointer is needed to get the file to the normal mode, which has been put into, write mode. Note the second and third parameter of fseek, which tells the fseek to stay where you are. At Line 32 and 33,

```
else
        ch = getc(fp1);
```

the else part of the if statement allows you to move forward when the character is not to be replaced.

6.6 USING COMMAND LINE PARAMETERS IN FILE I/O

We shall now present a program CATFILE.C in Program Listing 6.5, that takes file names as arguments and concatanate the files to the screen (show them on the screen).

```
/* Program Listing 6.5 :  CATFILE.c
Concatanate the files to the screen   */
#include <stdio.h>

void filecopy(FILE *, FILE *);

void main(int argc, char *argv[])
{
    FILE *fp1;
    int i;
    if(argc < 2)
          filecopy(stdin, stdout);
      else
          for(i = 1;i < argc;i++)
          {
              fp1 = fopen(*++argv, "r");
              if(fp1 == NULL)
              {
                fprintf(stderr,"\n%s not found ...", *argv);
                getch();
              }
              else
              {
                filecopy(fp1, stdout);
                fclose(fp1);
              }
          }
  }

  void filecopy(FILE *f1, FILE *f2)
  {
      int c;
      printf("\n");
      while((c = getc(f1)) != EOF)
          fputc(c, f2);
  }
```

```
C:\>CATFILE DATA.TXT DATA1.TXT
Welcome to the World of 'C'
'C' programming is very interesting
```

Program Listing 6.5 Program to concatanate files to the screen

At Line 9,

```
if(argc < 2)
```

if the argument count is less than 2, which means you have not specified any file. Therefore, we call filecopy with stdin and stdout which allows the program to print to screen, whatever you enter through the keyboard. At Line 12 to 25,

```
for(i = 1;i < argc;i++)
{
        fp1 = fopen(*++argv, "r");
        if(fp1 == NULL)
        {
                fprintf(stderr,"\n%s not found ...", *argv);
                getch();
        }
        else
        {
                filecopy(fp1, stdout);
                fclose(fp1);
        }
}
```

the for loop in the else part, will run from i = 1 to argc – 1 allowing each file on the command line to be opened. If the file is successfully opened the corresponding file ponter will be sent to the function filecopy. The filecopy is a simple function, which takes two file pointers fp1 and fp2, fp2 always being stdout, reads character by character from fp1 and sends it to the stdout.

At Line 14, notice the way in which argv is handled. Since argv is a pointer to the beginning of the array of argument strings, incrementing by 1 (++argv) makes it point to argv[1] instead of argv[0]. Each successive increment moves it along with the next argument. *argv is then the pointer to that argument.

SELF-REVIEW EXERCISES

1. A .... is a group of related records.
2. Function .... closes a file.
3. Function .... reads a line from a specified file.
4. Function .... opens a file.
5. Function .... repositions the file position pointer to a data from a file in random access applications.
6. The .... stream is normally connected to the input.
7. The .... and .... streams are normally connected to the computer screen.
8. In 'C' a file is basically a stream of ....

EXERCISES

1. Write a program that, given a seven digit number, writes to a file every possible seven-letter word corresponding to that number. There are 2187 (3 to the 7th power) such words. Avoid phone numbers with the digits 0 and 1.
2. Write a program that uses the ***sizeof()*** operator to determine the sizes in bytes of the various data types on your computer system. Write the results to the file "***datasize.dat*** " so you may print the results later.
3. Write statements that accomplish each of the following. Assume that the structure

```
struct person {
   char lastname[15], firstname[15], age[4];
};
```

has been defined and that the file is already open for writing.

(a) *Initialize the file " **nameage.dat**" so that there are 100 records with **lastname** = " **unassigned** ", **firstname** = " " and **age** = " 0 ".*

(b) *Input 10 last names, first names and ages and write them to the file.*

(c) *Update a record; if there is no information in the record, tell the user "* ***No Information*** *".*

(d) *Delete a record that has information by reinitializing that particular record.*

6. Implement complex Numbers - Subtraction, Division and multiplication using pointers and write the result to a data file.

7

Searching & Sorting

7.1 SEARCHING

Before we consider search techniques let us define some terms. A file is a collection of records, each record having one or more fields. The fields used to distinguish among the records are known as keys. Since the same file may be used for several different applications, the key fields for record identification will depend on the particular application. For instance, we may regard a telephone directory as a file, each record has three fields: name, address, and phone number. The key is usually the person's name. However, one may wish to locate the record corresponding to a given number, in which case the phone number field would be the key. In yet another application one may desire the phone number at a particular address, so this field too could be the key.

A search algorithm is an algorithm that accepts an argument k (the key value) and tries to find a record whose key is k. The algorithm may return the entire record or more commonly a pointer (location) of the record. It is possible that the search for a particular key in a file may be unsuccessful; that is there is no record in the file, whose key value matches with that of the search key k. In such cases, the algorithm may return a special value or a NULL pointer.

To be simple, we will present the searching algorithms assuming that the key values of the input set of records are stored in an array of integers. Further our searching algorithms will return the position within the array, in case the search key value is found (successful search), otherwise return a –1 (unsuccessful search). Normally, in a practical situation, if the key is found at a particular position, we can locate the actual record in the file using this information.

7.2 LINEAR SEARCH

In general there are two ways of organizing a file.

1. *The file is not ordered or sorted on the key values.*
2. *The file is ordered or sorted on the key values.*

In the first case, we have to compare the search key value with every key going through the entire array. This is called as *linear search*. The worst case time complexity of any algorithm that searches linearly, will be O(n), where n is the number of keys (records).

However, we have a better approach for the second case where it is possible to design a searching algorithm that has in worst case O(log n) time complexity which will be presented in next section.

Let us now present the linear search program in program listing 7.1.

```
/* Program Listing 7.1 :  linser.c
/* A program for linear searching      */

#include<stdio.h>
int lin_search(int [],int,int );
void main(void)
{
        int a[]={19,29,31,10,59,69,1245,89,109,234,345,348,456};
        int key,i;
        printf("enter the key to be searched:");
        scanf("%d",&key);
        i=lin_search(a,12,key);
        if(i != -1)
                printf(" %d is found at %d",key,i);
        else
                printf(" %d is not found ",key);
}
```

```
15.  int lin_search(int x[],int n, int k)
16.  {
17.       int i;
18.       for(i = 0;i < n;i++)
19.            if(x[i] ==k)
20.                 return i;
21.       return -1;
22.  }
```

```
enter the key to be searched: 31
31 is found at 2
enter the key to be searched: 999
999 is not found
```

Program Listing 7.1 Linear Search

For convenience we have declared an array of integers and initialized with key values. However in practice, these key values may be read from an index file into a buffer and the values could be even strings. This does not make any difference in the working of the algorithm. At Line 7 & 8,

```
printf("enter the key to be searched:");
scanf("%d",&key);
```

the search key is interactively accepted. At Line 9,

```
i=lin_search(a,12,key);
```

the routine lin_search is called by passing three parameters namely the address of the array containing the keys, the number of keys and the search key value. From Line 15 to 22,

```
int lin_search(int x[],int n, int k)
{
     int i;
     for(i = 0;i < n;i++)
          if(x[i] ==k)
               return i;
     return -1;
}
```

the lin_search routine, just contains a for loop, with the loop variable i running from 0 to n – 1. The if statement inside the loop returns the position if the key is found. Otherwise the routine returns –1 indicating to the calling routine that the search key is not found.

7.3 BINARY SEARCH

Usually, the keys are stored in an index file in a sorted order though the actual file is not sorted. The search in a sorted list could be much faster than in an unsorted list. In case of large file (a file with a huge number of records) where n is large and the search being used very frequently, it is necessary to keep the index in a sorted order. Now we can replace linear search (worst case complexity O(n)) with binary search (worst case complexity O(log n)). This will certainly improve the efficiency of search, which is absolutely necessary while searching large files. Now let us present a program in program listing 7.2, which uses the binary search to search on sorted keys.

```
/* Program Listing 7.2 :  binser.c
/* A program for binary searching      */

#include<stdio.h>
      int bin_search(int [],int,int );
void main(void)
{
      int a[]={19,29,39,49,59,69,79,89,109,234,345,348,456};
      int key,i;
      printf("enter the key to be searched:");
      scanf("%d",&key);
      i=bin_search(a,12,key);
      if(i != -1)
            printf(" %d is found at %d",key,i);
      else
            printf(" %d is not found ",key);
}
int bin_search(int x[],int n, int k)
{
      int low,high,mid;
      low=0;
      high=n;
      while(high>=low)
      {
            mid=(low+high)/2;
            if(x[mid]==k)
                  return(mid);
            if(x[mid]> k)
                  high=mid-1;
```

```
27.             else
28.                     low = mid+1;
29.         }
30.         return(-1);
31.     }
```

```
enter the key to be searched:39
39 is found at 2
enter the key to be searched:999
999 is not found
```

Program Listing 7.2 Binary Search

The routine bin_search from lines 15 to 31,

```
int bin_search(int x[],int n, int k)
{
    int low,high,mid;
    low=0;
    high=n;
    while(high>=low)
    {
        mid=(low+high)/2;
        if(x[mid]==k)
            return(mid);
        if(x[mid] > k)
            high=mid-1;
        else
            low = mid+1;
    }
    return(-1);
}
```

is a non-recursive routine, which takes three parameters namely the address of the array of keys, the number of keys and the search key value. The routine uses a while loop in which it computes a mid value at line 22. This allows the whole set of keys to be divided into two groups. One group between low and mid – 1 and the other mid + 1 and high. If the element is not found at mid, the search continues in one of these groups depending on the value of k.

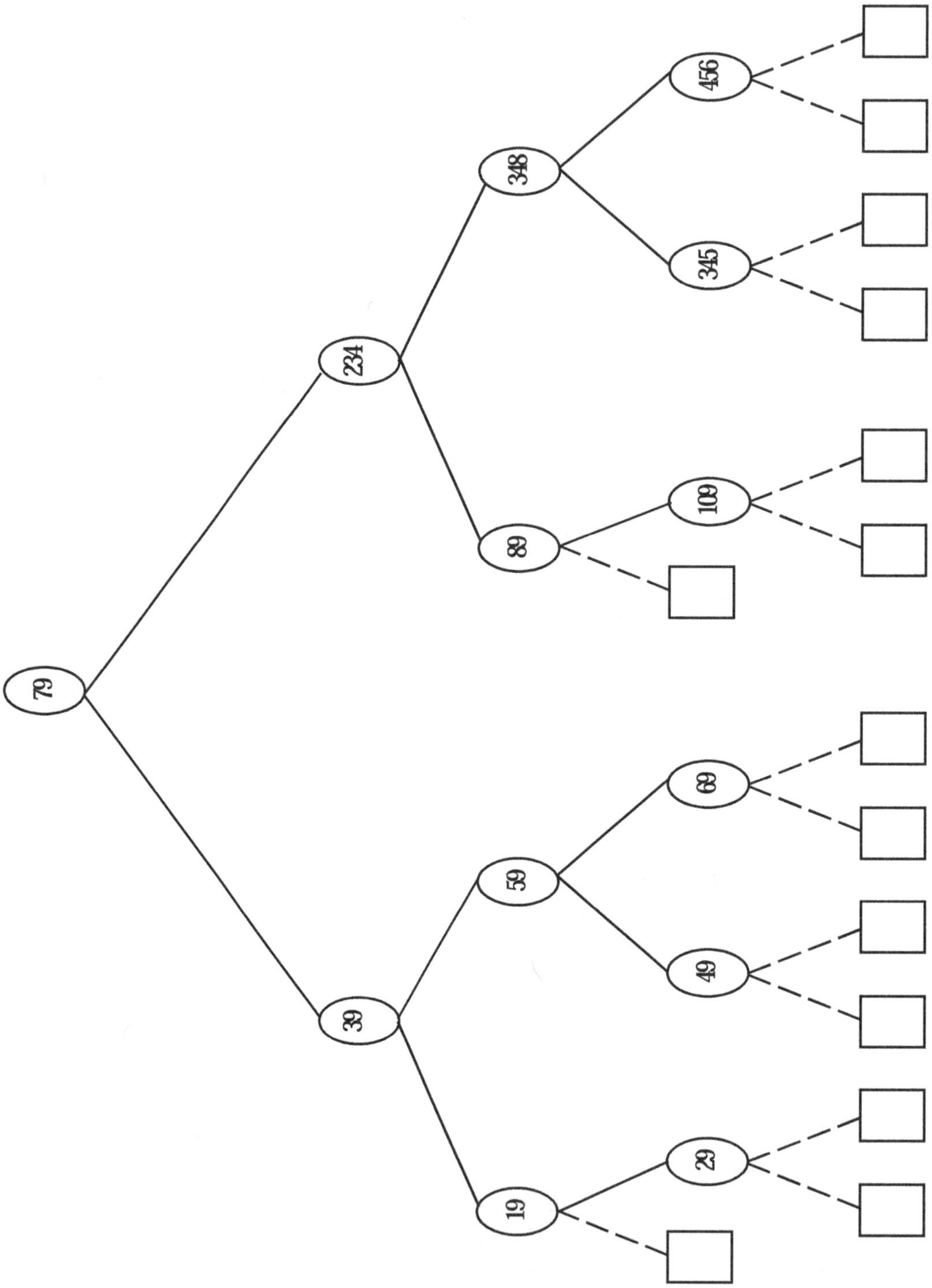
79
39
234
19
59
89
348
29
49
69
109
345
456

Fig. 7.1 Binary Search depicted through a Binary4 tree

If k has a value lower than x[mid], then the search should continue in the lower group, i.e., from low to mid – 1 else the search should continue in the upper group, i.e., from mid + 1 to high. This will continue till the element is found or till no longer the two groups exists (i.e., high < low). The entire search could be depicted using a binary tree. For the values given in the program how the search continues is illustrated in Fig 7.1

Any key value will follow a path from the root of this tree and exits from any one of the nodes along a single path. For example, let the search key be 59. The search starts at the root 79 as the mid, and the search continues with the mid as 39 and finally ends up when 59 matches the key value. This is a successful search and the while loop is iterated only for 3 times. Notice that 59 is at level 3 of the binary tree and the search exits from one of the internal node (marked as circles).

Lets try out now an unsuccessful search. Let k be 30. The search starts as usual at 79 and then proceeds to 39 then to 19 and finally to 29 where the search ends unsuccessfully. In fact all the unsuccessful searches will end up at one of the square nodes of the tree. These are called the external nodes. A binary tree with n internal nodes will have n + 1 external nodes. Notice that the while loop is iterated only for 4 times. Since the binary tree of Fig. 7.1 has a height of 4 which is equal to ***log 13 base 2***. Thus a worst case search will end up with 4 iterations. However the linear search on the same set of numbers will take 13 iterations for an unsuccessful search.

For example if there are 1024 elements in the set of keys to be searched, the binary search takes at most 10 iterations of the while loop, for an unsuccessful search. On the other hand the linear search will take 1024 iterations for an unsuccessful search. The student should notice the vast difference between the linear and binary searches, as n increases. However, the binary search needs the set of keys to be in a sorted order. It could be difficult to keep the records in a sorted order on the key value. But the key values which are usually stored in a separate index file along with physical address of the actual record will be in sorted order. And thus binary search could be applied on the index files to locate the desired key and get the physical address of the corresponding record.

Let us now present a recursive version of a binary search in program listing 7.3. The recursive algorithm is more natural to a binary search.

```
/* Program Listing 7.3 :  rbinser.c
/* A program for recursive binary searching      */
#include<stdio.h>
int rbin_search(int, int, int );
int a[]={19,29,39,49,59,69,79,89,109,234,345,348,456};
```

```c
void main(void)
{
      int key,i;
      printf("enter the key to be searched:");
      scanf("%d",&key);
      i=rbin_search(0, 12, key);
      if(i != -1)
            printf(" %d is found at %d",key,i);
      else
      printf(" %d is not found ",key);
}
int rbin_search(int low, int high, int k)
{
      int mid;
      if(high < low)
            return -1;
      mid = high + low / 2;
      if(a[mid] == k)
            return mid;
      if(k < a[mid])
            return rbin_search(low, mid - 1, k);
      else
            return rbin_search(mid + 1, high, k);
}
```

```
enter the key to be searched: 39
39 is found at 2
enter the key to be searched: 31
31 is not found
```

Program Listing 7.3 Recursive Binary Search

The routine rbin_search at line 15 to 27,

```
int rbin_search(int low, int high, int k)
{
        int mid;
        if(high < low)
                return -1;
        mid = high + low / 2;
        if(a[mid] == k)
                return mid;
        if(k < a[mid])
                return rbin_search(low, mid - 1, k);
        else
                return rbin_search(mid + 1, high, k);
}
```

will return −1, if high < low, i.e., an unsuccessful search. This is one base condition of the recursive program. The other one is the successful search at line 21, where the program returns the value of the mid when a[mid] == k. If both the base conditions are not satisfied, then we call recursively the rbin_search with the subset low to mid – 1 or mid + 1 to high depending on the value of k. The recursive calls of rbin_search will follow one path on the tree (Fig. 7.1) and exits either at one of the internal nodes (successful search) or at an external node (unsuccessful search). Thus the number of recursive calls are equivalent to the number of iterations in the previous program (the non recursive binary search).

7.4 SORTING

Now we will look into several sorting algorithms. Broadly a sorting algorithm can be classified as internal if the records that it is sorting are in the main memory or external if sum of the records that it is sorting are in auxiliary storage. In this chapter, we mainly restrict our attention to internal sorts. A file is said to be sorted on the key, if i < j implies that k[i] precedes k[j] in some order on the keys. Let us explain this with an example.

Consider a telephone directory as a file of records containing three fields name, address and telephone number. Let the file be sorted on the field name in alphabetical order, then it implies that any i^{th} name should be alphabetically lower than j^{th} name, where i < j. This order of sorting is known as ascending order. If for any i and j, i < j, the ith name is alphabetically greater than j^{th} name, then the file is said to be sorted in descending order.

We shall now present a number of sorting techniques, which are popular in Computer Science. All the algorithms that are presented in this chapter assume ascending order sorting. However you can always change an ascending sorting algorithm to a descending sorting algorithm by changing the comparison condition of the keys. We can classify the sorting algorithms into five categories.

1. *Exchange Sorts*
2. *Selection Sorts*
3. *Insertion Sorts*
4. *Merge Sorts*
5. *Distribution Sorts*

The basic idea behind ***exchange sorting technique*** is mainly, exchanging pairs of the items until the sequence is sorted. The examples of exchange sorters are The ***bubble sort*** and the ***quick sort.***

The ***selection sorting algorithms*** construct the sorted sequence one element at a time by adding elements to the sorted sequence in order. At each step the next element to be added to the sorted sequence is selected from the remaining elements. The examples are ***straight selection sort*** (normally known as selection sort) and ***heap sort*** under this category.

The category of algorithms that fall under ***insertion sort*** class consider element by element and insert it at the proper place in the sequence. The examples under this category are ***straight insertion sort*** (normally known as insertion sort) and ***binary insertion sort.***

The algorithms under merge sorting category combine two or more sorted sequences into a single sorted sequence. An example under this category is The Two Way Merge Sort.

The final class of sorting algorithms namely sort by distribution have a unique characteristic of not comparing the key values which normally all the other sorting algorithms do. Instead, distribution sorting algorithms rely on priori knowledge about the universal set from which the elements to be sorted are drawn. For example, if the keys are numbers, each digit must be between 0 and 9 and the keys are distributed examining the digits into buckets. The distribution continues till the correct sequence is achieved. The examples under this category are ***bucket sort*** and ***radix sort.***

In this chapter we will present only the following sorting algorithms

1. *Bubble Sort.*
2. *Selection Sort (Simple).*
3. *Insertion Sort (Straight).*
4. *Quick Sort.*
5. *Heap Sort.*
6. *Merge Sort (Two-way).*

The sorting techniques are presented in the above order in this chapter to facilitate the student to begin with an easier sorting technique and advance to more complex sorting techniques.

7.5 BUBBLE SORT

The simplest and perhaps the best known of the exchange sorts is the bubble sort. To sort a sequence of n elements, bubble sort makes n – 1 passes thorough the data. In each pass adjacent elements are compared and swapped if necessary. For example, the first and the second elements of the set are compared and exchanged if the first element is greater than the second element; next, the second and the third are compared and swapped if necessary and so on. The output shows various iterations of bubble sort for the sequence of numbers used in the program. Notice that after the first pass through the data the largest element in the sequence has bubbled up into the last position. In general after k passes through the data, the last k elements of the array are incorrect order and need not be considered any longer.

```
/* Program Listing 7.4 :  bubble.c
/* A program for Bubble Sorting      */

#include <stdio.h>
/*to sort the set of numbers using bubble sort a type of exchange sorting*/
void bsort(int [],int);
void print_list(int [],int);
void swap(int *, int *);

void main(void)
{
      int a[] = {56,28,84,66,78,23,90,156,12,27};
      printf("The Given List\n");
```

```
    print_list(a,10);/* prints the un-sorted  list */
    printf("\n");
    bsort(a,12);
    printf("\n");
    printf("The Final Sorted List\n");
    print_list(a,10);/* prints the sorted list */
}

void bsort(int x[],int n)
{ /* returns a sorted list */
    int  i, j;
    for(i = n;i >0;i–){
    /* bubble up the largest in the remaining list */
        printf("Iteration %2d  ", (n - i + 1));
        for(j=0;j<i-1;j++)
            if(x[j]>x[j+1]) swap(&x[j],&x[j+1]);
        print_list(x,n);
    }
}

void print_list(int y[],int n)
{
    int i;
    for(i=0;i<n;i++) printf("%5d",y[i]);
    printf("\n");
}
void swap(int *a, int *b)
{
    int t;
    t=*a;
    *a=*b;
    *b=t;
}
```

```
The Given List
  28   58   84   16  270   42   19   77   59   17   27   57


Iteration  1 28   58   16   84   42   19   77   59   17   27   57  270
Iteration  2 28   16   58   42   19   77   59   17   27   57   84  270
Iteration  3 16   28   42   19   58   59   17   27   57   77   84  270
Iteration  4 16   28   19   42   58   17   27   57   59   77   84  270
Iteration  5 16   19   28   42   17   27   57   58   59   77   84  270
Iteration  6 16   19   28   17   27   42   57   58   59   77   84  270
Iteration  7 16   19   17   27   28   42   57   58   59   77   84  270
Iteration  8 16   17   19   27   28   42   57   58   59   77   84  270
Iteration  9 16   17   19   27   28   42   57   58   59   77   84  270
Iteration 10 16   17   19   27   28   42   57   58   59   77   84  270
Iteration 11 16   17   19   27   28   42   57   58   59   77   84  270


The Final Sorted List
     16   17   19   27   28   42   57   58   59   77   84  270
```

Program Listing 7.4 Bubble Sort

In Program Listing 7.4, at Line 9,

```
int a[] = {56,28,84,66,78,23,90,156,12,27};
```

the array to be sorted is declared and initialized. This is as usual done for convenience. The student can modify the program to accept the key values interactively. At Line 13,

```
bsort(a,12);
```

the function bsort is called with two parameters namely the address of the array and the number of the elements in the array. From Line 19 to 29,

```
void bsort(int x[],int n)
{ /* returns a sorted list */
     int  i, j;
     for(i = n;i >0;i–){
     /* bubble up the largest in the remaining list */
          printf("Iteration %2d  ", (n - i + 1));
          for(j=0;j<i-1;j++)
               if(x[j]>x[j+1]) swap(&x[j],&x[j+1]);
          print_list(x,n);
     }
}
```

the bsort routine uses two for loops one within the other. The outer loop runs for n – 1 times, thus creates n – 1 passes through the data. The inner loop runs from 0 to i – 1, thus every time it does not consider the already sorted elements at the end of each pass. At Line 26, the swap function is used to exchange the elements if necessary. Notice that we are sending the actual addresses of the elements to the swap function to get true swap. At Line 27, we have included the print_list routine to show the set of elements after every pass.

The time complexity of bubble sort can be computed as follows. The outer loop at line 22 to 28 operates for n – 1 times. For each of the outer loop iteration, the inner loop is operated for n – 1, n – 2, and so on up to 1. Thus, the total number of iterations of the inner loop will be (n – 1) + (n – 2) + . . . + 2 + 1. This is nothing but the sum of n – 1 natural numbers and is equal to $n*(n - 1)/2$ or is equal to $n^2/2 - n/2$. Therefore, the running time Bubble sort is $O(n^2)$ ignoring as usual the lower order terms and constants.

7.6 SELECTION SORT

The simplest of the selection sorts is called the straight selection sort. At each step of the algorithm a linear search of the unsorted elements is made in order to determine the position of the largest element in the remaining elements. The element is then moved to the correct position of the array by swapping it with the element, which currently occupies that position. The output of program listing 7.5 shows various iterations of selection sort for the sequence of numbers used in the program. For example, in the first iteration shown in the output, a linear search of the entire array reveals that 156 is the largest element and is at position 7 (positions are counted from 0). Since this has to come to the last position (position 9), we swap 27, which is currently in position 9 with 156 at position 7. The second step of the algorithm (shown in the output) identifies 90 at position 6 as the largest in the remaining elements and is exchanged with 12 at position 8. Notice that in two passes the two largest numbers are in the right places. Therefore the algorithm after n – 1 such passes puts the entire list in a sorted order.

The program is illustrated in Program Listing 7.5.

```
/* Program Listing 7.5 :  selection.c
/* A program for Selection Sorting      */
#include <stdio.h>
/* to sort a set of numbers using selection sort*/
     void selection_sort(int [],int);
     void print_list(int [],int);
     void swap(int *, int *);
```

```
void main(void)
{
      int a[] = {56,28,84,66,78,23,90,156,12,27};
      printf(“\nThe Given List\n”);
      print_list(a,10);/* prints the un-sorted  list */
      printf(“\n”);
      selection_sort(a,10);
      printf(“\nThe Final List\n”);
      print_list(a,10);/* prints the sorted list */
}

void selection_sort(int x[],int n)
{ /* returns a sorted list */
      int  i, j,max;
      for(i = n;i > 1 ;i–){
            printf(“Iteration %2d  “, (n - i + 1));
            max=0; /* to select the max  each time we scan through*/
            for(j=1;j<i;j++)if(x[j]>x[max]) max=j;
            swap(&x[i-1],&x[max]);
            print_list(x,n);
      }
}

void print_list(int y[],int n)
{
      int i;
      for(i=0;i<n;i++) printf(“%5d”,y[i]);
      printf(“\n”);
}
void swap(int *a, int *b)
{
      int t;
      t=*a;
      *a=*b;
      *b=t;
}
```

```
The Given List
   56    28    84    66    78    23    90   156    12    27

Iteration  1      56    28    84    66    78    23    90    27    12   156
Iteration  2      56    28    84    66    78    23    12    27    90   156
Iteration  3      56    28    27    66    78    23    12    84    90   156
Iteration  4      56    28    27    66    12    23    78    84    90   156
Iteration  5      56    28    27    23    12    66    78    84    90   156
Iteration  6      12    28    27    23    56    66    78    84    90   156
Iteration  7      12    23    27    28    56    66    78    84    90   156
Iteration  8      12    23    27    28    56    66    78    84    90   156
Iteration  9      12    23    27    28    56    66    78    84    90   156

The Final List
   12    23    27    28    56    66    78    84    90   156
```

Program Listing 7.5 Selection Sorting

Observe the selection_sort routine from Lines 18 to 28,

```
void selection_sort(int x[],int n)
{ /* returns a sorted list */
      int  i, j,max;
      for(i = n;i > 1 ;i—){
            printf("Iteration %2d  ", (n - i + 1));
            max=0; /* to select the max  each time we scan through*/
            for(j=1;j<i;j++)if(x[j]>x[max]) max=j;
            swap(&x[i-1],&x[max]);
            print_list(x,n);
      }
}
```

wherein we have used two for loops one within the other, just similar to the bubble sort. However, the inner loop only determines where the position of the highest element exists in the remaining unsorted elements. After this the swapping is done in the outer loop only once, that is, in all we will have n – 1 swaps. But in bubble sort there could be as many as n * (n – 1) / 2 swaps.

The time complexity of this sorting algorithm will be $O(n^2)$as the inner loop operates for n * (n – 1) / 2, just similar to bubble sort. However you should note that the number of swaps could be considerably less for Selection Sort. The swap could be a costly process if large size record has to be swapped.

7.7 INSERTION SORT

The key step of an insertion sort algorithm involves the insertion of an item into a sorted sequence. There are two aspects to an insertion – finding the correct position in the sequence at which the new element could be inserted and moving all the elements over to make room for the new one.

This section presents the straight insertion sorting algorithm. Straight insertion sorting uses a linear search to locate the position at which the next element is to be inserted.

The output of program listing 7.6 shows various iterations of insertion sort for the sequence of numbers used in the program.. The Program Listing 7.6 gives the program for Straight Insertion Sort. As usual an array of unsorted elements are initialized in the program for convenience.

```
/* Program Listing 7.6 :  selection.c
/* A program for Insertion Sorting      */
#include <stdio.h>
/* to sort the set of numbers using insertion sort*/
void insertion_sort(int [],int);
void print_list(int [],int);
void swap(int *, int *);

void main(void)
{
      int a[] = {56,28,84,66,78,23,90,15,12,27};
      printf("\nThe Given List\n");
      print_list(a,10);/* prints the un-sorted  list */
      printf("\n");
      insertion_sort(a,10);
      printf("\nThe Final Sorted List\n");
      print_list(a,10);/* prints the sorted list */
}

void insertion_sort(int x[],int n)
{ /* returns a sorted list */
      int  i, j;
      for(i = 1;i < n ;i++)
      {
            printf("\nIteration %2d", (i - 1 + 1));
      /* inside for loop is not entered if the list is  sorted */
```

```
            for(j=i;j>0 && x[j-1] > x[j];j–)
                swap(&x[j],&x[j-1]);
            print_list(x,n);
        }
        printf("\n");
}

void print_list(int y[],int n)
{
        int i;
        for(i=0;i<n;i++)
        printf("%5d",y[i]);
}

void swap(int *a, int *b)
{
        int t;
        t=*a;
        *a=*b;
        *b=t;
}
```

```
The Given List
   56   28   84   66   78   23   90   15   12   27

Iteration  1   28   56   84   66   78   23   90   15   12   27
Iteration  2   28   56   84   66   78   23   90   15   12   27
Iteration  3   28   56   66   84   78   23   90   15   12   27
Iteration  4   28   56   66   78   84   23   90   15   12   27
Iteration  5   23   28   56   66   78   84   90   15   12   27
Iteration  6   23   28   56   66   78   84   90   15   12   27
Iteration  7   15   23   28   56   66   78   84   90   12   27
Iteration  8   12   15   23   28   56   66   78   84   90   27
Iteration  9   12   15   23   27   28   56   66   78   84   90

The Final Sorted List
   12   15   23   27   28   56   66   78   84   90
```

Program Listing 7.6 *Insertion Sort*

From Lines 18 to 30,

```
void insertion_sort(int x[],int n)
{ /* returns a sorted list */
      int  i, j;
      for(i = 1;i < n ;i++)
      {
            printf("\nIteration %2d", (i - 1 + 1));
      /* inside for loop is not entered if the list is  sorted */
            for(j=i;j>0 && x[j-1] > x[j];j—)
                  swap(&x[j],&x[j-1]);
            print_list(x,n);
      }
      printf("\n");
}
```

in the insertion_sort routine we make use of the outer for loop to make n – 1 passes through the data. The inner loop runs backwards from i to find proper position for insertion. Since the list is a sorted list up to i, the inner for loop is simply finding a place for the current element to be inserted into the already sorted list.

Notice that the inner for loop will operate just the number of times need to make a slot for current element in the already sorted list. In the extreme case, the inner loop is never operated if the list is already in the sorted order.

The algorithm in the worst case (sorted in descending order) will have a time complexity of order $O(n^2)$as the inner loop will operate for n * (n – 1) / 2. But in most practical places it would operate for much less number of times. For sorting small number of records insertion sort is always preferred as it has a very good average behavior.

7.8 QUICK SORT

We now turn our attention to a sorting scheme with a very good average behavior. The quick sort scheme developed by C.A. HOARE has the best average behavior among all the sorting algorithms covered in this chapter. The quick sort is a divide and conquer style algorithm. A divide and conquer algorithm solves a given problem by splitting it into two or more smaller sub-problems, recursively solving each of the sub-problems, and then combining the solutions to the smaller problems to obtain a solution to the original one.

To sort the sequence S = {s1, s2, s3, . . ., sn} quick sort performs the following steps:

1. *Select one of the elements of S. The selected element p, is called the pivot.*
2. *Remove p from S and partition the remaining elements of S into two distinct sequences, L & G, such that every element in L is less than or equal to the pivot and every element in G is greater than or equal to the pivot. In general, both L & G are unsorted.*
3. *Rearrange the elements of the sequence as follows*

$$S' = \{\underbrace{l_1, l_2, \ldots, l_{|L|}}_{L}, p, \underbrace{g_1, g_2, \ldots, g_{|G|}}_{G}\}$$

Notice that the pivot is now in the position to which it belongs in the sorted sequence, since all the elements to the left of the pivot are less than or equal to the pivot and all the elements to the right are greater than or equal to pivot.

4. *Recursively quick sort the unsorted sequences L and G.*

The first step of the algorithm is a crucial one. We have not specified how to select the pivot. Usually we select the first element of the set as the pivoting element. Fortunately, the sorting algorithm works no matter which element is chosen as the pivot. However, the pivot selection directly affects the running time of the algorithm. If we choose poorly the running time will be poor. We have chosen the first element of the list as the pivot to present the quick sort in a simple way. Note that this may not be the best solution.

The output of program listing 7.7 illustrates the detailed operation of quick sort as it sorts the sequence {26,5,37,1,61,11,59,15,48,19}. We will begin the sort with first element 26 as the pivot. Next, the remaining elements are partioned into two sequences, one which contains values less than or equal to 26 (L = {11,5,19,1,15}) and one which contains values greater than or equal to 26 (G = {59,61,48,37}). Notice that the partitioning is accomplished by exchanging elements. This is why quick sort is considered as an exchange sort.

After the partitioning, the pivot is inserted between the two sequences. This is called restoring the pivot. Notice that the 26 is in its correct position in the sorted sequence and it is not considered any further after the first iteration.

Now the quick sort algorithm calls itself recursively, first to sort the sequence L = {11,5,19,1,15}; second to sort the sequence G = {59,61,48,37}. The quick sort of L selects 11 as the pivot, and creates the two sub-sequences L' = {1,5} and G' = {19,15}. Similarly, the quick sort of G uses 59 as the pivot and creates the two subsequences L" = {48,37} and G" = {61}.

At this point in the example the recursion continues. The recursion continues till each sub-sequence becomes a size of 1. This means that when the algorithm terminates, the sequence is sorted. The program is presented in Program Listing 7.7.

```
/* Program Listing 7.7 :  qsort.c
/* A program for Quick Sorting       */
#include <stdio.h>
/* to sort the set of numbers using insertion sort*/
     void quick_sort(int [],int,int);
     void print_list(int [],int);
     void swap(int *, int *);

void main(void)
{
     int a[] = {26,5,37,1,61,11,59,15,48,19};
     printf("\nThe Given List\n");
     print_list(a,10);/* prints the un-sorted  list */
     printf("\n");
     quick_sort(a,0,9);
     printf("\nThe Final Sorted List\n");
     print_list(a,10);/* prints the sorted list */
}

void quick_sort(int x[],int m, int n)
{ /* returns a sorted list */
     int  i, j,k;
     if(m<n)
     {
          i=m;j=n+1;k=x[m]; /* k is the partitioning element */
          do
          {
               do
                    i++;
               while((x[i]<k)&&(i<=n));
               do
                    j–;
               while(x[j]>k);
               if(i<j)
                    swap(&x[i],&x[j]);
```

```
        } while(i<j);
        swap(&x[m],&x[j]);
        print_list(x,10);
        quick_sort(x,m,j-1);
        quick_sort(x,j+1,n);
    }
}
void print_list(int y[],int n)
{
    int i;
    for(i=0;i<n;i++)
        printf("%5d",y[i]);
    printf("\n");
}
void swap(int *a, int *b)
{
    int  t;
    t=*a;
    *a=*b;
    *b=t;
}
```

```
The Given List
   26    5   37    1   61   11   59   15   48   19

11    5   19    1   15   26   59   61   48   37
1    5   11   19   15   26   59   61   48   37
1    5   11   19   15   26   59   61   48   37
1    5   11   15   19   26   59   61   48   37
1    5   11   15   19   26   48   37   59   61
1    5   11   15   19   26   37   48   59   61

The Final Sorted List
   1    5   11   15   19   26   37   48   59   61
```

Program Listing 7.7 Quick Sort

At Lines 18 to 40,

```
void quick_sort(int x[],int m, int n)
{ /* returns a sorted list */
     int  i, j,k;
     if(m<n)
     {
          i=m;j=n+1;k=x[m]; /* k is the partitioning element */
          do
          {
               do
                    i++;
               while((x[i]<k)&&(i<=n));
               do
               j--;
               while(x[j]>k);
               if(i<j)
                    swap(&x[i],&x[j]);
          } while(i<j);
          swap(&x[m],&x[j]);
          print_list(x,10);
          quick_sort(x,m,j-1);
          quick_sort(x,j+1,n);
     }
}
```

the quick_sort routine is presented. The quick_sort routine is a recursive routine. So the routine must always start with the base condition (m < n). Line 21 ensures that the sub-sequence is at least of size 2 otherwise the recursion is terminated. The outer do-while loop together with the two inner do-while loops will partition the sub-sequence into two halves. The first half being less than or equal to the pivot and the other one greater than or equal to pivot. The condition i < j is to ensure that the partition is complete. Notice that while i < j, we swap the elements x[i] with x[j], thus collecting all elements less than the pivot on to one side (L) and all the elements greater than the pivot to the other side (G). At Line 35, the swap routine is called to move the pivot to the right place. The two groups are ready at this point and at lines 37 & 38, quick_sort is called recursively with the two groups (L & G).

The average running time of a quick sort algorithm under the assumption that each element of the sequence has an equal chance of being selected as a pivot is O(n log n).

7.9 MERGE SORT

The last sorting algorithm we consider is, the two-way merge sort. Merging is combinig two or more sorted sequence into a single sorted sequence. In a two-way merge, two sorted sequences are merged into one. Sorting by merging is a recursive, divide and conquer strategy (like quick sort). In the base case, we have a sequence with exactly one element in it. Since such a sequence is already sorted, there is nothing to be done. To sort a sequence of n > 1 elements,

1. *divide the sequence into two sequences of length* $\lfloor n/2 \rfloor$ *and* $\lceil n/2 \rceil$*;*
2. *recursively sort each of the two subsequences; and then,*
3. *merge the sorted subsequences to obtain the final result.*

Let us now look at an example. The input file {26, 5, 77, 1, 61, 11, 59, 15, 48, 19} is to be sorted using the recursive formulation of two-way merge sort. If the sub file from low to high is currently to be sorted then its two sub files are indexed from low to mid and from mid + 1 to high (where mid = (low + high)/2). The sub file partitioning that takes place is described by the binary tree of Fig. 7.2.

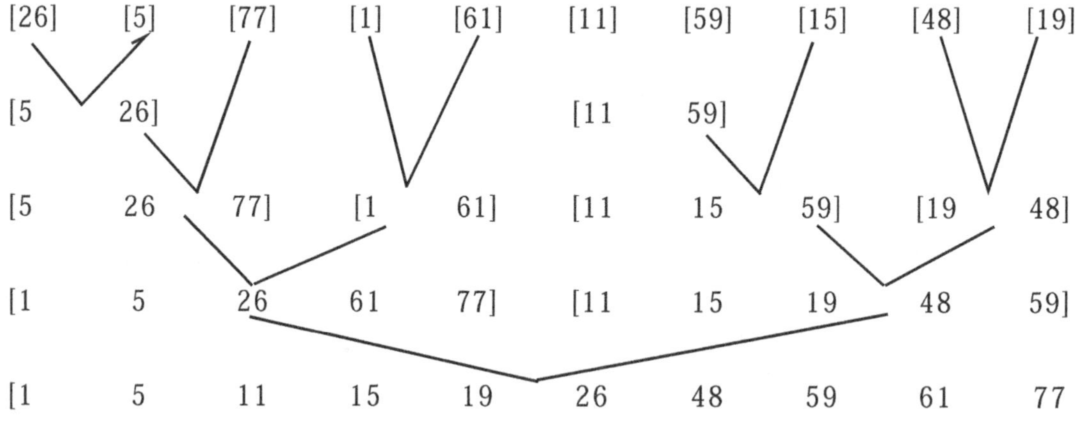
[26] [5] [77] [1] [61] [11] [59] [15] [48] [19]
[5 26] [11 59]
[5 26 77] [1 61] [11 15 59] [19 48]
[1 5 26 61 77] [11 15 19 48 59]
[1 5 11 15 19 26 48 59 61 77

Fig. 7.2 Merge Sort

From the preceding example, we may draw the following conclusion. If algorithm merge (merge routine of the program listing 7.8) is used to merge sorted sub files contained in one array, then it is necessary to copy the merging elements into an auxiliary array as inplace merge is not possible. For example to merge [5, 26, 77] and [1,61], we have to copy [1, 5, 26, 61, 77] in that order into an auxiliary array and copy them back to the original array. Notice the merge routine of program listing 7.8.

```
/* Program Listing 7.8 :  merge.c
/* A program for Merge Sorting       */

#include <stdio.h>
/* to sort the set of numbers using insertion sort*/
     void merg_sort(int [],int,int);
     void print_list(int [],int);
     void merge(int *, int, int,int);

void main(void)
{
     int a[] = {26,5,77,1,61,11,59,15,48,19};
     printf("\nThe Given List\n");
     print_list(a,10);/* prints the un-sorted  list */
     printf("\n");
     merg_sort(a,0,9);
     printf("\nThe Final Sorted List\n");
     print_list(a,10);/* prints the sorted list */
}

void merg_sort(int x[],int low,int high)
{ /* returns a sorted list */
     int mid;
     if(low<high)
     {
          mid=(high+low)/2;
          merg_sort(x,low,mid);
          merg_sort(x,mid+1,high);
          merge(x,low,mid,high);
     }
}
```

```
void print_list(int y[],int n)
{
      int i;
      for(i=0;i<n;i++)
            printf("%5d",y[i]);
      printf("\n");
}
void merge(int *a,int l,int m, int h)
{
      int b[50];
      int i,j,k;
      i=l;
      j=m+1;
      k=l;
      while(i<=m && j<=h)
            if(a[i] <= a[j])
                  b[k++]=a[i++];
            else
                  b[k++]=a[j++];
      while(i<=m)
            b[k++]=a[i++];
      while(j<=h)
            b[k++]=a[j++];
      for(k=l;k<=h;k++)
            a[k]=b[k];
}
```

```
The Given List
   26    5   77    1   61   11   59   15   48   19

5   26   77    1   61   11   59   15   48   19
5   26   77    1   61   11   59   15   48   19
5   26   77    1   61   11   59   15   48   19
1    5   26   61   77   11   59   15   48   19
1    5   26   61   77   11   59   15   48   19
1    5   26   61   77   11   15   59   48   19
```

```
1    5    26   61   77   11   15   59   19   48
1    5    26   61   77   11   15   19   48   59
1    5    11   15   19   26   48   59   61   77

The Final Sorted List
1    5    11   15   19   26   48   59   61   77
```

Program Listing 7.9 Merge Sorting

From Lines 36 to 54,

```
void merge(int *a,int l,int m, int h)
{
      int b[50];
      int i,j,k;
      i=l;
      j=m+1;
      k=l;
      while(i<=m && j<=h)
            if(a[i] <= a[j])
                  b[k++]=a[i++];
            else
                  b[k++]=a[j++];
      while(i<=m)
            b[k++]=a[i++];
      while(j<=h)
            b[k++]=a[j++];
      for(k=l;k<=h;k++)
            a[k]=b[k];
}
```

the merge routine, contains the declaration of an auxiliary array b, which is used for merge purpose. Notice at the end of the routine the elements that are merged, i.e., elements between l and h are copied back from b to a. The average time complexity for merge sort is O(n log n).

Table 7.1 summarizes the various sorting algorithms in terms of their time complexities.

Sorting Technique	Case	Time Complexity
Selection Sort	Average	$O(n^2)$
	Worst	$O(n^2)$
Bubble Sort	Average	$O(n^2)$
	Worst	$O(n^2)$
Insertion Sort	Average	$O(n^2)$
	Worst	$O(n^2)$
Merge Sort	Average	$O(n \log n)$
	Worst	$O(n \log n)$
Quick Sort	Average	$O(n \log n)$
	Worst	$O(n^2)$
Heap Sort	Average	$O(n \log n)$
	Worst	$O(n \log n)$

MORE EXAMPLES

1. Write a program sort the array elements using RADIX Sort Method.

```
/*----------------------------------------------------------------------------------------------------
        Elements of array are stored in a linked list and sorted as follows:

        Ten pockets corresponding to ten digits ( 0-9 ) are represented as
        linked FIFO Queues. On the first pass, ascending order sort is
        performed on the unit digit portion of each number. The numbers
        containing a given digit are placed in the appropriate queues. At
        the end of the pass these queues are combined in the proper order.
        On the second pass, sort is performed on the ten's digit portion of
        each number and so on.... If the maximum number in the given list
        of numbers is m, then m successive passes, from the unit digit to the
        most significant digit, are required in order to sort the list of numbers.
----------------------------------------------------------------------------------------------------*/

#include <stdio.h>
#include <malloc.h>
#define NULL 0
```

```
    struct list_element
    {
        int info;
        struct list_element *next;
    };
    typedef struct list_element node;
    node *first;
    node *bot[10], *top[10];
create(node *record)
{
    int num;
    printf("\nEnter -999 to Stop.\n");
    scanf("%d", &record->info);
    if(record->info == -999)
    {
        record->next = NULL;
        return;
    }
    else
    {
            record->next = (node *)malloc(sizeof(node));
        create(record->next);
    }
    return;
}
display(node *record)
{
    if(record != NULL)
    {
        if(record->info != -999)
        {
            printf("%8d", record->info);
            display(record->next);
        }
    }
    return;
}
```

```
int large(node *record)
{
      node *save;
      int p = 0;
      save = record;
      while(save->next != NULL)
      {
            if(save->info > p)
                  p = save->info;
            save = save->next;
      }
      printf("\n\nLargest Element in the List is: %d\n", p);
      return(p);
}
int numdig(int large)
{
      int temp, num = 0;
      temp = large;
      while(temp != 0)
      {
            ++num;
            temp = temp/10;
      }
      return(num);
}
int digit(int num, int j)
{
      int i, dig, temp;
      temp = num;
      for(i = 0;i < j;i++)
      {
            dig = temp % 10;
            temp = temp/10;
      }
      return(dig);
}
```

```
update(int dig, node *r)
{
      int i;
      if(top[dig] == NULL)
      {
            top[dig] = r;
            bot[dig] = r;
      }
      else
      {
            top[dig]->next = r;
            top[dig] = r;
      }
      r->next = NULL;
      return;
}
node *link(int poc, node *record)
{
      node *pr;
      int i;
      record = bot[poc];
      for(i = poc + 1;i < 10;i++)
      {
            pr = top[i - 1];
            if(top[i] != NULL)
                  pr->next = bot[i];
            else
                  top[i] = pr;
      }
      return(record);
}
node *radix(node *record)
{
      int lar, m, i, j, k, dig, poc;
      node *nex, *r, *prev;
      lar = large(record);
      m = numdig(lar);
```

```
        for(k = 0;k < 10;k++)
        {
              top[k] = (node *)malloc(9 * sizeof(node));
              bot[k] = (node *)malloc(9 * sizeof(node));
        }
        for(j = 1;j <= m;j++)
        {
              for(i = 0;i < 10;i++)
              {
                    top[i] = NULL;
                    bot[i] = NULL;
              }
              r = record;
              while(r->next != NULL)
              {
                    dig = digit(r->info, j);
                    nex = r->next;
                    update(dig, r);
                    r = nex;
              }
              if(r->info != -999)
              {
                    dig = digit(r->info, j);
                    update(dig, r);
              }
              poc = 0;
              while(bot[poc] == NULL)
                    poc++;
              record = link(poc, record);
        }
          return(record);
}
void main(void)
{
      node *start, *ptr;
      printf("\nEnter the Elements of the List.\n");
      start = (node *)malloc(sizeof(node));
      create(start);
```

```
        printf("\nThe Given List is:\n");
        display(start);
        first = start;
        start = radix(start);
        printf("\nRadix Sorted List is:\n");
        display(start);
}
OUTPUT:
        Enter the Elements of the List.
        Enter -999 to Stop. 345
        Enter -999 to Stop. 12
        Enter -999 to Stop. 4712
        Enter -999 to Stop. 96000
        Enter -999 to Stop. 1
        Enter -999 to Stop. 472
        Enter -999 to Stop. 46
        Enter -999 to Stop. 100000
        Enter -999 to Stop. 2565
        Enter -999 to Stop. 8
        Enter -999 to Stop. -999
        The Given List is:
        345   12   4712    96000   1    472    46   100000    2565    8
        Largest Element in the List is: 100000
        Radix Sorted List is:
        1  8  12   46   345   472   2565    4712    96000   100000
```

E.50 Write a program sort the array elements using RADIX Sort Method.

/*--

Shell Sort is a modification of Insertion Sort. The original array is divided into subfiles and sorted by the following technique:

A Particular Relation is considered to generate a sequence of increments. These increments decrease on successive passes. An increment of 'one' in the final pass will be Insertion Sort. Assume that starting increment is 5, then the subfile is made up of elements 1, 6, 11, 16, 21, ... < n (n is the size of the array). This subfile is sorted by swapping elements. Once this subfile is sorted, the next increment is taken and the subfile got from this is again sorted, till in the final pass the increment will be a 'one'.

--*/

```
#include <stdio.h>
shell(int b[100], int n)
{
      int i, j, inc, temp;
      inc = 1;
      while(inc <= n)
            inc = inc * 3 + 1;
      do
      {
            inc /= 3;
            i = inc + 1;
            printf("\nIncrement is %d\n", inc);
printf("\nElements at a distance %d are swapped if necessary.\n", inc);
            while(i <= n)
            {
                  temp = b[i];
                  j = i;
                  while((b[j - inc]) > temp)
                  {
                        printf("\nSwapping %d and %d", temp, b[j - inc]);
                        b[j] = b[j - inc];
                        j = j - inc;
                        if(j <= inc)
                                          break;
                  }
                  b[j] = temp;
                  i++;
            }
            printf("\nArray at End of pass:\n");
            for(j = 1;j <= n;j++)
                  printf("%8d", b[j]);
            printf("\n");
      }
      while(inc != 1);
      return;
}
```

```
void main(void)
{
     int a[110], i, n;
     printf("\nEnter the size of an Array.\n");
     scanf("%d", &n);
     for(i = 1;i <= n;i++)
     {
          printf("Enter the Elements in the Array at %d location.", i);
          scanf("%d", &a[i]);
     }
     printf("\nElements in the Array are:\n");
     for(i = 1;i <= n;i++)
     {
          printf("%8d", a[i]);
     }
     shell(a, n);
     printf("\nArray Elements after Shell Sorting:\n");
     for(i = 1;i <= n;i++)
     {
          printf("%8d", a[i]);
     }
}
```

OUTPUT:

```
     Enter the size of an Array. 10
     Enter the Elements in the Array at 1 location. 23
     Enter the Elements in the Array at 2 location. 45
     Enter the Elements in the Array at 3 location. 10
     Enter the Elements in the Array at 4 location. 9
     Enter the Elements in the Array at 5 location. 8
     Enter the Elements in the Array at 6 location. 56
     Enter the Elements in the Array at 7 location. 99
     Enter the Elements in the Array at 8 location. 22
     Enter the Elements in the Array at 9 location. 19
     Enter the Elements in the Array at 10 location.66
     Elements in the Array are:
23     45     10     9     8     56     99     22     19     66
     Increment is 4
     Elements at a distance 4 are swapped if necessary.
```

```
          Swapping 8 and 23
          Swapping 19 and 23
          Array at End of pass:
8         45      10      9       19      56      99      22      23      66
          Increment is 1
          Elements at a distance 1 are swapped if necessary.
          Swapping 10 and 45
          Swapping 9 and 45
          Swapping 9 and 10
          Swapping 19 and 45
          Swapping 22 and 99
          Swapping 22 and 56
          Swapping 22 and 45
          Swapping 23 and 99
          Swapping 23 and 56
          Swapping 23 and 45
          Swapping 66 and 99
          Array at End of pass:
8         9       10      19      22      23      45      56      66      99
          Array Elements after Shell Sorting:
8         9       10      19      22      23      45      56      66      99
```

SELF-REVIEW EXERCISES

1. .... is the worst case time complexity of linear search among n elements.
2. .... is the worst case time complexity of binary search among n elements.
3. The sorting algorithms can be classified into .... number of categories.
4. The worst case time complexity of bubble sort to sort n elements is ....
5. The worst case time complexity of quick sort to sort n elements is ....
6. The average and worst case time complexity of heap sort to sort n elements is ....
7. The average time complexity of Quick sort to sort n elements is ....
8. Quick sort comes under .... category of sorts.
9. Heap sort comes under .... category of sorts
10. The best case time complexity of an insertion sort is ....

State True or False

1. Bubble sort is an example of exchange sort.
2. The number of swaps in a bubble sort are far less than that of a selection sort.
3. In merge sort the merging operation is done using an auxilary array
4. One of the examples for Sort by distribution is Radix Sort.
5. Binary search can be used on an unsorted list.

EXERCISES

1. Write a recursive routine for terinary search algorithm which divides the elements into three parts unlike the binary search which divides into two parts.

2. For the above exercise write a non-recursive routine.

3. Work through algorithm binary search on an ordered file with keys {1, 2, 3, 4, 5, 6, 7, 8, 9, 10, 11, 12, 13, 14, 15, 16} and determine the number of key comparisions made while searching for the keys 2, 10 and 15.

4. A sorting algorithm is said to be unstable if it does not preserve the original order of records with equal key values. Suppose let r1 and r2 are two records in a file is sorted using each one of the sorting techniques which is stated in this chapter. Determine which of the string techniques are stable and which are not. Give sufficient reasoning for your conclusions.

5. Write the status of the F at the end of each iteration of the following :

   a. insertion sort

   b. quick sort

   c. heap sort

   F = { 20, 88, 32, 10, 35 56, 22, 90 }

8

Introduction to Data Structures

8.1 INTRODUCTION

We shall now present in this part of the book the basic data structures that are available in computer science to develop programs. In general, an effective computer program to solve a problem, can be developed, if a solution to the problem is conceived which is adoptable to a computer. Normally the solution to a problem is expressed as an algorithm. To translate an algorithm to a computer program, one needs an effective way to handle the data through designing proper data structure. Thus, developing the correct algorithm, to solve the problem and to choose an efficient data structures to implement the algorithm, could well computerize the solution to the problem. We shall deal with the efficiency of the algorithms/data structures at a later point of time in this chapter.

8.2 ABSTRACT DATATYPES

An useful data type for specifying the logical properties of a data type is the Abstract Data Type, or ADT. Fundamentally, a data type is a collection of values and a set of operations on those values. That collection and those operations form a mathematical construct that may be implemented using a particular hardware or software data structure.

The term Abstract Data Type refers to the basic mathematical concept that defines the data type. There are a number of methods for specifying an ADT. The advantage of such representation is to make clear the properties and operations of an abstract data type. For a formal mathematical description of ADT, you may refer to books listed in bibliography.

Several problems in computer science are solved using abstract data types like lists, queues, stacks, ... etc. In a simple way let us think that we want to multiply two matrices. We imagine the matrix as an ADT which could be described with its properties & operations. It is easy to conceive an algorithm that multiplies two matrices and get the result.

However, to translate this algorithm, into a computer program, the matrix must be represented within a computer program using the constructs (the basic data types of the language) in which the program is written. One way to represent a matrix which we have already seen in C programming is to choose two dimensional array. However, there could be other ways of representing a matrix. May be always the two dimensional array may not be efficient to represent a matrix, for example, sparse matrix (a large matrix where many elements are zeroes). We will present a number of examples of abstract data types as we go through with the various topics of Data Structures. However, the mathematical model of the ADT which defines the properties & operations is the key to select a proper data structure.

8.3 A SIMPLE EXAMPLE – POLYNOMIAL ADDITION

Let us straight away take up a problem that calls for a set of sub routines, which allow the manipulation of polynomials. For a mathematician, a polynomial is a sum of terms, where each term has the form ax^i where x is the variable a is coefficient and i is the exponent Two polynomials are shown below

$$A(x) = 5x^2 + 2x + 10$$

$$B(x) = x^5 + 3x^4 - 2x^3 + x^2 - 10x + 23$$

There are number of mathematical operations possible with polynomials. To start with we will consider only the basic arithmetic operations addition, subtraction, multiplication and division. The mathematical procedure for adding two polynomials is to add the coefficients of the terms with same exponents and obtain the results. For example, adding the above two polynomials A(x) and B(y) we get, $x^5 + 3x^4 - 2x^3 + 6x^2 - 8x + 33$. To be able to computerize this procedure, adding two polynomials, we have to find a way in which we can represent a polynomial.

One way to represent a polynomial is to declare an array of size MAXDEGREE, where MAXDEGREE is one more than the highest exponent in the polynomial. For example, to store B(x), we may need an array of size 6. We will store only the coefficients, at the respective locations, like the 0th location contain the constant term, 1st location will contain the coefficient of x, so on. If we represent the two polynomials A(x) and B(x) using two arrays A and B, we can obtain the sum by adding the corresponding elements of A and B and storing the sum in C. This "Symbolic" representation of a polynomial yields simple algorithms for various arithmetic operations on polynomials. However, consider the following polynomial.

$$C(x) = 2.5x^{100} + 2.3x^{13} - 3x$$

To represent the above polynomial, we need an array of size 101 in which most of the locations will be filled with zeroes. We quickly realize that, when we have to handle polynomials of this type, our earlier representation is not efficient. We should think of only storing the coefficients of non-zero terms, and not all terms with exponents 0 to MAXDEGREE. A better way is to store the exponent and coefficient together for all non-zero terms. We shall do this in C by declaring a structure like poly.

```
struct poly {
        int exp;
        float coef;
};
```

A polynomial can be represented using an array of above structure at most of size equal to the number of non-zero terms of the polynomial. This avoids storing lot of zeroes in the polynomials of the type C(x). With this representation, of polynomials let us now present a C program in the program listing 8.1, that adds two polynomials.

```
/* Program Listing 8.1 :  ADDPOLY.c
A Program to add Two Polynomials   */

#include <stdio.h>
struct poly{
        int exp;
        float coef;
};
void print_poly(struct poly [], int );
int poly_add(struct poly [],struct poly [],struct poly [],int ,int );
```

```
void main(void)
{
     int i;
     struct poly x[]={{10,2.0},{7,3.2},{2,-2.25}};
     /* 2.0x^10 + 3.2x^7 - 2.25x^2  */
     struct poly y[]={{17,-2.0},{12,3.2},{2,3.25},{0,-7.67}};
     /* -2.0x^17 + 3.2x^12 + 3.5x^2 - 7.67 */
     struct poly z[20];
     printf("X= ");
     print_poly(x,3);
     printf("Y= ");
     print_poly(y,4);
     i=poly_add(x,y,z,3,4);
     printf("Z= ");
     print_poly(z,i);
}
void print_poly(struct poly a[], int n){
     int i;
     for(i=0;i<n;i++) printf("(%d,%0.2f) ",a[i].exp,a[i].coef);
     printf("\n");
}
int poly_add(struct poly a[],struct poly b[],struct poly c[],int
               n1,int n2)
{
     int i,j,k;
     i=j=k=0;
     while((i<n1)&&(j<n2))
          if(a[i].exp==b[j].exp)
          {
               c[k].exp=a[i].exp;
               c[k++].coef=a[i++].coef+b[j++].coef;
          }
          else if(a[i].exp>b[j].exp)
          {
               c[k].exp=a[i].exp;
               c[k++].coef=a[i++].coef;
          }
```

```
40.             else
41.             {
42.                   c[k].exp=b[j].exp;
43.                   c[k++].coef=b[j++].coef;
44.             }
45.       while(i<n1)
46.       {
47.             c[k].exp=a[i].exp;
48.             c[k++].coef=a[i++].coef;
49.       }
50.       while(j<n2)
51.       {
52.             c[k].exp=b[j].exp;
53.             c[k++].coef=b[j++].coef;
54.       }
55.       return k;
56. }
```

```
X = (10, 2.0) (7, 3.20) (2, -2.25)
Y = (17, -2.0) (12, 3.20) (2, 3.25) (0, -7.67)
Z = (17, -2.0) (12, 3.20) (10, 2.0) (7, 3.20) (2, 1.00) (0, -7.67)
```

Program Listing 8.1 *Program to add two polynomial*

At Line 2 to 5,

```
struct poly{
      int exp;
      float coef;
};
```

the structure poly is declared with two members int exp and float coef, to store exponent and the corresponding the coefficient. At Line 10 and 11,

```
int i;
struct poly x[]={{10,2.0},{7,3.2},{2,-2.25}};
/* 2.0x^10 + 3.2x^7 - 2.25x^2  */
struct poly y[]={{17,-2.0},{12,3.2},{2,3.25},{0,-7.67}};
/* -2.0x^17 + 3.2x^12 + 3.5x^2 - 7.67 */
struct poly z[20];
```

we have declared and initialized two polynomials. Notice that we have stored the coefficients and the exponents of the corresponding non-zero terms of the polynomial in the decreasing order of the coefficients since index of the array does not bare any relationship to the exponent, unlike in the previously proposed representation. This is more convenient to handle the polynomial, as the program starts adding from the highest degree. For convenience, we have initialized the arrays with the polynomials. However a routine can be added which would interactively accept, these polynomials from the user. In such a routine, the user need to input coefficient-exponent pairs of non-zero terms of the polynomials. At Line 20 to 24,

```
void print_poly(struct poly a[], int n){
     int i;
     for(i=0;i<n;i++) printf("(%d,%0.2f) ",a[i].exp,a[i].coef);
     printf("\n");
}
```

the function print_poly takes the array of structure poly and the number of terms in the polynomial as arguments, and prints the pairs of exponent and corresponding coefficient, which is symbolic representation of a polynomial. At Line 16,

```
i=poly_add(x,y,z,3,4);
```

the function poly_add is called by passing x, y, z and the number of terms of x and y. The routine poly_add computes the sum of the polynomials in x and y and stores the result in z. Note that all the three address are passed along with the number of terms in x and y. poly_add returns the number of terms in z, which may not be equal to n1 + n2. The function poly_add declares three variables i, j, k to run through, the three polynomials a, b, c respectively. At Line 29,

```
while((i<n1)&&(j<n2))
```

the while loop is entered until you reach the end of at least one of the polynomials. At Line 30,

```
if(a[i].exp==b[j].exp)
```

observe the if else statement where three cases are considered. Note that both the polynomials are ordered lists. An ordered list is a list in which there exists an order among the elements stored. In this, example, we call the polynomial, an ordered list since, the exponent and coefficient pairs are stored, in non-increasing order of the exponents. Now let us present the three cases.

Case 1: is when the exponent of the current term of the first polynomial i.e., a[i].exp == b[j].exp. The corresponding action in this case would be to add both the coefficients (a[i].coef + b[j].coef) and store the result in c[k].coef. The exponent c[k].exp can either be a[i].exp or b[j].exp. i, j and k are all incremented.

Case 2: where a[i].exp > b[j].exp then evidently, we should copy a[i].coef to a[k].coef and a[i].exp to a[k].exp and increment i and k only.

Case 3: is the else part, where b[j].exp > a[i].exp, in which case, b[j].coef is copied into c[k].coef and b[j].exp is copied to c[k].exp and j and k are increment.

At Line 45 and 50,

```
while(i<n1)
while(j<n2)
```

the two while loops are necessary to take care of the case of polynomial that does not end first. The student should note that it is possible for one of the polynomials to end early, if it does not contain the lower order terms.

Time & Space Complexity of an Algorithm

After going through the above program, the student should understand that the following steps are adopted in writing a computer program for adding 2 polynomials.

1. *We have conceived a solution to problem of adding two polynomials.*
2. *We chose an efficient data structure to represent a polynomial in a computer program.*
3. *We designed addition of the polynomial, based on our data structures that represented a polynomial.*

The next thing that a student should investigate is how efficient is our poly_add ? Are there any more effective representation of polynomials that might lead to a more efficient poly_add routine? In computer science, this is known as analyzing your program (or algorithm). We shall now present a few ideas as to how a program/algorithm can be analyzed. Generally, there are three different types of analysis that one can perform on an algorithm/program. They are,

1. ***Correctness of an algorithm*** – *Does the algorithm work correctly according to the original specification of the task/problem.*
2. ***The time complexity of an algorithm*** – *How fast the algorithm executes.*
3. ***Space Complexity*** – *How much memory space the algorithm needs to execute.*

In this section, we shall concentrate only on time complexity of an algorithm. Consider, the following C function that computes n^{th} fibinocii numbers, which is already discussed in Chapter 3.

```
1.   unsigned int fib(int n)
2.   {                          /* iterative  or non-recursive program */
3.        unsigned int fn,fnm1,fnm2,i;
4.        if( n<=0 ) return(0);
5.        if( n==1 ) return(1);
6.        fnm1=1; fnm2=0;
7.        for(i=2;i<=n;i++)
8.        {
9.             fn= fnm1+fnm2;
10.            fnm2=fnm1;
11.            fnm1=fn;
12.       }
13.       return fn;
14.  }
```

To analyze the time complexity of the above function, we need to consider the two cases.

Case 1 *The executable statements outside the for loop.*

Case 2 *The executable statements inside the for loop.*

We shall count the total number of statements of execution and use this as a measure to compute the time complexity of program. Further only executable statements; contribute to time complexity of the program. Thus, Lines 1, 2, & 3, donot add to the time needed to compute the fibonacii number. The braces only indicate the begin and end of a block and therefore, do not contribute to the time complexity. When $n > 1$ the for loop at lines 7 to 12 gets executed for $n - 1$ times. All the lines within this loop get executed. The total number of statements executed by the function to compute n^{th} fibonacci number is $4 * (n - 1) + 4 = 4n$. In general, the program of above nature, need to execute, $k_1 n + k_2$ statements, where k_1 and k_2 are some constants. We often write this as O(n) ignoring the two constants k1 and k2. This notation means that the order of magnitude is proportional to n. For a formal definition of O(n), the student is advised to refer the books listed in the bibliography. We say the computing time of O(g(n) we mean that its execution takes no more than a constant times g(n). n is a parameter which characterizes the inputs and/or outputs. For example n might be the number of inputs or the number of outputs, their sum or the magnitude of one of them.

We write O(1) to mean a computing time which is a constant (independent of the problem size). O(n) is called linear. $O(n^2)$ is called quadratic, $O(n^3)$ is called cubic., and $O(2^n)$ is called exponential. If an algorithm takes time O(log n) it is faster, for sufficiently large n, than if it had taken O(n). Similarly, O(n log n) is better than $O(n^2)$ but not as good as O(n). These seven computing times, O(1), O(log n), O(n), O(n log n), $O(n^2)$, $O(n^3)$ and $O(2^n)$ are the ones we will see most often throughout the book.

If we have two algorithms which perform the same task, and the first has a computing time which is O(n) and second O(n^2), then we will usually take the first as superior. The reason for this is, that as n increases the time for the second algorithm will get far worse than the time for the first.

Now let us analyze the computing time of the program we have written for the function poly_add. For convenience, the function poly_add is shown below.

```
int poly_add(struct poly a[],struct poly b[],struct poly c[],int
                n1,int n2)
{
int i,j,k;
i=j=k=0;
while((i<n1)&&(j<n2))
      if(a[i].exp==b[j].exp)
      {
            c[k].exp=a[i].exp;
            c[k++].coef=a[i++].coef+b[j++].coef;
         }
         else if(a[i].exp>b[j].exp)
         {
               c[k].exp=a[i].exp;
               c[k++].coef=a[i++].coef;
         }
         else
         {
               c[k].exp=b[j].exp;
               c[k++].coef=b[j++].coef;
         }
         while(i<n1)
         {
               c[k].exp=a[i].exp;
               c[k++].coef=a[i++].coef;
         }
         while(j<n2)
         {
               c[k].exp=b[j].exp;
               c[k++].coef=b[j++].coef;
         }
         return k;
   }
```

It is natural to carry out this analysis in terms of non-zero terms in polynomials a and b. Let n1 and n2 be the non-zero terms in a and b respectively. In the worst case the while loops will operate for a total of n1 + n2 times, the case where the exponents of a and b do not match at all. Therefore the worst case time complexity of our algorithm is O(n1 + n2). Under normal circumstances (many exponents of a and b may match) the algorithm can do much better than this. Obviously this algorithm falls in the category of linear time complexity, i.e., O(n) where n = n1 + n2, the total size of the problem. Any other algorithm / program that can add the two polynomials would be considered better if and only if the algorithm at least has an order better than O(n) (may be O(log n)).

8.4 STACKS

Instead of considering individual problems, we try to study about various data structures that are most commonly used in Computer Science. Let us start with a abstract data structure (ADT) **Stack**. Stack is an ordered list in which all insertions and deletions are made at one end called the top. The ordering of elements in the stack imply that, if the elements a, b, c, d and e are added to the stack, in that order then the first element to be removed or deleted must be e. Equivalently we say, that the last element inserted into the stack is the first one to be removed. For this reasons stack is sometimes referred as **Last In First Out** or **LIFO** lists (see Fig. 8.1).

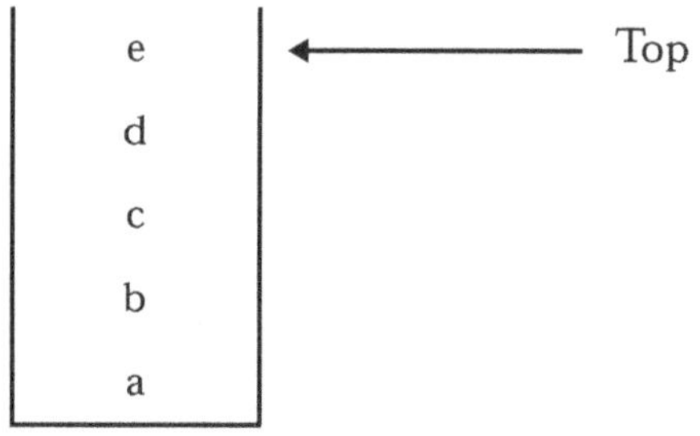
e
d
c
b
a
Top

Fig. 8.1 A Stack

A simple way to implement a stack is by using a one-dimensional array (stack[N]) of some size N, where N is the maximum number of allowable entries. The first or the bottom element in the stack will be stored at stack[0]. The second at stack[1] and so on and the ith at stack[i – 1]. This notation is very convenient since we implement these data structures in C and the indexing of an array starts from 0. Associated with the array will be variable top, which points to the top element in the stack. We shall now show how to implement a stack using an array and write procedures add_stack() (also known as push) and delete_stack() (also known as pop). The program is illustrated in Program Listing 8.2.

```
/* Program Listing 8.2 :  STACK.c
Illustration of operations on a Stacks  */
#include <stdio.h>
#include <conio.h>
#include <stdlib.h>
#define MAXSIZE 20
void print_stack(int [], int );
void add_stack(int [],int *,int );
int delete_stack(int [], int *);
void main(void)
{
    int stack[MAXSIZE], top=-1, i, k;
    clrscr();
    for(i = 1; i < 10; i++)
        add_stack(stack,&top,i);
    printf("\n");
    print_stack(stack,top);
    for(i = 1; i < 10; i++)
    {
        k = delete_stack(stack,&top);
        printf("%d ", k);
    }
}
void print_stack(int s[], int top)
{
    int i;
    for(i = 0;i <= top;i++) printf("%d ",s[i]);
    printf("\n");
}
void add_stack(int s[],int *top,int item)
{
    if(*top == MAXSIZE - 1)
        printf("\nStack Full. Not Adding %d", item);
```

```
35.         else
36.                 s[++*top]=item;
37.     }
38.     int delete_stack(int s[], int *top)
39.     {
40.         if(top < 0)
41.         {
42.                 printf("\nStack Empty.");
43.                 return -1;
44.         }
45.         return s[(*top)–];
46.     }
```

```
1 2 3 4 5 6 7 8 9
9 8 7 6 5 4 3 2 1
```

Program Listing 8.2 Illustration of operations on a Stack

At Line 13,

```
int stack[MAXSIZE], top=-1, i, k;
```

the stack is declared as an array of integers of MAXSIZE. The integer variable top is initialized to –1, which indicates an empty stack. Since the array indexing in C starts with 0, we have initialized top to –1. At Line 16,

```
add_stack(stack,&top,i);
```

the function add_stack is called in a for loop with 3 arguments. The first is the address of the array stack, the second is the address of the top and the third is the item to be pushed on to the stack. At Line 33,

```
if(*top == MAXSIZE - 1)
```

add_stack function tests for the stack full by comparing top with MAXSIZE – 1. Notice that in case the stack is full, it does not insert the element and simply returns back printing an error message ***Stack Full. Not Adding.*** At Line 36,

```
s[++*top]=item;
```

in the else part of the if statement (when the stack is not full), the element is added to the location one more than the current top. Notice that no parenthesis is needed around *top since the indirection or (dereferencing) operator * and the increment operator ++ have the same order of precedence and are evaluated right to left (Refer to the Table 2.8 in Chapter 2). The reason for passing the top as a pointer to the function add_stack, is to affect the change in the value of the top (when an element is added) in the main(). At Line 21,

```
k = delete_stack(stack,&top);
```

the function delete_stack is called in a for loop with two arguments. The first one is the stack and the second is the address of the top. At Line 40,

```
if(top < 0)
```

the function delete_stack, checks for empty stack. If the stack is empty, prints the error message ***Stack Empty*** and returns –1 and exits. At Line 45,

```
return s[(*top)--];
```

if the stack is not empty, it returns the element pointed by the current top and the top is decremented. Notice that a parenthesis is needed around *top, since the redirection operator and –– have the same precedence. If the parentheses are eliminated, the value of top will not be decremented. At Line 18,

```
print_stack(stack,top);
```

the print_stack routine is called. This routine prints the content of the stack from bottom to top. Usually stack may be holding just not integers. Most of the practical implementations require stack to be declared as an array of structures, each structure holding the composite information that is to be put on to the stack.

8.5 STACKS & DYNAMIC MEMORY ALLOCATION

In the stack implementation of Program Listing 8.2, the add_stack routine will not add an element if the stack is full. Now the question is, can we continue adding elements to the stack, inspite of the stack full condition is encountered. The answer is YES. In C we can manage a dynamic memory allocation which allows us to increase the size of the array dynamically. Let us look into a new version of the previous program that uses dynamic memory allocation in Program Listing 8.3.

```
/* Program Listing 8.3 :  STACK1.c
Illustrates Stacks and Dynamic Memory Allocation   */
#include <stdio.h>
#include <conio.h>
#include <stdlib.h>

#define MAXSIZE 15

typedef int *stack;

```

```
void print_stack(stack, int );
void add_stack(stack,int *,int );
int delete_stack(stack, int *);

void main(void)
{
      stack s;
      int top = -1, i, k;
      clrscr();
      s = (stack)calloc(MAXSIZE,sizeof(int));
      for(i = 1;i < 20;i++)
      add_stack(s, &top, i);
      printf("\n");
      print_stack(s,top);
      for(i = 1;i < 20;i++)
      {
            k = delete_stack(s, &top);
            printf("%d ", k);
      }
}
void print_stack(stack s, int top)
{
      int i;
      for(i = 0;i <= top;i++)
            printf("%d ",s[i]);
      printf("\n");
}
void add_stack(stack s, int *top, int item)
{
      static int size = MAXSIZE;
      if(*top == size - 1){
            print_stack(s, *top);
            fprintf(stderr, "\nReallocation Made\n");
            printf("\nSize before Reallocation = %d", size);
            size += MAXSIZE;
            s = (stack)realloc(s, size);
            printf("\nSize After Reallocation = %d", size);
      }
```

```
47.          s[++*top] = item;
48.     }
49.     int delete_stack(stack s, int *top)
50.     {
51.          if(*top < 0)
52.          {
53.               printf("\nStack Empty.");
54.               return -1;
55.          }
56.          return s[(*top)--];
57.     }
```

```
1 2 3 4 5 6 7 8 9 10 11 12 13 14 15
Reallocation Made
Size before Reallocation = 15
Size after Reallocation = 30
1 2 3 4 5 6 7 8 9 10 11 12 13 14 15 16 17 18 19
19 18 17 16 15 14 13 12 11 10 9 8 7 6 5 4 3 2 1
```

Program Listing 8.3 Illustrates Stacks and Dynamic Memory Allocation

At Line 7,

```
typedef int *stack;
```

the typedef statements renames int * as stack. Where ever stack is used, the compiler replaces it with int *. This is done to improve the readability of the program. At Line 15,

```
stack s;
```

declares s as an int *. At Line 18,

```
s = (stack)calloc(MAXSIZE,sizeof(int));
```

we have used the function, calloc() that allocates memory dynamically for what ever size we wanted. You should note the difference between the static allocation, which has been done in the earlier program, and the dynamic allocation using calloc(). In C, there are four important functions for dynamic memory management. The following is the syntax and the use of the four functions.

1. **void *calloc(size_t nobj, size_t size)**

calloc() returns a pointer to space for an array of nobj objects, each of size **size** or NULL if the request cannot be satisfied. The space is initialized to zero bytes. size_t is defined in stdio.h as unsigned int.

2. **void *malloc(size_t size)**

malloc() returns a pointer to space for an object of size size, or NULL if the request cannot be satisfied. The space is uninitialized.

3. **void *realloc(void *p, size_t size)**

realloc() changes the size of the object pointed by p to size. The contents will be unchanged up to the minimum of the old and new sizes. If the new size is larger, the new space is uninitialized. realloc() returns a pointer to the new space, or NULL if the request cannot be satisfied, in which case *p is unchanged.

4. **void free(void *p)**

free deallocates the space pointed to by p. It does nothing if p is NULL. p must be a pointer to space previously allocated by calloc(), malloc(), realloc().

In our program we shall make use of calloc() to get space allocated during runtime for an array of objects (here integers). Note that calloc returns a pointer to void. Let us explain, what we mean by this. In C a void pointer is used when we are not sure of, what object pointer the function is going to return. We can always cast the void pointer with a pointer of our choice.

At Line 18, we have called calloc with two parameters. The first one is the MAXSIZE, which is the size of an array we need, the second one is the ***sizeof(int)***, since we want here an array of integers. Note that size_t is type defined in stdio.h as unsigned. This is to prevent any negative number passed here in_advertantly. The function is type casted with stack i.e., int *. Hence, s will contain the starting address of dynamically allocated integer array of size MAXSIZE. We will now discuss add_stack routine where, we now try to tackle the stack full condition. In the earlier program the routine add_stack simply printed the error message and returned when the stack is full. At Lines 39 to 46,

```
if(*top == size - 1){
      print_stack(s, *top);
      fprintf(stderr, "\nReallocation Made\n");
      printf("\nSize before Reallocation = %d", size);
      size += MAXSIZE;
      s = (stack)realloc(s, size);
      printf("\nSize After Reallocation = %d", size);
}
```

observe how the stack full situation is handled. We use a function realloc to double the size of an array pointed by s and the return pointer we have assigned to s, since realloc may make a all together a fresh allocation in the memory. The variable size is declared as static in the function in order to retain its value across different calls to add_stack. Every time ***reaclloc()*** is called for additional space, the additional space is increased by MAXSIZE. The printf and print_stack statements in the if statement, helps the student to understand clearly what happens when a stack is full. Observe the output of the program carefully. We shall use malloc and free later on.

The function realloc may be used only once to increase the size rather than repeatedly. Mostly the memory allocation functions are implementation dependent. A better version of dynamic memory allocation, restricting the use of realloc only once is given in Program Listing 8.4.

```
/* Program Listing 8.4 :  STACK2.c
Illustrates Stacks and Dynamic Memory Allocation   */
#include <stdio.h>
#include <conio.h>
#include <stdlib.h>
#define MAXSIZE 10
typedef int *stack;
void print_stack();
void add_stack(int);
int delete_stack();
stack s;
int top=-1;
void main(void)
{
      int i, k;
      clrscr();
      s = (stack)calloc(MAXSIZE,sizeof(int));
      if(s==NULL)
      {
            printf("NO Allocation Possible\n");
            exit(1);
      }
```

```
        for(i = 1;i < 20;i++)
            add_stack(i);
        printf("\n");
        print_stack();
        for(i = 1;i < 20;i++)
        {
            k = delete_stack();
            printf("%d ", k);
        }
}
void print_stack()
{
        int i;
        for(i = 0;i <= top;i++)
            printf("%d ",s[i]);
        printf("\n");
}
void add_stack(int item)
{
        static int size = MAXSIZE;
        static int nrealloc=0;
        int ext_size;
        stack t;
        if(top < size-1)
            s[++top] = item;
        else if(!nrealloc){
            print_stack();
            fprintf(stderr, "\nReallocation beeing Made\n");
            printf("\nEnter the EXTRA SPACE NEEDED(not morethan
                  %d):",MAXSIZE);
            scanf("%d",&ext_size);
            size += ext_size;
            if((t=(stack)realloc(s,size))==NULL)
            {
                printf("NO Allocation Possible\n");
                exit(1);
            }
```

```
                nrealloc = 1;
                s[++top] = item;
                printf("\nSize After Reallocation = %d\n", size);
        }
        else
        {
                printf("STACK FULL NO MORE ALLOCATION POSSIBLE\n");
        }
}
int delete_stack()
{
        if(top < 0)
        {
        printf("\nFatal Error Trying to delete from Empty stack.");
                exit (1);
        }
        return s[top–];
}
```

```
1 2 3 4 5 6 7 8 9 10
Reallocation Made
Enter the EXTRA SPACE NEEDED(not morethan 10): 9
Size after Reallocation = 19
1 2 3 4 5 6 7 8 9 10 11 12 13 14 15 16 17 18 19
19 18 17 16 15 14 13 12 11 10 9 8 7 6 5 4 3 2 1
```

Program Listing 8.4 *An improved version of Dynamic Memory Allocation of Stacks*

Few more changes are made in this program. We chose the stack and top as the global variables avoiding passing these as the parameters to various functions. The student should note that the global variables are accessible to all the functions. This practice may not be desirable in larger programs. We have introduced another static variable, nrealloc which is initialized to zero. This variable will prevent in making use of the realloc for the second time. We are also allowing the user to interactively chose the extra space needed provided it is less than or equal to MAXSIZE. We have also changed delete stack routine. If an attempt is made to delete an empty stack the program is terminated prompting a fatal error. We have also incorporated in the program, testing of the pointers returned by calloc and realloc. If NULL is returned in either case, the program is terminated giving appropriate messages.

We can build a better routine stack_full to handle the overflow any number of times by using calloc function itself. The program is illustrated in Program Listing 8.5.

```
/* Program Listing 8.5 :  STACK3.c
Illustrates Stacks and Dynamic Memory Allocation   */
#include <stdio.h>
#include <conio.h>
#include <stdlib.h>

#define MAXSIZE 10

typedef int *stack;

void print_stack();
void add_stack(int );
int delete_stack();
void stack_full(int * );
stack s;
int top = -1;

void main(void)
{
      int i, k;
      clrscr();
      s = (stack)calloc(MAXSIZE,sizeof(int));
      if(s == NULL)
      {
            printf(“No Allocation Possible\n”);
            exit(0);
      }
      for(i = 1;i < 25;i++)
            add_stack(i);
      printf(“\n”);
      print_stack();
```

```
        for(i = 1;i < 25;i++)
        {
            k = delete_stack();
            printf("%d ", k);
        }
}
void print_stack()
{
        int i;
        for(i = 0;i <= top;i++)
            printf("%d ",s[i]);
        printf("\n");
}
void add_stack(int item)
{
        static int size = MAXSIZE;
        if(top == size - 1){
            print_stack();
            fprintf(stderr, "\nReallocation Made\n");
            printf("\nSize before Reallocation = %d", size);
            stack_full(&size);
            printf("\nSize After Reallocation = %d\n", size);
        }
        s[++top] = item;
}
int delete_stack()
{
        if(top < 0)
        {
        printf("\nFatal Error Trying to delete from Empty stack.");
            exit (1);
        }
        return s[top--];
}
```

```
64.  void stack_full(int *size)
65.  {
66.          stack t;
67.          int i, tsize;
68.          int isize;
69.          printf("\nEnter the Size to be allocated ...");
70.          scanf("%d", &isize);
71.          tsize = *size;
72.          *size += isize;
73.          t = (stack)calloc(*size, sizeof(int));
74.          if(t == NULL)
75.          {
76.                printf("No Allocation Possible\n");
77.                exit(0);
78.          }
79.          for(i = 0;i < tsize;i++)
80.          {
81.                t[i] = s[i];
82.          }
83.          free(s);
84.          s = t;
85.  }
```

```
1 2 3 4 5 6 7 8 9 10
Reallocation Made
Size before Reallocation = 10
Enter the Size to be allocated ...20
Size after Reallocation = 30
1 2 3 4 5 6 7 8 9 10 11 12 13 14 15 16 17 18 19 20 21 22 23 24
24 23 22 21 20 19 18 17 16 15 14 13 12 11 10 9 8 7 6 5 4 3 2 1
```

Program Listing 8.5 *STACK3.C*

In the routine stack_full, at Line 73,

```
t = (stack)calloc(*size, sizeof(int));
```

we are using calloc and asking for a fresh allocation of a required size of the stack. At Line 79,

```
for(i = 0;i < tsize;i++)
```

the for loop copies the elements of the old stack to new stack. At Line 83,

```
free(s);
```

we are also releasing the space of the old stack by using the function free, so that the space could be reused. Note that the old stack should be freed only after copying the elements of the old stack to the new stack. At Line 84,

```
s = t;
```

the value of s is replaced with the pointer to new stack, so that the other operations can be performed as usual.

8.6 EVALUATION OF EXPRESSIONS

An expression in a programming language such as C is made up of operators, operands and delimiters. Consider the following expression,

$$X = A/B*C+D*E$$

The above expression has 5 operands A, B, C, D and E. Though these are all oneletter variables, operands can be any legal variable name or constants permitted by C. In any expression the variables included must be consistent with operations performed on them. The operators describe these operations. In most programming languages, there are several kinds of operators, which correspond to different kinds of data, a variable can hold. To be simple, we shall only discuss expressions with the arithmetic operators *, /, +, –. The first problem in understanding the meaning of an expression is to decide in what order the operations to be carried out. Suppose, we take the values of A, B, C, D and E in the above expression as A = 4, B = C = 2, and D = E = 3 and evaluate the expression left to right operator by operator we get the following result.

$$X = 4 / 2 * 2 + 3 * 3 = 2 * 2 + 3 * 3 = 4 + 3 * 3 = 7 * 3 = 21$$

However, the true intention of the programmer is different. Since, the + operator has the lower precedence than *, the multiplication 3 * 3 should have been performed earlier than the addition, 4 + 3. The following is the correct way to evaluate the above expression

$$X = 4 / 2 * 2 + 3 * 3 = 2 * 2 + 3 * 3 = 4 + 9 = 13.$$

Any compiler that translates this expression into an executable code, has to scan till the end before it can decide the way in which the expression could be evaluated. This leads to a tedious logic for the compiler.

Now the question is how the compiler accepts the usual expression written by a programmer, (such as the one, given in the above example) and generates the correct code?

8.7 POSTFIX & PREFIX NOTATIONS

If e is an expression with operators and operands, the conventional way of writing e is called INFIX, because operators come in between the operands. On contrary if the operator comes after the operands, it is known as POSTFIX expression and if the operand comes before the operator it is called PREFIX expression. For example, the infix expression, A * B / C has a postfix equivalent A B * C /. Now imagine that A * B is computed and stored in T. Then we have division operator / coming immediately after its two operands T and C. Let us look at our original example and its postifix equivalent.

Infix	:	A / B * C + D * E
Postfix	:	A B / C * D E * +
Prefix	:	+ * / A B C * D E

Now let us present a simple procedure to convert Infix expression to Postfix and Prefix expressions. Given an Infix expression, first identify the first operation that would be performed in that expression. Parenthesise the operands and the operator of this operation. For example, consider the following expression.

A * B + C / D

In this expression, the first operation to be performed is A * B. Therefore, parenthesise this operation as follows

(A * B) + C / D

Convert the operation in the parenthesis as Postfix by placing the operator after the operands or as Prefix by placing the operator before the operands as follows

(A B *) + C / D   Postfix
(*A B) + C / D   Prefix

Identify the next operation to be performed treating what is existing in the parenthesis as a single operand. Obviously, the next operation that is to be performed is C / D and therefore we parenthesise and place the operator either after (Postfix) or before (Prefix) the operands as follows

(A B *) + (C D /)   Postfix
(*A B) + (/ C D)   Prefix

The last operation is the +, treating what is there in the parenthesises as single operands. We place the operand + either after or before the operands as follows

A B * C D / +   Postfix
+ *A B / C D   Prefix

The above procedure may be continued till all the operations to be performed are exhausted. Refer Table 8.1 for the steps in conversion of a more complex expression like

A * B + (C – D) / E

Step	PREFIX	POSTFIX
1	A * B + (– C D) / E	A * B + (C D –) / E
2	(* A B) + (– C D) / E	(A B *) + (C D –) / E
3	(* A B) + (/ – C D E)	(A B *) + (C D – E /)
4	+ * A B / – C D E	A B * C D – E / +

Note that, the postfix or infix expressions do not contain any parenthesises. The above procedure is quite useful to convert any infix expression into postfix or prefix expressions manually. However, we will present a more elegant way (for which a computer program can be easily written) of conversion from infix to postfix using a stack in later sections.

8.8 EVALUATION OF POSTFIX EXPRESSION USING STACKS

We can now comfortably evaluate from Left to Right and hope to get the correct result. With the assumption, that every time we compute a value we store in a temporary variable, we now go Left to Right on the postfix expression and evaluate in the following manner as shown in Table 8.1.

Table 8.1 Postfix Notation

Operation	Postfix
$T_1 = A / B$	T_1 C * D E *+
$T_2 = T_1 * C$	T_2 D E *+
$T_3 = D * E$	T_2 T_3 +
$T_4 = T_2 + T_3$	T_4

So T_4 will contain the result. We shall now show that a postfix expression could easily be evaluated by making a Left to right scan, stacking operands, and evaluating operators using the correct number of operands from the stack and finally placing the result on to the stack. This evaluation process is much simpler than attempting direct evaluation from the infix notation. The program presented in Program Listing 8.6 accepts an expression in postfix form and evaluates the same using a stack.

```
/* Program Listing 8.6 :  POSTFIX.c
Evaluate a Postfix Notation  using Stacks  */
#include <stdio.h>
#include <stdlib.h>
#include <string.h>
#define MAXSIZE 20
```

```
void add_stack(float [],int *,float );
float delete_stack(float [], int *);
char *getnexttoken(char *, int *);

void main(void)
{
    float stack[MAXSIZE], n1, n2, result;
    int top = -1, isoperand = 0;
    char ts[50], nexttoken[50], c;
    printf("Enter the Postfix Expression\n Delimited by spaces
                        between operators and operands...\n");
    scanf("%[^\n]", ts);
    while(1)
    {
        strcpy(nexttoken, getnexttoken(ts, &isoperand));
        if(strcmp(nexttoken, "#") == 0)
            break;
        if(isoperand)
            add_stack(stack, &top, atof(nexttoken));
        else
        {
            n1 = delete_stack(stack, &top);
            n2 = delete_stack(stack, &top);
            c = nexttoken[0];
            switch(c)
            {
                case '+':
                    add_stack(stack, &top, n2 + n1);
                    break;
                case '-':
                    add_stack(stack, &top, n2 - n1);
                    break;
                case '*':
                    add_stack(stack, &top, n2 * n1);
                    break;
```

```
                        case '/':
                            add_stack(stack, &top, n2 / n1);
                            break;
                        default:
                            printf("Invalid Operator.
                                                   Exiting.\n");
                            exit(0);
                    }
            }
        }
        result = delete_stack(stack, &top);
        printf("Result = %f", result);
}
void add_stack(float s[],int *top,float item)
{
        if(*top == MAXSIZE - 1)
            printf("\nStack Full. Not Adding %d", item);
        else
            s[++*top]=item;
}
float delete_stack(float s[], int *top)
{
        if(top < 0)
        {
            printf("\nStack Empty.");
            return -1;
        }
        return s[(*top)–];
}
char *getnexttoken(char *s, int *t)
{
        char ts[20];
        static int i = 0;
          int j = 0;
```

```
72.         while((s[i] == ' '))
73.             i++;
74.         if(s[i] == '\0')
75.         {
76.             ts[j++] = '#';
77.             ts[j] = '\0';
78.             return ts;
79.         }
80.         if(isdigit(s[i]) || s[i] == '.')
81.         {
82.             *t = 1;
83.             while(isdigit(s[i]) || s[i] == '.')
84.                 ts[j++] = s[i++];
85.             ts[j] = '\0';
86.             return ts;
87.         }
88.         else
89.         {
90.             *t = 0;
91.             ts[j++] = s[i++];
92.             ts[j] = '\0';
93.             return ts;
94.         }
95.     }
```

```
Enter the Postfix Expression
Delimited by spaces between operators and operands...3 3 * 5 /
Result = 1.800000
```

Program Listing 8.6 Evaluate Postfix Expression using Stacks.

At Line 11,

```
float stack[MAXSIZE], n1, n2, result;
```

we have declared a stack to hold floating-point numbers. Accordingly we have changed the routines add_stack and delete_stack. At Line 15,

```
scanf("%[^\n]", ts);
```

we are accepting the postfix expression using a scanf into ts. Note that in the postfix expression entered, the operands and the operators must be separated by space. Otherwise the program might end up with an error. For example, you can enter 6.2 3.5 * 7.2 + which is a postfix equivalent to a infix expression (6.2 * 3.5) + 7.2. At Line 18,

```
strcpy(nexttoken, getnexttoken(ts, &isoperand));
```

the call to getnexttoken takes the parameter ts and &isoperand, since we wish to get back into main whether the next token is an operand or operator. getnexttoken will set this value to 1 if it is an operand and 0 if it is an operator. getnexttoken returns a string containing the next token which is copied to nexttoken in the main. Now let us turn our attention to the function getnexttoken starting at Line 67. In the function getnexttoken, at Line 70,

```
static int i = 0;
```

we have declared a static int i and initialized it to 0. We need a static variable here, since we want to retain the value of i (i.e., the extent we have read the postfix expression contained in ts), for several entries and exits to getnexttoken. The getnexttoken skips all white spaces before it starts testing for an operand or an operator. At Line 72,

```
while((s[i] == ' '))
```

the while loop skips all the leading white spaces before proceeding further. At Line 74,

```
if(s[i] == '\0')
```

the if statement checks for the end of the postfix expression and if so returns a token which contains # signaling the end of the expression. At Lines 80 to 87,

```
if(isdigit(s[i]) || s[i] == '.')
{
    *t = 1;
    while(isdigit(s[i]) || s[i] == '.')
        ts[j++] = s[i++];
    ts[j] = '\0';
    return ts;
}
```

the if part of the if statement tests whether it is an operand and if so reads till the end of the operand using a while loop. Since an operand contains only a digit or decimal point, we are only testing for either of these characters and appending a '\0' at the end. The token is then returned. At Line 88 to 94,

```
else
{
        *t = 0;
        ts[j++] = s[i++];
        ts[j] = '\0';
        return ts;
}
```

the else part takes care of the operators. Since the operator is single character we have to read only one character into the local array ts and return it appending a '\0'. At Line 82, note that *t is set to 1, if it is an operand and at line 90, *t is set to 0 if it is an operator.

Let us now turn our attention once again to main() where token returned by getnexttoken is copied into nexttoken. At Line 19,

```
if(strcmp(nexttoken, "#") == 0)
```

nexttoken is compared with "#" and the while loop is terminated if nexttoken is equal to it. Note that getnexttoken returns a string with one character # when the input to getnexttoken reaches end. At Line 21 and 22,

```
if(isoperand)
```

the if statement, tests if the return token is operand and if so pushes (or adds) the string to the stack after converting it into a floating point number using atof(). atof() is a library function, (whose declaration is made in stdlib.h) which converts a string to floating-point number. At Line 23 to 46,

```
else
{
        n1 = delete_stack(stack, &top);
        n2 = delete_stack(stack, &top);
        c = nexttoken[0];
        switch(c)
        {
                case '+':
                        add_stack(stack, &top, n2 + n1);
                        break;
                case '-':
                        add_stack(stack, &top, n2 - n1);
                        break;
```

```
                    case '*':
                         add_stack(stack, &top, n2 * n1);
                         break;
                    case '/':
                         add_stack(stack, &top, n2 / n1);
                         break;
                    default:
                         printf("Invalid Operator.
                                                   Exiting.\n");
                         exit(0);
               }
          }
```

the else part of the if statement, takes care of the operators. For each operator, we delete (or pop out) two operands and store them in n1 and n2. Since all the operators we have assumed are binary operators we are deleting from stack two operands, with out bothering to test what the operand is. The switch statement tests for the operators and performs the appropriate operations between the operands and the result is added to stack. At Line 48 & 49,

```
result = delete_stack(stack, &top);
printf("Result = %f", result);
```

we pop out the result from the stack and print it. The student is advised to trace the contents of the stack for an example postfix expression like,

```
3 3 * 5 / 2 - 4 + 5 /
```

and observe the result.

8.9 INFIX TO POSTFIX CONVERSION USING STACKS

In the previous section, we have presented a program to compute the value of a postfix expression only scanning it once, from left to right. As discussed earlier, this is not possible with an infix expression. Therefore, every compiler translates an infix expression to a postfix expression and then uses the postfix expression for evaluation or to generate the necessary code for evaluation. We shall now present a program that scans the infix expression from left to right only once and produces the postfix equivalent of the expression.

Before we explain the program, we will present the basic idea involved in the conversion. For example, if we want A + B * C to yield A B C * +, we should perform the following sequence of stacking (These stacks will grow left to right.).

Next Token	Stack	Output
None	Empty	None
A	Empty	A
+	+	A
B	+	A B

At this point the algorithm must determine if * get placed on top of the stack or if the + gets taken off since * has greater priority we should stack.

*	+ *	A B
C	+ *	A B C

Now the input expression is exhausted, so we output all remaining operators in the stack to get

A B C * +

For another example, A * (B + C) * D has the postfix form A B C + * D *, and so the algorithm should behave as

Next Token	Stack	Output
None	Empty	None
A	Empty	A
*	*	A
(	* (	A
B	* (	A B
+	* (+	A B
C	* (+	A B C

At this point we want to unstack down to the corresponding left parenthesis and then delete the left and right parenthesis; this gives us:

)	*	A B C +
*	*	A B C + *
D	*	A B C + * D
Done	Empty	A B C + * D *

Note that the postfix expression does not contain a parenthesis. These examples should motivate the following hierarchy scheme for binary arithmetic operators and delimiters. The general case involving all the operators is left as an exercise.

Table 8.2 The instack and incoming priorities of various operators

Symbol	In-Stack Priority	In-Coming Priority
)	–	–
*, /	2	2
binary +, –	1	1
(	0	3

The rule will be that operators are taken out of the stack as long as their in-stack priority (isp), is greater than or equal to the in-coming priority(icp) of the new operator.

Now let us present the program in Program Listing 8.7.

```
/* Program Listing 8.7 :  INFIX.c
Convert an Infix Expression into a Postfix Expression*/
#include <stdio.h>
#include <conio.h>
#include <stdlib.h>
#include <string.h>

#define MAXSIZE 20

void add_stack(char [],int *,char );
char delete_stack(char [], int *);
char *getnexttoken(char *,int *);
int isp(char);
int icp(char);

void main(void)
{
        char stack[MAXSIZE];
        int top = -1, isoperand = 0;
```

```
        char ts[50], nexttoken[50], c,ch,postfix[50];
        int i=0,j;
        clrscr();
        add_stack(stack,&top,'#');
        printf("Enter An Expression\n Delimited by spaces between
                operators and operands...\n");
        scanf("%[^\n]", ts);
        while(1)
        {
            strcpy(nexttoken, getnexttoken(ts, &isoperand));
            if(strcmp(nexttoken, "#") == 0)
                break;
            if(isoperand)
            {
                j=0;
                while(nexttoken[j]!= '\0')
                    postfix[i++]=nexttoken[j++];
                postfix[i++]= ' ';
            }
            else
            {
                c = nexttoken[0];
                if(c==')') {
                    while((c=delete_stack(stack,&top)) != '(')
                    {
                        postfix[i++]=c;
                        postfix[i++]= ' ';
                    }
                }
                else {
                    while( isp(stack[top])>=icp(c))
                    {
                        ch= delete_stack(stack,&top);
                        postfix[i++]=ch;
```

```
                    postfix[i++]= ' ';
                }
            }
            add_stack(stack,&top,c);
        }


        /* printf("Result = %s", postfix);*/

    }
    while((c=delete_stack(stack,&top)) != '#')
    {
        postfix[i++]=c;
        postfix[i++]= ' ';
    }
    postfix[i]='\0';
    printf("Result = %s", postfix);
}
int isp(char c)
{
    switch(c)
    {
        case '*':
        case '/':return(2);
        case '+':
        case '-': return(1);
        case '(': return(0);
        case '#': return(-1);
        default : printf("Invalid Operator\n");
            exit(0);
    }
}
int icp(char c)
{
    switch(c)
    {
        case '*':
        case '/':return(2);
```

```
            case ‘+’:
            case ‘-’: return(1);
            case ‘(‘: return(3);
            default : printf(“Invalid Operator\n”);
                  exit(0);
      }
}

void add_stack(char s[],int *top,char item)
{
      if(*top == MAXSIZE - 1)
            printf(“\nStack Over Flow. Not Adding %d”, item);
      else
            s[++*top]=item;
}
char delete_stack(char s[], int *top)
{
      if(top < 0)
      {
         printf(“\nStack Empty.”);
         return -1;
      }
      return s[(*top)—];
}
char *getnexttoken(char *s, int *t)
{
      char ts[20];
      static int i = 0;
      int j = 0;
      while((s[i] == ‘ ‘))
            i++;
      if(s[i] == ‘\0’)
      {
            ts[j++] = ‘#’;
            ts[j] = ‘\0’;
            return ts;
      }
```

```
128.        if(isdigit(s[i]) || s[i] == '.')
129.        {
130.              *t = 1;
131.              while(isdigit(s[i]) || s[i] == '.')
132.                    ts[j++] = s[i++];
133.              ts[j] = '\0';
134.              return ts;
135.        }
136.        else
137.        {
138.              *t = 0;
139.              ts[j++] = s[i++];
140.              ts[j] = '\0';
141.              return ts;
142.        }
143. }
```

```
Enter An Expression
Delimited by spaces between operators and operands...3 * 3 / 5
Result = 3 3 * 5 /
```

Program Listing 8.7 Convert an infix expression into a postfix expression

At Line 16,

```
char stack[MAXSIZE];
```

we have declared a stack that can stack the operators. Essentially the routine getnexttoken() is same as that of the previous program. This routine returns as before, the next token of the inputted infix expression and sets isoperand accordingly. At Line 23,

```
scanf("%[^\n]", ts);
```

the infix expression is inputted. As usual we have selected an infinite while loop and break from it when getnexttoken sends an "#" signaling the end of the inputted expression. At Line 31 to 37,

```
if(isoperand)
{
      j=0;
      while(nexttoken[j]!= '\0')
            postfix[i++]=nexttoken[j++];
      postfix[i++]= ' ';
}
```

the nexttoken is tested for an operand and if so is copied into the array postfix which will be holding the postfix expression. If the nexttoken is not an operand it should be an operator. The else part of the above if statement, we are testing, if the operator is ')'. If so, at Line 40 to 44,

```
c = nexttoken[0];
if(c==')') {
      while((c=delete_stack(stack,&top)) != '(')
      {
            postfix[i++]=c;
```

we unstack all operators till '(' and copy them to the array postfix. If c is not a ')' then at Line 48 to 56,

```
else {
      while( isp(stack[top])>=icp(c))
      {
            ch= delete_stack(stack,&top);
            postfix[i++]=ch;
            postfix[i++]= ' ';
      }
}
add_stack(stack,&top,c);
```

we test for the in-stack priority and incoming priority and unstack all operators until the in-stack priority is greater than or equal to the incoming priority and copy them to the output array postfix. We then add the operator to the stack. At Line 21,

```
add_stack(stack,&top,'#');
```

note we have placed # as the first element in the stack with in-stack priority as −1. This is done to ensure that the first operator would get stacked, without any problem. The functions isp and icp reflect the Table 8.2 except for the inclusion # in isp.

At Line 63 to 67,

```
while((c=delete_stack(stack,&top)) != '#')
{
      postfix[i++]=c;
      postfix[i++]= ' ';
}
```

we are unstacking all the operators. At Line 69,

```
printf("Result = %s", postfix);
```

the result is printed.

Every time we are copying into the output array postfix we are ensuring that the operands and operators are separated by spaces. This is to make the output of this program to be given as an input to the program that evaluates a postfix expression in Program Listing 8.6. We shall now present a program in Program Listing 8.8, which takes an infix expression and converts it to a postfix and evaluates. In other words, we will combine the above two programs 8.6 and 8.7, and present a program that can perform the arithmetic operations +, - * and / on an infix expression containing floating point numbers in Program Listing 8.8.

```
/* Program Listing 8.8 :  INFPOST.c
 Converts a Infix Expression to Postfix and Evaluates using Stacks */
#include <stdio.h>
#include <conio.h>
#include <stdlib.h>
#include <string.h>

#define MAXSIZE 20

void add_stack1(float [],int *,float );
float delete_stack1(float [], int *);

void add_stack2(char [], int *, char );
char delete_stack2(char [], int *);

char *getnexttoken(char *, int *);

float postfix(char *);

char *infix(char *);
int isp(char );
int icp(char );

int flag = 0;
void main(void)
{
      char ts[50], post[50];
      float result;
```

```
        clrscr();
        printf("Enter An Expression: ");
        scanf("%[^\n]", ts);
        strcpy(post, infix(ts));
        printf("\nPostfix Expression = %s", post);
        result = postfix(post);
        printf("\nResult = %f\n", result);
}
char *infix(char *ts)
{
        char stack[MAXSIZE];
        int top = -1, isoperand = 0, j, i = 0;
        char nexttoken[50], c,ch,postfix[50];
        flag = 1;
        add_stack2(stack,&top,'#');
        while(1)
        {
                strcpy(nexttoken, getnexttoken(ts, &isoperand));
                if(strcmp(nexttoken, "#") == 0)
                        break;

                if(isoperand)
                {
                        j=0;
                        while(nexttoken[j]!= '\0') postfix[i++] =
                                                         nexttoken[j++];
                        postfix[i++]= ' ';
                }
                else
                {
                        c = nexttoken[0];
                        if(c==')')
                                while((c=delete_stack2(stack,&top)) != '(')
                                {
                                        postfix[i++]=c;
                                        postfix[i++]= ' ';
                                }
```

```
                    else {
                        while( isp(stack[top])>=icp(c))
                        {
                            ch= delete_stack2(stack,&top);
                            postfix[i++]=ch;
                            postfix[i++]= ‘ ‘;

                        }
                        add_stack2(stack,&top,c);
                    }
                }
        }/* end of while(1) */
        while((c=delete_stack2(stack,&top)) != ‘#’)
        {
            postfix[i++]=c;
            postfix[i++]= ‘ ‘;
        }
        postfix[i]=’\0';
        return postfix;
    }
    int isp(char c)
    {
        switch(c)
        {
            case ‘*’:
            case ‘/’:return(2);
            case ‘+’:
            case ‘-’: return(1);
            case ‘(‘: return(0);
            case ‘#’: return(-1);
            default : printf(“Invalid Operator\n”);
                exit(0);
        }
    }
```

```
int icp(char c)
{
        switch(c)
        {
                case ‘*’:
                case ‘/’:return(2);
                case ‘+’:
                case ‘-’: return(1);
                case ‘(‘: return(3);
                default : printf(“Invalid Operator\n”);
                   exit(0);
        }
}

void add_stack2(char s[],int *top,char item)
{
        if(*top == MAXSIZE - 1)
                printf(“\nStack Over Flow. Not Adding %d”, item);
        else
                s[++*top]=item;
}
char delete_stack2(char s[], int *top)
{
        if(top < 0)
        {
                printf(“\nStack Empty.”);
                return -1;
        }
        return s[(*top)–];
}
float postfix(char *ts)
{
        float stack[MAXSIZE], n1, n2, result;
        int top = -1, isoperand = 0;
        char nexttoken[50], c;
        flag = 1;
```

```
    while(1)
    {
        strcpy(nexttoken, getnexttoken(ts, &isoperand));
        if(strcmp(nexttoken, "#") == 0)
            break;
        if(isoperand)
            add_stack1(stack, &top, atof(nexttoken));
        else
        {
            n1 = delete_stack1(stack, &top);
            n2 = delete_stack1(stack, &top);
            c = nexttoken[0];
            switch(c)
            {
                case '+':
                    add_stack1(stack, &top, n2 + n1);
                    break;
                case '-':
                    add_stack1(stack, &top, n2 - n1);
                    break;
                case '*':
                    add_stack1(stack, &top, n2 * n1);
                    break;
                case '/':
                    add_stack1(stack, &top, n2 / n1);
                    break;
                default:
                    printf("Invalid Operator. Exiting.\n");
                    exit(0);
            }
        }
    }
    result = delete_stack1(stack, &top);
    return result;
}
```

```
void add_stack1(float s[],int *top,float item)
{
      if(*top == MAXSIZE - 1)
            printf("\nStack Full. Not Adding %d", item);
      else
            s[++*top]=item;
}
float delete_stack1(float s[], int *top)
{
      if(top < 0)
      {
            printf("\nStack Empty.");
            return -1;
      }
      return s[(*top)—];
}
char *getnexttoken(char *s, int *t)
{
      char ts[20];
      static int i = 0;
      int j = 0;
      if(flag == 1)
      {
            i = 0;
            flag = 0;
      }
      while((s[i] == ' '))
            i++;
      if(s[i] == '\0')
      {
            ts[j++] = '#';
            ts[j] = '\0';
            return ts;
      }
```

```
203.        if(isdigit(s[i]) || s[i] == '.')
204.        {
205.             *t = 1;
206.             while(isdigit(s[i]) || s[i] == '.')
207.                  ts[j++] = s[i++];
208.             ts[j] = '\0';
209.             return ts;
210.        }
211.        else
212.        {
213.             *t = 0;
214.             ts[j++] = s[i++];
215.             ts[j] = '\0';
216.             return ts;
217.        }
218. }
```

```
Enter An Expression: 3*3/5
Postfix Expression = 3 3 * 5 /
Result = 1.800000
```

Program Listing 8.8 *Converts a Infix Expression to Postfix and Evaluates using Stacks*

We have converted the above two program into two functions infix and postfix. The function infix converts the infix expression to postfix expression. At Line 30,

```
strcpy(post, infix(ts));
```

in the main, the function infix is called, by passing the infix expression accepted in ts and the string returned by this function is copied into an array post. At Line 32,

```
result = postfix(post);
```

we are calling postfix by passing the post to it. Postfix returns a float after evaluating the postfix expression which is stored in result. At Line 34,

```
printf("\nResult = %f\n", result);
```

the result is printed. Each of the functions postfix and infix use their own stacks. However, we need two different add_stack and delete_stack functions. add_stack1, delete_stack1 handle the stack of postfix function, which is an array of floats and add_stack2, delete_stack2 handle the stack of infix function, which is a array of characters. Both the functions make use of the getnexttoken function. However, we need to initialize the static variable i to 0, when each function, calls getnexttoken for the first time. This is accomplished by using a global variable flag, which is set to 1 by each function before it calls getnexttoken for the first time. From Lines 190 to 193, observe the code that initializes i to 0 and sets flag to 0.

```
if(flag == 1)
{
        i = 0;
        flag = 0;
}
```

8.10 QUEUE

A queue is an ordered list in which all insertions take place at one end rear while all the deletions take place on the other end called front. See Fig. 8.2. The restrictions on a queue require that the first element, which is inserted in the queue, will be the first one to be removed. Thus a queue is known as **First In First Out** (**FIFO**). Queues like stacks also arise quite naturally in computer solutions of many problems. Perhaps the most common occurrence of queue in computer applications is for the scheduling of jobs by an operating system. As mentioned earlier there are two distinct ends the front and a rear for a queue. Additions to a queue take place at the rear. Deletions are made at the front. Thus if a job is submitted for execution, joins at the rear of the queue and the job at the front of the queue is the next one to be executed. The representation of a queue using an array is somewhat more difficult than a stack. We need a one-dimensional array and two variables front and rear. The conventions we shall adopt for these two variable is that front is always one less than the actual front of the queue and the rear always points to the last element of the queue. Front will be equal to rear if and only if there are no elements in the queue. The initial condition then is front = rear = -1. With these assumptions and initial conditions let us now present a program in which we create a queue and add & delete elements using the routines add_q and delete_q. The program is presented in Program Listing 8.9

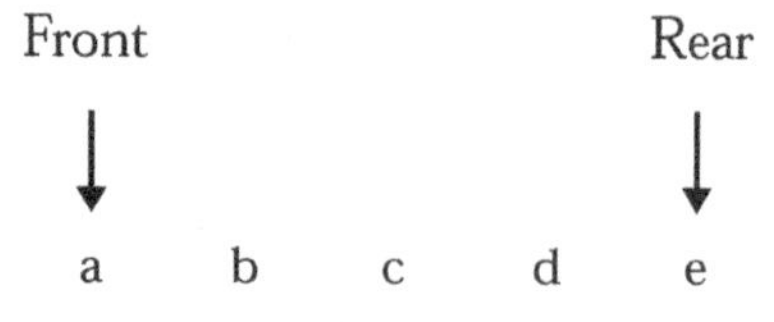
Front
Rear
a b c d e

Fig. 8.2 A Queue

```
/* Program Listing 8.9 :  QUEUE.c
Illustration of Queues  */
#include <stdio.h>
#include <conio.h>
#include <stdlib.h>

#define MAXSIZE 5


void print_q();
void add_q(int);
int delete_q();
int queue[MAXSIZE];
int front = -1,rear = -1;
void adjust_q();
void main(void)
{
      clrscr();
      add_q(12);
      add_q(34);
      add_q(56);
      print_q();
      delete_q();
      print_q();
      delete_q();
      print_q();
      delete_q();
      print_q();
      add_q(78);
      print_q();
      delete_q();
      print_q();
      delete_q();
      print_q();
      add_q(80);
```

```
        print_q();
        add_q(84);
        print_q();
        add_q(96);
        add_q(102);
        print_0q();
        delete_q();
        add_q(134);
        add_q(156);
        print_q();
}
void print_q()
{
        int i;
        if(front==rear)
              printf("There are no elements in the QUEUE");
        else
              for(i=front+1;i<=rear;i++) printf("%d ",queue[i]);
        printf("\n");
}
void add_q(int item)
{
        if(rear == MAXSIZE-1)/* we have reached the end */
        if(front>=0) /* adjustment can be made */
        {
              adjust_q();
              queue[++rear]=item ;/* add item */
        }
        else
              printf("\nStack Full. Not Adding %d\n", item);
        else
              queue[++rear]=item;
}
```

```
int delete_q()
{
      if(rear == front)
      {
            printf("QUEUE IS EMPTY\n");
            return(-1);
      }
      return queue[++front];      /* front always points to
                 one less than actual front */
}
void adjust_q()
{
      int i,j;
      for(i=front+1,j=0;i<=rear;i++,j++)
            queue[j]=queue[i];
 /* front and rear updated after adjustment */
      rear = —j;
      front = -1;
}
```

```
12
12 34
12 34 56
34 56
56
There are no elements in the QUEUE
78
There are no elements in the QUEUE
QUEUE IS EEMPTY
80
80 84
80 84 96 102
84 96 102 134 156
```

Program Listing 8.9 Illustration of a Queue

At Line 11,

```
int queue[MAXSIZE];
```

we have declared a queue as an array of integers of MAXSIZE. At Line 12,

```
int front = -1,rear = -1;
```

the front and rear are initialized to −1 and are made global along with the declaration of queue, so as to avoid passing these as parameters to functions add_q and delete_q for convinience.

From Line 54 to 66,

```
void add_q(int item)
{
      if(rear == MAXSIZE-1)/* we have reached the end */
      if(front>=0) /* adjustment can be made */
      {
            adjust_q();
            queue[++rear]=item ;/* add item */
      }
      else
            printf("\nStack Full. Not Adding %d\n", item);
      else
         queue[++rear]=item;
}
```

the function add_q takes one parameter, the item to be added. First the rear is tested for queue full condition. This is when the rear reaches MAXSIZE – 1. At this stage we cannot refuse to add because the queue may not be really full. Since some of the added items could have been deleted and there could be vacancy before the front.

If front is greater than or equal to 0, we have vacancies and adjust_q is called to shift all elements as shown in Fig. 8.3a. Further, adjust_q reassigns the values of rear and front with the new values Fig. 8.3b, thus providing place for the new insertions.

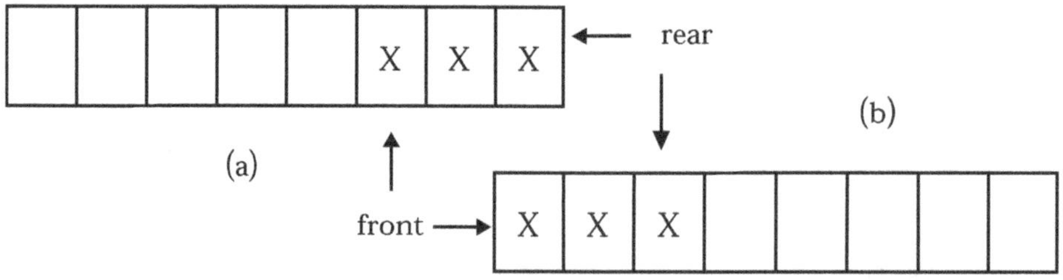
X
X
X
rear
(b)
(a)
front
X
X
X

Fig. 8.3 A Queue of MAXSIZE 8

From Lines 77 to 85,

```
void adjust_q()
{
      int i,j;
      for(i=front+1,j=0;i<=rear;i++,j++)
            queue[j]=queue[i];
 /* front and rear updated after adjustment */
      rear = —j;
      front = -1;
}
```

the adjust_q routine, sifts all the elements by using a for loop with two variables i and j and also assigns –1 to front and the position of the last element to rear (—j). From Lines 67 to 76,

```
int delete_q()
{
      if(rear == front)
      {
            printf("QUEUE IS EMPTY\n");
            return(-1);
      }
      return queue[++front];     /* front always points to
                 one less than actual front */
}
```

the delete_q routine first checks for emptiness of the queue by testing front = rear and returns –1. Otherwise front is incremented by one and the element is returned. Note that always front points one location less than the actual front. Another point at this stage the student must note is, the front and rear are always incremented and when front catches up the rear, the queue is empty. From Lines 45 to 54,

```
void print_q()
{
      int i;
      if(front==rear)
            printf("There are no elements in the QUEUE");
      else
            for(i=front+1;i<=rear;i++) printf("%d ",queue[i]);
      printf("\n");
}
```

the print_q routine runs through the queue provided front is not equal to rear and prints the contents. When the front is equal to rear, it prints "There are no elements in the QUEUE". In the main, we are calling several add_q, and delete_q and showing the output. Student is advised to physically draw a queue at every add, delete and verify the same with the output.

8.11 CIRCULAR QUEUES

One of the problems in the Linear Queue just discussed above is, that every time the queue full is signaled by add_q, the adjust_q is called. The worst case could be when the queue is really full and delete_q, add_q follow alternatively. For every add_q, adjust_q will be called. And thus becomes very inefficient. A more efficient queue is obtained regarding the queue (the array) as circular queue. When rear is equal to MAXSIZE – 1 the next element is entered at queue [0], incase the location is free. Using the same convention as before, front will always point to 1, counter clock-wise (anti-clockwise) from the first element in the queue. Again front is equal to rear, if and only if queue is empty. Initially front = rear = 0. In order to add an element move rear one position clock wise. Therefore, if rear = n – 1 then rear = 0 else rear++. The above statement could easily be implemented with modulo (%) operator. Similarly it is necessary to move front one position clockwise each time a deletion is made. We now present a circular queue in Program Listing 8.10

```
/* Program Listing 8.10 :  CQUEUE.c
Illustration of Circular Queues */
#include <stdio.h>
#include <conio.h>
#include <stdlib.h>
#define MAXSIZE 5
void print_q();
void add_q(int);
int delete_q();
int queue[MAXSIZE];
int front=0,rear=0;
void adjust_q();
void main(void)
{
       clrscr();
       add_q(12);
       add_q(34);
```

```
        add_q(56);
        print_q();
        delete_q();
        print_q();
        add_q(78);
        print_q();
        delete_q();
        print_q();
        delete_q();
        print_q();
        add_q(80);
        print_q();
        add_q(84);
        print_q();
        add_q(96);
        add_q(102);
        print_q();
        delete_q();
        add_q(134);
        add_q(156);
        print_q();
}
void print_q()
{
        int i;

        if(rear>front)
             for(i=front+1;i<=rear;i++)
                  printf("%d ",queue[i]);
        else
        {
             for(i=front+1;i<MAXSIZE;i++) printf("%d ",queue[i]);
             for(i=0;i<=rear;i++) printf("%d ",queue[i]);
        }
        printf("\n");
}
```

```
void add_q(int item)
{
      int temp;
      temp = (rear+1)%MAXSIZE;

      if(temp == front)
            printf("\nStack Full. Not Adding %d\n", item);
      else
      {
            rear=temp;
            queue[rear]=item;
      }
}
int delete_q()
{
      if(rear==front)
      {
            printf("QUEUE IS EEMPTY\n");
            return(-1);
      }
      front=(front+1)%MAXSIZE;
      return queue[front];
}
```

```
12 34 56
34 56
34 56 78
56 78
78
78 80
78 80 84
78 80 84 96

Stack Full. Not Adding 102
78 80 84 96
80 84 96
80 84 96 134
```

```
Stack Full. Not Adding 156
80 84 96 134
84 96 134
96 134
134
No elements in the Queue.
```

Program Listing 8.10 *Circular Queue*

In the add_q routine, at Line 52 to 64,

```
void add_q(int item)
{
        int temp;
        temp = (rear+1)%MAXSIZE;

        if(temp == front)
              printf("\nStack Full. Not Adding %d\n", item);
        else
        {
              rear=temp;
              queue[rear]=item;
        }
}
```

rear is incremented by 1 and modulo to MAXSIZE is taken. The result is stored in temp. This is done to check the queue full condition i.e., front = rear. The student should not get confused here, because for queue empty also we test for front = rear condition. However, the difference is that when the front catches the rear the queue is empty and when the rear catches the front the queue is full. Since we do not want to mix up both the conditions, we will not allow, rear to actually catch up with the front. Therefore, we will make rear = temp if and only if the front does not become equal to rear. Note that the location being pointed by front is in fact vacant when a queue full condition is encountered, since the front points to one less than the actual front. If we try to use this location, front will become equal to rear and the delete_q routine will consider this as an empty queue. Since we do not want this confusion, we are using one place less in the queue. Thus in the circular queue, we will use only MAXSIZE – 1 locations as against MAXSIZE locations in the linear queue. However, we can use upto MAXSIZE in a circular queue by setting a variable **flag**, which is made 0 when front catches rear and 1 when the rear catches the front. In conjunction with this variable if you test front = rear, then we can distinguish between queue empty and queue full conditions.

In the delete_q routine from Lines 66 to 75,

```
int delete_q()
{
      if(rear==front)
      {
            printf("QUEUE IS EEMPTY\n");
            return(-1);
      }
      front=(front+1)%MAXSIZE;
      return queue[front];
}
```

the front is incremented and modulo to MAXSIZE is taken if and only if the queue is not empty. It is quite interesting to look at print_q routine from Lines 38 to 51,

```
void print_q()
{
      int i;

      if(rear>front)
            for(i=front+1;i<=rear;i++)
                  printf("%d ",queue[i]);
      else
      {
            for(i=front+1;i<MAXSIZE;i++) printf("%d ",queue[i]);
            for(i=0;i<=rear;i++) printf("%d ",queue[i]);
      }
      printf("\n");
}
```

which cannot now run through the array from front + 1 to rear. It has to distinguish with two cases. Case 1 is if rear is greater than front then, the rear has not crossed the boundary of array yet. And therefore, we print contents as we did before. Case 2 is If front less than rear then rear has crossed MAXSIZE – 1, which is the upper limit of the array. Therefore, we need two for loops to print elements of the queue, one running from front + 1 to MAXSIZE – 1 and the other running from 0 to rear.

There are several applications for queues in computer science. An example of usage of a queue is presented in Chapter 8, "***Trees and Graphs***" to implement Breath First Search.

SELF-REVIEW EXERCISES

1. ADT stands for .... (Abstract Data Type)
2. Time complexity of an algorithm is represented using .... notation. (big O)
3. The three types of analysis that can be performed on an algorithm are ...., ... and .... (correctness, time, space)
4. The postfix equivalent of an infix expression A * (B + C) is .... (ABC + *)
5. The infix equivalent of a postfix expression A BC * / is ....

   (A*B + C)
6. .... function is used in C to dynamically allocate space for one object. (Malloc)
7. .... function is used in C to dynamically allocate space for more than one object. (Calloc)
8. .... function is used in C to release dynamically allocated memory.

   (Free)
9. The type of pointer returned by calloc is .... (Woid)
10. Postfix expression allows you to compute the expression in .... number of scans. (1)

State whether true or false.

1. Stack is also known as a LIFO structure. (T)
2. Queue is also known as a FIFO structure.
3. add_queue() routine for queue is also referred as push.
4. A Circular Queue of size n can only use n - 1 locations.
5. To manuplate a queue, we need two variables top and rear.

EXERCISES

1. Write the postfix form of the following expressions.

   A + B – C + D

   A * B / C + D

   (A + B) * D + E / (F + A * D) + C

   A + B % C + D

2. Another form of representing an expression is a prefix notation, where the operators preceed the operands. For example, A * B / C could be written as / * A B C. Notice that the order of the operands is not changed in going from infix to prefix. Write an algorithm / C program to transform a prefix expression to postfix expression.

3. Write an algorithm / C program to transform a postfix to prefix expression.

4. Two stacks are to be implemented on a single array of size m. Write routines add_stack(i, x) and delete_stack(i) to add x and delete an element from stack i. Note that you should not use fixed partitioning for stack1 and stack2.

5. Re-write the program to convert infix expression to postfix expression (program listing 8.7) including all relational operators.

6. Modify program of program lists 8.10 (circular queue) to use all the location of the array as suggested.

9

Linked Lists

9.1 SINGLY LINKED LIST

In the previous chapter we have studied the representation of ordered list using arrays and sequential mapping. The sequential mapping has the property that successive data objects are stored at fixed distance apart. Thus, the successive locations in the memory are ensured for the list.

However, when a sequential mapping is used for ordered lists, operations such as insertion and deletion of arbitrary elements become expensive. This is because, we want to insert an element somewhere in the middle of the list, and we have to shift half the number of elements to right to make the insertion. When an element is deleted somewhere in the middle of the list, to avoid the vacant place, we have to shift the elements after the deleted items to one place to the left. To avoid the data movement while deleting and inserting in sequential representation, we now offer an alternative.

The alternative is using linked instead of sequential representation. Unlike a sequential representation, where successive items of a list are located, a fixed distance apart, in a linked representation, these items may be placed anywhere in the memory. To access elements in the list in the correct order, with each element we store the address or location of the next element in that list. Thus, associated with each data object in a linked representation is a pointer to the next object. This pointer is often referred as a **link**.

In C, we have the structures, which can be made self-referential. A self-referential structure is one that includes within its structure at least one member which is a pointer to the same structure type. Thus, a node in a linked list can be defined as a self-referential structure with at least one data item. For example,

```
struct slink {
        char name[50];
        struct slink *next;
};
```

We have chosen one data item in the structure. There could be any number of them. It is customary to draw linked list as an ordered sequence of nodes with links being represented by arrows as in Fig 9.1.

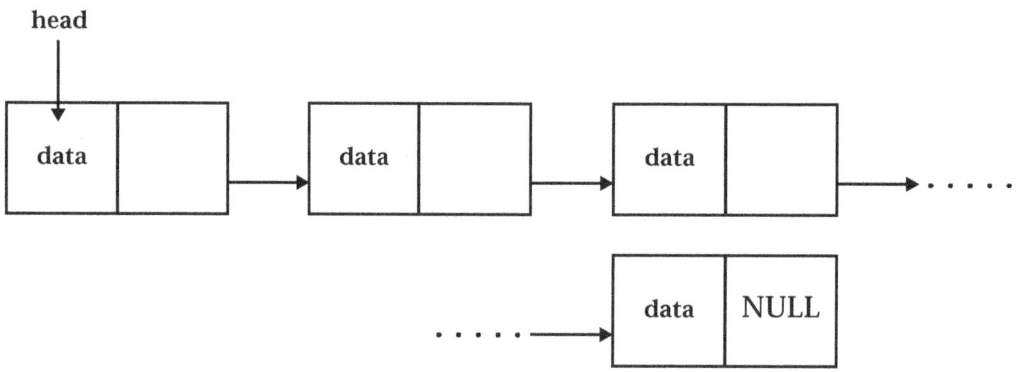
head
data
data
data
data
NULL

Fig 9.1 Linked List Representation

We shall refer to the pointer variable that points to the first element of the list as head. In fact head itself represents the list. Notice that in Fig 9.1 we did not explicitly put into the values of the pointers but simply drew arrows, indicating that they are there. Note that the last node in the list does not point to anything. Now we can show that an insertion / deletion somewhere within the list could easily be affected.

Let us now see why it is easier to make arbitrary insertions and deletions using a linked list rather than a sequential list. To insert the data item C between B and D in the linked list shown in Fig 9.2. the following steps are adequate:

(i) Get a new node; let its address be x;

(ii) Set the data field of this node as C;

(iii) Set the link field of x to point to the node after B which contains D;

(iv) Set the link field of the node containing B to x.

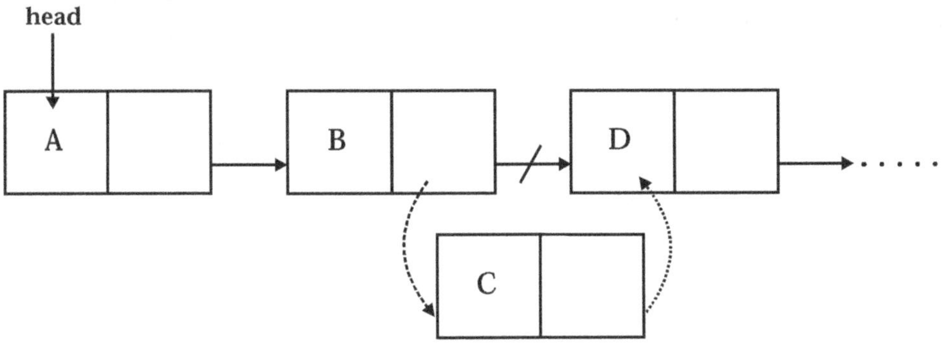
head
A
B
D
C

Fig 9.2 Insertion of Data into a Linked List

Fig 9.2 shows how we can draw the insertion using our arrow notation. The new arrows are dashed. The important thing to notice is that when we insert C we do not have to move any other elements, which are already in the list, contrary to sequential data representation.

Now suppose we want to delete C from the list. All we need to do is find the element which immediately precedes C, which is B, and set the pointer next of B to point to D. Again there is no need to move the data around. Even though the next field of C still contain a pointer to D, C is no longer in the list (see Figure 9.3).

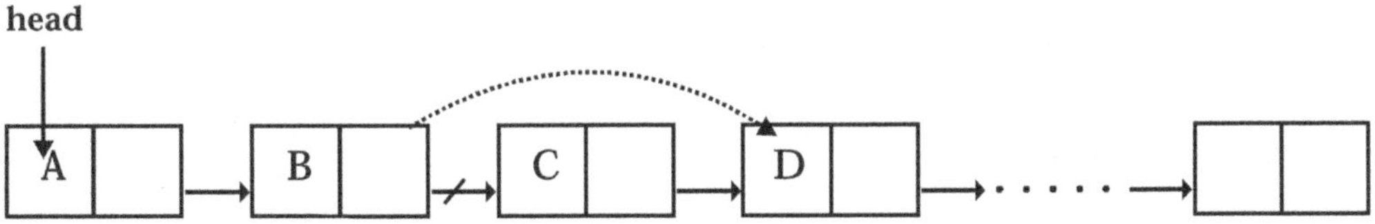
head
A
B
C
D

Fig 9.3 Deletion of Data from a Linked List

From our brief discussion of linked lists, we see that the following capabilities are needed to make linked representations possible.

(i) A mechanism to define the structure of a node (The self referential structures of C).

(ii) A way to create nodes as needed. (malloc function in C)

(iii) A way to free nodes that are no longer in use. (free function in C)

These capabilities are provided in the programming language C as indicated above. Let us present a program in Program Listing 9.1 which illustrates the capabilities of C language, to create linked list and handle operations such as insertions and deletions.

```
/*      Program Listing 9.1: LLINK.C
        A program to illustrate Singly Linked List      */
#include<stdio.h>
#include<string.h>
#include <stdlib.h>
#include <conio.h>

struct slink{
        char name[50];
        struct slink *next;
};
        struct slink * insertfront(struct slink *,char *);
        struct slink * insertrear( struct slink *,char *);
        struct  slink * insertpos( struct slink *,char *,int );
        struct  slink * deletefront( struct slink *,char *);
        struct slink * deleterear( struct slink *,char *);
        struct  slink * deletepos( struct slink *,char *,int );
        void printlist(struct slink *);

void main(void)
{
        struct slink *head;
        int i;
        char sname[50];
        head=NULL;
        while (1)
        {
                printf("Enter 1 to cont. 0 to break: ");
                scanf("%d",&i);
```

```
            fflush(stdin);
            if(i==0) break;
            printf("Enter the name: ");
            scanf("%[^\n]",sname);
            fflush(stdin);
            head = insertrear(head,sname);
        }
        clrscr();
        printf("List of Names after Insertion into List ...\n");
        printlist(head);
        getch();
        head=insertfront(head,"Krishna Rao");
        head=insertpos(head,"Rama Rao",3);
        head=insertpos(head,"Ranga Rao",6);
        printf("End of Insertion in a Position.  List is\n");
        printlist(head);
        getch();
        printf("Deleting of Ist Name.  List is\n");
        head = deletepos(head, sname, 1);
        printlist(head);
        printf("Deleting of 2nd Name.  List is\n");
        head = deletepos(head, sname, 2);
        printlist(head);
        printf("Deleting of 6th Name.  List is\n");
        head = deletepos(head, sname, 6);
        printlist(head);
}

struct slink * insertfront( struct slink *head,char *sname)
{
        struct slink *t;
        t  = (struct slink*)malloc(sizeof(struct slink));
        strcpy(t->name,sname);
        t->next=head;
        return t;
}
struct slink * insertrear( struct slink *head,char *sname)
{
        struct slink *t,*temp;
        t  = (struct slink*)malloc(sizeof(struct slink));
```

```
      strcpy(t->name,sname);
      t->next=NULL;
      if(head==NULL) return t; /* if list is empty */
      temp=head;
   /* traverse the list till end */
      while(temp->next != NULL) temp=temp->next;
   /* insert the new node */
      temp->next=t;
      return head;
}
struct slink *insertpos( struct slink *head,char *s,int pos)
{
   /* inserts at a position pos if pos is within the list
   or inserts at the end if pos is greater than the position
   of the last element in the list */
      int i=1;
      struct slink *t,*temp;
      if(pos<1) return head;
      t  = (struct slink*)malloc(sizeof(struct slink));
      strcpy(t->name,s);
      if(pos==1)
      {
            t->next=head;
            return t;
      }
      temp=head;
      while((temp->next != NULL)&&(i<pos-1))
   /* stop one position ahead of pos or end of list */
      {
            temp=temp->next;
            i++;
      }
      /* insert */
      t->next=temp->next;
      temp->next=t;
      return head;
}
struct slink *deleterear( struct slink *head,char *s)
{
```

```
        struct slink *t,*temp;
        if(head==NULL)strcpy(s,"\0"); /* if list is empty */
        temp=head;
        t=head;
    /* traverse the list till end */
        while(temp->next != NULL)
        {
             t=temp;
             temp=temp->next;
        }
        strcpy(s,temp->name);
        if(temp==head) head=NULL;
        else t->next=NULL;
    /* delete the new node */
        free(temp);
        return head;
}
struct  slink * deletefront( struct slink *head,char *s)
{
        struct slink *t,*temp;
        if(head==NULL) strcpy(s,"\0"); /* if list is empty */
        else
        {
             temp=head;
             head=temp->next;
             strcpy(s,temp->name);
             free(temp);
        }
        return head;
}
struct  slink * deletepos( struct slink *head,char *s,int pos)
{
/* deletes a node at a position pos if pos is within the list
   or does not delete if pos is greater than the position
   of the last element in the list */
        int i=1;
        struct slink *t,*temp;
```

```
        t = head;
        if((pos < 1) || (head == NULL)) return head;

        if(pos==1)
             head = t->next;
        else
        {
             temp = head;
             while((t != NULL)&&(i < pos))
                  /* stop at node to be deleted
             temp points one node preceeding */
             {
                  temp = t;
                  t=t->next;
                  i++;
             }
             if(t != NULL)/* deletion possible. do it */
                  temp->next = t->next;
             else   /* deletion not possible */
             {
                  strcpy(s, "\0");
                  return head;
             }
        }
        strcpy(s, t->name);
        free(t);
        return head;
}
void printlist(struct slink *head)
{
        struct slink *t;
        t = head;
        printf("\n");
        while(t != NULL)
        {
             printf("%s \n",t->name);
             t=t->next;
        }
}
```

```
Enter 1 to cont. 0 to break:1
Enter the name:ravi
Enter 1 to cont. 0 to break:1
Enter the name:kiran
Enter 1 to cont. 0 to break:1
Enter the name:padmanabham
Enter 1 to cont.0 to break:1
Enter the name:naresh
Enter 1 to cont. 0 to break:0

List of Names after Insertion into List ...
ravi
kiran
padmanabham
naresh
End of Insertion in a Position.  List is

Krishna Rao
ravi
Rama Rao
kiran
padmanabham
Ranga Rao
naresh
Deleting of Ist Name.  List is
ravi
Rama Rao
kiran
padmanabham
Ranga Rao
naresh

Deleting of 2nd Name.  List is
ravi
kiran
padmanabham
Ranga Rao
naresh
```

```
Deleting of 6th Name.  List is
ravi
kiran
padmanabham
Ranga Rao
naresh
```

Program Listing 9.1 Program to demonstrate various operations on a Singly Linked List

At Line 8,

```
struct slink {
      char name[50];
      struct slink *next;
};
```

we have defined a self-referential structure to represent each node of singly linked list. The structure contains only one data field, name a character array to hold a string apart from the self-referential pointer **next**. As said previously we can have any number of data fields. But for convenience we have restricted it to one. In the main() we have declared head as a pointer to structure slink and initialized the value of head to NULL, which means the list is empty. At lines 26 to 36,

```
while (1)
{
      printf("Enter 1 to cont. 0 to break: ");
      scanf("%d",&i);
      fflush(stdin);
      if(i==0) break;
      printf("Enter the name: ");
      scanf("%[^\n]",sname);
      fflush(stdin);
      head = insertrear(head,sname);
}
```

the while loop interactively accepts data from the user and inserts into the list. At Line 35, within the while loop we are calling the function insertrear(). At Lines 66 to 79,

```
struct slink * insertrear( struct slink *head,char *sname)
{
      struct slink *t,*temp;
      t= (struct slink*)malloc(sizeof(struct slink));
      strcpy(t->name,sname);
      t->next=NULL;
```

```
        if(head==NULL) return t; /* if list is empty */
        temp=head;
    /* traverse the list till end */
        while(temp->next != NULL) temp=temp->next;
    /* insert the new node */
        temp->next=t;
        return head;
    }
```

the ***insertrear*** function takes two parameters, a pointer to the head of the list and the string to be copied into the data field. The function also returns the new head of the list. It is essential to return the head as the list is empty, when the first time we call insertrear. Let us explain the routine insertrear.

We have used malloc to create a new node and the address of the new node is stored in t. The data is copied into t->name using strcpy(). If it is an empty list, we will make the new node itself as the head, otherwise we traverse the list till the end using a while loop, since the insertion is to made in the rear. Note that the while loop exits when temp->next becomes NULL. Now temp points to the last node of the list. We assign temp->next with the value of t. Now that, temp points to t and t->next is already NULL (assigned at the beginning of the routine) t becomes the last node in the list. Thus, we have accomplished adding t in the rear. Since, the value of head doesn't changed, the same is returned.

Let us now look at the routine insertfront at lines 58 to 65,

```
    struct slink * insertfront( struct slink *head,char *sname)
    {
        struct slink *t;
        t= (struct slink*)malloc(sizeof(struct slink));
        strcpy(t->name,sname);
        t->next=head;
        return t;
    }
```

which takes same parameters as insertrear and always returns the new head. Since the insertion is at the front, the address of the new node created will be the new head. As usual malloc function is used to create a new node t and t->next is assigned the value of head after copying the data into the node. The new head is returned.

We have seen the insertion at the rear and at the front. These routines are quite useful to implement queues and stacks later on. Now let us look at the routine insertpos at lines 80 to 106,

```
struct  slink * insertpos( struct slink *head,char *s,int pos)
{
     /* inserts at a position pos if pos is within the list
     or inserts at the end if pos is greater than the position
     of the last element in the list */
       int i=1;
     struct slink *t,*temp;
     if(pos<1) return head;
     t= (struct slink*)malloc(sizeof(struct slink));
     strcpy(t->name,s);
     if(pos==1)
     {
          t->next=head;
          return t;
     }
     temp=head;
     while((temp->next != NULL)&&(i<pos-1))
  /* stop one position ahead of pos or end of list */
     {
          temp=temp->next;
          i++;
     }
  /* insert */
     t->next=temp->next;
     temp->next=t;
     return head;
}
```

which inserts a node arbitrarily at any specified position. The routine insertpos takes a parameter more than insertrear and insertfront. The extra parameter is necessary to specify the position where the insertion is to be made. We shall design our routine insertpos to insert the node at the specified position if and only if the position is with in the list. If the specified position is greater than the number of elements that exist in the list, the insertion is made at the end. If the position is less than 1 then we do not insert the node and we simply return the old head. This routine also has to return the new head because if position 1 is specified then the head will get changed. This is treated as special case in the routine and is resolved with an if statement.

The else part of the if statement has a while loop which has two conditions. The first condition fails if you reach the end of the list. The second condition fails when you reach a position 1 less than the specified position. Now, at this stage, temp points to one node before the actual position, where insertion has to be made or the last node in the list. However, we are not interested to check whether we have reached the end or the actual position. In any case, we wanted to insert a node at the end of the list if the position specified is outside the list. The node is inserted by assigning t->next with the value of temp->next and t->next with the value of t. This insertion will be correct, even if temp is pointing to the last node.

Let us now turn our attention to the 3 routines that will enable us to delete nodes from the list. Let us start with deleterear at lines 107 to 125

```
struct slink * deleterear( struct slink *head,char *s)
{
        struct slink *t,*temp;
        if(head==NULL)strcpy(s,"\0"); /* if list is empty */
        temp=head;
        t=head;
/* traverse the list till end */
        while(temp->next != NULL)
        {
                t=temp;
                temp=temp->next;
        }
        strcpy(s,temp->name);
        if(temp==head) head=NULL;
        else t->next=NULL;
/* delete the new node */
        free(temp);
        return head;
}
```

which takes two parameters. The first one is as usual the head and the second is pointer to a character string in which the data of the deleted node can be copied. The routine also returns possibly a new head. First the routine tests for an empty list and if the list is empty, it copies an empty string to s and returns, otherwise the list is traversed till the end using a while loop. The important point to note here is, when a node is to be deleted, we need to have the address of the preceding node. In the while loop, we are storing the address of the preceding node in t and current node in temp. We normally refer to this as “t trials temp”. When we come out of the loop, temp points to last node and t points to the last but one of the nodes. If temp is the only node, we make head as NULL, other wise, we make t->next as NULL. We now release the space occupied by the node pointed by temp by using the function free(), of course after copying the data contained in temp to s.

The routine deletefront from lines 126 to 138,

```
struct  slink * deletefront( struct slink *head,char *s)
{
        struct slink *t,*temp;
        if(head==NULL) strcpy(s,"\0"); /* if list is empty */
        else
        {
                temp=head;
                head=temp->next;
                strcpy(s,temp->name);
                free(temp);
        }
        return head;
}
```

is much similar to deleterear except the deletions would now take place at the beginning of the list. The routine deletefront, deletes node pointed by head, provided head is not NULL. The node pointed by head is deleted by assigning head to temp and temp->next to head (new value of head) and releasing temp after copying the data into s.

The routine deletepos which is presented from lines 139 to 174,

```
struct  slink * deletepos( struct slink *head,char *s,int pos)
{
        /* Deletes a node at a position pos if pos is within the list
        and does not delete if pos is greater than the position
        of the last element in the list */
        int i=1;
        struct slink *t,*temp;
        t = head;
        if((pos < 1) || (head == NULL)) return head;

        if(pos==1)
                head = t->next;
```

```
        else
        {
            temp = head;
            while((t != NULL)&&(i < pos))
        /* stop at node to be deleted
        temp points one node preceding */
            {
                temp = t;
                t=t->next;
                i++;
            }
            if(t != NULL)/* deletion possible. do it */
                temp->next = t->next;
            else   /* deletion not possible */
            {
                strcpy(s, "\0");
                return head;
            }
        }
        strcpy(s, t->name);
        free(t);
        return head;
    }
```

deletes the node at the specified position if and only if the specified position is within the list. Otherwise it does not delete any node. If position is specified as 1 then the deletion changes the address of the head, which is taken care by the if part of the if statement testing the position for 1. The else part uses a while loop to traverse to the position specified or to the end of the list incase the position is greater than the list length. Since we are affecting a deletion we set a pointer temp which trails t. We test whether we have reached the end of the list, if so, we do not affect the deletion. Otherwise we have reached the specified position and therefore we affect the deletion as usual by assigning t->next to temp->next. We free t after copying the data into s.

The printlist is a simple routine from line 175 to 185,

```
    void printlist(struct slink *head)
    {
        struct slink *t;
        t = head;
        printf("\n");
```

```
        while(t != NULL)
        {
              printf("%s \n",t->name);
              t=t->next;
        }
  }
```

which runs through the list using a while loop and prints the contents of the list. The routine is extensively used in main to show the contents of the list whenever insertions and deletions are performed on the list.

9.2 IMPLEMENTING STACKS & QUEUES USING LINKED LISTS

We have already seen how to represent stacks and queues sequentially using arrays in the previous chapter. In this section, we will present linked stacks and queues. Fig. 9.4a and Fig. 9.4b depict the linked stacks and queues respectively. Notice that the direction of links for both the stacks and queues are such as to facilitate easy insertion and deletion of the nodes. In case of Stacks (Figure 9.4a), one can easily add a node at the top or delete one from the top using more or less the same routines as insertfront and deletefront. We can also see in the case of Queues (Figure 9.4b), one can easily add a node at the rear and a deletion can be performed at the front using insertrear and deletefront. The implementation of linked stack is presented in Program Listing 9.2.

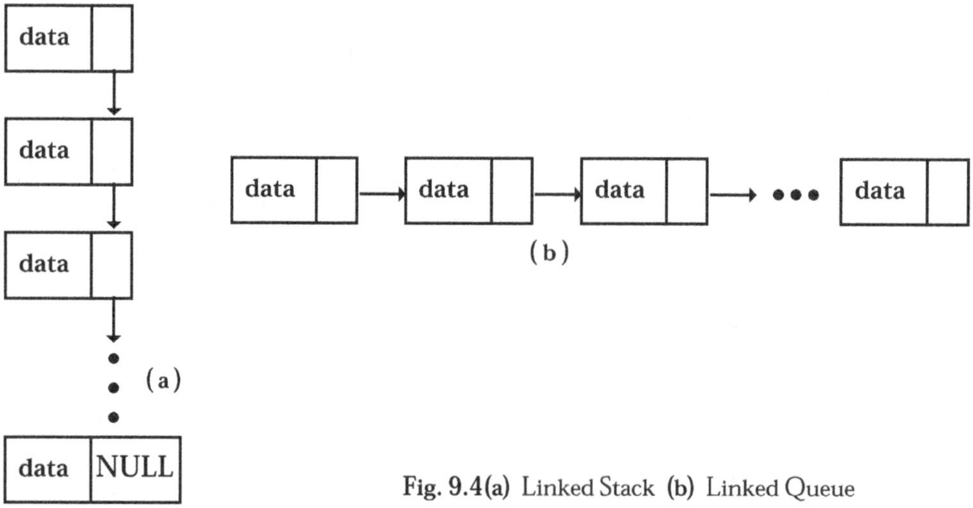
data
data
data
(a)
data
NULL
data
data
data
data
(b)

Fig. 9.4(a) Linked Stack **(b)** Linked Queue

```
/*      Program Listing 9.2: LINKSTAC.C
        A program to Implement Linked Stacks      */

#include <stdio.h>
#include <conio.h>
#include <string.h>
#include <stdlib.h>
struct slink{
      char name[50];
      struct slink *next;
};

struct slink * add_stack( struct slink *top,char *sname)
{
      struct slink *t;
      t = (struct slink*)malloc(sizeof(struct slink));
      strcpy(t->name,sname);
      t->next=top;
      return t;
}
struct  slink * delete_stack( struct slink *top,char *s)
{
      struct slink *t,*temp;
      if(top==NULL) strcpy(s,"\0"); /* if list is empty */
      else
      {
            temp=top;
            top=temp->next;
            strcpy(s,temp->name);
            free(temp);
      }
      return top;
}
```

```
void print_stack(struct slink *top){
    struct slink *t;
    t = top;
    printf("\n");
    while(t != NULL){
        printf("%s \n",t->name);
        t=t->next;
    }
}

void main(void){
    struct slink *top;
    int i;
    char sname[50];
    clrscr();
    top=NULL;
    printf("\nStacks Implementation using Linked List\n");
    top = add_stack(top,"Rama Rao");
    top = add_stack(top,"Krishna Rao");
    top = add_stack(top,"Laxman Rao");
    printf("Data in the Stack is\n");
    print_stack(top);
    top = delete_stack(top, sname);
  printf("Data in the Stack after deleting \'%s\' is\n", sname);
    print_stack(top);
    top = delete_stack(top, sname);
  printf("Data in the Stack after deleting \'%s\' is\n", sname);
    print_stack(top);
    top = delete_stack(top, sname);
  printf("Data in the Stack after deleting \'%s\' is\n", sname);
    print_stack(top);
}
```

```
Stacks Implementation using Linked List

Data in the Stack is
Laxman Rao
Krishna Rao
Rama Rao

Data in the Stack after deleting 'Laxman Rao' is
Krishna Rao
Rama Rao

Data in the Stack after deleting 'Krishna Rao' is
Rama Rao

Data in the Stack after deleting 'Rama Rao' is
```

Program Listing 9.2 Implementation of Linked Stacks

At Lines 5 to 8,

```
struct slink{
      char name[50];
      struct slink *next;
};
```

we declare a self referential structure which will be the node structure of a stack. At Line 46, we have initialized top to NULL to start with. The stack is empty if and only if top is equal to NULL.

From Lines 10 to 17, the add_stack routine,

```
struct slink * add_stack( struct slink *top,char *sname)
{
      struct slink *t;
      t = (struct slink*)malloc(sizeof(struct slink));
      strcpy(t->name,sname);
      t->next=top;
      return t;
}
```

is just similar to insertfront routine of Program Listing 9.1. The routine returns the new top every time it is called, since the new node is inserted on the top of the stack (Figure 9.4a).

From Line 18 to 30,

```
struct  slink * delete_stack( struct slink *top,char *s)
{
        struct slink *t,*temp;
        if(top==NULL) strcpy(s,"\0"); /* if list is empty */
        else
        {
                temp=top;
                top=temp->next;
                strcpy(s,temp->name);
                free(temp);
        }
        return top;
}
```

the delete_stack is just similar to deletefront routine of Program Listing 9.1. The routine at the beginning tests for stack empty condition by testing if top equals to NULL. Note that this routine also should return new top.

From Lines 31 to 39, the routine print_stack, prints the contents of the stack whenever called.

```
void print_stack(struct slink *top){
        struct slink *t;
        t = top;
        printf("\n");
        while(t != NULL){
                printf("%s \n",t->name);
                t=t->next;
        }
}
```

In the main, several add_stacks and delete_stacks are included alternatively, to allow the student to understand the implementation clearly. Next we implement a queue using linked list. The program for linked queue is presented in Program Listing 9.3.

```
/*      Program Listing 9.3: LINKQUEU.C
        A program to Implement Linked Queues      */
#include<stdio.h>
#include <conio.h>
#include <stdlib.h>
#include<string.h>

struct slink{
        char name[50];
        struct slink *next;
};
struct slink *front=NULL, *rear = NULL;
void add_queue(char *sname)
{
        struct slink *t;
        t  = (struct slink*)malloc(sizeof(struct slink));
        strcpy(t->name,sname);
        t->next=NULL;
        if(front==NULL)front=t;
        else rear->next=t;
        rear=t;
}
void delete_queue( char *s)
{
        struct slink *t,*temp;
        if(front==NULL) strcpy(s,"\0"); /* if list is empty */
        else
        {
                temp=front;
                strcpy(s,temp->name);
                front=temp->next;
                if( front == NULL) rear = NULL;
                                            /*Deleting the last node   */
                free(temp);
        }
}
```

```
void print_queue(void){
      struct slink *t;
      t = front;
      printf(“\n”);
      while(t != NULL){
            printf(“%s \n”,t->name);
            t=t->next;
      }
}

void main(void){
      int i;
      char sname[50];
      clrscr();
      printf(“Queues Implementation using Linked List\n”);
      add_queue(“RAMA RAO”);
      add_queue(“KRISHNA RAO”);
      add_queue(“LAXMAN RAO”);
      printf(“Printing Data in the Queue\n”);
      print_queue();
      printf(“Deleting Data from the Queue\n”);
      delete_queue(sname);
      printf(“Printing Data in the Queue\n”);
      print_queue();
      delete_queue(sname);
      printf(“Printing Data in the Queue\n”);
      print_queue();
      delete_queue(sname);
      printf(“Printing Data in the Queue\n”);
      print_queue();
}
```

```
Queues Implementation using Linked List

Printing Data in the Queue
RAMA RAO
KRISHNA RAO
LAXMAN RAO

Deleting Data from the Queue
Printing Data in the Queue
KRISHNA RAO
LAXMAN RAO

Printing Data in the Queue
LAXMAN RAO

Printing Data in the Queue
RAMA RAO
KRISHNA RAO
LAXMAN RAO
```

Program Listing 9.3 Implementation of Queues using Linked List

We have made a change in implementing queues. We have declared the front and rear as global variables, in order to avoid passing these as parameters to add_queue and delete_queue. Note that the return types of add_queue and delete_queue routines will now be void as front and rear are global. However, the student is reminded that this is not a good practice, if you are using multiple queues.

From Lines 11 to 20,

```
void add_queue(char *sname)
{
      struct slink *t;
      t= (struct slink*)malloc(sizeof(struct slink));
      strcpy(t->name,sname);
      t->next=NULL;
      if(front==NULL)front=t;
      else
            rear->next=t;
      rear=t;
}
```

the routine add_queue is somewhat similar to insertrear routine of Program Listing 9.1. However, we need not have to traverse the list to find the end of the list, since we are holding the address of the last node of the queue in **rear**. We simply test whether the insertion is a first insertion or not (front == NULL) and if so update front, otherwise we add the node at the end using rear (rear->next = t). The rear is always updated (rear = t).

From Lines 21 to 33, the delete_queue routine is somewhat similar to deletefront routine of Program Listing 9.1. In the beginning we test for the emptiness of the queue before affecting the deletion. Note the if statement with in the else which tests for the deletions of the last node and appropriately makes rear null.

```
void delete_queue( char *s)
{
        struct slink *t,*temp;
        if(front==NULL) strcpy(s,"\0"); /* if list is empty */
        else
        {
                temp=front;
                strcpy(s,temp->name);
                front=temp->next;
                if( front == NULL) rear = NULL; /*Deleting the last node   */
                free(temp);
        }
}
```

From Lines 31 t 41.

```
void print_queue(void){
        struct slink *t;
        t = front;
        printf("\n");
        while(t != NULL){
                printf("%s \n",t->name);
                t=t->next;
        }
}
```

The print_queue routine is just the same as print_stack routine of the previous program and doesn't need any explanation.

9.3 CIRCULAR LINKED LIST

One problem, you must have noticed with the earlier programs on linked list is that every time we make an insertion or deletion, we have to update the head of the list. Another problem is to check when exactly, the head should change. For example, consider the insertrear routine of Program Listing 9.1. The head of list does not change except when you are inserting the first node. This condition is to be explicitly checked in the program. As an other example, consider, insertfront. Every time the new node is inserted, the value of head will change and we need not have to explicitly test for the first insertion. To be able to make these routines consistent, we introduce the concept of Circular Linked List. In circular list, we create a dummy node called head and this node does not contain any data. This is simply the head of the list. The representation of the empty Circular list is shown in the Fig 9.5a.

Note that, the value of next field of the head node for the empty list is head itself. Fig 9.5b represents a circular list with three nodes inserted into the list. Now with these ideas let us present a program in Program Listing 9.4 to illustrate the implementation of circular linked list.

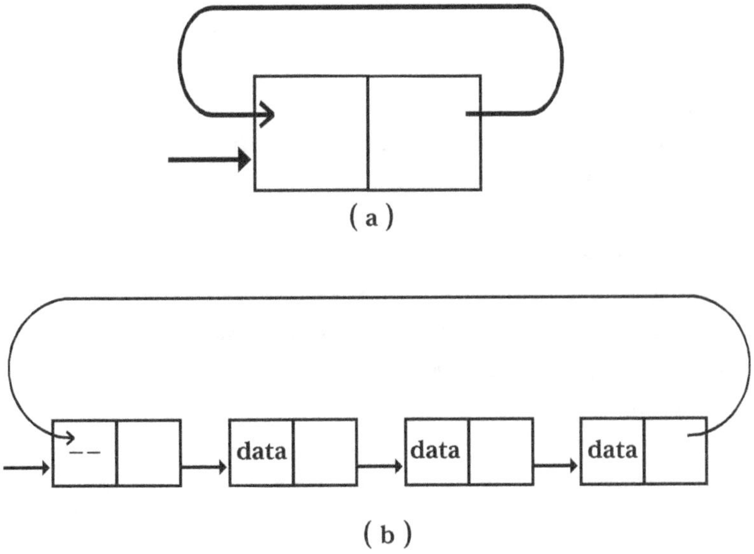
(a)
--
data
data
data
(b)

Figure 9.5 Circular Linked List

```
/*      Program Listing 9.4: CLINK.C
        A program to Implement Circular Linked Lists      */

#include<stdio.h>
#include<string.h>
#include <stdlib.h>
#include <conio.h>

struct slink{
        char name[50];
        struct slink *next;
};
    /* circular list */
void insertfront( struct slink *head,char *sname)
{
        struct slink *t;
        t  = (struct slink*)malloc(sizeof(struct slink));
        strcpy(t->name,sname);
        t->next=head->next;
        head->next=t;
}
void insertrear( struct slink *head,char *sname)
{
        struct slink *t,*temp;
        t  = (struct slink*)malloc(sizeof(struct slink));
        strcpy(t->name,sname);
        t->next=head;
        temp=head;
/* traverse the list till end */
        while(temp->next != head) temp=temp->next;
/* insert the new node */
        temp->next=t;
}
void deleterear( struct slink *head,char *s)
{
        struct slink *t,*temp;
        if(head->next==head) strcpy(s,"\0"); /* if list is empty */
            temp  =  head;
```

```
            t  =  head;
    /* traverse the list till end */
      while(temp->next != head)
      {
            t=temp;
            temp=temp->next;
      }
      strcpy(s,temp->name);
      t->next=head;
    /* delete the new node */
      free(temp);
}
void deletefront( struct slink *head,char *s)
{
      struct slink *t,*temp;
      if(head->next==head) strcpy(s,"\0"); /* if list is empty */
      else
      {
            temp=head->next;
            head->next=temp->next;
            strcpy(s,temp->name);
            free(temp);
      }
}
void insertpos( struct slink *head,char *s,int pos)
{
    /* inserts at a position pos if pos is within the list
    or inserts at the end if pos is greater than the position
    of the last element in the list */
      int i=1;
      struct slink *t,*temp;
      if(pos<1) exit(0);
      t = (struct slink*)malloc(sizeof(struct slink));
      strcpy(t->name,s);
      temp=head;
      while((temp->next != head)&&(i++<pos)) temp=temp->next;
      t->next=temp->next;
```

```
        temp->next=t;
}
void deletepos( struct slink *head,char *s,int pos)
{
    /* deletes at a position pos if pos is within the list
    or deletes at the end if pos is greater than the position
    of the last element in the list */
        int i=1;
        struct slink *t,*temp;
        if(pos<1)
                exit(0);
        t=head;
        temp=head->next;
        while((temp != head)&&(i++<pos))
        {
                t = temp;
                temp = temp->next;
        }
        if(temp != head)
        {
                t->next=temp->next;
                strcpy(s, t->name);
                free(temp);
        }
}

void printlist(struct slink *head)
{
        struct slink *t;
        t = head->next;
        printf("\n");
        while(t != head)
        {
                printf("%s\n",t->name);
                t=t->next;
        }
}
```

```
void main(void)
{
        struct slink *head;
        int i;
        char sname[50];
        head = (struct slink*)malloc(sizeof(struct slink));
        strcpy(head, "\0");
        head->next=head;
        while (1)
        {
              printf("enter 1 to cont. 0 to break: ");
              scanf("%d",&i);
              fflush(stdin);
              if(i==0) break;
              printf("enter the name: ");
              scanf("%[^\n]",sname);
              fflush(stdin);
              insertrear(head,sname);
        }
        clrscr();
        printf("Adding at Rear\n");
        printlist(head);
        printf("\nBegin of Insertion\nInserting at Front");
        printlist(head);
        printf("\nInserting at Pos 3 & 6\n");
        insertpos(head,"Laxman Rao",3);
        insertpos(head,"Rama Rao",6);
        printlist(head);
        printf("\nEnd of Insertion\n");
        printf("\nDeleting at Pos 1");
        deletepos(head, sname, 1);
        printlist(head);
        printf("\nDeleting at Pos 3 & 7");
        deletepos(head, sname, 3);
        printlist(head);
```

```
        deletepos(head, sname, 7);
        printlist(head);
        printf("\nDeleting at Rear");
        deleterear(head,sname);
        printf("\nDeleting at Front");
        deletefront(head,sname);
        printlist(head);
}
```

```
enter 1 to cont. 0 to break:1
enter the name:Ravi
enter 1 to cont. 0 to break:1
enter the name:Kiran
enter 1 to cont. 0 to break:1
enter the name:Padmanabham
enter 1 to cont. 0 to break:1
enter the name:Naresh
enter 1 to cont. 0 to break:1
Adding at Rear

Ravi
Kiran
Padmanabham
Naresh

Begin of Insertion
Inserting at Front
Krishna Rao
Ravi
Kiran
Padmanabham
Naresh
```

```
Inserting at Pos 3 & 6

Krishna Rao
Ravi
Laxman Rao
Kiran
Padmanabham
Rama Rao
Naresh

End of Insertion

Deleting at Pos 1
Ravi
Laxman Rao
Kiran
Padmanabham
Rama Rao
Naresh

Deleting at Pos 3 & 7
Ravi
Laxman Rao
Padmanabham
Rama Rao
Naresh

Ravi
Laxman Rao
Padmanabham
Rama Rao
Naresh

Deleting at Rear
Deleting at Front
Laxman Rao
Padmanabham
Rama Rao
```

Program Listing 9.4 Implementation of Circular Linked List

At Lines 116 to 118,

```
head= (struct slink*)malloc(sizeof(struct slink));
strcpy(head, "\0");
head->next=head;
```

we have created the dummy node head, which will be the head of the list always. The dummy node has been made into an empty list by making head->next as head and copying an empty string to the data field (Fig 9.5 a). Now for all the routines the return type is void as no routine alters the address of the head node.

Another point to be observed is that the list empty condition need not be checked in insertfront or insertrear. In the routine insertpos also we are not checking specially for position 1 as we did in the previous programs. Position 1 will also be taken care by remaining logic of the program. In the deletefront routine, since we are not changing the value of the head, we need not have to return it. Further, in deleterear, we need not have to check for the last node being removed since, the head will not become NULL. The deletepos routine will also be simpler now, since we need not have to check explicitly for position 1 and handle it seperately.

9.4 DOUBLY LINKED LIST

So far we have been working with singly linked linear lists. For some problems these would be too restrictive. One difficulty with these lists is that if we are pointing to a specific node, say p, then we can easily move only in the direction of the links. The only way to find the node which precedes p is to start back at the beginning of the list. The same problem arises when one wishes to delete an arbitrary node from a singly linked list. As seen earlier, in order to easily delete an arbitrary node one must know the preceding node. If we have a problem, where moving in either direction is often necessary, then it is useful to have doubly linked lists. Each node now has two link fields, one linking in the forward direction and one in the backward direction.

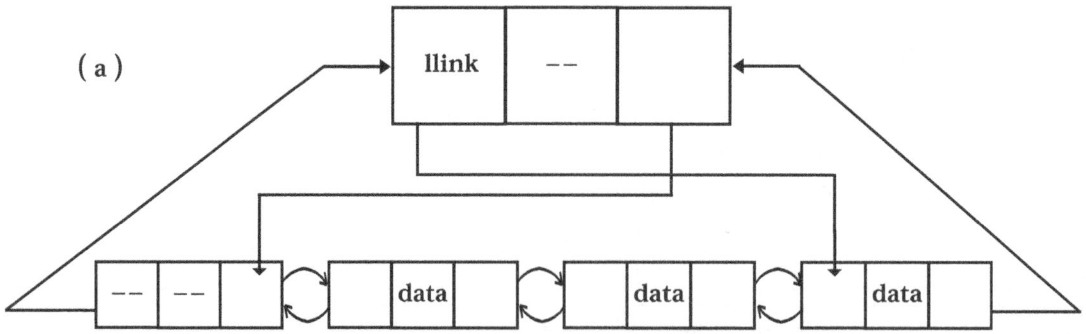
(a)
llink
--
--
--
data
data
data

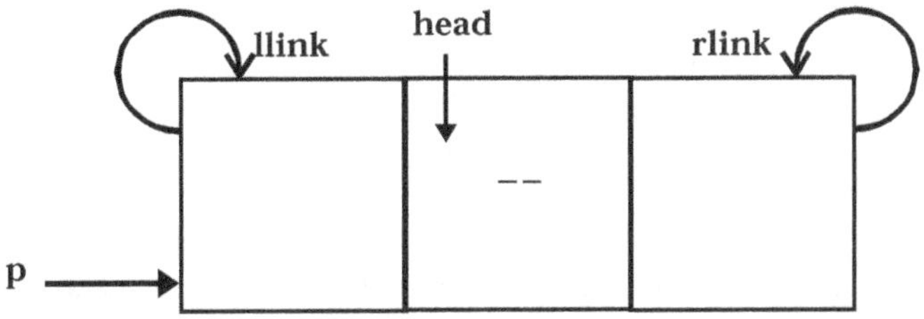
head
llink
rlink
--
p

Figure 9.6 a Doubly Linked List **b** Empty Doubly Linked List

A node in a doubly linked list has at least 3 fields, say data, llink (left link) and rlink (right link). A doubly linked list may or may not be circular. A sample doubly linked circular list with 3 nodes is given in Fig 9.6a. Besides these three nodes, a special node has been added called a head node. As was true in the earlier sections, head nodes are again convenient for the algorithms. The data field of the head node will not usually contain information. Now suppose that p points to any node in a doubly linked list, then it is the case that, p is equal to p->llink->rlink and also equal to p->rlink->llink. This reflects the essential virtue of this structure namely, that one can go back and forth with equal ease. An empty list is not really empty since it will always have its head node and it will look like Fig. 9.6b

Now to work with these lists, we must be able to insert and delete nodes. In Program Listing 9.4, we present the program to create a doubly linked list and the associated routines.

```
/*      Program Listing 9.5: DLINK.C
        A program to Implement Doubly Linked Lists      */

#include<stdio.h>
#include <conio.h>
#include <stdlib.h>
#include<string.h>
struct dlink{
        char name[50];
        struct dlink *llink;
        struct dlink *rlink;
};
void insert(struct dlink *head,char *sname)
{
        struct dlink *t;
        t= (struct dlink*)malloc(sizeof(struct dlink));
```

```
        strcpy( t->name, sname);
        head->rlink->llink=t;
        t->rlink=head->rlink;
        t->llink=head;
        head->rlink=t;
}
struct dlink *search(struct dlink *head, char *sname)
{
        struct dlink *t;
        t = head->rlink;
        while(t != head)
        {
                if((strcmp(t->name, sname)) == 0)
                        return t;
                t = t->rlink;
        }
        return NULL;
}
int delete(struct dlink *head,char *sname)
{
        struct dlink *t;
        t = search(head, sname);
        if(t == NULL)
                return 0;
        t->llink->rlink = t->rlink;
        t->rlink->llink = t->llink;
        free(t);
        return 1;
}
void printlistfwd(struct dlink *head){
        struct dlink *t;
        t = head->rlink;
        while(t != head){
                printf("%s \n",t->name);
                t=t->rlink;
        }
}
```

```
void printlistrev(struct dlink *head){
      struct dlink *t;
      t = head->llink;
      while(t != head){
            printf("%s \n",t->name);
            t=t->llink;
      }
}

void main(void){
      struct dlink *head;
      int i;
      char sname[50];
      head = (struct dlink*)malloc(sizeof(struct dlink));
      strcpy(head, "\0");
      head->llink =head->rlink = head;
      insert(head, "Rama");
      while (1){
            printf("enter the name ");
            scanf("%s",sname);
            insert(head,sname);
            printf("enter 1 to cont. 0 to break");
            scanf("%d",&i);
            if(i==0) break;
      }
      clrscr();
      printf("\nAfter Insertion\nForward List\n");
      printlistfwd(head);
      printf("\nAfter Insertion\nBackward List\n");
      printlistrev(head);
      printf("\n");
      getchar();
      fflush(stdin);
      printf("\nEnter the name to be deleted from the list: ");
```

```
        scanf("%[^\n]", sname);
        if(!delete(head, sname))
        fprintf(stderr, "\nUnable to delete the %s ", sname);
        printf("\nAfter Deletion\nForward List\n");
        printlistfwd(head);
        printf("\nAfter Deletion\nBackward List\n");
        printlistrev(head);
}
```

```
enter the name Ravi
enter 1 to cont. 0 to break 1
enter the name Kiran
enter 1 to cont. 0 to break 1
enter the name Padmanabham
enter 1 to cont. 0 to break 1
enter the name Naresh
enter 1 to cont. 0 to break 1

After Insertion
Forward List
Naresh
Padmanabham
Kiran
Ravi
Rama

After Insertion
Backward List
Rama
Ravi
Kiran
Padmanabham
Naresh
```

```
Enter the name to be deleted from the list: Kiran
After Deletion
Forward List
Naresh
Padmanabham
Ravi
Rama

After Deletion
Backward List
Rama
Ravi
Padmanabham
Naresh
```

Program Listing 9.5 Implementation of Doubly Linked List

At Lines 5 to 9,

```
struct dlink{
    char name[50];
    struct dlink *llink;
    struct dlink *rlink;
};
```

we have declared a self-referential structure dlink which has now two links llink and rlink as required for a doubly linked list. The data field is as usual taken as an array of character to hold a string which could always be changed or more fields can be added as per the requirement.

From Lines 64 to 66, in main,

```
head = (struct dlink*)malloc(sizeof(struct dlink));
strcpy(head, "\0");
head->llink =head->rlink = head;
```

we have created a head node and set the pointers of right link and left link to point to head itself as shown in Fig 9.6b to constitute an empty list.

From Lines 10 to 19,

```
void insert(struct dlink *head,char *sname)
{
    struct dlink *t;
    t= (struct dlink*)malloc(sizeof(struct dlink));
```

```
        strcpy( t->name, sname);
        head->rlink->llink=t;
        t->rlink=head->rlink;
        t->llink=head;
        head->rlink=t;
}
```

the insert routine, inserts the node to the right of the head node as shown in Figure 9.7.

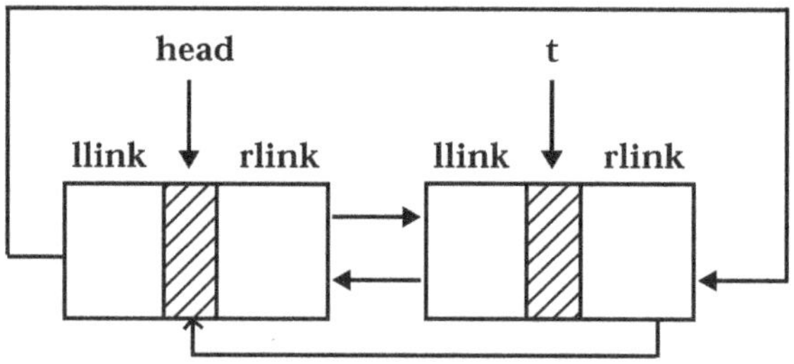
head
t
llink
rlink
llink
rlink

Figure 9.7 Insertion of first node into a Doubly Linked List

In the routine, as usual we are creating a node by using malloc and storing the address into t. To insert a new node, we have to affect changes in four pointers as marked and shown in the Fig. 9.7. The following is the order in which the four pointers have to be changed to affect the correct insertion without loosing any links.

(1) *head->rlink->llink = t;*
(2) *t->rlink = head->rlink;*
(3) *t->llink = head;*
(4) *head->rlink = t*

where head is the head of the list and t is the node to be inserted. The student is advised to be sure about the above pointer manipulations before proceedings further.

Since arbitrary deletions are possible in a doubly linked list. We now present a delete routine, which searches for a specified node and deletes it. There are number of ways in specifying the node to be deleted like, specifying the position or specifying the address or specifying the data content of the node. We shall use in the last one, i.e., specifying the data content in our routine delete.

The delete routine, at Line 32 to 42,

```
int delete(struct dlink *head,char *sname)
{
        struct dlink *t;
        t = search(head, sname);
```

```
        if(t == NULL)
        return 0;
        t->llink->rlink = t->rlink;
        t->rlink->llink = t->llink;
        free(t);
        return 1;
    }
```

takes two parameters head and sname and returns 1, if the deletion is successful and 0 if unsuccessful. Delete calls the function search. The routine search at line 20 to 31,

```
    struct dlink *search(struct dlink *head, char *sname)
    {
        struct dlink *t;
        t = head->rlink;
        while(t != head)
        {
            if((strcmp(t->name, sname)) == 0)
            return t;
            t = t->rlink;
        }
    return NULL;
}
```

using a while loop, traverses the list and looks for the data at each node, and compares with the specified data. This comparison is done using strcmp and when the data at any node is found search returns the address of the node. Otherwise search will return NULL.

The delete routine returns a 0, if search returns NULL, otherwise affects deletion (Fig. 9.8) of the node whose address is in t (returned by search). To affect the deletion, the following are the two pointers to be changed

(1) *t->llink->rlink = t->rlink;*

(2) *t->rlink->llink = t->llink;*

The above two pointer changes will simply bridge out t and thus t can be freed. Once again the student is advised to be sure of these changes.

Now we have two print routines printlistfwd and printlistrev. We have already said that we can traverse a doubly linked list in either direction. The printlistfwd routine at Lines 43 to 50,

```
void printlistfwd(struct dlink *head){
      struct dlink *t;
      t = head->rlink;
      while(t != head){
            printf("%s \n",t->name);
            t=t->rlink;
      }
}
```

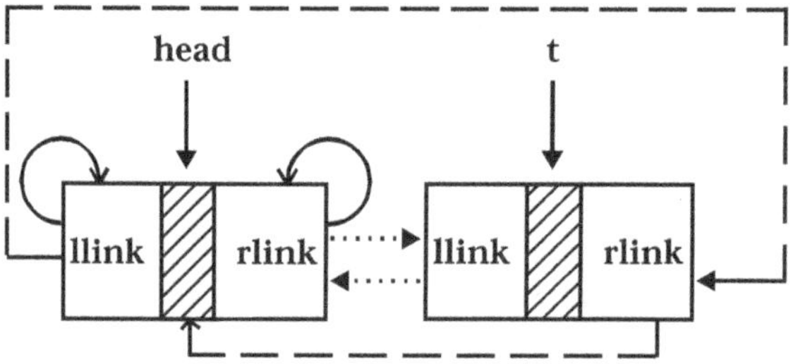
head
t
llink
rlink
llink
rlink

Figure 9.8 Deletion of Last Node from Doubly Linked List

picks up the right link of the head node, uses a while loop to traverse all the nodes printing the contents of each node. Note the while loop terminating condition is t != head will terminate the while loop at the end of the list.

The only change in the printlistrev is it picks left link of the head instead of the right link and traverses the list in the opposite direction.

9.5 INPLACE REVERSAL OF SINGLY LINKED LIST

It is often necessary and desirable to build a variety of routines for manipulating singly linked list. Some of these routines are slightly intricate. One of them is to invert a chain. This routine is especially interesting because, it has to do the reversal ***inplace***. By inplace we mean no new node should be created while reversing the list. We will present the program in Program Listing 9.6.

```
/*      Program Listing 9.6: REVLIST.C
     A program to Implement Inplace Reversal Lists      */

#include<stdio.h>
#include<string.h>
#include <stdlib.h>
```

```
#include <conio.h>

struct slink{
        char name[50];
        struct slink *next;
};
struct slink * invertlist( struct slink *head)
{
        struct slink *p,*q,*r;
        p=head;
        q=NULL;
        while(p != NULL)
        {
                r=q;
                q=p;
                p=p->next;
                q->next=r;
        }
        return q;
}
struct slink * insertfront( struct slink *head,char *sname)
{
        struct slink *t;
        t= (struct slink*)malloc(sizeof(struct slink));
        strcpy(t->name,sname);
        t->next=head;
        return t;
}

void printlist(struct slink *head)
{
        struct slink *t;
        t = head;
        printf("\n");
```

```
        while(t != NULL)
        {
            printf("%s \n",t->name);
            t=t->next;
        }
}

void main(void)
{
        struct slink *head;
        int i;
        char sname[50];
        head=NULL;
        while (1)
        {
            printf("enter 1 to cont. 0 to break: ");
            scanf("%d",&i);
            fflush(stdin);
            if(i==0) break;
            printf("enter the name: ");
            scanf("%[^\n]",sname);
            fflush(stdin);
            head = insertfront(head,sname);
        }
        clrscr();
        printf("\nThe List is \n");
        printlist(head);
        printf("\nThe Reversed List is \n");
        head=invertlist(head);
        printlist(head);
}
```

```
enter 1 to cont. 0 to break:1
enter the name: Ravi
enter 1 to cont. 0 to break:1
enter the name: Kiran
enter 1 to cont. 0 to break:1
enter the name: Padmanabham
enter 1 to cont. 0 to break:1
enter the name: Naresh
enter 1 to cont. 0 to break:0

The List is
Naresh
Padmanabham
Kiran
Ravi

The Reversed List is

Ravi
Kiran
Padmanabham
Naresh
```

Program Listing 9.6 Implementation of Inplace Reversal Lists

Since, we cannot reverse a list unless we create one first. Therefore, we have used the routine insertfront (which has already been discussed earlier) to create a list. This is done at the beginning of the main using a while loop and calling insertfront repeatedly. At Line 66, the invert list is called from main passing the head of the list as a parameter. The invertlist returns the new head which is the head of the reversed list. It is interesting to look at invertlist from Line 10 to 23,

```
struct slink * invertlist( struct slink *head)
{
    struct slink *p,*q,*r;
    p=head;
    q=NULL;
    while(p != NULL)
    {
        r=q;
        q=p;
```

```
                p=p->next;
                q->next=r;
            }
            return q;
        }
```

which uses three pointers p, q, r. q trails p and r trails q. Initially p is assigned with head and q with NULL. The while loop has a termination condition, p != NULL. Within the while loop, r is given the value q, since r trails q. q is given the value p, since q trails p. p moves to the next node (p = p->next) and only one pointer need to be manipulated i.e., you have to link q (possibly the middle node) to the previous node r. The while loop comes to an end when p is equal to NULL i.e., when q points to the last node. Therefore, we return the value q as the new head of the inverted list.

The student should try this program out on at least 3 examples, the empty list, list of 1 and 2 to clearly understand the mechanism.

9.6 MERGING OF TWO SORTED LISTS

Another useful program in linked list is merging of two sorted lists. Given two sorted lists L_1 and L_2 to produce a list L that contains all the elements of L_1 and L_2 in a sorted order. This can be produced with an algorithm / program with linear time complexity of the order O(n) where n is the number of total elements. Program Listing 9.7 presents a program for merging two sorted lists.

```
/*      Program Listing 9.7: MERGE.C
    A program to Implement Inplace Reversal Lists      */

#include<stdio.h>
#include<string.h>
#include <stdlib.h>
#include <conio.h>

struct slink{
    char name[50];
    struct slink *next;
};
struct slink * insertrear( struct slink *head,char *sname)
{
    struct slink *t,*temp;
    t = (struct slink*)malloc(sizeof(struct slink));
```

```
        strcpy(t->name,sname);
        t->next=NULL;
        if(head==NULL) return t; /* if list is empty */
        temp=head;
    /* traverse the list till end */
        while(temp->next != NULL) temp=temp->next;
        /* insert the new node */
        temp->next=t;
        return head;
    }

    struct slink * mergelist(struct slink *list1, struct slink *list2)
    {
        struct slink *p,*q, *r;
        p=list1;
        q=list2;
        r=NULL;
        while(p != NULL && q != NULL)
        {
            if(strcmp(p->name, q->name) < 0)
            {
                r=insertrear(r,p->name);
                p = p->next;
            }
            else
            {
                r=insertrear(r,q->name);
                q = q->next;
            }
        }
        while(p != NULL)
        {
            r=insertrear(r,p->name);
            p = p->next;
        }
```

```
        while(q != NULL)
        {
            r=insertrear(r,q->name);
            q = q->next;
        }
        return r;
}
void printlist(struct slink *head)
{
        struct slink *t;
        t = head;
        printf("\n");
        while(t != NULL)
        {
            printf("%s \n",t->name);
            t=t->next;
        }
}

void main(void)
{
        struct slink *head, *head1, *head2;
        int i;
        head = head1 = NULL;
        printf("\nMerge Listing ...\n");
        head = insertrear(head,"AAA");
        head = insertrear(head, "BBB");
        head = insertrear(head, "QQQ");
        head = insertrear(head,"RRR");

        head1 = insertrear(head1,"FFF");
        head1 = insertrear(head1,"GGG");
        head1 = insertrear(head1,"QQQ");
        head1 = insertrear(head1,"SSS");
        head1 = insertrear(head1,"TTT");

        clrscr();
        printf("The List1 is \n");
```

```
        printlist(head);
        printf("The List2 is \n");
        printlist(head1);
        printf("The Merged List is \n");
        head2=mergelist(head, head1);
        printlist(head2);
}
```

```
Merge Listing ...
The List1 is

AAA
BBB
QQQ
RRR

The List2 is

FFF
GGG
QQQ
SSS
TTT

The Merged List is

AAA
BBB
FFF
GGG
QQQ
QQQ
RRR
SSS
TTT
```

Program Listing 9.7 Implementation of Merge Lists

We use insertrear routine to create the two-sorted lists. Insertrear is called a number of times to construct two sorted lists, which are pointed, by head and head1. At Line 91, mergelist is called by the main with two lists as parameters. Mergelist returns the list obtained by merging List1 and List2.

Now let us look at mergelist from Lines 25 to 55,

```
struct slink * mergelist(struct slink *list1, struct slink *list2)
{
      struct slink *p,*q, *r;
      p=list1;
      q=list2;
      r=NULL;
      while(p != NULL && q != NULL)
      {
      if(strcmp(p->name, q->name) < 1)
      {
            r=insertrear(r,p->name);
            p = p->next;
      }
      else
      {
            r=insertrear(r,q->name);
            q = q->next;
      }
  }
  while(p != NULL)
  {
      r=insertrear(r,p->name);
      p = p->next;
  }
  while(q != NULL)
  {
      r=insertrear(r,q->name);
      q = q->next;
  }
  return r;
}
```

We have declared 3 pointers p, q, r. p holds the starting address of list1 and q that of list2. The variable r points to the third list obtained by merging list1 and list2. In the first while loop, we compare p->name with q->name using strcmp. If strcmp returns a value less than 1, we insert p->name into the new list and advance p, else we insert q->name into the new list and advance q. The while loop is exited when one of the lists exhaust (while p!= NULL && q != NULL).

The next two while loops are necessary to copy the remaining list of either list1 or list2 which ever has not exhausted. The head of the merged list r is returned by the routine.

9.7 INSERTIONS & DELETIONS IN A SORTED CIRCULAR LISTS

As a last program in this chapter we shall present a sorted circular list into which insertions and deletions are made. The program listing 9.8 presents the insertion and deletion into a sorted list.

```
/*      Program Listing 9.8      CSL.c
A program to insert and delete from a circular sorted list     */

#include<stdio.h>
#include<string.h>
#include <stdlib.h>
#include <conio.h>

struct slink{
int data;
struct slink *next;
};
void insertlist(struct slink *);
void deletelist( struct slink *);
void printlist(struct slink *);

void main(void)
{
        struct slink *head;
        int i;
        head=(struct slink*)malloc(sizeof(struct slink));
        head->data=0;
        head->next=head;/* create the head node */
        clrscr();
```

```
    while (1)
    {
        printf(“1.insert\n2.delete\n3.print list\n4.exit\n”);
        printf(“enter your choice:”);
        scanf(“%d”,&i);
        fflush(stdin);
        switch(i)
        {
            case 1: insertlist(head);break;
            case 2: deletelist(head);break;
            case 3: printlist(head); break;
            case 4: exit(0);/* program terminates here*/
            default :printf(“invalid option\n”);
        }
    }
}

void insertlist( struct slink *head)
{
    struct slink *t,*p,*q;
    int n;
    p=head->next;
    q=head; /* q lags p */
    t= (struct slink*)malloc(sizeof(struct slink));
    printf(“enter the numberto be inserted:”);
    scanf(“%d”,&n);
    t->data=n;
    while(p!=head)
    {
        if(p->data>n) break;
        q=p;
        p=p->next;
    }
    q->next=t;
    t->next=p;/* insert the new node */
}
```

```
void deletelist( struct slink *head)
{
	struct slink *p,*q;
	int n;
	p=head->next;
	q=head;
	printf("enter the number to be deleted:");
	scanf("%d",&n);
	while(p!=head)
	{
		if(p->data==n) /* node is found delete */
		{
			q->next=p->next;
			free(p);
			break;
		}
		if(p->data>n) break; /* no use searching further */
			q=p;
		p=p->next;
	}

}
void printlist(struct slink *head)
{
	struct slink *t;
	t = head->next;
	printf("\n");
	while(t != head)
	{
		printf("%d ",t->data);
		t=t->next;
	}
	printf("\n");
}
```

```
1.insert
2.delete
3.print list
4.exit
enter your choice:1
enter the numberto be inserted:2

1.insert
2.delete
3.print list
4.exit
enter your choice:1
enter the numberto be inserted:4

1.insert
2.delete
3.print list
4.exit
enter your choice:1
enter the numberto be inserted:6

1.insert
2.delete
3.print list
4.exit
enter your choice:1
enter the numberto be inserted:7

1.insert
2.delete
3.print list
4.exit
enter your choice:1
enter the numberto be inserted:8
```

```
1.insert
2.delete
3.print list
4.exit
enter your choice:3
2 4 6 7 8

1.insert
2.delete
3.print list
4.exit
enter your choice:2
enter the number to be deleted:2

1.insert
2.delete
3.print list
4.exit
enter your choice:2
enter the number to be deleted:4

1.insert
2.delete
3.print list
4.exit
enter your choice:2
enter the number to be deleted:8

1.insert
2.delete
3.print list
4.exit
enter your choice:3
6 7

1.insert
2.delete
3.print list
4.exit
enter your choice:4
```

Program Listing 9.8 *Implementation of Insertion & Deletion in a Sorted Circular Queue*

In this program we chose to work with a circular linked list. At lines 20 to 22,

```
head=(struct slink*)malloc(sizeof(struct slink));
head->data=0;
head->next=head;/* create the head node */
```

in the main() we have created the head node and made it into the empty circular list (refer Fig. 9.5a). From lines 24 to 38,

```
while (1)
{
      printf("1.insert\n2.delete\n3.print list\n4.exit\n");
      printf("enter your choice:");
      scanf("%d",&i);
      fflush(stdin);
      switch(i)
      {
            case 1: insertlist(head);break;
            case 2: deletelist(head);break;
            case 3: printlist(head); break;
            case 4: exit(0);/* program terminates here*/
            default :printf("invalid option\n");
      }
}
```

an user interface giving different choices to the user is created using a switch statement in a while loop. Note that the while loop is an infinite loop and the program can only be exited by selecting choice 4. The inserlistt routine from lines 41 to 59,

```
void insertlist( struct slink *head)
{
      struct slink *t,*p,*q;
      int n;
      p=head->next;
      q=head; /* q lags p */
      t= (struct slink*)malloc(sizeof(struct slink));
      printf("enter the numberto be inserted:");
      scanf("%d",&n);
      t->data=n;
```

```
        while(p!=head)
        {
            if(p->data>n) break;
            q=p;
            p=p->next;
        }
        q->next=t;
        t->next=p;/* insert the new node */
    }
```

inserts the integer data entered by the user into a sorted list. At line 43, three node pointers t, p, q are declared. At line 47, a new node is created and its address is stored in t. The while loop at line 51, allows traversal through the list and find the proper position for insertion. Note that ***q*** is set to trail ***p***, as we need the address of the node prior to the position where insertion has to take place. If all the numbers in the sorted list are less than the number to be inserted, the new number will be inserted at the last position. This is the case when the while loop terminates with the condition when ***p*** equals to ***head***. If the number to be inserted falls somewhere in the list, then the while loop is terminated through the **break** statement at line 53. The last part of the routine (at lines 57 and 58), inserts the new node into the sorted list. The deletelist routine from lines 60 to 81,

```
    void deletelist( struct slink *head)
    {
        struct slink *p,*q;
        int n;
        p=head->next;
        q=head;
        printf("enter the number to be deleted:");
        scanf("%d",&n);
        while(p!=head)
        {
            if(p->data==n) /* node is found delete */
            {
                q->next=p->next;
                free(p);
                break;
            }
            if(p->data>n) break; /* no use searching further */
            q=p;
            p=p->next;
        }
    }
```

deletes the node specified by the user if it exists in the list, otherwise, it simply does nothing. While effecting a deletion in a singly linked list, we need the address of the node preceeding the node to be deleted. So we set ***q*** to trail ***p***. Once again, if the node is found it is deleted(lines 70 to 75) and the while loop is terminated through a **break** statement. The if statement at line 76, terminates the search for the node to be deleted, should the number entered by the user exceeds the current value. The reason for this is, the list is a sorted list and there is no use traversing the list beyond this point.

The printlist routine is just the same which we have been using in the earlier programs.

SELF-REVIEW EXERCISES

1. A self .... structure in C is used to form a node of a linked list.
2. In a circular empty list, head->next points to ....
3. A linked list that enables you to travel in an either direction is a ....
4. To create a node dynamically in a singly linked list .... function in C is used.
5. In a singly linked list, the next field of the last node points to ....
6. In a circular linked list, the next field of the last node points to ....
7. For any node X, in a doubly linked list, X->llink->rlink is the address of ....
8. The node structure of a linked list must contain atleast one .... field and one .... field
9. To make and arbitrary insertions into a linked list, we need either the position number or address of .... node, where insertion has to be made.
10. For any node X, in a doubly linked list, X->rlink->llink is the address of ....

State True or False

1. Stack full situation in a linked stack is not explicitly handled.
2. To delete a node from a singly linked list, we should know the address of the node that succeeds the node to be deleted.
3. The Linked list is not an ordered list.

4. A linked list cannot be rversed inplace.

5. A linked list is a linear data structure.

EXERCISES

1. Write a C program to multiply two long positive integers, represented by two singly linked circular lists. Assume each digit is stored in one node.

2. Write an algorithm / C routine length(p) to count the number of nodes in a singly linked list p, where p points to the first node in the list. The last node has link field NULL.

3. Repeat the above exercise for a circularly linked list. Note you should not count the head node.

4. Implement a queue using circularly linked list and write algorithms/C routines to add and delete elements from a queue.

5. Give an algorithm / C program, to reverse a singly linked circular list inplace.

6. An unrestricted DQueue is a double ended Queue, where insertions & deletions can be made in either ends of the Queue. Write a program, using linked list to implement a DQueue.

7. An input restricted DQueue, is a double ended queue where insertions can be made at one end only and deletions can be made at both the ends. Similarly, an output restricted DQueue, is a double ended queue where insertions can be made at both the ends and deletions can be made at only one end. Using linked lists implement the above two Queues.

Lab Manual

WEEK - 1

a. Write a C program to find the sum of individual digits of a positive integer.

```
#include<stdio.h>
/* to compute sum of digits of a number */
void main(){
int i,n,sum=0;;
printf("\nEnter the number:");
scanf("%d",&n);
if(n<0){ printf( "ERROR \n"); exit(1);}
i=n;
while(i!=0){
sum+=i%10;
i/=10;
}
printf("\nsum of digits of %d is %d\n",n,sum);
}
```

OUTPUT:

```
Enter the number:1234
sum of digits of 1234 is 10
```

b. A Fibonacci Sequence is defined as follows: the first and second terms in the sequence are 0 and 1. Subsequent terms are found by adding the preceding two terms in the sequence. Write a C program to generate the first n terms of the sequence.

```
#include<stdio.h>
void main(){
int n,i,f1=0,f2=1,fn;
printf("Enter n:");
scanf(" %d",&n);
printf("%4d%4d",f1,f2);
for(i=2;i<n;i++){   /* to generate 3 rd to n terms */
fn=f1+f2;
printf("%4d",fn);
f1=f2;
f2=fn;
}
printf("\n\n");
}
```

OUTPUT:

```
Enter n:5
0  1   1   2   3
```

c. Write a C program to generate all the prime numbers between 1 and n, where n is a value supplied by the user.

```
#include<stdio.h>
void main(){
int n,i,j,flg;
printf("\nEnter the number:");
scanf("%d",&n);
if(n<0){ printf( "ERROR \n"); exit(1);}
for(i=1;i<=n;i++){
if(i<4){printf("%4d",i);continue;}
flg=1; /* flg will not become 0 if i is prime */
for(j=2;j<=i/2;j++)if(i%j==0){flg=0;break;}
if(flg)printf("%4d",i);
}
}
```

OUTPUT:

```
Enter the number:10
1  2  3  5  7
```

WEEK - 2

a. Write a C program to calculate the following sum:

$Sum=1-x^2/2!+x^4/4!+x^6/6!+x^8/8!-x^{10}/10!$

```
#include<stdio.h>
/* to compute a series */
void main(){
int i,sign=1;
float x,sum=1,term=1.0,fact=1;
printf("Enter the value of x:");
scanf("%f",&x);
printf("x=%f\n",x);
for(i=2;i<=10;i+=2){
term=term*x*x;
fact=fact*(i-1)*i;
printf("\nterm=%f fact=%f\n", term,fact);
if(sign % 2 == 0) sum=sum+term/fact;
else sum=sum-term/fact;
printf("\nsum=%f\n", sum);
sign++;
}
printf("\nsum=%f",sum);
}
```

OUTPUT:

```
Enter the value of x:1
X=1.000000
term=1.000000 fact=2. .000000
sum=0.500000
term=1.000000 fact=24.000000
sum=0.541667
term=1.000000 fact=720.000000
sum=0.540278
term=1.000000 fact=40320.000000
sum=0.540303
term=1.000000 fact=3628800.000000
sum=0.540302
sum=0.540302
```

b. Write a C program to find the roots of a quadratic equation.

```
#include<stdio.h>
#include<math.h>
void main(){
float a,b,c,disc,r1,r2;
printf("Enter a b c:");
scanf("%f %f %f",&a,&b,&c);
disc=b*b-4*a*c;
if(disc>=0){/* roots are real */
r1=(-b+sqrt(disc))/(2*a);
r2=(-b-sqrt(disc))/(2*a);
printf("\nthe roots are Real:\n\n %f,%f",r1,r2);
}
else{
disc=(-1)*disc;
r1=-b/(2*a);
r2=sqrt(disc)/(2*a);
printf("\nthe roots are coplex:\n\n %f+i%f ,%f-i%f ",r1,r2,r1,r2);
}
printf("\n\n");
}
```

OUTPUT:

```
Enter a b c:1 6 7
the roots are Real:
-1.585786, -4.414214
```

WEEK - 3

a. Write a C program that use both recursive and non-recursive functions

I. To find the factorial of a given integer.

```
#include<stdio.h>
double rfact(int i){
if(i<2) return 1;
return(double)(i*rfact(i-1));
}
double ifact(int n){
int i;
double fact=1;
for(i=2;i<=n;i++)fact=fact*i;
return fact;
}
void main(){
int n;
printf("Enter n:");
scanf("%d",&n);
printf("\nFactorial of %d is %5.0f\n",n,ifact(n));
printf("\nFactorial of %d is %5.0f\n",n,rfact(n));
}
```

OUTPUT:

```
Enter n:5
Factorial of 5 is   120
Factorial of 5 is   120
```

II. To find the GCD (greatest common divisor) of two given integers.

```
#include<stdio.h>
/* to compute gcd */
int gcd_r(int i,int j){
if(i%j==0) return j;
return (gcd_r(j,i%j));
}
int gcd_nr(int i,int j){
int t;
while(i%j!=0){
t=i%j;
i=j;
j=t;
}
```

```
return j;
}
void main(){
int u,v;
printf("Enter the values of u and v:");
scanf("%d %d",&u,&v);
printf("\ngcd of %d and %d is %d\n",u,v,gcd_nr(u,v));
printf("\ngcd of %d and %d is %d\n",u,v,gcd_r(u,v));
}
```

OUTPUT:

```
Enter the values of u and v: 12 6
gcd of 12 and 6 is 6
gcd of 12 and 6 is 6
```

III. To solve Towers of Hanoi problem.

```
#include<stdio.h>
int i=0;
void hanoi(int n,char source, char by , char dest){
if(n==1)printf("\n %d.move disk from %c to
c\n",++i,source,dest);
else {
hanoi(n-1, source,dest,by);
hanoi(1, source,by,dest);
hanoi(n-1, by,source,dest);
}
}
void main(){
char s='a',b='b',d='c';
int n;
printf("enter n:");
scanf("%d",&n);
hanoi(n,s,b,d);
}
```

OUTPUT:

```
enter n:3
1.move disk from a to c
2.move disk from a to b
3.move disk from c to b
4.move disk from a to c
5.move disk from b to a
6.move disk from b to c
7.move disk from a to c
```

WEEK - 4

a. The total distance traveled by vehicle in 't' seconds is given by distance=ut+1/2at² where 'u' and 'a' are the initial velocity (m/sec), and acceleration (m/sec²). Write C program to find the distance traveled at regular intervals of time given the values of 'u' and 'a'. The program should provide the flexibility to the user to select his own time intervals and repeat the calculations for different values of 'u' and 'a'.

```
#include<stdio.h>
/* to compute distance travelled */
void main(){
float s,u,t,a,time,itvel;
char c;
while(1){
printf("\nEnter intial velocity u(mts/sec):");
scanf("%f",&u);
printf("\nEnter acceleration a(mts/sec2):");
scanf("%f",&a);
printf("\nEnter time(secs):");
scanf("%f",&time);
printf("\nEnter time intervel(secs):");
scanf("%f",&itvel);
printf("\n    TIME      DISTANCE\n:");
for(t=itvel;t<=time;t+=itvel){
s=u*t+0.5*a*t*t;
printf("\n%10.4f %10.4f\n", t,s);
}
printf("\npress any key to continue/ space bar to quit...");
c=getch();
if(c==' ') break;
}
}
```

OUTPUT:

```
Enter initial velocity u(mts/sec):3
Enter acceleration a(mts/sec2):2
Enter time(secs):5
Enter time interval(secs):1
        TIME          DISTANCE:
        1.0000            4.0000
        2.0000           10.0000
        3.0000           18.0000
        4.0000           28.0000
        5.0000           40.0000
press any key to continue/space bar to quit...
```

b. Write a C program, which takes two integer operands and one operator from the user, performs the operation and then prints the result. (Consider the operators +, -, *, /, % and use switch statement)

```
#include<stdio.h>
/* to compute arithmetic op between two ints */
void main(){
int i,j,r;
char c;
while(1){
printf("\nEnter expression(ex:23 * 12)");
scanf("%d %c %d",&i,&c,&j);
switch(c){
case '+':r=i+j;break;
case '-':r=i-j;break;
case '*':r=i*j;break;
case '/':r=i/j;break;
case '%':r=i%j;break;
default :r=0;
}
printf("\n%d %c %d = %d\n",i,c,j,r);
printf("\npress any key to continue/ space bar to quit...");
c=getch();
if(c==' ') break;
}
}
```

OUTPUT:

```
Enter expression(ex:23*12)34/17
34 / 17 = 2
press any kley to continue/ space bar to quit...
```

WEEK - 5

a. Write a C program to find both the largest and smallest number in a list of integers.

```
#include<stdio.h>
#include<string.h>
/*find largest and smallest numbers */
void enter_list(int l[],int n){
int i;
for(i=0;i<n;i++){
printf("\nenter no %d:",i+1);
scanf("%d",&l[i]);
```

```
}
}
void main(){
int list[25],c,n,largest,smallest,i;
while(1){
printf("\nEnter How many?:");
scanf("%d",&n);
enter_list(list,n);
largest=smallest=list[0];
for(i=1;i<n;i++){
if(list[i]>largest)largest=list[i];
else if(list[i]<smallest)smallest=list[i];
}
printf("\nLargest=%d Smallest=%d\n",largest,smallest);
printf("\npress any key to continue/ space bar to quit...");
c=getch();
if(c==' ') break;
}
}
```

OUTPUT:

```
Enter How many?:5
enter no 1:1
enter no 2:3
enter no 3:456
enter no 4:2
enter no 5:76
Largest=456 Smallest=1
press any key to continue/ space bar to quit...
```

b. Write a C program that uses functions to perform the following:

I. Addition of two matrices

II. Multiplication of two matrices

```
#include<stdio.h>
#include<string.h>
#define MSIZE 10
/*matrix addition and multiplication */
void enter_matrix(int mat[][MSIZE],int row,int col){
int i,j;
for(i=0;i<row;i++)
for(j=0;j<col;j++){
printf("\nenterelement [%d][%d]:",i,j);
scanf("%d",&mat[i][j]);
}
```

```
}
void print_matrix(int mat[][MSIZE],int row,int col){
int i,j;
printf("\n\n");
for(i=0;i<row;i++){
for(j=0;j<col;j++)printf("%4d",mat[i][j]);
printf("\n\n");
}
}
void add_matrix(int mat1[][MSIZE],int mat2[][MSIZE],int mat3[][MSIZE],int
row,int col){
int i,j;
for(i=0;i<row;i++)
for(j=0;j<col;j++)mat3[i][j]=mat1[i][j]+mat2[i][j];
}
void mult_matrix(int mat1[][MSIZE],int mat2[][MSIZE],int mat3[][MSIZE],int
row,int col){
int i,j,k;
for(i=0;i<row;i++)
for(j=0;j<col;j++){mat3[i][j]=0;
for(k=0;k<col;k++) mat3[i][j]+=mat1[i][k]*mat2[k][j];
}
}
void main(){
int matrix1[MSIZE][MSIZE], matrix2[MSIZE][MSIZE];
int matrix3[MSIZE][MSIZE];
int nr,nc;
char c;
while(1){
printf("\nHow many rows?:");
scanf("%d",&nr);
printf("\nHow many colums?:");
scanf("%d",&nc);
printf("\n ENTER MATRIX 1\n");
enter_matrix(matrix1,nr,nc);
printf("\n ENTER MATRIX 2\n");
enter_matrix(matrix2,nr,nc);
printf("\n MATRIX 1\n");
print_matrix(matrix1,nr,nc);
printf("\n MATRIX 2\n");
print_matrix(matrix2,nr,nc);
add_matrix(matrix1,matrix2,matrix3,nr,nc);
printf("\n  MATRIX 1 + MATRIX 2\n");
```

```
print_matrix(matrix3,nr,nc);
mult_matrix(matrix1,matrix2,matrix3,nr,nc);
printf("\n  MATRIX 1 * MATRIX 2\n");
print_matrix(matrix3,nr,nc);
printf("\npress any key to continue/ space bar to quit...");
c=getch();
if(c==' ') break;
}
}
```

OUTPUT:

```
How many rows?:3

How many colums?:3

   ENTER MATRIX 1

enterelement [0][0]:1

enterelement [0][1]:2

enterelement [0][2]:3

enterelement [1][0]:4

enterelement [1][1]:5

enterelement [1][2]:6

enterelement [2][0]:7

enterelement [2][1]:8

enterelement [2][2]:9

   ENTER MATRIX 1

enterelement [0][0]:1

enterelement [0][1]:1

enterelement [0][2]:1

enterelement [1][0]:1
```

```
enterelement [1][1]:1

enterelement [1][2]:1

enterelement [2][0]:1

enterelement [2][1]:1

enterelement [2][2]:1

MATRIX 1 + MATRIX 2

2       3       4

5       6       7

8       9       10

MATRIX 1 * MATRIX 2


6       6       6

15      15      15

24      24      24

press any key to continue/ space bar to quit...
```

WEEK - 6

a. Write a C program that uses functions to perform the following operations:

I. To insert a sub-string in to a given main string from a given position.

II. To delete n characters from a given position in a given string.

```
#include<stdio.h>
#include<string.h>
#define MSIZE 256
```

```
/*insert substring-delete n chars from a string */
void insert_str(char *s1, char *s2, int n){
int l1,l2,i,j;
l1=strlen(s1);
l2=strlen(s2);
if(n>l1) n=l1;/* if n is larger insert at the end */
i=l1;
j=l1+l2;
while(i>n-1)s1[j--]=s1[i--]; /* make space for insertion in s1 */
i=n;
j=0;
while(s2[j])s1[i++]=s2[j++];/* insert s2 into string s1 */
}
void delete_str(char *s, int p,int n){
int l,i,j;
l=strlen(s);
i=p-1;
j=i+n;
while(j<=l)s[i++]=s[j++];
}
void main(){
char str[MSIZE],sub[MSIZE];
int n,p;
printf("\nEnter the string:");
gets(str);
fflush(stdin);
printf("\nEnter the sub string:");
gets(sub);
printf("\nEnter Position:");
scanf("%d",&n);
insert_str(str,sub,n);
printf("\n After insertion: %s",str);
printf("\n\nenter position to delete from:");
scanf("%d",&p);
printf("\nenter no of chars to delete:");
scanf("%d",&n);
delete_str(str,p,n);
 printf("\n After deletion: %s",str);
}
```

OUTPUT:

```
Enter the string:Computer Engineering
Enter the sub string:Science
Enter Position:8
  After insertion: ComputerScience Engineering
enter position to delete from:14
enter no of chars to delete:5
   After deletion: ComputerSciengineering
```

b. Write a C program to determine if the given string is a palindrome or not.

```
#include<stdio.h>
#include<conio.h>
#include<string.h>
/* palindrome */
int palin(char st[]){
int i=0,j;
j=strlen(st)-1;
while(i++<j--)if(st[i]!=st[j])return 0;
return 1;
}
void main(){
char s[25],c;
while(1){
printf("\nEnter String:");
gets(s);
if(palin(s))printf("\n%s is a palindrome\n",s);
else printf("\n%s is  NOT a palindrome\n",s);
printf("\npress any key to continue/ space bar to quit...");
c=getch();
if(c==' ') break;
}
}
```

OUTPUT:

```
Enter String:madam
madam is a palindrome
press any key to continue/ space bar to quit...
```

WEEK - 7

a. Write a C program that displays the position or index in the string S where the string T begins or -1 if S doesn't contain T.

```
#include<stdio.h>
#include<string.h>
#define MSIZE 256
#define YES 1
#define NO 0
/*search for substring */
int search_str(char *s1, char *s2){
int l1,l2,i,j,flg;
l1=strlen(s1);
l2=strlen(s2);
if(l2>l1) return -1;/* if sub-string is longer */
for(i=0;i<=l1-l2;i++){
flg=YES;
for(j=0;j<l2;j++)
if(s1[i+j]!=s2[j]){flg=NO;break;}
if(flg==YES)return i;
}
return -1;
}
void main(){
char str[MSIZE],sub[MSIZE];
int p;
printf("\nEnter the string:");
gets(str);
fflush(stdin);
printf("\nEnter the sub string:");
gets(sub);
p=search_str(str,sub);
if(p!=-1)printf("\n substring found at: %d",p);
else
printf("\n substring not found");
}
```

OUTPUT:

```
Enter the string:information technology

Enter the sub string:techno

 substring found at: 12
```

b. Write a C program to count the lines, words, characters in a given text.

```
#include<stdio.h>
#include<conio.h>
#define OUT 0
#define IN 1
/*word count */
void main(){
int c,nw,nl,nc,flg;
while(1){
clrscr();
nc=nl=nw=0;
flg=OUT;
printf("\nEnter Text at end type ctrl-z:");
while((c=getchar())!=EOF){
nc++;
if(c=='\n')nl++;
if((c==' ')||(c=='\t')||(c=='\n'))flg=OUT;
else if(flg==OUT){flg=IN;nw++;}
}
printf("\nWord     Count=%d     Line     Count=%d     Charecter
Count=%d\n",nw,nl,nc);
printf("\npress any key to continue/ space bar to quit...");
c=getch();
if(c==' ') break;
}
}
```

OUTPUT:

```
Enter Text at end type ctrl-z:hello,
how are you?
This is a sample test to test the program which counts
number of lines, words, and characters present in the
given text.
Word Count=25 Line Count=2 Character Count=137

press any key to continue/ space bar to quit...
```

WEEK - 8

a. Write a C program to generate the Pascal's triangle.

```
#include<stdio.h>
void main(void)
{
int binom=1,p,q=0,r,x;
printf("Enter the number of rows:");
scanf("%d",&p);
while(q<p)
{
for(r=40-3*q;r>0;--r)
{
printf(" ");
}/*end of for*/
for(x=0;x<=q;++x)
{
if(x==0||q==0)
binom=1;
else
binom=(binom*(q-x+1))/x;
printf("%6d",binom);
}/*end of for*/
printf("\n");
++q;
}/*end of while*/
printf("\n");
}/*end of main*/
```

OUTPUT:

```
Enter the number of rows:5
                                                 1
                                              1     1
                                           1     2     1
                                        1     3     3     1
                                     1     4     6     4     1
```

b. Write a C program to construct a pyramid of numbers.

```
#include<stdio.h>
void main(void)
{
int p,m,q,n;
```

```
printf("Enter the number of lines:");
scanf("%d",&n);
for(p=1;p<=n;p++)
{
for(q=1;q<=n-p;q++)
printf(" ");
m=p;
for(q=1;q<=p;q++)
printf(" %d",m++);
m-=2;
for(q=1;q<p;q++)
printf(" %d",m--);
printf("\n\n");
}/*end of for*/
}/*end of main*/
```

OUTPUT:

```
Enter the number of lines:5
        1

      2 3 2

    3 4 5 4 3

  4 5 6 7 6 5 4

5 6 7 8 9 8 7 6 5
```

WEEK - 9

Write a C program to read in two numbers, x and n, and then compute the sum of this geometric progression: $1+x+x^2+x^3+\ldots\ldots\ldots\ldots+x^n$. For example: if n is 3 and x is 5, then the program computes 1+5+25+125. Print x, n, sum. Perform error checking. For example, the formula does not make sense for negative exponents – if n is less than 0. have your program print an error message if n<0, then go back and read in the next pair of numbers without computing the sum. Are any values of x also illegal? If so, test for them too.

```
#include<stdio.h>
#include<stdio.h>
#include<conio.h>
#define OUT 0
#define IN 1
/*word count */
```

```
void main(){
 int c,x,n,i,sum,term;
 while(1){
  clrscr();
  sum=1;
  term=1;
  printf("\nEnter n:");
  scanf("%d",&n);
  if(n<0){
   printf("\n\nERROR Press any key to continue");
   getch();
   continue;
  }
  printf("\nEnter x:");
  scanf("%d",&x);
  for(i=0;i<n;i++){
  term*=x;
  sum+=term;
  }
  printf("\nx=%d,n=%d, sum=%d\n",x,n,sum);
  printf("\npress any key to continue/ space bar to quit...");
  c=getch();
  if(c==' ') break;
 }
}
```

OUTPUT:

```
Enter n:3

Enter x:5

x=5,n=3, sum=156

press any key to continue/ space bar to quit..._
```

WEEK - 10

a. 2's complement of a number is obtained by scanning it from right to left and complementing all the bits after first appearance of a 1. thus 2's complement of 11100 is 00100. Write a C program to find the 2's complement of a binary number.

```
#include<stdio.h>
#include<string.h>
 /* 2's complement of binary numbers */
```

```
void complement(char bn[],int i){
 if(bn[i]=='1')bn[i]='0';
 else bn[i]='1';
}
void tows_complement(char st[]){
 int i,flg=0;
 i=strlen(st)-1;
 while(i>=0){
  if(flg)complement(st,i);
  if((!flg)&&(st[i]=='1'))flg=1;
  i--;
 }
}
void main(){
 char s[25],c;
 while(1){
  clrscr();
  printf("\nEnter a binary no:");
  gets(s);
  tows_complement(s);
  printf("\nThe 2s Coplement is: %s",s);
  printf("\npress any key to continue/ space bar to quit...");
  c=getch();
  if(c==' ') break;
 }
}
```

OUTPUT:

```
Enter a binary no:101

The 2s Coplement is: 011
press any key to continue/ space bar to quit..._
```

b. Write a C program to convert a Roman numeral to its decimal equivalent.

```
#include<stdio.h>
#include<conio.h>
#include<stdlib.h>
#include<string.h>
/*convert Roman numbers to decimal */
int valof(char c){
switch(c){
case'\0': return 0;
```

```
case 'I':
case 'i': return 1;
case 'V':
case 'v': return 5;
case 'X':
case 'x': return 10;
case 'L':
case 'l': return 50;
case 'C':
case 'c': return 100;
case 'D':
case 'd': return 500;
case 'M':
case 'm': return 1000;
}
printf("\nERROR Press any key to exit\n");getch();exit(1);
}

void main(){
char romon[25],c;
int i,j,vali,valj,sum;
while(1){
clrscr();
printf("\nEnter a valid roman number:");
gets(romon);
sum=0;
i=0;
j=1;
vali=valof(romon[i]);
for(;;i++,j++){
valj=valof(romon[j]);
if(vali>=valj)sum+=vali;
else sum-=vali;
if(valj==0)break;
vali=valj;
}
printf("\n%d\n",sum);
printf("\npress any key to continue/ space bar to quit...");
c=getch();
if(c==' ') break;
}
}
```

OUTPUT:

```
Enter a valid roman number:IX

9

press any key to continue/ space bar to quit..._
```

WEEK - 11

Write a C program that uses functions to perform the following operations:

I. Reading a complex number
II. Writing a complex number
III. Addition of two complex numbers
IV. Multiplication of two complex numbers

(Note: represent complex number using a structure)

```
#include<stdio.h>
#include<conio.h>
 /* complex numbers */
struct Complex{
 float real;
 float imag;
};
void enter_complex(struct Complex *a){
 char sign,filler;
 float re,im;
 printf("\n\nEnter a complex number(Ex:2.3-j3.5):");
 scanf("%f%c%c%f",&re,&sign,&filler,&im);
 if(sign=='-')im*=-1;
 a->real=re;
 a->imag=im;
}
void print_complex(struct Complex a){
 char sign='+';
 if(a.imag<0){sign='-';a.imag*=-1;}
 printf("%3.2f",a.real);
 if(a.imag != 0)
  printf("%cj%3.2f\n",sign,a.imag);
}
struct Complex add_complex(struct Complex x,struct Complex y){
 struct Complex z;
```

```
 z.real=x.real+y.real;
 z.imag=x.imag+y.imag;
 return z;
}
struct Complex mult_complex(struct Complex x,struct Complex y){
 struct Complex z;
 z.real=x.real*y.real-(x.imag*y.imag);
 z.imag=x.imag*y.real+x.real*y.imag;
 return z;
}

void main(){
 struct Complex a,b,c;
 clrscr();
 enter_complex(&a);
 printf("\na=");
 print_complex(a);
 enter_complex(&b);
 printf("\nb=");
 print_complex(b);
 c=add_complex(a,b);
 printf("\n\na+b=");
 print_complex(c);
 c=mult_complex(a,b);
 printf("\n\na*b=");
 print_complex(c);
 getch();
}
```

OUTPUT:

```
Enter a complex number(Ex:2.3-j3.5):3.1+j1.2
a=3.10+j1.20

Enter a complex number(Ex:2.3-j3.5):1.2-j3.1
b=1.20-j3.10

a+b=4.30-j1.90

a*b=7.44-j8.17
_
```

WEEK - 12

a. Write a C program which copies one file to another.

```
#include<stdio.h>
#include<conio.h>
#include<stdlib.h>
void main(int argc,char *argv[]){
FILE *f1,*f2;
int c,i;
clrscr();
if(argc<3) exit(2);
for(i=2;i<argc;i++){
 if((f1=fopen(argv[1],"r"))==NULL) {printf("\n\nERROR");exit(1);}
 if((f2=fopen(argv[i],"w"))==NULL) {printf("\n\nERROR");exit(1);}
 while((c=fgetc(f1)) != EOF) fputc(c,f2);
 fclose(f1);
 fclose(f2);
 }
printf("\n\n\n DONE");
getch();
}
```

OUTPUT:

```
DONE
```

(Contents of the first file are copied into the second file)

b. Write a C program to reverse the first n characters in a file. (Note: The file name and n are specified on the command line)

```
#include<stdio.h>
#include<conio.h>
#include<stdlib.h>
#define FSIZE 2048
 /* to reverse first n chars of a file */
 void reverse(char *s, int n){
 int i=0,j=n-1,c;
 while(i<j){
 c=s[i];
 s[i++]=s[j];
 s[j--]=c;
 }
}

void main(int arc, char *arg[]){
 int i=0,j=0,n;
 char buf[FSIZE],c;
 FILE *fp;
 clrscr();
 if(arc<2){
  printf("FILE NAME NOT SPCEFIED:");
  exit(1);
 }
 if(arc<3){
  printf("N NOT SPCEFIED:");
  exit(1);
 }
 fp=fopen(arg[1],"r");
 if(fp==NULL){
  printf("FILE NOT FOUND :");
  exit(2);
 }
 while((c=fgetc(fp))!=EOF)buf[i++]=c;
 fclose(fp);
 n=atoi(arg[2]);
 if(i<n){
  printf("FILE NOT FOUND :");
  exit(2);
 }
 reverse(buf,n);
```

```
fp=fopen(arg[1],"w");
if(fp==NULL){
 printf("FILE NOT FOUND :");
 exit(2);
}
while(j<=i)fputc(buf[j++],fp);
fclose(fp);
printf("\nDONE");
getch();
}
```

OUTPUT:

```
DONE
```

(first n characters of the given file are reversed)

WEEK - 13

a. Write a C program to display the contents of a file.

```
#include<stdio.h>
void main(){
FILE *fp;
int c;
clrscr();
if((fp=fopen("my.dat","w"))==NULL) {printf("\n\nERROR");exit(1);}
while((c=getc(stdin)) != EOF) putc(c,fp);
printf("\n\n\n DONE");
fclose(fp);
getch();
}
```

OUTPUT:

```
DONE
```

b. Write a C program to merge two files into a third file (i.e., the contents of the first file followed by those of the second are put in the third file.)

```
#include<stdio.h>
#include<conio.h>
```

```
#include<stdlib.h>
void main(int argc,char *argv[]){
FILE *f1,*f2,*f3;
int c,i;
clrscr();
if(argc<3) exit(2);
if((f1=fopen(argv[1],"r"))==NULL) {printf("\n\nERROR");exit(1);}
 if((f2=fopen(argv[2],"r"))==NULL) {printf("\n\nERROR");exit(1);}
if((f3=fopen(argv[3],"w"))==NULL) {printf("\n\nERROR");exit(1);}
 while((c=fgetc(f1)) != EOF) fputc(c,f3);
 fclose(f1);
while((c=fgetc(f2)) != EOF) fputc(c,f3);
 fclose(f2);
fclose(f3);
 }
printf("\n\n\n DONE");
getch();
}
```

OUTPUT:

```
DONE
```

WEEK - 14

Write a C program that uses functions to perform the following operations on singly linked list:
I. Creation II. Insertion III. Deletion IV. Traversal

```
#include<stdio.h>
#include<conio.h>
#include<alloc.h>
#include<stdlib.h>
struct node{
 int data;
 struct node * next;
};
struct node *head=NULL;
void print_list(){
 struct node *t;
 printf("\n");
 if(head==NULL){
```

```
 printf("*****LIST EMPTY*****\n");
 return;
}
t=head;
while(t){
 printf("%d ",t->data);
 t=t->next;
}
printf("\n");
}
void insert(int d){
 struct node *t,*p,*c;
 t=(struct node *) malloc(sizeof(struct node));
 if(t==NULL){
  printf("FATAL ERROR\n");
  exit(1);
 }
 t->data=d;
 if(head==NULL){ // insertion into an empty list
  t->next=NULL;
  head=t;
  return;
 }
 p=NULL;
 c=head;
 while((c!=NULL)&&(c->data>d)){
  p=c;
  c=c->next;
 }
 if(p==NULL){ // first node
  t->next=c;
  head=t;
 }
 else{ // not the first node
  t->next=c;
  p->next=t;
 }
}
int delete_ls(int e){
 struct node * tmp,*p;
 int i;
 if(head==NULL) {printf("LIST EMPTY ERROR\n"); return -1;}
 tmp = head;
```

```
 p=NULL;
 while((tmp->data!=e)&&(tmp!=NULL)){p=tmp;tmp=tmp->next;}
 if(tmp!=NULL){
 i=tmp->data;
  if(p!=NULL)p->next=tmp->next;
   else head=tmp->next;
          free(tmp);
   printf("\n%d deleted\n",e);
   return i;
 }
 printf("\n%d not found\n",e);
 return -1;
}
void main(){
int i,j;
clrscr();
 for(i=0;i<6;i++){
  printf("enter a number:");
  scanf("%d",&j);
  insert(j);
 }
 print_list();
 delete_ls(5);
 print_list();
 delete_ls(5);
 print_list();
 delete_ls(9);
 print_list();
 delete_ls(7);
 print_list();
 for(i=1;i<10;i++)delete_ls(i);
 print_list();
 getch();
}
```

OUTPUT:

```
enter a number:1
enter a number:2
enter a number:3
enter a number:4
enter a number:5
enter a number:6

6 5 4 3 2 1

5 deleted

6 4 3 2 1
```

WEEK - 15

Write a C program that uses functions to perform the following operations on doubly linked list:
I. Creation II. Insertion III. Deletion IV. Traversal in both ways

```
#include<stdio.h>
#include<conio.h>
#include<stdlib.h>
#include<alloc.h>
struct node{
 int data;
 struct node * llink, *rlink;
};
struct node *head;
void print_fwd(){
 struct node *t;
 printf("\n");
 if(head->rlink==head){
  printf("*****LIST EMPTY*****\n");
  return;
 }
 t=head->rlink;
 while(t!=head){
  printf("%d ",t->data);
  t=t->rlink;
 }
 printf("\n");
}
void print_bwd(){
 struct node *t;
 printf("\n");
 if(head->llink==head){
  printf("*****LIST EMPTY*****\n");
  return;
 }
 t=head->llink;
 while(t!=head){
  printf("%d ",t->data);
  t=t->llink;
 }
 printf("\n");
}
void insert(int d){
 struct node *t,*p,*c;
 t=(struct node *) malloc(sizeof(struct node));
 if(t==NULL){
```

```
  printf("FATAL ERROR\n");
  exit(1);
 }
 t->data=d;
 c=head->rlink;
 while((c!=head)&&(c->data>d))c=c->rlink;
 t->llink=c->llink;
 c->llink->rlink=t;
 t->rlink=c;
 c->llink=t;
}
int delete_ls(int e){
 struct node * tmp;
 int i;
 if(head->rlink==head) {printf("LIST EMPTY ERROR\n"); return -1;}
 tmp = head->rlink;
 while((tmp->data!=e)&&(tmp!=head)) tmp=tmp->rlink;
 if(tmp!=head){
  i=tmp->data;
  tmp->rlink->llink=tmp->llink;
  tmp->llink->rlink=tmp->rlink;
  free(tmp);
  printf("\n%d deleted\n",e);
  return i;
 }
 printf("\n%d not found\n",e);
 return -1;
}
void main(){
int i,j;
head= (struct node *) malloc(sizeof(struct node));
if(head==NULL){
  printf("FATAL ERROR\n");
  exit(1);
 }
 head->llink=head->rlink=head;
clrscr();
 for(i=0;i<6;i++){
  printf("enter a number:");
  scanf("%d",&j);
  insert(j);
 }
 print_fwd();
 delete_ls(5);
 print_fwd();
 delete_ls(5);
 print_bwd();
 delete_ls(9);
 print_bwd();
```

```
 delete_ls(7);
 print_fwd();
 for(i=1;i<10;i++)delete_ls(i);
 print_fwd();
 getch();
}
```

OUTPUT:

```
enter a number:1
enter a number:2
enter a number:3
enter a number:4
enter a number:5
enter a number:6

6 5 4 3 2 1

5 deleted

6 4 3 2 1

5 not found

1 2 3 4 6

9 not found

1 2 3 4 6

7 not found
6 4 3 2 1

1 deleted

2 deleted

3 deleted

4 deleted

5 not found

6 deleted
LIST EMPTY ERROR
LIST EMPTY ERROR
LIST EMPTY ERROR

*****LIST EMPTY*****
```

WEEK- 16

Write C programs that implement stack (its operations) using

I. Arrays

```
#include <stdio.h>
#include <conio.h>
#define SIZE 20
int s[SIZE];
int top=-1;

int push(int e){
if(top==SIZE-1)return -1;
  s[++top]=e;
            return 1;
    }

int pop(){
if(top!=-1)return s[top--];
return -1;
}
void main(){
 int op,n,poped;
 clrscr();
do{
printf("1.Push\n2.Pop\n3.Quit\nEnter your option:");
scanf("%d",&op);
switch(op)
{
case 1:printf("entera number:");
scanf("%d",&n);
push(n);
break;
case 2:
poped=pop();
if(poped==-1){
printf("There are not items to pop\n");
getch();
}
else{
printf("%d\n",poped);
getch();
}
break;
```

```
}
}while(op!=3);
 getch();
}
```

OUTPUT:

```
1.Push
2.Pop
3.Quit
Enter your option:1
entera number:1
1.Push
2.Pop
3.Quit
Enter your option:1
entera number:2
1.Push
2.Pop
3.Quit
Enter your option:1
entera number:3
1.Push
2.Pop
3.Quit
Enter your option:2
3
1.Push
2.Pop
3.Quit
Enter your option:2
2
1.Push
2.Pop
3.Quit
Enter your option:2
1
1.Push
2.Pop
3.Quit
Enter your option:2
There are not items to pop
1.Push
2.Pop
3.Quit
Enter your option:3
```

II. Pointers

```
#include<stdio.h>
#include<conio.h>
#include<stdlib.h>
#include<alloc.h>
struct node{
 int data;
```

```
 struct node * next;
};
struct node *top=NULL;
void print_ls(){
 struct node *t;
 printf("\n");
 if(top==NULL){
  printf("*****STACK EMPTY*****\n");
  return;
 }
 t=top;
 while(t){
  printf("%d ",t->data);
  t=t->next;
 }
 printf("\n");
}
void push(int d){
 struct node *t;
 if(t==NULL){printf("FATAL ERROR\n"); exit(1);}
 t=(struct node *) malloc(sizeof(struct node));
 t->data=d;
 t->next=top;
 top=t;
}
int pop(){
 struct node * tmp;
 int i;
 if(top==NULL) {printf("STACK EMPTY ERROR\n"); return -1;}
 tmp = top;
 i=top->data;
 top=tmp->next;
 free(tmp);
 return i;
}
void main(){
int i;
clrscr();
for(i=1;i<15;i++)push(i);
print_ls();
for(i=1;i<10;i++) printf("\n%d \n",pop());
print_ls();
getch();
}
```

OUTPUT:

```
14 13 12 11 10 9 8 7 6 5 4 3 2 1
14
13
12
11
10
9
8
7
6
5 4 3 2 1
```

WEEK - 17

Write C programs that implement Queue (its operations) using
I. Arrays

```
#include<stdio.h>
#include<conio.h>
#define MAXSIZE 10
int  queue[MAXSIZE];
int front= -1,rear= -1;
void print_q(){
 int i;
 for(i=front+1;i<=rear;i++)printf("%d ",queue[i]);
 printf("\n");
}
void adjust_q(){
int i,j;
for(i=0,j=front+1;j<=rear;i++,j++)queue[i]=queue[j];
front=-1; rear=--i;
}

void add_q(int e){
 if(rear==MAXSIZE-1)
  if(front>=0) adjust_q();
  else{printf("QUEUE full ERROR\n"); return ;}
  queue[++rear]=e;
}
int delete_q(){
 if(front==rear){printf("QUEUE empty ERROR\n");return -1;}
  else return queue[++front];
}
```

```
void main(){
int i;
clrscr();
for(i=1;i<13;i++)add_q(i);
print_q();
for(i=0;i<5;i++)delete_q();
print_q();
for(i=1;i<13;i++)add_q(i);
print_q();
 getch();
}
```

OUTPUT:

```
QUEUE full ERROR
QUEUE full ERROR
1 2 3 4 5 6 7 8 9 10
6 7 8 9 10
QUEUE full ERROR
QUEUE full ERROR
QUEUE full ERROR
QUEUE full ERROR
QUEUE full ERROR
QUEUE full ERROR
QUEUE full ERROR
6 7 8 9 10 1 2 3 4 5
```

II. Pointers

```
#include<stdio.h>
#include<conio.h>
#include<stdlib.h>
#include<alloc.h>
struct node{
 int data;
 struct node * next;
};
struct node *front=NULL,*rear=NULL;
void print_q(){
 struct node *t;
 printf("\n");
 if(front==NULL){
  printf("*****queue EMPTY*****\n");
  return;
 }
 t=front;
 while(t){
  printf("%d ",t->data);
  t=t->next;
 }
 printf("\n");
```

```
}
void add_q(int d){
 struct node *t;
 if(t==NULL){printf("FATAL ERROR\n"); exit(1);}
 t=(struct node *) malloc(sizeof(struct node));
 t->data=d;
 if(front==NULL)front=t;
 else rear->next=t;
 t->next=NULL;
 rear=t;
}
int delete_q(){
 struct node * tmp;
 int i;
 if(front==NULL) {printf("QUEUE EMPTY ERROR\n"); return -1;}
 tmp = front;
 i=front->data;
 front=front->next;
 if(front==NULL) rear=NULL;
 free(tmp);
 return i;
}
void main(){
int i;
clrscr();
for(i=1;i<5;i++) add_q(i);
print_q();
for(i=1;i<3;i++) printf("\n%d \n",delete_q());
print_q();
for(i=1;i<5;i++) add_q(i+10);
print_q();
getch();
}
```

OUTPUT:

```
1 2 3 4

1

2

3 4

3 4 11 12 13 14
```

WEEK - 18

Write a C program that uses Stack operations to perform the following:

I. Converting infix expression into postfix expression

```
#include<stdio.h>
#include<conio.h>
#include<stdlib.h>
#include<ctype.h>
#define MAXSIZE 10
char  stack[MAXSIZE];
int top= -1;
void print_stack(){
 int i;
 for(i=0;i<=top;i++)printf("%c ",stack[i]);
 printf("\n");
}
int getnexttoken( char *s,char *t){
 static int i=0;
 int j=0;
 while(s[i]==' ')i++;
 if(s[i]=='\0') return -1;
 while((s[i]!=' ')&&(s[i]!='\0')) t[j++]=s[i++];
 t[j]='\0';
 if(isdigit(t[0])||t[0]=='.') return 1;
  else return 0;
}
void push(char e){
 if(top==MAXSIZE-1){ printf("Stack full ERROR\n");exit(3);}
  else stack[++top]=e;
}
char pop(){
 if(top==-1){printf("Stack empty ERROR\n");return -1;}
  else return stack[top--];
}
int isp(){
 if(top==-1) return -1;
 switch (stack[top]){
  case '(' : return 0;
  case '*' :
  case '/' : return 2;
  case '+' :
  case '-' : return 1;
 }
 return -1;
}
int icp(char c){
```

```
 switch (c){
  case '(' : return 3;
  case '*' :
  case '/' : return 2;
  case '+' :
  case '-' : return 1;
 }
 return -1;
}
void main(){
 char exp[50],token[10],postfix[50];
 int k,i=0,j;
 char c;
 clrscr();
 printf("\n\n enter infix expression:");
 gets(exp);
 printf("%s\n",exp);
 getch();
 while(1){
  k=getnexttoken(exp,token);
  if(k==-1) break;
  if(k==1)
   for(j=0;token[j]!='\0';j++) postfix[i++]=token[j];
   postfix[i++]=' ';
  if(k==0){
   if(token[0]==')')
    while((c=pop())!='('){
     postfix[i++]=c;
       postfix[i++]=' ';
      }
     else{
      while(icp(token[0])<= isp()){
       postfix[i++]=pop();
       postfix[i++]=' ';
      }
       push(token[0]);
     }
  }
 }
 while(top>=0){
  postfix[i++]=pop();
  postfix[i++]=' ';
 }
 postfix[i]='\0';
 printf("%s",postfix);
 getch();
}
```

OUTPUT:

```
 enter infix expression:2 + 3 / 4
2 + 3 / 4
2  3  4 / +
```

II. Evaluating the postfix expression

```
#include<stdio.h>
#include<conio.h>
#include<stdlib.h>
#include<ctype.h>
#define MAXSIZE 10
int  stack[MAXSIZE];
int top= -1;
 void print_stack(){
 int i;
 for(i=0;i<=top;i++)printf("%4d",stack[i]);
 printf("\n");
}
int getnexttoken( char *s,char *t){
 static int i=0;
 int j=0;
 while(s[i]==' ')i++;
 if(s[i]=='\0') return -1;
 while((s[i]!=' ')&&(s[i]!='\0')) t[j++]=s[i++];
 t[j]='\0';
 if(isdigit(t[0])) return 1;
  else return 0;
 }
void push(int e){

 if(top==MAXSIZE-1){ printf("Stack full ERROR\n");exit(3);}
  else stack[++top]=e;
  }
 int pop(){
  if(top==-1){printf("Stack empty ERROR\n");exit(2);}
     else return stack[top--];
     return(-1);
  }
void main(){
 char exp[50],token[10];
 int k;
 int t1,t2;
 clrscr();
 printf("enter postfix expression:");
 gets(exp);
```

```
printf("%s\n",exp);
getch();
while(1){
k=getnexttoken(exp,token);
printf("%d   %s \n" , k,token);
if(k==-1) break;
printf("%d\n",atoi(token));
if(k==1)push(atoi(token));
print_stack();
getch();
if(k==0){
 t2=pop();
 t1=pop();
 switch(token[0]){
  case '+':push(t1+t2);break;
  case '*':push(t1*t2);break;
  case '-':push(t1-t2);break;
  case '/':push(t1/t2);break;
  default: printf("operator error"); exit(1);
 }
}

}
printf("\n%d",pop());
getch();
}
```

OUTPUT:

```
enter postfix expression:2 4 8 / +
2 4 8 / +
1    2
2
   2
1    4
4
   2    4
1    8
8
   2    4    8
0    /
0
   2    4    8
0    +
0
   2    0
-1    +

2
```

WEEK - 19

Write a C program that implements the following sorting methods to sort a given list of integers in ascending order.

I. Bubble Sort

```
#include<stdio.h>
void xchange(int *n1,int *n2){
 int t;
 t=*n1;
 *n1=*n2;
 *n2=t;
 }
 void print_array(int *a,int n){
 int i;
 for(i=0;i<n;i++)printf("%d ",a[i]);
 printf("\n");
}
void main(){
 int s[]={200,122,67,23,90,12,68,34,56,99,33};
 int i=0,j;
 clrscr();
 for(i=10;i>=0;i--){
  for(j=0;j<i;j++) if(s[j]>s[j+1])xchange(&s[j],&s[j+1]);
   print_array(s,11);
   }
 getch();
}
```

OUTPUT:

```
122 67 23 90 12 68 34 56 99 33 200
67 23 90 12 68 34 56 99 33 122 200
23 67 12 68 34 56 90 33 99 122 200
23 12 67 34 56 68 33 90 99 122 200
12 23 34 56 67 33 68 90 99 122 200
12 23 34 56 33 67 68 90 99 122 200
12 23 34 33 56 67 68 90 99 122 200
12 23 33 34 56 67 68 90 99 122 200
12 23 33 34 56 67 68 90 99 122 200
12 23 33 34 56 67 68 90 99 122 200
12 23 33 34 56 67 68 90 99 122 200
```

II. Selection Sort

```
#include<stdio.h>
#include<conio.h>
void xchange(int *n1,int *n2){
```

```
int t;
t=*n1;
*n1=*n2;
*n2=t;
}
void print_array(int *a,int n){
int i;
for(i=0;i<n;i++)printf("%4d",a[i]);
printf("\n");
}
void main(){
int s[]={43,122,67,23,90,12,168,34,56,99,333};
int i=0,j,max;
clrscr();
for(i=10;i>0;i--){
 max=0;
 for(j=1;j<=i;j++) if(s[j]>s[max]) max=j;
 xchange(&s[max],&s[i]);
 print_array(s,11);
}
getch();
}
```

OUTPUT:

```
 43 122  67  23  90  12 168  34  56  99 333
 43 122  67  23  90  12  99  34  56 168 333
 43  56  67  23  90  12  99  34 122 168 333
 43  56  67  23  90  12  34  99 122 168 333
 43  56  67  23  34  12  90  99 122 168 333
 43  56  12  23  34  67  90  99 122 168 333
 43  34  12  23  56  67  90  99 122 168 333
 23  34  12  43  56  67  90  99 122 168 333
 23  12  34  43  56  67  90  99 122 168 333
 12  23  34  43  56  67  90  99 122 168 333
```

WEEK - 20

Write C program that use both recursive and non-recursive functions to perform the following searching operations for a Key value in a given list of integers:

I. Linear search

II. Binary search

```
#include<stdio.h>
#include<stdlib.h>
#include<conio.h>
struct student{
      int rno;
```

```
    char name[25];
    };
int lsearch(struct student s[],int i,int k){
 int j;
 for(j=0;j<i;j++){printf("%d ",j);if(s[j].rno==k)return j;}
 return -1;
}
int bsearch(int l, int h, int k, struct student s[]){
 int m;
 printf("%d\t%d\t%d\n",l,(l+h)/2,h);
 if(h<l) return -1;
 m=(h+l)/2;
 if(s[m].rno==k)return(m);
 if( s[m].rno<k) l=m+1;
 if( s[m].rno>k) h=m-1;
 return bsearch(l,h,k, s);
 }
void main(){
 struct student s[20];
 FILE *fp;
 char filename[20];
 int i=0,j,k,key;
 clrscr();
 printf("\nenterfilename:");
 gets(filename);
 fp=fopen(filename,"r");
 if(fp==NULL) exit(1);
 while((fscanf(fp,"%d %[^\n]",&s[i].rno,s[i].name) != EOF))i++;
 fclose(fp);
 for(j=0;j<i;j++)printf("%d\t%s\n",s[j].rno,s[j].name);
 while(1){
  printf("\nenter rno or 0 to quit:");
  scanf("%d",&key);
  if(key==0) break;
  printf("Linear\n");
  k=lsearch(s,i,key);
  if(k!=-1)printf("\n%d\t%s\n\n",s[k].rno,s[k].name);
  printf("Binary\n");
  j=bsearch(0,i-1,key,s);
  if(j!=-1)printf("\n%d\t%s\n",s[j].rno,s[j].name);
   else printf("\n%d not found\n",key);
 }
}
```

OUTPUT:

```
enterfilename:j:\x.txt
101      V.V.RAO
152      Rama Rao
102      Ranga Rao
108      Pandu
143      Ramesh
133      Kumar
167      Pratap
201      Krishna Rao
234      K.K.Murthy
222      Pramod

enter rno or 0 to quit:201
Linear
0 1 2 3 4 5 6 7
201      Krishna Rao

Binary
0        4        9
5        7        9

201      Krishna Rao

enter rno or 0 to quit:0
```

WEEK - 21

Write C program that implements the following sorting method to sort a given list of integers in ascending order.

I. Quick sort

```
#include<stdio.h>
#include<conio.h>
#define RECS 10
void xchange(int *n1,int *n2){
 int t;
 t=*n1;
 *n1=*n2;
 *n2=t;
 }
 void print_array(int *a,int n){
 int i;
 for(i=0;i<n;i++)printf("%4d",a[i]);
 printf("\n");
}
```

```
void qsort(int l,int h,int a[]){
int i,j,p;
i=l;j=h+1;
p=a[i];
if(h>l){
 do{
  do{
      i++;
      }while(a[i]<=p&&i<=h);
     do{
              j--;
       }while(a[j]>p);
     if(i<j)xchange(&a[i],&a[j]);
     printf("i=%d j=%d\n",i,j);
     } while(i<j);
  xchange(&a[l],&a[j]);
  print_array(a,RECS);
  getch();
  qsort(l,j-1,a);
  qsort(j+1,h,a);

 }
}
void main(){
 int s[]={26,5,37,1,61,11,59,15,48,19};
 clrscr();
 qsort(0,RECS-1,s);
 print_array(s,RECS);
 getch();
}
```

OUTPUT:

```
i=2 j=9
i=4 j=7
i=6 j=5
  11   5  19   1  15  26  59  61  48  37
i=2 j=3
i=3 j=2
   1   5  11  19  15  26  59  61  48  37
i=1 j=0
   1   5  11  19  15  26  59  61  48  37
i=5 j=4
   1   5  11  15  19  26  59  61  48  37
i=7 j=9
i=9 j=8
   1   5  11  15  19  26  48  37  59  61
i=8 j=7
   1   5  11  15  19  26  37  48  59  61
   1   5  11  15  19  26  37  48  59  61
```

WEEK - 22

Write C program that implement the following sorting method to sort a given list of integers in ascending order:

I. Merge sort

```
#include<stdio.h>
#include<conio.h>
#define RECS 12
void xchange(int *n1,int *n2){
 int t;
 t=*n1;
 *n1=*n2;
 *n2=t;
 }
 void print_array(int *a,int n){
 int i;
 printf("\n");
 for(i=0;i<n;i++)printf("%4d",a[i]);
 printf("\n");
 }
void merge(int low,int mid,int high, int a[]){
 int i,j,k;
 int b[RECS];
 i=low;
 j=mid+1;
 k=low;
 while(i<=mid&&j<=high)
  if(a[i]<a[j])b[k++]= a[i++];
   else b[k++]=a[j++];
 while(i<=mid)b[k++]= a[i++];
 while(j<=high)b[k++]=a[j++];
 for(i=low;i<=high;i++)a[i]=b[i];
}
void msort(int l,int h,int a[]){
 int m;
 if(l<h){
  m=(l+h)/2;
  msort(l,m,a);
  msort(m+1,h,a);
  merge(l,m,h,a);
  printf("\nlow=%d  mid=%d   high=%d\n",l,m,h);
  print_array(a,RECS);
  getch();
 }
}

void main(){
 int s[]={26,25,37,10,61,11,59,15,48,19,34,56};
```

```
    clrscr();
    print_array(s,RECS);
    msort(0,RECS-1,s);
    getch();
}
```

OUTPUT:

[redacted]

```
  26  25  37  10  61  11  59  15  48  19  34  56
low=0  mid=0   high=1
  25  26  37  10  61  11  59  15  48  19  34  56
low=0  mid=1   high=2
  25  26  37  10  61  11  59  15  48  19  34  56
low=3  mid=3   high=4
  25  26  37  10  61  11  59  15  48  19  34  56
low=3  mid=4   high=5
  25  26  37  10  11  61  59  15  48  19  34  56
low=0  mid=2   high=5
  10  11  25  26  37  61  59  15  48  19  34  56
low=6  mid=6   high=7
  10  11  25  26  37  61  15  59  48  19  34  56
low=6  mid=7   high=8
  10  11  25  26  37  61  15  48  59  19  34  56
low=9  mid=9   high=10
  10  11  25  26  37  61  15  48  59  19  34  56
low=9  mid=10   high=11
  10  11  25  26  37  61  15  48  59  19  34  56
low=6  mid=8   high=11
  10  11  25  26  37  61  15  19  34  48  56  59
low=0  mid=5   high=11
  10  11  15  19  25  26  34  37  48  56  59  61
```

WEEK - 23

Write C programs to implement the Lagrange interpolation and Newton-Gregory forward interpolation.
Lagrange interpolation

```
#include<stdio.h>
#include<conio.h>
#define SIZE 50
void main()
{
int i=0,j=0,n;
float x[SIZE],fx[SIZE],sum=0,product=1,x1;
clrscr();
printf("Enter n:");
scanf("%d",&n);
while(i<n)
{
printf("Enter x,f(x):");
scanf("%f%*[,]%f",&x[i],&fx[i]);
i++;
}
printf("Enter x to find f(x):");
scanf("%f",&x1);
i=0;
while(i<n)
{
printf("%f,%f\n",x[i],fx[i]);
i++;
}
i=0;
while(i<n)
{
product=1;
while(j<n)
{
if(j!=i)
product*=(x1-x[j])/ (x[i]-x[j]);
j++;}
j=0;
sum+=fx[i]*product;
i++;
}
```

```
printf("Result:%f",sum);
getch();
}
```

OUTPUT:

```
Enter n:3
Enter x,f(x):1,1
Enter x,f(x):2,4
Enter x,f(x):3,9
Enter x to find f(x):6
1.000000,1.000000
2.000000,4.000000
3.000000,9.000000
Result:36.000000
```

Newton-Gregory forward interpolation

```
#include<stdio.h>
#include<conio.h>
#define SIZE 50
#define ORDER 2

void main ()
{
 float x[SIZE], y[SIZE], nrator=1, dnator=1, x1, y1, p, h, dt[SIZE][ORDER];
 int i,j,n,k;
 clrscr();

 printf("Enter the value of n \n");
 scanf("%d",&n);
 printf("Enter the values of x and y");

 for(i=0; i<=n; i++)
 scanf("%f%f", &x[i], &y[i]);
 printf("Enter the value of x at which value of y is to be calculated");
 scanf("%f", &x1);
 h=x[1]-x[0];

 for(i=0; i<=n-1; i++)
dt[i][1]=y[i+1]-y[i];
 for(j=2; j<=ORDER; j++)
 for(i=0; i<=n-j; i++)
dt[i][j]=dt[i+1][j-1] - dt[i][j-1];
 i=0;
```

```
while(!(x[i]>x1))
i++;
i--;
p=(x1-x[i])/h;
y1=y[i];

for (k=1; k<=ORDER; k++)
{
 nrator *=p-k+1;
 dnator *=k;
 y1 +=(nrator/dnator)*dt[i][k];
}
printf("When x=%6.1f, y=%6.2f\n",x1, y1);
getch();
}
```

OUTPUT:

```
Enter the value of n
2
Enter the values of x and y1 1
2 4
3 9
Enter the value of x at which value of y is to be calculated2.5
When x=   2.5, y=  6.50
```

WEEK - 24

Write C programs to implement the linear regression and polynomial regression algorithms.

Linear Regression

```
#include<stdio.h>
#include<conio.h>
#include<math.h>
void main()
{
int i=1,n,x;
float xsum=0,xsqsum=0,ysum=0,xysum=0,y,denom,a0,a1;
clrscr();
printf("Enter n:");
scanf("%d",&n);
while(i<=n)
{
printf("Enter x,y:");
scanf("%d%*[,]%f",&x,&y);
```

```
xsum+=x;
xsqsum+=pow(x,2);
ysum+=y;
xysum+=x*y;
i++;
}
denom=n*xsqsum-xsum*xsum;
a0=(ysum*xsqsum-xsum*xysum)/denom;
a1=(n*xysum-xsum*ysum)/denom;
printf("a0:%f\na1:%f",a0,a1);
getch();
}
```

OUTPUT:

```
Enter n:3
Enter x,y:1,1
Enter x,y:2,4
Enter x,y:3,9
a0:-3.333333
a1:4.000000_
```

WEEK - 25

Write C programs to implement Trapezoidal and Simpson methods.
Trapezoidal Method

```
#include<stdio.h>
#include<conio.h>
#include<math.h>
double func(double x)
{
return(pow(x,3)+1);
}
void main()
{
double a,b,h,sum,ict;
int n,i=1;
clrscr();
printf("Enter a:");
scanf("%lf",&a);
printf("Enter b:");
scanf("%lf",&b);
printf("Enter h:");
scanf("%lf",&h);
n=(b-a)/h;
sum=(func(a)+func(b))/2.0;
```

```
while(i<n)
{
sum+=func(a+i*h);
i++;
}
ict=sum*h;
printf("a=%lf\nb=%lf\nh=%lf\nResult:%lf\n",a,b,h,ict);
getch();
}
```

OUTPUT:

```
Enter a:2
Enter b:3
Enter h:1
a=2.000000
b=3.000000
h=1.000000
Result:18.500000
```

Simpson Method

```
#include<stdio.h>
#include<conio.h>
#include<math.h>
double func(double x)
{
return(pow(x,3));
}
void main()
{
double x,a,b,h,sum,ict,f1,f2,f3;
int n,m,i=1;
clrscr();
printf("Enter a:");
scanf("%lf",&a);
printf("Enter b:");
scanf("%lf",&b);
printf("Enter h:");
scanf("%lf",&h);
n=(b-a)/h;
m=n/2;
x=a;
f1=func(x);
while(i<m)
{
```

```
f2=func(x+h);
f3=func(x+2*h);
sum+=f1+4*f2+f3;
f1=f3;
x=x+2*h;
i++;
}
ict=(sum*h)/3.0;
printf("a=%lf\nb=%lf\nh=%lf\nResult:%lf\n",a,b,h,ict);
getch();
}
```

Output:

```
Enter a:2
Enter b:3
Enter h:1
a=2.000000
b=3.000000
h=1.000000
Result:0.000000
```

A

Number Systems

A.1 INTRODUCTION

In this appendix, we introduce the key number systems that programmers use, especially, when they are working on software projects that require close iteration with ***machine-level*** hardware. Projects like this include operating systems, computer networking software, compilers, database systems, and applications requiring high performance.

When we write an integer such as 227 and –63 in a program, the number is assumed to be in the ***decimal*** (base 10) ***number system***. The ***digits*** in the decimal number system are 0, 1, 2, 3, 4, 5, 6, 7, 8 and 9. The lowest digit is 0 and the highest digit is 9 - on less than the base of 10. Internally, computers use the ***binary*** (base 2) ***number system***. The binary number system has only two digits, namely 0 and 1. Its lowest digit is 0 and its highest digit is 1 - one less than the base of 2. Table. A.1 summarizes the digits used in the binary, octal, decimal and hexadecimal number systems.

As we will see, binary numbers tend to be much longer than their decimal equivalents. Programmers who work in assembly languages and in high-level languages that enable programmers to reach down to the ***machine level***, find it cumbersome to work with binary numbers. So two other number systems the ***octal*** (base 8) ***number system*** and the ***hexadecimal*** (base 16) ***number system*** - popular primarily because they make it convenient to abbreviate binary numbers.

In the octal number system, the digits range from 0 to 7. Because both the binary number system and the octal number system have fewer digits than the decimal number system, their digits are the same as the corresponding digits in decimal.

The hexadecimal number system poses a problem because it requires sixteen digits - a lowest digit of 0 and highest digit with a value equivalent to decimal 15 (one less than the base of 16). By convention, we use the letters A through F to represent the hexadecimal digit corresponding to decimal values 10 through 15. Thus in hexadecimal we can have numbers like 876 consisting solely of decimal-like digits, numbers like 8A55F consisting of digits and letters, and numbers like FFE consisting solely of letters. Occasionally, hexadecimal number spells a common word such as FACE or FEED - this can appear strange to programmers accustomed to working with numbers. Table B.2 summarizes each of the number systems.

Each of these number systems uses ***positional notation*** - each position in which a digit is written has a different ***positional value***. For example, in the decimal number 937 (the 9, the 3 and the 7 are referred to as ***symbol values***), we say that the 7 is written in the ***ones position***, the 3 is written in the ***tens position***, and the 9 is written in the ***hundreds position***. Notice that each of these positions is a power of the base (base 10), and that these powers begin at 0 and increase by 1 as we move left in the number (Table A.3).

Table A.1 Digits of the Binary, Octal, Decimal and Hexadecimal Number Systems

Binary Digit	Octal Digit	Decimal Digit	Hexadecimal Digit
0	0	0	0
1	1	1	1
	2	2	2
	3	3	3
	4	4	4
	5	5	5
	6	6	6
	7	7	7
		8	8
		9	9
			A (decimal value of 10)
			B (decimal value of 11)
			C (decimal value of 12)
			D (decimal value of 13)
			E (decimal value of 14)
			F (decimal value of 15)

Table A.2 Comparison of the Binary, Octal, Decimal and Hexadecimal Number Systems

Attribute	Binary Digit	Octal Digit	Decimal Digit	Hexadecimal Digit
Base	2	8	10	16
Lowest Digit	0	0	0	0
Highest Digit	7	9	9	F

Table A.3 Positional Values in the Decimal Number System

Positional Values in the Decimal Number System			
Decimal Digit	9	3	7
Position Name	Hundreds	Tens	Ones
Positional Value	100	10	1
Positional Value as a power of the base (10)	10^2	10^1	10^0

For longer decimal numbers, the next positions to the left would be the ***thousands position*** (10 to the 3rd power), the ***ten-thousands position*** (10 to the 4th power), the ***hundred-thousands position*** (10 to the 5th power), the ***millions position*** (10 to the 6th power), the ***ten-millions position*** (10 to the 7th power), and so on.

In the binary number 101, we say that the rightmost 1 is written in the ***ones position***, the 0 is written in the ***twos position***, and the leftmost 1 is written in the ***fours position***. Notice that each of these positions is a power of the base (base 2), and that these powers begin at 0 and increase by 1 as we move left in the number (Table A.4).

Table A.4 Positional Values in the Binary Number System

Positional Values in the Binary Number System			
Binary Digit	1	0	1
Position Name	Fours	Twos	Ones
Positional Value	4	2	1
Positional Value as a power of the base (2)	2^2	2^1	2^0

For longer binary numbers, the next positions to the left would be the ***eights position*** (2 to the 3rd power), the ***sixteens position*** (2 to the 4th power), the ***thirty twos position*** (2 to the 5th power), the ***sixty-fours positions*** (2 to the 6th power) and so on.

In the octal number 425, we say that the 5 is written in the ***ones positions***, the 2 is written ***eights position***, and the 4 is written in the ***sixty-fours position***. Notice that each of these positions is a power of the base (base 8), and that these powers begin at 0 and increase by 1 as we move left in the number (Table A.5).

Table A.5 Positional Values in the Octal Number System

Positional Values in the Octal Number System			
Octal Digit	4	2	5
Position Name	Sixty-fours	Eighties	Ones
Positional Value	64	8	1
Positional Value as a power of the base (8)	8^2	8^1	8^0

For longer octal numbers, the next positions to the left would be the ***five-hundred-and-twelves positions*** (8 to the 3rd power), the ***four-thousand-and=ninety sixes position*** (8 to the 4th power), the ***thirty-two-thousand-seven-hundred-and-sixty-eights positions*** (8 to the 5th power), so on.

In the hexadecimal number 3DA, we say that the A is written in the ***ones position***, the D is written in the ***sixteens position***, and the 3 is written in the ***two-hundred-and-fifty-sixes position***. Notice that each of these positions is a power of the base (base 16), and that these powers begin at 0 and increase by 1 as we move left in the number (Table A.6).

Table A.6 Positional Values in the Hexadecimal Number System

Positional Values in the Hexadecimal Number System			
Hexadecimal Digit	3	D	A
Position Name	Two-hundred-and -fifty-sixes	Sixteens	Ones
Positional Value	256	16	1
Positional Value as a power of the base (16)	16^2	16^1	16^0

For longer hexadecimal numbers, the next positions to the left would be the ***four-thousand-and-ninety-sixes position*** (16 to the 3rd power), the ***sixty-five-thousand-five-hundred-and-thirty-six position*** (14 to the 4th power), and so on.

A.2 ABBREVIATING BINARY NUMBERS AS OCTAL NUMBERS AND HEXADECIMAL NUMBERS

The main use of octal and hexadecimal numbers is computing is for abbreviating lengthily binary representations. Table A.7 highlights the fact that lengthy binary numbers can be expressed concisely in number systems with higher bases than the binary number system.

Table A.7 Decimal, Binary, Octal and Hexadecimal Equivalents

Decimal Digit	Octal Digit	Binary Digit	Hexadecimal Digit
0	0	0	0
1	1	1	1
2	2	10	2
3	3	11	3
4	4	100	4
5	5	101	5
6	6	110	6
7	7	111	7
8	10	1000	8
9	11	1001	9
10	12	1010	A
11	13	1011	B
12	14	1100	C
13	15	1101	D
14	16	1110	E
15	17	1111	F
16	20	10000	10

A particularly important relationship that both the octal number system and the hexadecimal number system have to the binary system is that the bases of octal and hexadecimal (8 and 16 respectively) are powers of the base of the binary number system (base 2). Consider the following 12-digit binary number and its octal and hexadecimal equivalents. Se if you can determine how this relationship makes it convenient to abbreviate binary numbers in octal or hexadecimal. The answer follows the numbers.

Binary Number	Octal Equivalent	Hexadecimal Equivalent
100011010001	4321	8D1

To see how the binary number converts easily to octal, simply break the 12-digit binary number into groups of three consecutive bits each, and write those groups over the corresponding digits of the octal number as follows

100	011	010	001
4	3	2	1

Notice that the octal digit you have written under each group of the bits corresponds precisely to the octal equivalent of that 3-digit binary number as shown in Table A.7

The same kind of relationship may be observed in converting numbers from binary to hexadecimal. In particular, break the 12-digit binary number into groups of four consecutive bits each and write those groups over the corresponding digits of the hexadecimal number as follows.

1000	1101	0001
8	D	1

Notice that the hexadecimal digit you wrote under each group of four bits corresponds precisely to the hexadecimal equivalent of that 4-digit binary number as shown in Fig. A.7.

A.3 CONVERTING OCTAL NUMBERS AND HEXADECIMAL NUMBERS TO BINARY NUMBERS

In the previous section, we saw how to convert binary numbers to their octal and hexadecimal equivalents by forming groups of binary digits and simply rewriting these groups as their equivalent octal digit values or hexadecimal digit values. This process may be used in reverse to produce the binary equivalent of a given octal or hexadecimal number.

For example, the octal number 653 is converted to binary simply by writing the 6 as its 3-digit binary equivalent 110, the 5 as its 3-digit binary equivalent 101, and the 3 as its 3-digit binary equivalent 011 to form the 9-digit binary number 110101011.

The hexadecimal number FAD5 is converted to binary simply by writing the F as its 4-digit binary equivalent 1111, the A as its 4-digit binary equivalent 1010, the D as its 4-digit binary equivalent 1101, and the 5 as its 4-digit binary equivalent 0101 to form the 16-digit 1111101011010101.

A.4 CONVERTING FROM BINARY, OCTAL OR HEXADECIMAL TO DECIMAL

Because we are accustomed to working in decimal, it is often convenient to convert a binary, octal or hexadecimal number to decimal to get a sense of what the number is ***really*** worth. Our tables in section A.1 express the positional values in decimal. To convert a number to decimal from another base, multiply the decimal equivalent of each digit by its positional value, and sum these products. For example, the binary number 110101 is converted to decimal 53 as shown in Table A.8.

To convert octal 7614 to decimal 3930, we use the same technique, this time using appropriate octal positional values as shown in Table A.9.

To convert hexadecimal AD3B to decimal 44347, we use the same technique, this time using appropriate hexadecimal positional values as shown in Table A.10.

Table A.8 Converting a Binary Number to Decimal

Converting a Binary Number to Decimal						
Positional Values :	32	16	8	4	2	1
Symbol Values :	1	1	0	1	0	1
Products :	1*32 = 32	1*16 = 16	0*8 = 0	1*4 = 4	0*2 = 0	1*1 = 1
Sum :	= 32 + 16 + 0 + 4 + 0 + 1 = 53					

Table A.9 Converting a Octal Number to Decimal

Converting a Octal Number to Decimal				
Positional Values :	512	64	8	1
Symbol Values :	7	6	1	1
Products :	7*512 = 3584	6*64 = 384	1*8 = 8	1*4 = 4
Sum :	= 3584 + 384 + 8 + 4 = 3980			

Table A.10 Converting a Hexadecimal Number to Decimal

Converting a Hexadecimal Number to Decimal				
Positional Values :	4096	256	16	1
Symbol Values :	A	D	3	B
Products :	A*4096 = 4096D	D*256 = 3328	3*16 = 48	1*B = 11
Sum :	= 4096D + 3328 + 48 + 11 = 44347			

A.5 CONVERTING FROM DECIMAL TO BINARY, OCTAL OR HEXADECIMAL

The conversions of the previous section follow naturally from the positional notation conventions. Converting from decimal to binary, octal or hexadecimal also follows these conventions.

Suppose we wish to convert decimal 57 to binary. We begin by writing the positional values of the columns right to left until we reach a column whose positional value is greater than the decimal number. We do not need that column, so we discard it. Thus, we first write:

Positional Values :   64   32   16   8   4   2   1

The we discard the column with positional value 64 leaving:

Positional Values :   32   16   8   4   2   1

Next we work from the left most column to the right. We divide 32 into 57 and observe that there is one 32 in 57 with a remainder of 25, so we write 1 in the 32 column. We divide 16 into 25 and observe that there is one 16 in 25 with a remainder of 9 and write 1 in the 16 column. We divide 8 into 9 and observe that there is one 8 in 9 with a remainder of 1. The next two columns each produce quotients of zero when their positional values are divided into 1. So we write 0s in the 4 and 2 columns. Finally, 1 into 1 is 1, so we write 1 in the 1 column. This yields:

Positional Values :	32	16	8	4	2	1
Symbol Values :	1	1	1	0	0	1

and thus decimal 57 is equivalent to binary 111001.

To convert decimal 103 to octal, we begin by writing the positional values of the columns until we reach a column whose positional value is greater than the decimal number. We do not need that column, so we discard it. Thus, we first write:

Positional Values :	512	64	8	1

Then we discard the column with positional value 512, yielding:

Positional Values :	64	8	1

Next we work from the leftmost column to the right. We divide 64 into 103 and observe that there is one 64 in 103 with a remainder of 39, so we write 1 in the 64 column. We divide 8 into 39 and observe that there are four 8s in 39 with a remainder of 7 and write 4 in the 8 column. Finally, we divide 1 into 7 and observe that there are seven 1s in 7 with no remainder, so we write 7 in the 1 column. This yields:

Positional Values :	64	8	1
Symbol Values :	1	4	7

and thus decimal 103 is equivalent to octal 147.

To convert decimal 375 to hexadecimal, we begin by writing the positional values of the columns until we reach a column whose positional value is greater than the decimal number. We do not need that column, so we discard it. Thus, we first write,

Positional Values :	4096	256	16	1

Then we discard the column with positional value 4096, yielding :

Positional Values :	256	16	1

Next we work from the leftmost column to the right. We divide 256 into 375 and observe that there is one 256 in 375 with a remainder of 119, so we write 1 in the 256 column. We divide 16 into 119 and observe that there are seven 16s in 119 with a remainder of 7 and write 7 in the 16 column. Finally, we divide 1 into 7 and observe that there are seven 1s in 7 with no remainder, so we write 7 in the 1 column. This yields:

Positional Values :	256	16	1
Symbol Values :	1	7	7

and thus decimal 375 is equivalent to hexadecimal 177.

A.6 NEGATIVE BINARY NUMBERS: TWO'S COMPLEMENT NOTATION

The discussion in this appendix has been focussed on positive numbers. In this section, we explain how computers represent negative numbers using ***two's complement notation***. First we explain how the two's complement of a binary number is formed, and then we show why it represents the negative value of the given binary number.

Consider a machine with 32-bit integers. Suppose,

int value = 13;

The 32-bit representation of value is

00000000 00000000 00001101

To form the negative of value we first form its ***one's complement*** by applying C's bitwise complement operator(~), which is also called the ***bitwise NOT operator***.

onescomplementofvalue = ~value;

Internally, ***~value*** is now value with each of its bits reversed -- ones become zeroes and zeroes become ones as follows:

value:

00000000 00000000 00001101

~value:

11111111 11111111 11110010

To form the two's complement of value we simple add one to value's one's complement. Thus,

11111111 11111111 11110011

Now if this is infact fact equal to −13, we should be able to add it to binary 13 and obtain a result of 0. Let us try this:

```
00000000 00000000 00000000 00000000
11111111 11111111 11111111 11110011
-----------------------------------
00000000 00000000 00000000 00000000
-----------------------------------
```

The carry bit coming out of the leftmost column is discarded and we indeed get zero as a result. If we add the one's complement of a number to the number, the result would be all 1s. The key to getting a result of all zeros is that the twos complement is 1 more than the one's complement. The addition of 1 causes each column to ad to 0 with a carry of 1. The carry keeps moving leftward until it is discarded from the leftmost bit, and hence the resulting number is all zeroes.

Computer actually perform a subtraction such as

x = a − value;

by adding the two's complement of value to a as follows:

x = a + (~value + 1);

Suppose a is 27 and value is 13 as before. If the two's complement of value is actually the negative of value, then adding the two's complement of value to a should produce the result 14. Let use try this:

```
a ( i.e., 27 )     00000000 00000000 00000000 00011011
+ ( ~value + 1)    11111111 11111111 11111111 11110011
                   -----------------------------------
                   00000000 00000000 00000000 00001110
                   -----------------------------------
```

which is indeed equal to 14.

A.7 FLOATING - POINT NUMBER SYSTEMS

Earlier we described number representation systems in which positive and negative integers are stored in binary form. In this representation system, the binary point is ***fixed*** in that it lies at the end of each word, so each value represented is an integer. When computers calculate with binary numbers in this format, the operations are called ***fixed-point arithmetic***.

In science it is often necessary to calculate with very large or very small numbers, so scientists have adopted a convenient notation in which a ***mantissa*** and an ***exponent*** represent a number. For instance, 4,900,000 may be written as 0.49×10^7, where 0.49 is the mantissa and 7 is the value of exponent. Similarly, 0.00023 may be written as 0.23×10^{-3}. The notation is based on the relation $y = a \times r^p$, where y is the number to be represented, a is the mantissa, r is the base of the number system (r = 10 for decimal and r = 2 for binary), and p is the power to which the base is raised.

It is possible to calculate using this representation system. To multiply $a \times 10^n$ and $b \times 10^m$, we form a $a \times b \times 10^{m+n}$. To divide $a \times 10^m$ by $b \times 10^n$, we form $a/b \times 10^{m-n}$. To add $a \times 10^m$ and $b \times 10^n$, we must first make m equal to n. If $m = n$, then $a \times 10^m + b \times 10^n$ is equal to $a + b \times 10^m$. The process of making m equal to n is called ***scaling*** the numbers.

Considerable book keeping can be involved in scaling numbers, and it can be difficult to maintain precision during computations when numbers vary over a very wide range of magnitudes. For computer usage these problems are alleviated by means of two techniques whereby the computer (not the programmer) keeps track of the radix point, automatically scaling the numbers. In the first, programmed ***floating-point routines*** automatically scale the numbers used during the computations while maintaining the precision of the results and keeping track of the scale factors. These routines are used with small computers having only fixed-point operations. A second technique lies in building what are called ***floating-point operations*** into the computer's hardware. The logic circuitry of the computer is then used to perform the scaling automatically and to keep track of the exponents when calculations are performed. To effect this, a number representation system called the ***floating-point system*** is used.

A floating-point number in a computer uses the exponential notation system described. During calculations, the computer keeps track of the exponent as well as the mantissa. A computer number is a floating-point system may be divided into three pieces; the first is the sign bit, indicating whether the number is negative or positive; the second part contains the exponent for the number to be represented; and the third part is the mantissa.

As an example, let us consider a computer with a 12-bit word length. Fig. A.1 shows a floating-point word for such a computer. It is common practice to call the exponent part of the word the ***characteristic*** and the mantissa section the ***integer part.***

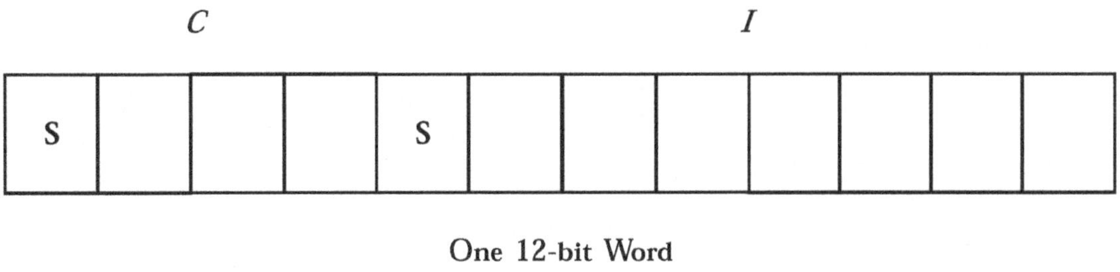
C
I
S
S
One 12-bit Word

Fig. A.1 A 12-bit Floating-Point Word

The integer part of the floating-point word represents its value in signed magnitude form (rather than 2s complement, although this has been used). The characteristic is also in signed-magnitude form. The value of the number expressed is $I \times 2^C$, where I is the value of the integer part and C is the value of the characteristic.

Fig. A.2 shows several values of floating-point numbers, both in binary form and after conversion to decimal. Since the characteristic has 5 bits and is in signed magnitude form, C can have values from −15 to +15. The value of I is a sign-plus-magnitude binary integer of 7 bits, and so I can have a value from −63 to +63. The largest number represented by this system is thus 63×2^{15}. This shows the use of the floating-point number representation system to store ***real*** numbers of considerable range in a binary word.

C *I*

0	0	1	1	1	0	0	0	1	0	1	1

$C = +7$ $I = +11$

Value is $2^7 \times 11 = 1408$

0	0	0	1	1	1	0	0	0	1	1	1

$C = +3$ $I = -7$

Value is $2^3 \times (-7) = -56$

$C = -5$ $I = +5$

Value is $2^{-5} \times 7 =$

1	0	1	1	0	1	0	0	1	0	0	1

$C = -6$ $I = -9$

Value is $2^{-6} \times (-9) =$

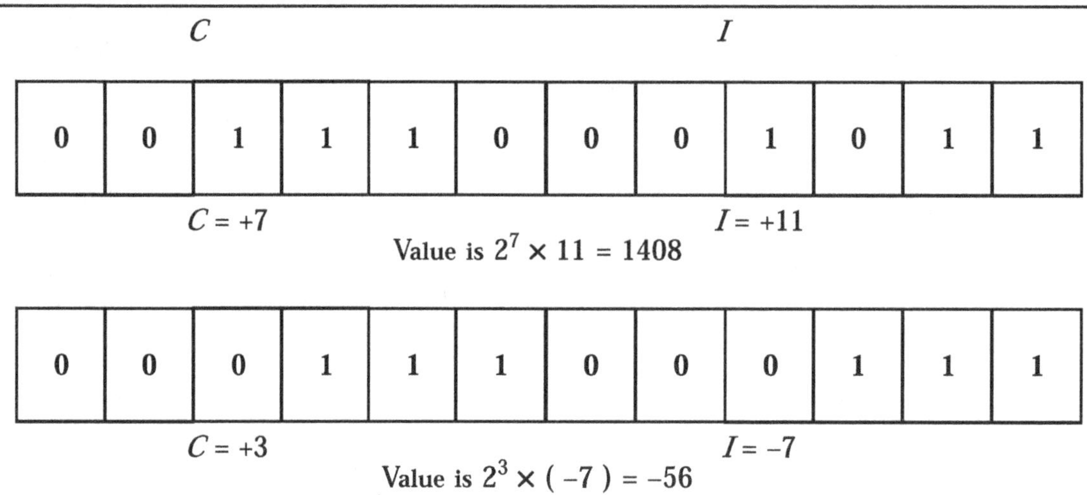

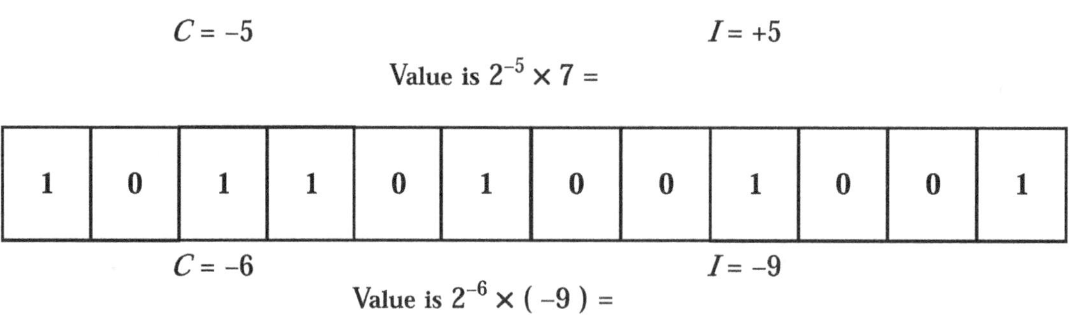

Fig. A.2 Values of floating-point numbers in 12-bit all-integer systems.

Another widely followed practice is to express the mantissa of the word as a fraction instead of as an integer. This is in accord with common scientific usage, since 0.93×10^4 is the normal form for exponential notation (and not 93×10^2). In this usage a mantissa is decimal normally has a value from 0.1 to 0.999. Similarly, a binary mantissa in normal form would have a value from 0.5 (decimal) to less than 1. Most computers maintain their mantissa sections in normal form, continually adjusting words so that a significant (1) bit is always in the leftmost mantissa position.

When the mantissa is in fraction form, this section is called the ***fraction***. For our 12-bit example, we can express floating-point numbers with characteristic and fraction by simply supposing the binary point is to the left of the magnitude (and not to the right, as in integer representation). In this system, a number to be represented has value $F \times 2^C$, where F is the binary fraction and C is the characteristic.

For the 12-bit word considered before, fractions would have values from 1 to 2^{-6}, which is 0111111, to $-(1 - 2^{-6})$, which is 1111111, where the leftmost bin in each number is the sign bit. Thus numbers from $(1 - 2^{-6}) \times 2^{15}$ to $-(1 \times 2^{-6}) \times 2^{15}$, or about +32,000 to −32,000, can be represented. The smallest value the fraction part could have is 01000000, which is 2^{-1}, and the smallest characteristic is 2^{-15}, so the smallest positive number representable is $2^{-1} \times 2^{-16}$. Most computers use this fractional system for the mantissa, although Burroughs and NCR use the integer system.

An example of computers with internal circuitry that performs floating-point operations is the IBM series. IBM calls the exponent part the ***characteristic*** and the mantissa part the ***fraction***. In the IBM series, floating-point data words can be either 32 or 64 in length. The basic format for a short or single-word floating-point number is:

S	Characteristic	Fraction
0	1→7	8→31

The format for a long or double-word floating-point number is:

S	Characteristic	Fraction
0	1→7	8→63

In both cases, the sign bit, S is in the leftmost position and gives the sign of the number. The characteristic part of the word comprises bits 1 to 7 and is simply a binary integer, which we call C, ranging from 0 to 127. The actual value of the scale factor is formed by subtracting 64 from this integer and raising 16 to this power. Thus, the value 64 in bits 1 to 7 gives a scale factor of $16^{C-64} = 16^{93-64}$, which is 16^{29}; and a 24 in bits 1 to 7 gives 16^{-40}.

The magnitude of the actual number represented in a floating-point word is equal to this scale factor times the fraction contained in bits 8 to 31 (for the short number) or 8 to 63 (for a long number). The radix point is assumed to be to the left of bit 8 in either case. So if bits 8 to 31 contain 1000 . . . 00, the fraction has value ½(decimal); that is, the fraction is .1000 . . .000 in binary. Similarly, if bits 8 to 31 contain 11000 . . . 000, the fraction value is ¾(decimal), or 0.11000 . . .000 binary.

The number represented then had magnitude equal to the value of the fraction times the value determined by the characteristic. Consider a short number:

Floating-point Number:	0	1	0	0	0	0	0	1	1	1	1	0	0	...	0
Bit Position :	0	1	2	3	4	5	6	7	8	9	10	11	12	...	31

The sign bit is a 0, so the number represented is positive. The characteristic has binary value 1000001, which is 65 decimal, so the scale factor is 16^1. The fraction part has the value 0.111 binary, or $\frac{7}{8} \times 16$, or 14 decimal.

Floating-point Number:	0	1	0	0	0	0	0	1	1	1	1	0	0	...	0
Bit Position :	0	1	2	3	4	5	6	7	8	9	10	11	12	...	31

Consider the following number:

This has value –14, since every bit is the same as before, except for the sign bit.

Most PCs (and Microprocessors) now use the IEEE standard for Binary Floating-point Arithmetic. This standard is the result of work by several organizations (not just IEEE) and is widely supported.

The principle feature of the standard is the ***hidden 1*** principle. Floating-point numbers generally have their fraction (magnitude) part stored with a leading 1 in the leftmost position. This is called ***normalized form***; it ensures that the maximum number of significant bits is carried in the number. The reasoning behind the ***hidden 1*** principle is that if that leftmost bit in the fraction (magnitude) section is always a 1, why carry it? Instead, this section of the floating-point number is shifted left one more bit, and the 1 is discarded. However, in any reconstruction of the number for external use or during calculations, the 1 is replaced.

There is a single format and a double format. The single format is:

1	← 8 →	← 23 - bits →
S	E	F

where S is the sign bit, E is a binary integer, and F is a binary fraction of length 23. However, the value of F is formed by adding 1 to this fraction. Thus, if F is this format is stored as 11000 . . . 00, the value of F is 1.11000 . . . 00, which is 1¾ in decimal. The value of a floating-point number in this system is

$$V = (-1)^S \times 2^{E-127} \times 1.F$$

Notice that this system uses an offset of 127 for the exponent (characteristic value. Here are three examples of the single-format system:

Floating-point Number	$(-1)^S \times 2^{E-127} \times 1.F$	Decimal Value
3F800000	$1 \times 2^0 \times 1.0$	+1
BF800000	$-1 \times 2^0 \times 1.0$	−1
40400000	$1 \times 2^0 \times 1.5$	+3

Note that fraction values for *F* range from 1 to slightly less than 2 ($1 \le F < 2$).

The double format is:

1	← 11 →	← 52 - bits →
S	E	F

where S is the sign bit, E is a 11-bit integer, and F is a 52-bit binary fraction with the binary point to the far left. However, as before, the value for F is formed by adding 1 to the left of this fraction. So if F is stored as 101000 . . . 00, then, the value of F is 1.10100 . . . 00, or $1\frac{5}{8}$ in decimal. The value of a number stored is then

$$V = (-1)^S \times 2^{E-1023} \times F$$

Here are examples :

Floating-point Number	$(-1)^S \times 2^{E-127} \times 1.F$	Decimal Value
3DF0000	$1 \times 2^2 \times 1.0$	+0.25
C03E000	$-1 \times 2^4 \times 1.875$	-30
401C000	$1 \times 2^2 \times 1.75$	+7

There is also a single extended format, with $E \geq 11$ bits and $F \geq 31$ bits and a double extended format, with $E \geq 15$ bits and $F \geq 63$ bits. These are used only in particular implementations.

Since a 1 is assumed to be ***invisibly*** stored with each number, the representation for 0 must be special. The standard 0 is represented by all 0s in the E and F sections (there is a +0 and a –0). Furthermore, infinity is represented by all 1s in the E section and all 0s in the F section. There is, therefore, also a $+\infty$ and a $-\infty$.

When numbers are so small that they cannot be represented in normalized form, because E would need to be less than 1, the F part is handled in denormalized form, and the 1 is not added when the numbers are evaluated.

The results of invalid operations are signaled as follows: E is all 0s; S can be anything; and if F is nonzero, the 1s in F signal an illegal operation.

B

Standard Library Functions In C

The appendix presents a list of functions and their use. The actual syntax may be obtained from the "help" of the complier under which you are working. Note that all function may not be available under all compliers.

B.1 ARITHMETIC FUNCTIONS

Function	Use
double abs(double *x*);	returns the absolute value of an integer
double cos(double *x*);	calculates cosine
double exp(double *x*);	raises the exponential e to the power x
double floor(double *x*);	finds largest integer less than or equal to argument
double log(double *x*);	calculates natural logarithm
double log10(double *x*);	calculates base 10 logarithm
double pow(double *x*, double *y*);	calculates a value raised to a power
double sin(double *x*);	calculates sine
double sqrt(double *x*);	calculates square root
double tan(double *x*);	calculates tangent

B.2 DATA CONVERSION FUNCTION

Function	Use
double atof(const char **nptr*);	converts string to float
int atoi(const char **nptr*);	converts string to int
long int atol(const char **nptr*);	converts string to long

B.3 CHARACTER FUNCTIONS

Function	Use
int isalnum(int *c*);	tests for alphanumeric character
int isalpha(int *c*);	tests for alphabetic character
int isdigit(int *c*);	tests for decimal digit
int islower(int *c*);	tests for lowercase character
int isspace(int *c*);	tests for white space character
int isupper(int *c*);	tests for uppercase character
int tolower(int *c*);	converts to lowercase if uppercase
int toupper(int *c*);	converts to uppercase if lowercase

B.4 STRING FUNCTIONS

Function	Use
char *strcat(char **s1*, const char **s2*);	appends one string to another
char *strchr(const char **s*, int *c*);	finds first occurrence of a given character in a string
int strcmp(const char **s1*, const char **s2*);	compares two strings
char *strcpy(char **s1*, const char **s2*);	copies two strings without regard to case

size_t strlen(const char *s);	finds length of a string
char *strlwr(char *s1);	converts a string to lowercase
char *strrev(char *s1);	reverses a string
char *strupr(char *s1);	converts a string to uppercase

B.5 I/O FUNCTIONS

Function	Use
int fclose(FILE *stream);	closes a file
int fgetc(FILE *stream);	reads a character from a file
char *fgets(char *s, int n, FILE *stream);	reads a string from a file
FILE *fopen(const char *filename, const char *mode);	opens a file
int fprintf(FILE *stream, const char *format, ...);	writes formatted data to a file
int fputc(int c, FILE *stream);	writes a character to a file
int fputs(const char *s, FILE *stream);	writes a string to a file
int fscanf(FILE *stream, const char *format, ...);	reads formatted data from a file
int fseek(FILE *stream, long int offset, int whence);	repositions file pointer to given location
long int ftell(FILE *stream);	gets current file pointer position
int getc(FILE *stream);	reads a character from a file
getch	reads a character from the keyboard
int getchar(void);	reads a character from keyboard
char *gets(char *s);	reads a line from keyboard
int printf(const char *format, ...);	writes formatted data to screen
int putc(int c, FILE *stream);	writes a character to a file

int putchar(int *c*);	writes a character to screen
int puts(const char *s*);	writes a line to file
void rewind(FILE **stream*);	repositions file pointer to beginning of a file
int scanf(const char **format*, ...);	reads formatted data from keyboard

B.6 MEMORY ALLOCATION FUNCTIONS

Function	Use
void *calloc(size_t *nmemb*, size_t *size*);	allocates a block of memory
void *malloc(size_t *size*);	allocates a block of memory
void *realloc(void **ptr*, size_t *size*);	reallocates a block of memory
void free(void **ptr*);	frees a block allocated with malloc

C

ASCII Character Set

	0	1	2	3	4	5	6	7	8	9
0	nul	soh	stx	etx	eot	enq	ack	bel	bs	ht
1	nl	vt	ff	cr	so	si	dle	dc1	dc2	dc3
2	dc4	nak	syn	etb	can	em	sub	esc	fs	gs
3	rs	us	sp	!	"	#	$	%	&	'
4	(	)	*	+	,	-		/	0	1
5	2	3	4	5	6	7	8	9	:	;
6	<	=	>	?	@	A	B	C	D	E
7	F	G	H	I	J	K	L	M	N	O
8	P	Q	R	S	T	U	V	W	X	Y
9	Z	[	\	]	^	_	`	a	b	c
10	d	e	f	g	h	i	j	k	l	m
11	n	o	p	q	r	s	t	u	v	w
12	x	y	z	{	|	}	~	del		

Fig. C.1 ASCII Character Set

The digits at the left of the table are the left digits of the decimal equivalent (0-127) of the character code, and the digits at the top of the right digits of the character code. For example, the character code for "F" is 70, and the character code for "&" is 38.

D

Objective Type Questions

1. Consider the following C function :

```
void  foo_1(char * s)
{
   while(*s)
   {
      if((*s >= 'a')&&(*s <= 'z'))
         *s-=32;
      s++;
   }
}
```

When a pointer to a string is passed to the above C function it,

(a) *Converts all the digits of the string to 0's*
(b) *Converts all lower case alphabets of the string into upper case*
(c) *Converts all uppercase alphabets of the string to lower case*
(d) *Reverses the string*

2. Consider the following C function

```
int  foo_2(int n)
{
   if n==0
      return 1;
   else
      return  n*foo_2(n-1);
}
```

If the above function, is called with n=3,it returns

(a) *0* (b) *3* (c) *6* (d) *goes into infinite loop*

3. If the foo_2 function is called with n=-3, it returns

(a) *0* (b) *3* (c) *6* (d) *goes into infinite loop*

4. Consider the following C declaration

```
int  (*b) [3];
```

The above declares,

(a) *a 2 dimensional array b of size 3*
(b) *a pointer to a group of one dimensional arrays of size 3*
(c) *an array of integer pointers of size 3*
(d) *is an error*

5. Consider the following C program,

```
void main(void)
{
   char name1[] = "Computer Science";
   char name2[] = {'C','o','m','p','u','t','e','r',' ',
                   'S','c','i','e','n','c','e','\0'};
   printf(" %d , %d", sizeof(name1), sizeof(name2));
}
```

The above C program prints,

(a) *17,17* (b) *16,17* (c) *17,16* (d) *16,16*

6. Consider the following C program

```
void foo_3(char *s)
{
   char *s1;
   char c;
   s1 = s + (strlen(s) - 1);
   while(s<s1)
   {
      c=*s;
      *s=*s1;
      *s1=c;
      s++;
      s1–;
   }
}
```

When a pointer to a string is passed to the above C function it,

(a) *Converts the string from uppercase to lower case*
(b) *Converts the string from lowercase to uppercase*
(c) *Reverses the string*
(d) *is an error*

7. Consider the statements below:

(a) In C, any operation that can be achieved by array subscripting can also be done with pointers.
(b) Structures in C may be compared for equivalence.

Which of the following statements is correct?

(a) *only (a) is true*
(b) *only (b) is true*
(c) *both (a) and (b) are true*
(d) *both (a) and (b) are false*

8. Which of the following functions are not found in string.h?

(a) *strcat(s,t)*
(b) *strncat(s,t,n)*
(c) *strlength(s)*
(d) *strchar(s,c)*

9. Consider the statements below:

(a) In C, a pointer to a function can be defined but cannot be passed to another function
(b) When a function is declared static in C its name is visible outside of the file in which it is declared.

Which of the following statements is correct?

(a) *only (a) is true*
(b) *only (b) is true*
(c) *both (a) and (b) are true*
(d) *both (a) and (b) are false*

10.

```
union{
        int a;
        float b;
        char c;
    } abc;
```

Assuming that the size of int is 4bytes, float is 8bytes and char is 1byte.

sizeof(abc) returns

(a) *1* (b) *4* (c) *8* (d) *13*

11. Observe the following code segment of C

```
int i  = 10;
int b = ++i;
```

The value of i and b at the end of this segment are respectively.

(a) *10,10* (b) *11,10* (c) *10,11* (d) *11,11*

12. Consider the following C expression

```
z = (a > b) ? a : b;
```

If a = 10 and b = 11 and z = 12 before the above statement was executed, then the values of a,b,z after the execution of above statement are

(a) *10,11,11* (b) *11,11,12* (c) *11,10,12* (d) *10,10,12*

13. Consider the following statements,

(a) *A break statement is used within a control structure like while ,for, do while or switch to cause immediate exit from the control structure.*

(b) *The function* fopen *takes two string arguments 'a file name' and 'read-write permissions on that file'.*

Which of the following statement is true?

(a) *only (a) is true* (b) *only (b) is true*
(c) *both (a) and (b) are true* (d) *both (a) and (b) are false*

14. The only use of an identifier declared as a label in C is

(a) *as a target of goto* (b) *to indicate the beginning of the block*
(c) *to indicate an end of a block* (d) *none of the above*

15. Which of the following sorting algorithms does not have a worst case running time of $O(n^2)$?

(a) *Insertion sort* (b) *Merge sort*
(c) *Quick sort* (d) *Bubble sort*

16. A tree, for which at every node the height of its left sub tree and right sub tree differ at most by one is a/an

(a) *Binary search tree* (b) *AVL tree*
(c) *Complete binary tree* (d) *Threaded binary tree*

17. The postfix form of the infix expression

$(A + B) * (C * D - E) * F$ is

(a) $AB + CD + E - * F *$ (b) $AB + CDE + - * F *$
(c) $AB + CD - EF + - * *$ (d) $ABCDEF * - + * +$

18. A full binary tree with n leaf nodes contains

(a) *n nodes* (b) $log_2 n$ *nodes* (c) $2n - 1$ *nodes* (d) 2^n *nodes*

19. Which data structure is needed to convert infix notations to postfix notation?

(a) *B-Tree* (b) *Queue* (c) *Tree* (d) *Stack*

20. A sorting technique is called *stable* if :

(a) *It takes O (n log n) time*
(b) *It maintains the relative order of occurrence of non-distinct elements*
(c) *It uses divide and conquer paradigm*
(d) *It takes O (n) space*

21. Which one of the following statements is false?

(a) *A tree with n nodes has (n – 1) edges*
(b) *A labeled rooted binary tree can be uniquely be constructed given its post order and inorder traversal results.*
(c) *A complete binary tree with n internal nodes has (n + 1) leaf nodes.*
(d) *The maximum number of nodes in a binary tree of height h is* $(2^{h+1} - 1)$ *(the height of the root is reckoned as 0).*

22. If each node in a tree has a value greater than every value in its left sub tree and has value less than every value in its right sub tree, the binary tree is known as

(a) *Complete binary tree* (b) *Full binary tree*
(c) *Binary search tree* (d) *Threaded binary tree*

23. The five items: A, B, C, D and E are pushed in a stack, one after the other starting from A. The stack is popped four times and each element is inserted in a queue. Then two elements are deleted from the queue and pushed back on the stack. Now one item is popped from the stack. The popped item is

(a) *A* (b) *B* (c) *C* (d) *D*

24. The time required to search an element in a binary search tree having n elements is

(a) $O(1)$ (b) $O(log_2 n)$ (c) $O(n)$ (d) $O(nlog_2 n)$

25. A binary tree in which if all its levels except possibly the last, have the maximum number of nodes and all the nodes at the last level appear as far as possible, is known as

(a) *full binary tree* (b) *2-tree*
(c) *threaded tree* (d) *complete binary tree*

26. A list of integers is read in, one at a time, and a binary search tree is constructed. Next the tree is traversed and the integers are printed. Which traversed would result in a printout which duplicates the original order of the list of integers?

(a) *preorder* (b) *postorder* (c) *inorder* (d) *none of the above*

27. The infix expression A+((B-C)*D) is correctly represented in prefix notation as

(a) *A+B-C*D* (b) *+A*-BCD* (c) *ABC-D*+* (d) *A+BC-D**

28. A graph G with n nodes is bipartite if it contains

(a) *n edges* (b) *a cycle of odd length*
(c) *no cycle of odd length* (d) n^2 *edges*

29. For merging two sorted lists of sizes m and n into a sorted list of size m+n, we require comparisons of

(a) *O(m)* (b) *O(n)* (c) *O(m+n)* (d) *O(logm+logn)*

30. A binary tree T has n leaf nodes. The number of nodes of degree 2 in T is

(a) $log_2 n$ (b) *n-1* (c) *n* (d) 2^n

31. Let LASTPOST, LASTIN and LASTPRE denote the last vertex visited in a post order, in order and pre order traversal, respectively, of a complete binary tree. Which of the following is always true?

(a) *LASTIN=LASTPOST* (b) *LASTIN=LASTPRE*
(c) *LASTPRE=LASTPOST* (d) *none of the above*

32. Let G be an undirected graph. Consider a depth-first traversal of G, and let T be the resulting depth-first search tree. Let *u* be a vertex in G and let *v* be the first new (unvisited) vertex visited after visiting *u* in the traversal. Which of the following statements is always true?

(a) *{u,v} must be an edge in G, and u is a descendant of v in T*
(b) *{u,v} must be an edge in G, and v is a descendant of u in T*
(c) *If {u,v} is not an edge in G then u is a leaf in T*
(d) *If {u,v} is not an edge in G then u and v must have the same parent in T*

33. The value of j at the end of the execution of the following C program

```
int incr(int i)
{
   static int count =0;
   count = count + i;
   return (count);
}
main()
{
   int i,j;
   for(i=0;i<4;i++)
      j=incr(i);
}
```

is

(a) *10* (b) *4* (c) *6* (d) *7*

34. The number of swappings needed to sort the numbers 8, 22, 7, 9, 31, 19, 5, 13 in ascending order using bubble sort is

(a) *11* (b) *12* (c) *13* (d) *14*

35. The differences between ***malloc() and calloc()*** **are**

(a) *malloc is used for dynamic allocation of memory, while calloc can't be used for that purpose*
(b) *malloc needs only one argument, while calloc needs two*
(c) *Unlike calloc, malloc allocates memory and initializes it to 0*
(d) *malloc needs two arguments and calloc only one*

Answers to Objective Type Questions

1. (d)	2. (c)	3. (d)	4. (a)	5. (a)
6. (a)	7. (d)	8. (d)	9. (b)	10. (d)
11. (b)	12. (a)	13. (a)	14. (c)	15. (b)
16. (b)	17. (a)	18. (c)	19. (d)	20. (b)
21. (b)	22. (c)	23. (d)	24. (b)	25. (d)
26. (c)	27. (b)	28. (a)	29. (c)	30. (b)
31. (b)	32. (d)	33. (a)	34. (a)	35. (b)

Bibliography

1. Computer Algoriths Introduction to Design and Analysis,
   Sara Bause & Allen Van Gelder, Addison Wesley.

2. C How to Program,
   Dietel & Dietel, Pearson.

3. Data Structures & Algoriths,
   Bruno R. Preiss, John Wiley.

4. Fundamentals of Algorithimics,
   Gilles Brassard & Paul Bratley, PHI.

5. The C Programming Language,
   Brian W. Kernighan & Dennis M. Ritchie, PHI.

6. Fundamentals of Data Structures in Pascal,
   Ellis Horowitz, Sartaj Sahni, GB.

7. Fundamentals of Data Structures,
   Ellis Horowitz, Sartaj Sahni, GB.

8. Data Structures using C and C++,
   Yedidyah Langsam & Moshe J. Augenstein and Aaron M. Tenenbaum, PHI.

www.ingramcontent.com/pod-product-compliance
Lightning Source LLC
LaVergne TN
LVHW080849240726
843527LV00052B/283